'Famous in my time'

BYRON'S LETTERS AND JOURNALS
VOLUME 2
1810–1812

The World is all before me—or behind;
 For I have seen a portion of that same,
And quite enough for me to keep in mind ;—
 Of passions, too, I have proved enough to blame,
To the great pleasure of our friends, Mankind,
 Who like to mix some slight alloy with fame;
For I was rather famous in my time,
Until I fairly knocked it up with rhyme.

DON JUAN, 14, 9

BYRON
From an engraving, by H. Meyer in 1812,
of a portrait by George Sanders

'Famous in my time'

BYRON'S LETTERS AND JOURNALS

Edited by
LESLIE A. MARCHAND

VOLUME 2
1810–1812

*The complete and unexpurgated text of
all the letters available in manuscript and
the full printed version of all others*

THE BELKNAP PRESS OF
HARVARD UNIVERSITY PRESS
CAMBRIDGE, MASSACHUSETTS

ISBN 0–674–08941–3
Library of Congress Catalog Card
Number 73–81853

Printed in the United States of America

CONTENTS

EDITORIAL NOTE

Since the first two volumes of this edition were prepared together, it will be useful to consider them as a unit for any purposes of research in the letters. It has not seemed either possible or desirable to divide the acknowledgments or the bibliography between the two volumes. The reader will find the acknowledgments for the two volumes at the end of the Editorial Note in Volume 1. The Bibliography for the volumes is in Appendix II of Volume 1. Additional appropriate acknowledgments and bibliography will be added in future volumes.

BYRON CHRONOLOGY

1810 July 18—Arrived in Athens.
July 21—Left for the Morea.
July 25—Took Greek boy Eustathius into entourage at Vostitza.
July 26—Arrived at Patras.
Aug.—Visit to Veli Pasha at Tripolitza.
Aug. 19?—Back in Athens; at Capuchin monastery.
Sept.—Second excursion to Morea; ill with fever at Patras.
Oct. 13—Returned to Athens.
Dec.—Second trip to Sunium.

1811 Jan. 14—Sent valet Fletcher home.
March—Wrote *Hints from Horace* and *The Curse of Minerva*.
April 22—Sailed on the *Hydra*.
April 30–June 2—At Malta.
June 2—Sailed for England on the *Volage* frigate.
July 14—Landed at Sheerness; At Reddish's Hotel, St. James's Street.
Aug. 1—Byron's mother died.
Aug. 3—At Newstead; Matthews drowned at Cambridge.
Oct. [5?]—Left with Hanson for Rochdale.
Oct. 9—Returned to Newstead; news of Edleston's death.
Oct. 16—Visit with Davies at Cambridge.
Oct. 28—At 8 St. James's Street, London.
Nov. 4—Dinner with Samuel Rogers to meet Moore.
Nov.—Visited Cambridge again.
Dec.—Back in London.
Dec. 19—Left for Newstead with Hodgson and Harness; enamoured of Welsh maid, Susan Vaughan.

1812 Jan. 11—Left for London.
Feb. 27—Maiden speech in House of Lords.
March 10—*Childe Harold* I and II published; famous overnight.
March 25—First saw Annabella Milbanke.
April—Liaison with Lady Caroline Lamb begun.
June 4—To Newstead with Hobhouse.
June 13—Returned to London.
July 29—Hobhouse prevented Byron from eloping with Caroline.

Aug. 14—Newstead offered at auction but bought in.

Aug. 15—Thomas Claughton offered £140,000 for Newstead, but repented after agreement was signed and delayed payment.

Aug. 23—At Cheltenham with Jerseys, Melbournes, Hollands.

Sept.—Wrote Drury Lane Address at request of Lord Holland.

Oct.—Proposed to Annabella Milbanke through Lady Melbourne and was rejected; wrote *The Waltz*.

Oct. 24—Left for Eywood, Presteign, to visit the Oxfords.

Nov. 21—Left Eywood for Jerseys at Middleton.

Nov. 30—At Batt's Hotel, Dover Street, London.

Dec. [14?]—Back at Eywood.

Sir,—The Marquis of Sligo[2] has informed me that previous to his departure from England you wished to forward through his means a letter to me which you stated to be of some consequence.—What the contents may be I am at a loss to conjecture unless they refer to an account which I hope has been long liquidated.—If by any mistake, which I should regret as much as you can possibly do, this has not taken place, I request you will carry this letter to Messrs Hanson & Birch No. 6 Chancery Lane who will take care to see it paid off immediately. I have not received any letter from you, amongst my English papers, though several were forwarded to me during my stay both at Smyrna, and Constantinople.—If however you address to Malta my Banker will send your letter on to the Morea.—I remain, Sir,

your very obedt. & very humble Servant
BYRON

[TO MRS. CATHERINE GORDON BYRON]   *Athens. July 20th. 1810*

Dear Mother.—I have arrived here in four days from Constantinople which is considered as singularly quick particularly for the season of the year; *you Northern Gentry* can have no conception of a Greek Summer, which however is a perfect Frost compared with Malta, and Gibraltar, where I reposed myself in the *shade* last year after a gentle Gallop of four hundred miles without intermission through Portugal & Spain.—You see by my date that I am at Athens again, a place which I think I prefer upon the whole to any I have seen.—I left Constantinople with Adair at whose audience of leave I saw Sultan Mahmout, and obtained a firman to visit the Mosques of which I think I gave you some description in my last letter, now voyaging towards England in the Salsette frigate in which I visited the plains of Troy, and Constantinople.—My next movement is tomorrow into the Morea, where I shall probably remain a month or two, and then return to winter here if I do not change my plans, which however are very variable as you may suppose, but *none* of them verge to England.—The Marquis of Sligo my old fellow collegian is here, and wishes to accompany me into the Morea, we

---

1 William Miller was a bookseller at 50 Albemarle Street from whom Byron bought a large quantity of books before he went abroad.

2 Lord Sligo, who had been at Cambridge with Byron, arrived in Athens before Byron returned from Constantinople.

shall go together for that purpose, but I am already woefully sick of travelling companions after a years experience of Mr. Hobhouse who is on his way to Great Britain.—Ld. S[ligo] will afterwards pursue his way to the Capitol, and Ld. *B.* having seen all the wonders in that quarter, will let you know what he does next, of which at present he is not quite certain.—Malta is my perpetual post-office from which my letters are forwarded to all parts of the habitable Globe, by the bye, I have now been in Asia, Africa [sic],[1] and the East of Europe, and indeed made the most of my time, without hurrying over the most interesting scenes of the ancient world.—Fletcher, after having been toasted and roasted, and baked and grilled, and eaten by all sorts of creeping things begins to philosophise, is grown a refined as well as resigned character, and promises at his return to become an ornament to his own parish, and a very prominent person in the future family pedigree of the Fletchers whom I take to be Goths by their accomplishments, Greeks by their acuteness, and ancient Saxons by their appetite.—He (Fletcher) begs leave to send half a dozen sighs to Sally his spouse, and wonders (though I do not) that his ill written and worse spelt letters have never come to hand, as for that matter there is no great loss in either of our letters, saving and except, that I wish you to know we are well and warm enough at this present writing God knows.—You must not expect long letters at present for they are written with the sweat of my brow, I assure you.—It is rather singular that Mr. Hanson has not written a syllable since my departure, your letters I have mostly received, as well as others, from which I conjecture that the man of law is either angry or busy.—I trust you like Newstead and agree with your neighbours, but you know *you* are a *vixen*, is not that a dutiful appellation?—Pray take care of my Books, and several boxes of papers in the hands of Joseph, and pray leave me a few bottles of Champagne to drink for I am very thirsty, but I do not insist on the last article without you like it.—I suppose you have your house full of silly women, prating scandalous things;—have you ever received my picture in oil from Sanders London? it has been paid for these 16 months, why do you not get it?—My Suite consisting of two Turks, two Greeks, a Lutheran, and the nondescript Fletcher, are making so much noise that I am glad to sign myself yours &c.

BYRON

[1] This is a strange statement. There is no evidence that Byron ever set foot in Africa. He had intended to cross over while he was in Gibraltar, but a contrary wind prevented it, and he left soon after for Malta. His days at Gibraltar are all accounted for in Hobhouse's diary, in which there is no mention of a trip to Africa.

Dear Hobhouse,—The same day, which saw me ashore on Zea, set me forth once more upon the high seas, where I had the pleasure of seeing the frigate in the *Doldrums* by the light of Sun and Moon.— Before daybreak I got into the Attics at Thaskalio whence I dispatched men to Keratia for horses and in ten hours from landing I was at Athens.—There I was greeted by my Ld. Sligo, and next day Messrs North, Knight, and Fazakerly[1] paid me formal visits.—Sligo has a brig with 50 men who wont work, 12 guns that refuse to go off, and sails that have cut every wind except a contrary one, and then they are as willing as may be.—He is sick of the concern but an Engagement of six months prevents him from parting with this precious Ark.—He *would* travel with me to Corinth, though as you may suppose I was already heartily disgusted with travelling in company.—He has "en suite" a painter, a captain, a Gentleman misinterpreter (who boxes with the painter) besides sundry idle English Varlets.—We were obliged to have 29 horses in all.—The Captain and the *Drogueman* [*Dragoman*] were left at Athens to kill bullocks for the crew, and the Marquis & the limner with a ragged Turk by way of Tartar, and the ship's carpenter in the capacity of linguist, with two servants (one of whom had the gripes) clothed both in *leather breeches* (the *Thermometer 125!!*) followed over the hills and far away.—On òur route, the poor limner in these gentle latitudes was ever and anon condemned to bask for half an hour that he might produce what he himself termed a "bellissimo sketche" (pardon the orthography of the last word) of

---

[1] Frederick North, later fifth Earl of Guilford (1766–1827) was an enthusiastic Philhellene. He had already travelled widely in Greece and the Ionian Islands and learned to speak and write the Romaic or modern Greek language. He later founded the Ionian University in Corfu and was its first Chancellor. He continually wore the classical Greek costume adopted as the academic garb, which excited ridicule in England. Byron shared in the general English view, calling him later: "the most illustrious humbug of his age and country". (Letter of Nov. 15, 1817, to Murray.)

Henry Gally Knight (1786–1846) was on tour of Greece, Egypt, and Palestine with North and Fazakerly. Byron had known him at Cambridge and saw him again at Cadiz. Later, when Knight published his *Ilderim, a Syrian Tale* (1816), and *Phrosyne, a Grecian Tale* (1817), Byron ridiculed him in occasional verse and in letters to his friends: ". . . I despise the middling mountebank's mediocrity . . ." (Aug. 31, 1820, to Murray). Knight later gained some renown for his books on architecture.

John Nicholas Fazakerly (1787–1852) became known as a scholar and antiquary. He was a witness at the Select Committee inquiry into the Elgin Marbles in 1816, and expressed the view, contrary to Byron's, that the marbles at Athens were in danger of deterioration (thus justifying Lord Elgin's bringing them to England).

the surrounding country.—You may also suppose that a man of the Marchesa's kidney was not very easy in his seat, as for the *servants* they and their *leather breeches* were equally immoveable at the end of the first stage.—Fletcher too with his usual acuteness contrived at Megara to ram his damned clumsy foot into a boiling teakettle.—At Corinth we separated, the M[arquis] for Tripolitza, I for Patras.— Thus far the ridiculous part of my narrative belongs to others, now comes my turn.—At Vostitza I found my dearly-beloved Eustathius [2] —ready to follow me not only to England, but to Terra Incognita, if so be my compass pointed that way.—This was four days ago, at present affairs are a little changed.—The next morning I found the dear soul upon horseback clothed very sprucely in Greek Garments, with those ambrosial curls hanging down his amiable back, and to my utter astonishment and the great abomination of Fletcher, a *parasol* in his hand to save his complexion from the heat.—However in spite of the *Parasol* on we travelled very much enamoured, as it should seem, till we got to Patras, where Strané received us into his new house where I now scribble.—Next day he went to visit some accursed cousin and the day after we had a grand quarrel, Strané said I spoilt him, I said nothing, the child was as froward as an unbroken colt, and Strané's Janizary said I must not be surprised, for he was too *true* a *Greek* not to be disagreeable.—I think I never in my life took so much pains to please any one, or succeeded so ill, I particularly *avoided* every thing which *could possibly give* the *least offence* in any *manner*, somebody says that those who try to please will please, this I know not; but I am sure that no one likes to fail in the attempt.—At present he goes back to his father, though he is now become more tractable.—Our *parting* was vastly pathetic, as many kisses as would have sufficed for a boarding school, and embraces enough to have ruined the character of a county in England, besides tears (not on *my* part) and expressions of "Tenerezza" to a vast amount.—All this and the warmth of the weather has quite overcome me. Tomorrow I will continue, at present "to bed, "to bed, "to bed".—The youth insists on seeing me to-morrow, the issue of which interview you shall hear.—I wish you a pleasant sleep.—

Sheet second. July 30th. 1810—
I hope you have slept well, I have only dosed, for this last six days I

---

[2] Eustathius Georgiou, whom Byron had probably met at the time he visited the Cogia Basha Andreas Londos in Vostitza in 1809, wrote several letters to him. One seems to indicate that Byron had sent for him to come to Athens, but he was ill and could not come. Another expresses a wish to accompany him on his travels.

have slept little and eaten less, the heat has burnt me brown, and as for Fletcher he is a walking Cinder.—My new Greek acquaintance has called thrice, and we improve vastly, in good truth, so it ought to be, for I have quite exhausted my poor powers of pleasing, which God knows are little enough, Lord help me!—We are to go on to Tripolitza and Athens together, I do not know what has put him into such good humour unless it is some Sal Volatile I administered for his headach and a green shade instead of that effeminate parasol, but so it is, we have *redintegrated* (a new *word* for you) our affections at a great rate.—Now is not all this very ridiculous? pray tell Matthews it would do his heart good to see me travelling with my Tartar, Albanians, Buffo, Fletcher and this amiable παιδη[3] prancing by my side.—Strané hath got a steed which I have bought, full of spirit, I assure you, and very handsome accoutrements, my *account* with him was as I stated on board the Salsette.—Here hath just arrived the Chirurgeon of the Spider[4] from Zante who will take this letter to Malta.—I hope it will find you warm.—You cannot conceive what a delightful companion you are now you are gone.—Sligo has told me some things, that ought to set you and me by the ears, but they shan't, and as a proof of it, I wont tell you what they are till we meet, but in the mean time I exhort you to behave well in polite society.—His Lordship has been very kind, and as I crossed the Isthmus of Corinth, offered if I chose to take me to that of Darien but I liked it not, for you have cured me of "villainous company".—I am about, after a Giro of the Morea, to move to Athens again, and thence I know not where, perhaps to Englonde, Malta Sicily, Ægypt, or the Low Countries.—I do suppose you are at Malta, or Palermo, I amuse myself alone very much to my satisfaction riding, bathing, sweating, hearing Mr. Paul's[5] musical clock, looking at his red breeches, we visit him every evening, there he is, playing at Stopper with the old Cogia Bashi,[6] when these amusements fail there is my Greek to quarrel with, and a Sofa to tumble upon.—Nourse and Darwin[7] had been at Athens scribbling all sorts of ribaldry over my old apartment, where Sligo

[3] boy.
[4] The vessel on which Byron and Hobhouse first came to Greece from Malta in September 1809.
[5] Mr. Paul, a cousin of the British Vice-Consul Strané, was the Imperial Consul in Patras.
[6] Cogia Bashi (or Basha) was the official designation or title of a Greek holding a provincial governing post under the Turks.
[7] Dr. Francis Darwin, son of the author of *The Botanic Garden*, and uncle of the author of *The Origin of Species*, was a passenger with Byron and Hobhouse on the *Pylades* sloop-of-war when they left Athens for Smyrna in March 1810.

before my arrival had added to your B. A. an A. S. S. and scrawled the compliments of Jackson, Devville [D'Egville?], Miss Cameron,[8] and "*I am very unappy, Sam Jennings.*"—Wallace is incarcerated,[9] and wanted Sligo to bail him, at the Bell and Savage Fleet Rules.—The news are not surprising. What think you? Write to me from Malta, the Mediterranean or Ingleterra, to the care of ο. κονσολοσ Στρανέ[10] Have you cleansed my pistols? and dined with the "*Gineral*"? My *compts.* to the church of St. Johns,[11] and peace to the ashes of Ball.[12]— How is the Skipper? I have drank his cherry Brandy, and his Rum has floated over half the Morea.—Plaudite et Valete.

yours ever
BYRON

[TO MRS. CATHERINE GORDON BYRON] *Patras. July 30th. 1810*

Dear Madam,—In four days from Constantinople with a favourable wind I arrived in the frigate at the island of Zea, from whence I took a boat to Athens where I met my friend the Marquis of Sligo who expressed a wish to proceed with me as far as Corinth.—At Corinth we separated he for Tripolitza I for Patras where I had some business with the Consul Mr. Stranè in whose house I now write, he has rendered me every service in his power since I quitted Malta on my way to Constantinople, whence I have written to you twice or thrice.— In a few days I visit the Pacha at Tripolitza, make the tour of the Morea, and return again to Athens, which at present is my head-quarters.—The heat is at present intense, in England if it reaches 98 you are all on fire, the other day in travelling between Athens and Megara the thermometer was at 125!!—Yet I feel no inconvenience, of course I am much bronzed, but I live temperately, and never enjoyed better health.—Before I left Constantinople I saw the Sultan (with Mr. Adair) and the interior of the Mosques, things which rarely happen to travellers.—Mr. Hobhouse is gone to England.—I am in no hurry to return, but have no particular communications for your country, except my surprise at Mr. Hanson's silence, and my desire that he will remit regularly.—I suppose some arrangement has been made with regard to Wymondham and Rochdale.—Mr. Hobhouse has

[8] The girl Byron had kept in lodgings in Brompton in 1808.
[9] See April 26, 1808, to Augusta Leigh.
[10] The consul Strané.
[11] St. John's church, Malta.
[12] Sir Alexander John Ball, governor of Malta, died shortly after Byron's visit there in 1809.

letters for you from me.—Malta is my post office, or to Mr. Stranè Consul General Patras, Morea.—You complain of my silence, I have written twenty or thirty times within the last year, never less than twice a month, and often more. If my letters do not arrive you must not conclude that we are eaten, or that there is a war, or a pestilence, or famine, neither must you credit *silly* reports, which I dare say, you have in Notts as usual.—I am very well, and neither more or less happy than I usually am, except that I am very glad to be once more alone, for I was sick of my companion (not that he was a bad one) but because my nature leads me to solitude, and that every day adds to this disposition.—If I chose, here are many men who would wish to join me, one wants me to go to Ægypt, another to Asia, of which I have seen enough, the greater part of Greece is already my own, so that I shall only go over my old ground, and look upon my old seas and mountains, the only acquaintances I ever found improve upon me.— I have a tolerable suite, a Tartar, two Albanians, and interpreter, besides Fletcher, but in this country, these are easily maintained.—Adair received me wonderfully well, and indeed I have no complaints against any one, hospitality here is necessary, for inns are not.—I have lived in the houses of Turks, Greeks, Italians, and English, today in a palace, tomorrow in a cowhouse, this day with the Pacha, and the next with a Shepherd.—I shall continue to write briefly but frequently, and am glad to hear from you, but you fill your letters with things from the papers, as if English papers were not found all over the world, I have at this moment a dozen before me.—Pray take care of my books, and believe me

my dear Mother yours very faithfully
BYRON

[TO JOHN CAM HOBHOUSE]   *Tripolitza. August 16th. 1810*

Dear Hobhouse,—I am on the rack of setting off for Argos amidst the usual creaking swearing loading and neighing of sixteen horses and as many men [serving us? servingers?] included.—You have probably received one letter dated Patras and I send this at a venture. —Velly Pacha received me even better than his Father did, though he is to join the Sultan, and the city is full of troops and confusion, which as he said, prevents him from paying proper attention.—He has given me a very pretty horse and a most particular invitation to meet him at Larissa, which last is singular enough as he recommended a different route to Ld. Sligo who asked leave to accompany him to the Danube.

9

—I asked no such thing, but on his enquiring where I meant to go, and receiving for answer that I was about to return to Albania for the purpose of penetrating higher up the country, he replied, "no you must not take that route, but go round by Larissa where I shall remain some time on my way. I will send to Athens, and you shall join me, we will eat and drink well, and go a hunting."—He said he wished all the old men (specifying under that epithet *North*, *Forresti*,[1] and *Stranè*) to go to his father, but the young ones to come to him, to use his own expression "vecchio con vecchio, Giovane con Giovane."—He honored me with the appellations of his *friend* and *brother*, and hoped that we should be on good terms not for a few days but for Life.—All this is very well, but he has an awkward manner of throwing his arm round one's waist, and squeezing one's hand in *public*, which is a high compliment, but very much embarrasses *"ingenuous youth"*.—The first time I saw him he received me *standing*, accompanied me at my departure to the door of the audience chamber, and told me I was a παλικαρι[2] and an εὔμορφω παιδι[3]—He asked if I did not think it very proper that as *young* men (he has a *beard* down to his middle) we should live together, with a variety of other sayings, which made Stranè stare, and puzzled me in my replies.—He was very facetious with Andreas and Viscillie,[4] and recommended that my Albanians' heads should be cut off if they behaved ill.—I shall write to you from Larissa, and inform you of our proceedings in that city.—In the mean time I sojourn at Athens.———

I have sent Eustathius back to his home, he plagued my soul out with his whims, and is besides subject to *epileptic* fits (tell *M*[atthews] this) which made him a perplexing companion, in *other* matters he was very tolerable, I mean as to his *learning*, being well versed in the Ellenics.— You remember Nicolo[5] at Athens Lusieri's wife's brother.—Give my *compliments* to *Matthews* from whom I expect a congratulatory letter.

———I have a thousand anecdotes for him and you, but at present Τι να καμω?[6] I have neither time nor space, but in the words of Dawes, "I have things in store."—I have scribbled thus much, where shall I send

---

[1] Byron met George Forresti at Malta. He was later (1810) British Resident at Janina. He was a Greek by birth, but with a Western education.

[2] brave young man.

[3] beautiful boy.

[4] Andreas Zantachi and Viscillie (Vascillie) were Byron's Greek and Albanian servants.

[5] Nicolo Giraud, a boy in his teens, had attached himself to Byron before he went to Constantinople, and became his companion-dragoman on his second excursion to the Morea in September.

[6] Τι να καμω? [Τι να κανω? = What to do?]

it, why to Malta or Paternoster Row. Hobby you wretch how is the Miscellany? that damned and damnable work, "what has the learned world said to your paradoxes? I hope you did not forget the importance of Monogamy."[7]—Stranè has just arrived with bags of piastres, so that I must conclude by the usual phrase of

yours &c. &c.
BYRON

P.S.—You knew young Bossari at Yanina, he is a piece of Ali Pacha's!! well did Horace write "Nil Admirari"

[TO JOHN CAM HOBHOUSE]

The Convent. Athens. August 23d. 1810

My dear Hobhouse,—Ld Sligo's unmanageable Brig being re-manded to Malta with a large quantity of vases amounting in value (according to the depreciation of Fauvel)[1] to one hundred and fifty piastres, I cannot resist the temptation of assailing you in this third letter, which I trust will find you better than your deserts, and no worse than my wishes can make you.—I have girated the Morea, and was presented with a very fine horse (a stallion) and honoured with a number of squeezes and speeches by Velly Pacha, besides a most pressing invitation to visit him at Larissa in his way to the wars.—But of these things I have written already.—I returned to Athens by Argos where I found Ld. Sligo with a painter who has got a fever with sketching at mid day, and a dragoman who has actually lied himself into a lockjaw, I grieve to say the Marchesa has done a number of young things, because I believe him to be a clever, and I am sure he is a good man.—I am most auspiciously settled in the Convent,[2] which is

[7] *Vicar of Wakefield*, Chapter 20.

[1] Louis François Sebastian Fauvel (1753–1838) had an art education in France before coming to the Near East under the patronage of Count Choiseul-Gouffier, the French Ambassador at Constantinople, in 1787. He gathered material and prepared illustrations for his patron's *Voyage Pittoresque de la Grèce* (1787; 1809). Fauvel settled in Athens and became the French Consul, continuing his archaeo-logical and artistic pursuits. In a note to *Childe Harold*, Byron referred to him as one "to whose talents as an artist, and manners as a gentleman, none who have known him can refuse their testimony". But he took exception to Fauvel's state-ment that the Greeks did not deserve to be emancipated because of their "national and individual depravity". (*Poetry*, II, 190.)

[2] On his return from his first journey to the Morea, Byron left his lodgings with the Macri family and lived for the remainder of his stay in Athens at the Capuchin convent (monastery) at the foot of the Acropolis. It was built around the fourth-century monument to Lysicrates. In Byron's time it served as a school for some of the sons of Frank families, and, in the absence of hotels, as a hostelry for travellers.

11

more commodious than any tenement I have yet occupied, with room for my *suite*, and it is by no means solitary, seeing there is not only "il Padre Abbate" but his "schuola" consisting of six "Regatzi" all my most particular allies.—These Gentlemen being almost (saving Fauvel and Lusieri) [3] my only associates it is but proper their character religion and morals should be described.—Of this goodly company three are Catholics and three are Greeks, which Schismatics I have already set a boxing to the great amusement of the Father who rejoices to see the Catholics conquer.—Their names are, Barthelemi, Giuseppe, *Nicolo*,[4] Yani, and two anonymous at least in my memory.— Of these Barthelemi is a "simplice Fanciullo" according to the account of the Father, whose favourite is Guiseppe who sleeps in the lantern of Demosthenes.[5]—We have nothing but riot from Noon till night.— The first time I mingled with these Sylphs, after about two minutes reconnoitering, the amiable Signor Barthelemi without any previous notice seated himself by me, and after observing by way of compliment, that my "Signoria" was the "pieu bello" of his English acquaintances saluted me on the left cheek, for which freedom being reproved by Giuseppe, who very properly informed him that I was "μεγαλοσ"[6] he told him I was his "φιλοσ"[7] and "by his beard," he would do so again, adding in reply to the question of "διατι ασπασετε?"[8] you see he laughs, as in good truth I did very heartily.—But my friend as you may easily imagine is Nicolo, who by the bye, is my Italian master, and we are already very philosophical.—I am his "Padrone" and his "amico" and the Lord knows what besides, it is about two hours since that after informing me he was most desirous to follow *him* (that is me) over the world, he concluded by telling me it was proper for us not only to live but "morire insieme."—The latter I hope to avoid, as much of the former as he pleases.—I am awakened in the morning by these imps shouting "venite abasso" and the friar gravely observes it is "bisogno bastonare" every body before the studies can possibly commence.—Besides these lads, my suite, to which I have added a

[3] Giovanni Battista Lusieri, a Neapolitan painter, had been employed by William Richard Hamilton, secretary to Lord Elgin when he was Ambassador at Constantinople, to make topographical studies in the Near East. Lord Elgin employed him to make drawings of the antiquities in Athens, and he stayed on as Elgin's agent in gathering and shipping the Elgin marbles to England.

[4] Nicolo Giraud, brother of Lusieri's wife.

[5] The hollow monument to Lysicrates in the court yard of the monastery was commonly called the "Lantern of Demosthenes".

[6] "a great one", *i.e.*, a lord.

[7] loved one, dear friend.

[8] Why did you embrace (kiss) him?

Tartar and a youth to look after my two new saddle horses, my suite I say, are very obstreperous and drink skinfuls of Zean wine at 8 paras the oke daily.—Then we have several Albanian women washing in the "giardino" whose hours of relaxation are spent in running pins into Fletcher's backside.—"*Damnata di mi if I have seen such a spectaculo in my way from Viterbo.*"[9]—In short what with the *women*, and the *boys*, and the *suite*, we are very disorderly.—But I am vastly happy and childish, and shall have a world of anecdotes for you and the "Citoyen."—Intrigue flourishes, the old woman Teresa's mother was mad enough to imagine I was going to marry the girl, but I have better amusement, Andreas[10] is fooling with Dudu[11] as usual, and Mariana[12] has made a conquest of Dervise Tahiri, Viscillie Fletcher and Sullee my new Tartar have each a mistress, "Vive l'Amour!"—I am learning Italian, and this day translated an ode of Horace "Exegi monumentum"[13] into that language[.] I chatter with every body good or bad and tradute prayers out of the Mass Ritual, but my lessons though very long are sadly interrupted by scamperings and eating fruit and peltings and playings and I am in fact at school again, and make as little improvement now as I did then, my time being wasted in the same way.—However it is too good to last, I am going to make a second tour of Attica with Lusieri who is a new ally of mine, and Nicolo goes with me at his own most pressing solicitation "per mare, per terras"—"Forse" you may see us in Inghilterra, but "non so, come &c."—For the present, Good even, Buona sera a vos signoria, Bacio le mani.——August 24th. 1810.—I am about to take my daily ride to the Piraeus where I swim for an hour despite of the heat, here hath been an Englishman ycleped Watson,[14] who died and is buried in the Tempio of Theseus. I knew him not, but I am told that the Surgeon of Ld. Sligo's brig slew him with an improper potion and a cold bath.—Ld. Sligo's crew are sadly addicted to liquor.—He is in some apprehension of a scrape with the Navy concerning certain mariners of the King's ships.—He himself is now at Argos with his

[9] Unidentified.

[10] Andreas Zantachi, Byron's servant, hired at Patras in 1809 because he spoke Turkish, Greek, French, Italian, and bad Latin.

[11] Dudu Roque, daughter of Phokion Roque, a French merchant living in Athens. Byron later used her name for the innocent buxom odalisque, whose bed Don Juan shared in the harem.

[12] Mariana, the eldest of the Macri sisters.

[13] Horace's closing song to his Muse, beginning "exegi monumentum aere perennius . . ." ("A monument I've achieved more strong than brass . . .").

[14] George Watson died on September 17, 1810. Byron wrote a Latin epitaph which was engraved on a stone placed over his body in the Theseum.

hospital but intends to winter in Athens. I think he will be sick of it, poor soul he has all the indecision of your humble servant, without the relish for the ridiculous which makes my life supportable.——I wish you were here to partake of a number of waggeries which you can hardly find in the Gunroom or in Grub-street, but then you are so very crabbed and disagreeable that when the laugh is over, I rejoice in your absence.—After all I do love thee, Hobby, thou hast so many good qualities and so many bad ones it is impossible to live with or without thee.—

Nine in the Evening.—

I have as usual swum across the Piraeus, the Signore Nicolo also laved, but he makes as bad a hand in the water as L'Abbe Hyacinth at Falmouth,[15] it is a curious thing that the Turks when they bathe wear their lower garments as your humble servant always doth, but the Greeks not, however questo Giovane e vergogno.—Ld. Sligo's surgeon has assisted very materially the malignant fever now fashionable here, another man *died* to day, two men a week like fighting Bob Acres in the country.—Fauvel says he is like the Surgeon whom the Venetians fitted out against the Turks with whom they were then at war.—I have been employed the greater part of today in conjugating the verb "$\alpha\sigma\pi\alpha\zeta\omega$'[16] [$\alpha\sigma\pi\alpha\zeta o\mu\alpha\iota$] (which word being Ellenic as well as Romaic may find a place in the *Citoyen's* Lexicon) I assure you my progress is rapid, but like Caesar "nil actum reputans dum quid superesset agendum"[17] I must arrive at the pl & opt C,[18] and then I will write to ——— [Matthews], I hope to escape the fever, at least till I finish this affair, and then it is welcome to try, I dont think without its friend the drunken Poticary it has any chance, take a quotation. —"Et Lycam *nigris* oculis, nigroque *Crine* decorum."—[19]

yours & the *Sieur's* ever

B.

[TO JOHN CAM HOBHOUSE]   *Patras. Septr. 25th. 1810*

My Dear Hobhouse—I am at present in a very ridiculous situation, under the hands of Dr. Romanelli and a fever which hath confined me

---

15 See June 22, 1809, to Matthews, and Nov. 2, 1811, to Hobhouse.

16 To embrace, kiss.

17 Lucan in the *Pharsalia* (II, 656) wrote: "Caesare in omnia praeceps, nil actum credens, cum quid superesset agendum." ("Caesar, always prompt to act, believed nothing had been done while anything was left to be done.")

18 See June 22, 1809, to Matthews, note 1.

19 Horace, *Odes* I, xxxii, 11: "et Lycum nigris oculis nigroque crine decorum". ("And Lycus beautiful for black eyes and raven locks." Translation by C. E. Bennet, Loeb Classical Library.)

BYRON'S LETTERS AND JOURNALS

to my bed for these three days past, but by the blessing of God and two glysters, I am now able to sit up, but much debilitated.—I will describe my situation in a parody on Pope's lines on the Duke of Buckingham,[1] the which I composed during an Interval for your edification.—

> On a cold room's floor, within a bed
> Of iron, with three coverlids like lead,
> A coat and breeches dangling o'er a nook,
> Where sits a doctor, and prescribes a puke,
> Poor B-r-n sweats—alas! how changed from him
> So plump in feature, and so round in limb,
> Grinning and gay in Newstead's monkish fane
> The scene of profanation and Champagne,
> Or just as gay with scribblers in a ring
> Of twenty hungry authors banqueting,
> No whore to fondle left of half a score,
> Yet one thing left him, which he values more,
> Here victor of a fever and it's friends
> Physicians and their art, his lordship *mends*.

I have been vomited and purged according to rule, and as my fever has almost subsided, I hope to weather this bout, which has been pretty tight I assure you.—Yet if I do fall by the Glyster pipe of Romanelli, recollect my injunction.

> Odious! in boards, twould any Bard provoke,
> (Were the last words that dying Byron spoke)
> No let some charming cuts and frontispiece
> Adorn my volume, and the sale increase,
> One would not be unpublished when one's dead
> And, Hobhouse, let my works be bound in *Red*.

Patras. October 2d. 1810

Dear Yani,[1]—By this second date you will perceive that I have been again ill, indeed I have had this fever very violently, and five days bed-riding with Emetics glysters, Bark, all the host of Physic, showed how vain were my former hopes of complete recovery.—But being well toasted and watered &c. I shall endeavour to conclude this letter of two

---

[1] Byron's parody is on the lines beginning: "In the worst inn's worst room" in Pope's lines to Allen Lord Bathurst (*Moral Essays*, III, 299–314), referring to the 2nd Duke of Buckingham, who died in 1687.
[1] See P.S. Dec. 5, to Hobhouse, note 17.

beginnings, which I must do quickly and attend poor Nicolo who has waited on me day and night till he is worse than I was and is now undergoing the same process for his recovery.—I believe you recollect him, he is the brother of Lusieri's spouse, and has been with me nearly two months, at his own particular request.—He is now my sole dragoman (I have commenced Italian) for the moment I received yours, Andreas was dismissed at the instance of *Dominus* Macgill.—) [2] —I have made a tolerable tour of the Morea, and visited Vely Pacha who gave me a very pretty horse.—The other day I went to Olympia. —Argos, Napoli and Mantinea [3] I saw in my route to and from Tripolitza.—I have seen a good deal of Ld. Sligo, by the bye there is a silly report all over the Morea that he and I quarreled fought and were wounded at Argos, there is not a word of truth in it from beginning to end.—If I kept any journal, your request would be immediately complied with, but I have none.—Vely is gone to the Danube.—I have been here on business with Stranè, but the moment Nicolo and myself are enough recovered to set out, I shall proceed again to Athens.—I lodge in the Convent.—Perhaps I am in possession of anecdotes that would amuse you and the Citoyen, [4] but I must defer the detail till we meet.—I have written to you three times since I left you in Zea, and direct my letters to Ridgeway's [5] where I presume you will be found on Sundays.—You are now in England.—What you tell me of the Miscellany grieves me (in spite of Rochefoucault) [6] I commend your design of not letting the Public off so easily, come out as a tourist, prose must go down.—But dont ask half a guinea for your next book, consider half a guinea carries a man to the opera, and if he goes to Hookham's [7] tis odds but he buys more tickets than books, aye and cheaper too, try seven shillings, Mr. Hobhouse, seven shillings, Sir, stick to that, and let me tell you, when you have received seven hundred seven shilling pieces, they will cut a figure on your little deal

---

[2] Unidentified.

[3] Mantinea was an ancient town in Arcadia not far from modern Tripolis (Tripolitza). The Theban general Epaminondas defeated the Spartans there but died after his victory.

[4] This was a playful name which Byron gave to Charles Skinner Matthews.

[5] James Ridgway, the bookseller.

[6] Byron was fond of quoting the statement in La Rochefoucauld's Maximes: "Dans l'adversité de nos meilleurs amis, nous trouvons toujours quelque chose qui ne nous déplait pas." ("There is something in the misfortunes of our best friends which does not displease us.")

[7] Thomas Hookham, Jr. (1787–1867) with his brother Edward conducted a publishing and bookselling business at their father's circulating library at 15 Old Bond Street. He sold opera tickets it seems as well as books. He is best known now for his association with Shelley.

writing table, I have a regard for you, Sir, a regard, and out of it I beg you to strike off the odd three and sixpence.——I have nothing to request in England, every body with whom I am at all connected seems asleep, as far as regards me, and I shant awake them.—Hanson you may just fillip on the nose, and ask him from me if he is insane, not to have answered my letters.—As to the others, their conduct is optional, and I have nothing to say. I shall certainly be in England, in a few months, perhaps before, but I do not wish this to go forth, as it will only make Hanson more dilatory.—If you hear any thing you will write, and I will apprise you of my intentions as they rise and subside, for it would be very absurd in me to pretend to any regular plan.—You have no doubt a deal to do and say and hear and reply, wishing you well through it I am yours

very sincerely &c.
B.—

[TO MRS. CATHERINE GORDON BYRON] *Patras. October second. 1810*

Dear Madam,—It is now several months since I have received any communication from you, but at this I am not surprised, nor indeed have I any complaint to make since you have written frequently, for which I thank you. But I very much condemn Mr. Hanson, who has not taken the smallest notice of my many letters, nor of my request before I left England, which I sailed from on this *very day* fifteen months ago.—Thus one year and a quarter have passed away, without my receiving the least intelligence on the state of my affairs, and they were not in a posture to admit of neglect, and I do conceive and declare that Mr. H. has acted negligently and culpably in not apprising me of his proceedings, I will also add uncivilly.—His letters were there any could not easily miscarry, the communications with the Levant are slow but tolerably secure, at least as far as Malta, and there I left proper directions which I know would be observed.—I have written to you several times from Constantinople and Smyrna, you will perceive by my date I am returned into the Morea, of which I have been making the tour and visiting the Pacha, who gave me a fine horse, and paid me all possible honours and attention.—I have now seen a good portion of Turkey in Europe and Asia Minor, and shall remain at Athens and in the vicinity till I hear from England.—I have punctually obeyed your injunctions of writing frequently, but I shall not pretend to describe countries which have been already amply treated of, I believe before this time Mr. Hobhouse will have arrived in England, and he brings letters from me written at Constantinople.—In these I mention having seen the Sultan & the Mosques, and that I swam from Sestos to Abydos an exploit of which I take care to boast.—I am here on business, at present, but Athens is my head quarters, where I am very pleasantly situated in a Franciscan convent.—Believe me to be with great sincerity

yrs. very affectly.

BYRON

P.S.—Fletcher is well and discontented as usual.—his wife dont write, at least her scrawls have not arrived.—You will address to Malta [.] Pray have you never received my picture in oil from Sanders, Vigo Lane, London?—

[TO JOHN HANSON]   *Patras. Morea. October 2d. 1810*

Sir,—On this day fifteen months ago I sailed from England, and since that period I have not been favoured with the slightest intimation from you or any of your family.—I am willing to think your letters must have miscarried, yet I have received some from other quarters, but I wish to suppose anything rather than that you are negligent and uncivil, both of which terms might be applied to such an instance of wilful neglect.—I have written from Spain, Malta, Athens, Yanina, Smyrna, Constantinople and the Morea, and I write once more to enforce the former request of

your very obedt. humble Sert.

BYRON

P.S.—Address to Malta.—I return to Athens in a few days.—

[TO FRANCIS HODGSON]   *Patras. Morea. Octr. 3d. 1810*

My dear Hodgson—As I have just escaped from a physician and a fever which confined me five days to bed, you wont expect much "allegrezza" in the ensuing letter.—In this place there is an indigenous distemper, which, when the wind blows from the Gulph of Corinth (as it does five months out of six) attacks great and small, and makes woeful work with visitors.—Here be also two physicians, one of whom trusts to his Genius (never having studied) the other to a campaign of eighteen months against the sick of Otranto, which he made in his youth with great effect.—When I was seized with my disorder, I protested against both these assassins, but what can a helpless, feverish, toasted and watered poor wretch do? in spite of my teeth & tongue, the English Consul, my Tartar, Albanians, Dragoman forced a physician upon me, and in three days vomited and glystered me to the last gasp. —In this state I made my epitaph, take it,

> Youth, Nature, and relenting Jove
> To keep my *lamp in* strongly strove,
> But *Romanelli* was so stout
> He beat all three—and *blew* it *out*.—

But Nature and Jove being piqued at my doubts, did in fact at last beat Romanelli, and here I am well but weakly, at your service.—Since I left Constantinople I have made a tour of the Morea, and visited Vely Pacha who paid me great honours and gave me a pretty stallion.— Hobhouse is doubtless in England before even the date of this letter, he bears a dispatch from me to your Bardship.—He writes to me from Malta, and is desperate of his Miscellany, but has other plots against the public, and requests my journal if I keep one, I have none or he should have it, but I have replied in a consolatory and exhortatory epistle, wherein I do recommend him to turn his hand to prose, which must go down or the Devil's in't, at the same time praying him to abate three and sixpence in the price of his next boke, seeing that half a guinea is a price not to be given for any thing save an opera ticket.— As for England, it is long since I have heard from it, every one at all connected with my concerns, is asleep, and you are my only correspondent, agents excepted.—I have really no friends in the world, though all my old school companions are gone forth into the world, and walk about in monstrous disguises, in the garb of Guardsmen, lawyers, parsons, fine gentlemen, and such other masquerade dresses. —So I have shaken hands and cut with all these busy people, none of whom write to me, indeed I asked it not, and here I am a poor traveller and heathenish philosopher, who hath perambulated the greatest part of the Levant, and seen a great quantity of very improveable land and sea, and after all am no better than when I set out, Lord help me.—I have been out fifteen months this very day and I believe my concerns will draw me to England soon, but of this I will apprise you regularly from Malta. On all points Hobhouse will inform you if you are curious as to our adventures.—I have seen some old English papers up to the

15th. of May, I see the "Lady of the Lake" advertised[;] of course it is in his old ballad style, and pretty, after all Scott is the best of them.— The end of all scribblement is to amuse, and he certainly succeeds there, I long to read his new Romance.—And how does Sir Edgar?[1] and your friend Bland?[2] I suppose you are involved in some literary squabble, the only way is to despise all brothers of the quill, I suppose you wont allow me to be an author, but I contemn you all, you dogs! I do.—You dont know Dallas, do you? he had a farce ready for the stage before I left England, and asked me for a prologue, which I promised, but sailed in such a hurry I never penned a couplet.—I am afraid to ask after his drama for fear it should be damned, Lord forgive me for using such a word, but the pit, Sir, you know the pit, they will do those things in spite of merit.—[3] I remember this farce from a curious circumstance; when Drury Lane was burnt to the Ground,[4] by which accident Sheridan and his Son lost the few remaining shillings they were worth, what doth my friend D— do? why, before the fire was out, he writes a note to Tom Sheridan[5] the Manager of this combustible concern, to enquire whether this *farce* was not converted into fuel with about two thousand other unactable manuscripts which of course were in great peril if not actually consumed.—Now was not this characteristic? the ruling passions of Pope are nothing to it.—Whilst the poor distracted manager was bewailing the loss of a building only worth 300 000 £, together with some twenty thousand pounds worth of rags and tinsel in the tiring rooms, Bluebeard's elephants and *all that*;[6] in comes a note from a scorching author requiring at his hands two acts and odd scenes of a farce!!!—Dear H. remind Drury that I am his wellwisher, and let Scrope Davies be well affected towards me.—I look forward to meeting you at Newstead and renewing our old Champagne evenings with all the Glee of anticipation.—I have written by every opportunity, and expect responses as regular as those of the liturgy, and somewhat longer.—As it is impossible for a man in his senses to hope for happy days, let us at least look forward

[1] *Sir Edgar* was Hodgson's novel.

[2] An assistant master at Harrow while Byron was there, a friend of Hodgson, Drury, and other friends of Byron.

[3] Dallas's farce was acted at the Lyceum, by the Drury Lane Company, in November, 1809. The prologue, which Byron did not write, was written by Walter Rodwell Wright, author of *Horae Ionicae*.

[4] Drury Lane was twice destroyed by fire, first in 1791 and again in 1809.

[5] Thomas Sheridan (1775–1817) was assisting his father Richard Brinsley Sheridan as manager of Drury Lane when it burned in 1809.

[6] *Bluebeard, or Female Curiosity*, by George Colman the Younger was being acted at Drury Lane in January, 1809. The elephants were made of wickerwork.

to merry ones which come nearest to the other in appearance if not in reality, and in such expectations I remain yours very affecty.

BYRON

[TO JOHN CAM HOBHOUSE]   *Patras. Morea. October 4th. 1810*

My dear Hobhouse,—I wrote to you two days ago, but the weather and my friend Strane's conversation being much the same, and my ally Nicolo in bed with a fever, I think I may as well talk to you, the rather, as you cant answer me and excite my wrath with impatient observations, at least for 3 months to come.—I will try not to say the same things I have set down in my other letter of the 2d. but I cant promise, as my poor head is still giddy with my late fever.—I saw the Lady Hesther Stanhope[1] at Athens, and do not admire "that dangerous thing a female wit."[2]—She told me (take her own words) that she had given you a good set down at Malta, in some disputation about the Navy, from this of course I readily inferred the contrary, or in the words of an *acquaintance* of *ours*, that "you had the best of it."—She evinced a similar disposition to argufy with me, which I avoided by either laughing, or yielding, I despise the sex too much to squabble with them, and I rather wonder you should allow a woman to draw you into a contest, in which however I am sure you had the advantage she abuses you so bitterly.—I have seen too little of the Lady to form any decisive opinion, but I have discovered nothing different from other she things, except a great disregard of received notions in her conversation as well as conduct. I dont know whether this will recommend her to our sex, but I am sure it won't to her own.—She is going on to Constantinople.—Ali Pacha is in a scrape, Ibrahim Pacha, and the Pacha of Scutari have come down upon him with 20000 Gegdes and Albanians, retaken Berat, and threaten Tepaleni,[3] Adam Bey is dead,[4] Vely Pacha was on his way to the Danube, but has gone off suddenly to Yanina, and all Albania is in an uproar.—The Mountains we crossed

[1] Lady Hester Lucy Stanhope, a niece of William Pitt, and an independent and eccentric woman, was then starting on her Eastern travels with her friend Michael Bruce and her physician Charles Lewis Meryon, who afterward published her memoirs. Byron's brief encounter with her is best described in his letters. Her impression of him was not very favourable, according to Meryon. (See Meryon, III, 218–19.)

[2] Perhaps adapted from Pope's *Rape of the Lock*: "Parent of Vapours and of female wit" (IV, 59).

[3] Tepelene (variously spelled) was the seat of Ali Pasha's castle and stronghold in the mountains of Albania when Byron visited him in October, 1809.

[4] See Nov. 3, 1811, to Hobhouse.

last year are the Scene of warfare, and there is nothing but carnage and cutting of throats.—In my other letter I mentioned that Vely had given me a fine horse on my late visit, he received me with great pomp, standing, conducted me to the door with his arm round my waist, and a variety of civilities, invited me to meet him at Larissa and see his army, which I should have accepted, had not this rupture with Ibrahim taken place.—Sultan Mahmout is in a phrenzy because Vely has not joined the army, we have a report here that the Russians have beaten the Turks and taken Muchtar Pacha[5] prisoner, but it is a Greek Bazar rumour and not to be believed.—I have now treated you with a dish of Turkish politics, you have by this time gotten into England, and your ears and mouth are full of "Reform Burdett, Gale Jones, minority, last night's division, dissolution of parliament, battle in Portugal,"[6] and all the cream of forty newspapers.—In my t'other letter to which I am perpetually obliged to refer, I have offered some moving topics on the head of your Miscellany, the neglect of which I attribute to the half guinea annexed as the indispensable equivalent for the said volume.—Now I do hope notwithstanding that exorbitant demand, that on your return you will find it selling, or, what is better, sold, in consequence of which you will be able to face the public with your new volume, if that intention still subsists.—My journal, did I keep one, should be yours, as it is I can only offer my sincere wishes for your success, if you will believe it possible for a brother scribbler to be sincere on such an occasion. Will you execute a commission for me? Ld. Sligo tells me it was the intention of Miller in Albemarle Street to send by him a letter to me, which he stated to be of consequence, now, I have no concern with Mr. M. except a bill which I hope is paid before this time, will you visit the said M. and if it be a pecuniary matter, refer him to Hanson, and if not, tell me what he means, or forward his letter.—I have just received an epistle from Galt[7] with a Candiot poem which it seems I am to forward to you, this I would willingly do, but it is too large for a letter and too small for a parcel, and besides appears to be damned nonsense, from all which considerations I will deliver it in person.—It is entitled the "fair Shepherdess" or rather "Herdswoman"[;] if you don't like the trans-

[5] Ali Pasha's eldest son.

[6] A composite of newspaper stories.

[7] John Galt (1779–1839), a Scottish miscellaneous writer, was on a voyage to promote the export of British goods when he met Byron on the journey from Gibraltar to Malta. They met again in Athens. Galt later wrote an undistinguished life of Byron (1830) and made some fame as a novelist, his most successful work being *Annals of the Parish* (1821).

lation take the original title "η βοσκοπούλα".—Galt also writes something not very intelligible about a "Spartan state paper" which by his account is anything but *Laconic*, now the said Sparta having some years ceased to be a state, what the devil does he mean by a paper? he also adds mysteriously that the *affair* not being *concluded* he cannot at present apply for it.—Now, Hobhouse, are you mad? or is he? are these documents for Longman & Co.? Spartan state papers! and Cretan rhymes! indeed these circumstances superadded to his house at[Mycone?][8] (whither I am invited) and his Levant wines, make me suspect his sanity.—Athens is at present infested with English people, but they are moving, Dio benedetto!—I am returning to pass a month of two, I think the Spring will see me in England, but do not let this transpire, nor cease to urge the most dilatory of mortals, Hanson. I have some idea of purchasing the Island of Ithaca. I suppose you will add me to the Levant Lunatics.—I shall be glad to hear from your Signoria of your welfare, politics and Literature.— Tell M[atthews] that I have obtained above two hundred pl & opt Cs[9] and am almost tired of them, for the history of these he must wait my return, as after many attempts I have given up the idea of conveying information on paper.—You know the monastery of Mendele,[10] it was there I made myself master of the first.—Your last letter closes pathetically with a postscript about a nosegay, I advise you to introduce that into your next sentimental novel—I am sure I did not suspect you of any fine feelings, and I believe you are laughing, but you are welcome.—Vale, I can no more like Ld. Grizzle—yrs.

μπαιρων[11]

[TO STRATFORD CANNING[1]]   *Athens. October. 13th. 1810*

Sir,—I cannot address you without an apology the more especially as I write in the character of a complainant.—In travelling from the

---

[8] Mycone seems to have been the then accepted spelling (probably Italian) of the island of Mykonos.

[9] See June 22, 1809, to Matthews, note 1.

[10] Probably the monastery of Pendele, founded in 1578 at the foot of the mountain from which the Pendelic marble of the Acropolis was quarried.

[11] Here and frequently thereafter Byron signed his letters to friends in the Greek letters, the μπ being the common Greek transliteration of the English *B*.

[1] Stratford Canning, cousin of the statesman George Canning, had been first secretary of the British Embassy in Constantinople under Robert Adair, the Ambassador, while Byron was there. When Adair left for England on the ship that took Byron back to Greece, Canning became head of the Embassy without being named Ambassador.

Morea to Athens, the Bey of Corinth for some time refused me a lodging, and this at a time when the inclemency of the weather made it an act not only of impoliteness, but of inhumanity. It was indeed one of those days when "an enemy's dog" would have been sheltered.— The Greek Cogia Bachi[2] was equally unwilling to order a house, and I at last with difficulty procured a miserable cottage.—As the last circumstance has happened *twice* to myself in the same place, and once to *others*, I have nothing left but to request your interference.—I know no circumstance of extenuation, as a word from the Bey or the Cogia Bachi, would have admitted me into any house in the village, where I had before (in the time of Vely Pacha) found much better accommodation.—I therefore do hope and venture to request that this "circumcised dog" may not pass (I cannot say unpunished) but *unreprimanded*. —I believe it to be the inclination, as I know it to be in the power of the British minister to protect the subjects of his Sovereign from Insult.—I conceive that brutality will not be countenanced even by the Turks, as we are taught that hospitality is a Barbarian's virtue.— Your interference may be esteemed a favour not only to me but to all future travellers.—By land or sea we must pass the Isthmus in our excursions from Athens to the Morea, and you will be informed of the accuracy of my statement of the Bey's conduct, by the Marquis of Sligo, who does me the honour to deliver this letter.—I again solicit your interposition, and have the honour to be, Sir,

your most obedient humble Servant
BYRON

[TO J[OHN] FOSTER[1]]   [*Nov., 1810?*]

No written agreement exists between the owner of the horse in question & myself, but I assure you upon my *honour*, the horse was to be mine at a certain sum a day during my stay in Athens and so far from its being in George's option to let him to another, he obtained him under the pretext of his fatigue after a journey to rest for a few days only.—As for the man he is a liar & a rascal, and has contradicted himself today twenty times before the Waywode, and also before me, pretending "that the horse was taken by force, that he wanted to sell

---

[2] The Cogia Bachi was a Greek provincial official under the Turks.
[1] John Foster (1787?–1846), a Liverpool architect, met Cockerell in 1810 in Constantinople and continued his travels and research with him in Greece. He was one of the travelling Englishmen with whom Byron was associated in Athens in 1810–11.

him &c. &c."—His object at present appears to be that of causing a quarrel between the parties, in which if he succeeds it will not be the. . . . [Remainder of manuscript missing.]

[TO JOHN HANSON] *Athens. Novr. 4th. 1810*

Dear Sir,—The Bearer of this, William Fletcher, has lived with me some years and served me very faithfully; the whole sum I owe him for wages and other accounts is *two* hundred and *fifty* pounds which I desire may be *paid* him as *soon* as possible.—As he was brought up originally to farming, if anything falls at Newstead which may chance to suit, let him have the refusal.—

Believe me dr. Sir yrs. very truly
BYRON

[TO JOHN HANSON] *Athens. Novr. 11th. 1810*

Dear Sir,—Yours arrived on the first Inst. it tells me I am ruined.— It is in the power of God, the Devil, and Man, to make me poor and miserable, but neither the *second* nor *third* shall make me sell Newstead, and by the aid of the *first* I will persevere in this resolution.—My "father's house shall *not* be made a den of thieves."—Newstead shall *not* be sold.—I am some thousand miles from home with few resources, and the prospect of their daily becoming less, I have neither friend nor counsellor, my only English servant departs with this letter, my situation is forlorn enough for a man of my birth and former expectations; —do not mistake this for complaint however, I state the simple fact, and will never degrade myself by lamentations. You have my answer. —Commend me to your family, I perceive Hargreaves is your partner, he always promised to turn out well, and Charles I am sure is a very fine fellow.—As for the others I can't pretend to prophecy, I present my respects to all the ladies, and I suppose I may *kiss* Harriet as you or Mrs. Hanson will be my proxy, provided she is not grown too tall for such a token of remembrance.—I must not forget Mrs. Hanson who has often been a mother to me, and as you have always been a friend I beg you to believe me with all sincerity

yours
BYRON

Dear Hobhouse,—I wrote to you to apprise Mr. Hanson (as I have done in a letter, but wish you to repeat my refusal) that I will *not* sell Newstead according to his suggestion.—I shall enter into no details but state the sum total, viz, that I am ruined.—For further particulars enquire at No. 6.—My compts to Matthews and Davies, send Mrs. Pigot a copy of your miscellany,[1] and believe me

yours very truly
BYRON

P.S.—I beg you will repeat very seriously for me, that let the consequence be as it may, ruin to myself and all connected with me (D. and the old women inclusive) I will not sell Newstead, *No, oXi, yok, yeo* (Albanesico) *Noa* (Nottinghamshirico) [*Naw?*], μὴ, οὐκ, having now given my negative in all the tongues I can refuse in, I call Christ, Mahomet, Confucius and Zoroaster to witness my sincerity and Cam Hobhouse to make it manifest to the ears and eyes of men, and I further ask his pardon for a long postscript to a short letter.

P.S. 2d.—If any body is savage and wants satisfaction for my satire, write, that I may return, and give it.—

My dear Hodgson,—This will arrive with an English servant whom I send homewards with some papers of consequence.—I have been journeying in different parts of Greece for these last four months, and you may expect me in England somewhere about April, but this is very dubious.—Hobhouse you have doubtless seen, he went home in August to look after his Miscellany, and to arrange materials for a tour he talks of publishing.—You will find him well and scribbling, that is scribbling if well, and well if scribbling.—I suppose you have a score of new works, all of which I hope to see flourishing, with a hecatomb of reviews.—*My* works are likely to have a powerful effect with a vengeance, as I hear of divers angry people, whom it is proper I should shoot at, by way of satisfaction.—Be it so, the same impulse which made "Otho a warrior," will make me one also.—My domestic affairs being moreover considerably deranged, my appetite for travelling pretty well satiated with my late peregrinations, my various

---

[1] Hobhouse's *Imitations and Translations* contained nine of Byron's poems, some of which, such as his poem to his Newfoundland dog Boatswain, would be of special interest to the Pigots.

hopes in this world almost extinct, and not very brilliant in the next, I trust I shall go through the process with a creditable "sang froid" and not disgrace a line of cut-throat ancestors.—I regret in one of your letters to hear you talk of domestic embarrassments,[1] indeed I am at present very well calculated to sympathise with you on that point.—I suppose I must take to dram drinking as a succedaneum for philosophy, though as I am happily not married I have very little occasion for either just yet.—Talking of marriage puts me in mind of Drury, who I suppose has a dozen children by this time all fine fretful brats; I will never forgive Matrimony for having spoiled such an excellent Bachelor. If any body honours my name with an enquiry tell them of "my whereabouts" and write if you like it.—I am living alone in the Franciscan monastery with one Fri*ar* (a Capuchin of course) and one Fri*er* (a bandy legged Turkish Cook) two Albanian savages, a Tartar, and a Dragoman, my only Englishman departs with this and other letters.—The day before yesterday, the Waywode (or Governor of Athens) with the Mufti of Thebes (a sort of Mussulman Bishop) supped here and made themselves beastly with raw Rum, and the Padrè of the convent being as drunk as *we*, my *Attic* feast went off with great eclât.—I have had a present of a stallion from the Pacha of the Morea.—I caught a fever going to Olympia.—I was blown ashore on the Island of Salamis, in my way to Corinth through the gulph of Ægina.—I have kicked an Athenian postmaster, I have a friendship with the French Consul, and an Italian painter, and am on good terms with five Teutones & Cimbri, Danes and Germans, who are travelling for an Academy.[2]—Vale!

yours ever,

μπαιρων

[TO JOHN CAM HOBHOUSE]   *Athens. Novr. 26th. 1810*

Dear Hobhouse,—Five or six letters are already on their passage, or perhaps arrived, since July, and I suppose after all your delays, they

---

1 Hodgson's father, Rector of Barwick-in-Elmet, Yorkshire, died in October, 1810, leaving only burdensome debts to his son. Byron later relieved Hodgson of some of his financial embarrassments with several large "loans" never meant to be repaid.

2 The French Consul was Louis François Sébastien Fauvel; the Italian painter was Giovanni Battista Lusieri, Lord Elgin's agent; The five foreigners were Peter Oluf Brønsted, Karl Freiherr Haller von Hallerstein, Jacob Linckh, Otto Magnus Freiherr von Stackelberg, and H. C. Koës. (Details concerning them are given in Borst, pp. 136–38.)

will find you in London.—I have in my former sheets told you where I have been and what I have been doing, or rather not doing, for my life has, with the exception of a very few moments, never been anything but a *yawn*.—Here have been Lords and Ladies with many others of good report.—Some have seen you at Malta & some have not.—They tell me sad news of my good for nothing acquaintances; Sir G. W. & Sir B. G.[1] are ruined (by the bye so am I but I wrote you that news by Fletcher) and Wallace[2] is incarcerated; your friend Baillie[3] is the only lucky man I hear of, his stepmother is dead, can't you inoculate yours with the same disorder?—Letters I have had, yours of Cagliari, and two billets from Hanson, he wants me to sell Newstead, but I wont, and pray repeat my negative as strongly as possible.—My affairs are greatly embarrassed, & I see no prospect of their ever being better, but I will not sell my abbey for man or the Devil.—Tell Davies, in a very few months I shall be at home to relieve him from his responsibility[4] which he would never have incurred so long, had I been aware "of the law's delay" and the (not Insolence) but "Indolence of office."—I presume he is very wroth and in that mood, to use his frequent quotation, in which the "Dove would peck the *Es*tridge."—I shall be glad to meet him on friendly terms, & it will not be my fault if we meet on others, but I cannot "truckle to his maudlin humours."— You refresh me greatly with the tidings of my Satire, if there be any of that martial spirit to require trial by combat, you will inform me which be they, the same impulse which made *"Otho a warrior"* will make me one too.—And so Lucien B[onaparte] is "lagged" to Malta,[5] he is really a Philosopher.—I have now seen the World, that is the most ancient of the ancient part, I have spent my little all, I have

[1] Sir G. W. was probably Sir Godfrey Webster; Sir B. G. was Sir B. Graham. They and Captain Wallace were companions of Byron's roistering days in 1808. See April 15, 1808, to Hobhouse.

[2] See April 26, 1808, to Augusta Leigh, note 2.

[3] "Long" Baillie, a friend of Hobhouse and Matthews, had been at Harrow with Byron.

[4] Scrope Davies had made Byron a loan before the poet's first journey abroad in 1809. An undated letter from Davies to Byron in the Murray MSS. says: "The bond debt is £4633." Davies apparently raised the money by borrowing on his own signature from the usurers. Byron paid off the debt on his return, from Claughton's down payment on Newstead, first £1500 and a final payment of £4800 on March 27, 1814. (See diary of March 28, 1814.) The sum repaid included interest.

[5] In 1809 Lucien Bonaparte, brother of Napoleon, left Italy, where he had been living in exile after disagreements with his brother, for America, but was captured by the British and taken to Malta and later to England where he was kept under surveillance until the end of the war with France.

tasted of all sorts of pleasure (so tell the Citoyen) I have nothing more to hope, and may begin to consider of the most eligible way of walking out of it, probably I may find in England, somebody inclined to save me the trouble.—Mention to M[atthews], that I have found so many of his antiques[6] on this classical soil, that I am tired of pl & opt Cs,[7] the last thing I could be tired of, I wish I could find some of Socrates's Hemlock, but Lusieri tells me it dont poison people nowadays.—I had a fever in the Morea, but my Constitution beat both it & the Doctors.——You talk of a tour (in print) I have told Cockerell[8] to paint for you, but I have no Journal or any thing worth journalising. —Why Man! you have materials enow without ramming in my damned nonsense, as Diggory says.—Here is a Scotch Surgeon going to write on Greece,[9] you must be before hand with him; *his* will be very heavy work I am sure if I may judge by his jargon; it will make admirable subject for a review should you feel venomous.—I expect to find you in the press, pray what's become of the Miscellany?— Where is Hodgson? where Dallas? your prize essay? and the 40 pounds annexed?—That timber-head Fletcher is sent home with a paper of some consequence to my mother.—I dont miss him at all, Viscillie and Dervise are admirable waiters, I have a bandy legged Turkish Cook, and *Nicolo Giraud* is my Dragoman and Major Domo.—I have preferred your petition of marbles to Fletcher, who hath consented to take them, but he hath an ill memory, Heaven help him!—You will write to Malta, till you hear of my arrival, and I will answer as well as I can.———Sandford Graham[10] whom you remember at Trinity dines with me tomorrow (the 28th). He tells me that Davies is to be married to an heiress whom he picked up at Bath.——I am now an Italoquist having been taught that tongue by necessity and Nicolo Giro the brother of Lusieri's should be wife.—Andreas Zantachi[11] I sent off after your Malta letter, so I had no choice left between pantomime or silence, except gabbling Romaic and Italian in which last I am

[6] Byron probably means the ancient Greek penchant for boy love.

[7] See June 22 [1809], to Matthews, note 1.

[8] Charles Robert Cockerell (1788–1863), an architect who later achieved renown, was starting on a course of professional studies by exploring the architectural antiquities of Greece. He spent the winter of 1810–11 in Athens where he saw much of Byron. With other explorers he discovered the Ægina Marbles.

[9] Unidentified; it may have been the Dominus Macgill mentioned in this letter.

[10] Sandford Graham (1788–1852), whom Byron had known at Trinity College, was one of the English travellers in Athens during the winter of 1810–11. He was in Byron's party on the visit to Sounion described in this letter. Graham was later a member of Parliament and a Fellow of the Society of Antiquaries.

[11] Byron's Greek servant who spoke many languages.

intelligible, my Greek is ϵτϛη και ϵτϛη,[12] and my Latin of course walked off with the late dragoman of Dominus Macgill.[13]—Cockerell, Foster, Graham, Baron Haller[14] (a Teutonic and Cimbrian traveller) Lusieri, and myself are to set off μεθαυριον[15] for Cape Colonna in great force.—— A Bolognese physician is to be presented to me tomorrow at his own petition having heard that I am the *celebrated aquatic genius* who swam across the Hellespont when he was at Abydos. I believe the fellow wants to make experiments with me in diving.——You are now, Yani Hobhouse, digesting your remarks for Lintot or Jacob Tonson, and anticipating publication with your tongue to Matthews, or some such patient listener.—I suppose you have made the tour of Longman's back-shop, and sunned yourself in the smiles of Mrs. Ridgway.[16]—If you hear any thing of your own or my works good or bad, let us have it.—I shall be glad to hear that they are all alive.—You have sailed so long in the Salsette you must be quite a Tarpaulin.—Kill your step-mother and reconcile yourself to your father, I hope your brother was not in that damned advance Guard which has lately taken up its ever-lasting position at some place in Portugal according to the Frankfort Gazette.—Fletcher I have sent home with dispatches, he is in great tribulation with his numskull full of Gales of wind, French privateers, Galliots, Black john lugger, pressing at home, thieves in the Morea, row at his castle with Sally, and a world of woes.—As for me I am finished, for I will not sell, and have nothing left for the "Gemman as goes round for the tax upon income" according to the Salsette song,— believe me dear Yani, yours ever

B......n.—

P.S.—Decr. 5th. 1810.

Dear Cam,—I open my letter to mention an escape; Graham, Cockerell, Lusieri, myself, and a Bavarian Baron, went to Cape Colonna where we spent a day.—At that time five and twenty Main-notes (pirates) were in the caves at the foot of the cliff with some Greek boatmen their prisoners.—They demanded of these who were the

---

[12] so-so.

[13] See note 9.

[14] Karl Freiherr Haller von Hallerstein (1774–1817) was architect to Prince Louis of Bavaria. He was on an expedition financed (meagrely) by the Prince. He joined in the archaeological researches of Cockerell and others on Ægina in 1811, and assisted Cockerell and Stackelberg in the excavations at Bassae of the Temple of Apollo.

[15] day after tomorrow.

[16] Ridgeway was a London bookseller who executed various commissions for Byron. His wife must have smiled on Byron as well as Hobhouse.

Franks above? one of the Greeks knew *me*, and they were preparing to attack us, when seeing my Albanians and conjecturing there were others in the vicinity, they were seized with a panic and marched off.— We were all armed (about 12 with our attendants) some with fusils & all with pistols and ataghans, but though we were prepared for resistance, I am inclined to think we are rather better without a battle.— Some of the Greeks whom they had taken, told me afterwards they saw me with my double barrell mounted on a chestnut horse, and described the rest of our party very accurately.—Two of them arrived yesterday, released, but stripped of every thing by the Mainnotes.——These last deliberated some time, but as we were in a very advantageous position among the columns, ignorant of our numbers, and alarmed by some balls which whizzed over their heads by accident, they kept to the shore, and permitted us to depart in peace.—The Albanians, my Turkish bandy legged Cook, a servant of Lusieri's & myself had guns and pistols, the rest side arms and pistols, but how we should have carried on the war is very doubtful, I rather think we should have been taen like Billy Taylor and carried off to Sea.—We are all snug in our winter quarters after the same tour we made last year.—Graham and myself got drunk at Keratia, the former in his Bacchanism decapitated a large pig with a Highland Broadsword to the horror of Lusieri, and after all we could not eat him.—Good bye, Yani,[17]

yrs. a second time

B x x x x x x x x x x x x x x x x x x x x x x N.—

[TO JOHN CAM HOBHOUSE]
Capuchin Convent. Athens. January 10th. 1811

Dear Hobhouse,—I have written at intervals several letters, some of which it is probable you have received.—Two have arrived of yours dated Malta and Cagliari, & I conceive there be others *on* the Sea or *in* it, for you must have been months in England.—Since your departure from the Cyclades, I have been principally in Attica, which I have traversed more than once, besides two tours in the Morea of the particulars of which Mr. Fletcher now on his voyage with dispatches will apprise you.—Here be many English, and there have been more, with all of whom I have been and *am* on dining terms, & we have had balls and a variety of fooleries with the females of Athens.——I am very undecided in my intentions, though stationary enough as you perceive

---

[17] A phonetic spelling of the Greek Giannis (from older Greek Ioannis) = John.

by my date.—I sometimes think of moving homewards in Spring & sometimes of not moving at all till I have worn out my shoes which are all as good as new.—Hanson has at last written, and wants *me* to sell Newstead. I *will not*, and though I have in more than one letter to you requested you to corroborate and assist this *negative*, I beg in this and all subsequent communications to entreat you to tell him and all whom it may concern, that I will *not* sell my patrimony.—I suppose however the adjustment of that and other damned affairs will drag me to England.—Well, Sir, & so I suppose you are holding forth to your acquaintance on the subject of your travels, and they are all very glad to see you, and you have been tipsy and loquacious as usual on such occasions, and are just beginning to subside into the old track of living after shaking about sixty pair of hands, and seeing the play & such like all of which must be very new to a voyager from the Levant.—You will present my respects to Matthews and Davies who is I hear about to throw himself away on a rich wife, and none of the seemliest according to my reporter.—Pray what profits make ye of the Miscellany? ey, ey, I warrant you now, you are preparing a tome of travel for the press.—I have no journal or you should have it to abet your design.—I am now tolerable in Italian, and am studying the Romaic under a Master,[1] being obliged to cashier my Latin with my last Dragoman,[2] and betake myself to the moderns.—I have sent a bark to Smyrna in the faint hope of letters, & shall not fill up this sheet till it's return.—January 14th. 1811.—My boat is returned with some newspapers & duplicates of letters already received.—None from you, but all in good time.—I shall certainly not (without something very novel occurs) move towards your Island till Spring, nor even then if I receive any further remittances, a business which I hope you did not fail to urge to my agent.—You have I humbly presume forwarded all my epistles to their respective destinations.—I certainly wish to hear how you go on, and what plan you have chalked out, five and twenty is almost too late in life for anything but the Senate or the Church, I wish you was a parson, or a counsellor at law, by the bye Ld. Erskine[3] did not com-

[1] In the first edition of *Childe Harold* (1812), pp. 224–25, Byron included "the prospectus of a translation of Anacharsis into Romaic, by my Romaic master Marmarotouri, who wished to publish it in England". Marmarotouri was a leader among the Greek patriots, who no doubt influenced Byron's views of the Greeks and of Greek nationalism.

[2] Andreas Zantachi, Byron's servant, whom he took on in Patras in 1809 as dragoman because he spoke many languages.

[3] Thomas Erskine, first Baron Erskine (1750–1823), later Lord Chancellor, was first called to the bar and won an important case against Lord Sandwich, first lord of the Admiralty, when he was only 28.

mence till nearly thirty.—I do not think your Sire so blameable, the fault lies of course with the Stepdame, the old story, Baillie has got rid of his "injusta Noverca" see what it is to have luck![4]—As you are fond of scribbling, and are said to have a talent that way. Why dont you, and *Matthews* & some other wits, undertake some periodical, hebdomadal, or diurnal concern, I leave you to find out what, but I think you might bring such a scheme to bear.—Fyott[5] is this day arrived from Mt. Athos ("ἅγιον ὄρος") he has discovered nothing to signify in the manuscript way.—Graham & Haygarth[6] are to depart shortly, one for Stambol, Haygarth for Sicily.—I shall send this by the latter.— Galt is in Pera full of his Sour Wine Company speculation. I shall look at him in Mycone[7] in the "Prima Vera".—He sent me a Candiot poem for you, but being the worst Romaic & the vilest nonsense ever seen, it was not worth the carriage.—As you know Athens and all its peculiarities, I shall not afflict you with description.—I have three horses (one a gift of Vely Pacha) and live rather better and cheaper than last winter.—I see a good deal of the English & Lusieri, chiefly of late, and have had no disputes with any one.—I am tranquil & as contented as I suppose one can be in any situation. I have also a Bavarian Baron & celebrated painter, taking views for me.[8]—yrs. very affectly. & truly

B.—

P.S.—This goes by Haygarth who moves in a few days to Malta by way of the Morea & Zante.—Graham is off too.—I stay till Spring, at all events till I receive letters, which as usual take their time on the way.—Good night, you Port-drinking fellow, I am just returned from dining with Haygarth.
January 17th. 1811——

---

[4] "injusta Noverca" (Virgil, *Eclogue* III, 33) "Unjust (or harsh) step-mother".

[5] John Fiott (1783–1866), a graduate of St. John's College, Cambridge, toured the Near East in 1807–10 as a "travelling Bachelor" of his college, collecting antiquities, including manuscripts, coins, and medals. He later gained eminence as a collector and man of science and was a member of the Society of Antiquaries and president of the Royal Astronomical Society.

[6] Sandford Graham and William Haygarth were among the English travellers and antiquaries in Athens during Byron's residence.

[7] John Galt had been in Athens on Byron's return from Constantinople. He had taken a house on the island of Mykonos. Byron did not visit him there.

[8] Baron Haller, an architect and archaeologist, also had talent as an artist, and produced many drawings and landscape paintings of Greece.

Athens January 14th. 1811

My dear Madam,—I seize an occasion to write to you as usual shortly but frequently, as the arrival of letters where there exists no regular communication is of course very precarious.—I have received at different intervals several of yours, but generally six months after date, some sooner, some later, and though lately tolerably stationary, the delays appear just the same.—I have lately made several small tours of some hundred or two miles about the Morea, Attica &c. as I have finished my grand Giro by the Troad Constantinople &c. and am returned down again to Athens.—I believe I have mentioned to you more than once that I swam (in imitation of Leander though without his lady) across the Hellespont from Sestos to Abydos. Of this and all other particulars Fletcher whom I have sent home with papers &c. will apprise you.—I cant find that he is any loss, being tolerably master of the Italian & modern Greek languages, which last I am also studying with a master, I can order and discourse more than enough for a reasonable man.—Besides the perpetual lamentations after beef & beer, the stupid bigotted contempt for every thing foreign, and insurmountable incapacity of acquiring even a few words of any language, rendered him like all other English servants, an incumbrance.—I do assure you the plague of speaking for him, the comforts he required (more than myself by far) the pilaws (a Turkish dish of rice & meat) which he could not eat, the wines which he could not drink, the beds where he could not sleep, & the long list of calamities such as stumbling horses, want of tea!!! &c. which assailed him, would have made a lasting source of laughter to a spectator, and of inconvenience to a Master.—After all the man is honest and in Christendom capable enough, but in Turkey—Lord forgive me, my Albanian soldiers, my Tartars & Janizary worked for him & us too as my friend Hobhouse can testify.——It is probable I may steer homewards in Spring, but to enable me to do that I must have remittances.—My own funds would have lasted me very well, but I was obliged to assist a friend, who I know will pay me, but in the meantime I am out of pocket.—At present I do not care to venture a winter's voyage, even if I were otherwise tired of travelling, but I am so convinced of the advantages of looking at mankind instead of reading about them, and of the bitter effects of staying at home with all the narrow prejudices of an Islander, that I think there should be a law amongst us to set our young men abroad for a term among the few allies our wars have left us.—Here

I see and have conversed with French, Italians, Germans, Danes, Greeks, Turks, Armenians, &c. &c. &c. and without losing sight of my own, I can judge of the countries and manners of others.—Where I see the superiority of England (which by the bye we are a good deal mistaken about in many things) I am pleased, and where I find her inferior I am at least enlightened.—Now I might have staid smoked in your towns or fogged in your country a century without being sure of this, and without acquiring anything more useful or amusing at home.—I keep no journal, nor have I any intention of scribbling my travels.—I have done with authorship, and if in my last production I have convinced the critics or the world, I was something more than they took me for, I am satisfied, nor will I hazard *that reputation* by a future effort.—It is true I have some others in manuscript, but I leave them for those who come after me, and if deemed worth publishing, they may serve to prolong my memory, when I myself shall cease to remember.—I have a famous Bavarian Artist taking some views of Athens &c. &c. for me.—This will be better than scribbling, a disease I hope myself cured of.—I hope on my return to lead a quiet and re-cluse life, but God knows and does best for us all, at least so they say, and I have nothing to object, as on the whole I have no reason to com-plain of my lot.—I am convinced however that men do more harm to themselves than ever the Devil could do to them. I trust this will find you well and as happy as we can be, you will at least be pleased to hear that I am so &

yours ever
BYRON.—

[TO JOHN HANSON]   *Athens. January 18th. 1811*

Dear Sir,—I have written my negative to your proposal on the sub-ject of Newstead, by my servant Fletcher, which I presume is de-livered by this time, and I write now for the purpose of repeating it.—I will *not* sell Newstead, come what may!—As I am distressed for money, you will send me remittances if you can, if you cannot, I must stem the tide as well as possible, I however cannot return to England without a further supply.—You perceive I have made my principal tour i.e. to Constantinople &c.—& am returned into Greece again; I am now very undecided, but determined not to return if I can help it.—You will present my respects to all your family, but I suppose there are others in it *not* of my acquaintance since my departure.—You will be good enough when you hear from me always to apprise Mrs Byron, as she will be anxious, and the arrival of my letters to her is uncertain.—I write when I can, but you will glance at the Map, and perceive that it is a long voyage for a "single Sheet".—You wont expect a long letter from these outlandish places, & as you are a man of business it would be wrong to take up your time with observations on Turks, and Greeks. —I have travelled a good deal, and seen a good deal, & shall be very glad some of these days to take a bottle of your port in Chancery Lane, and hear how your live stocks go on at Farleigh, and how much Bacon your hinds consume, which article you see I have not forgotten, though I am in a country where it is a damnable sin to think of it.—It is a pity you can't make a Mussulman of Manchester, who would then swallow less of that expensive dainty, by the bye, I hope that his master dont take so many of Dr. Hill's diet-draughts as formerly & that he leaves off business (to Hargreaves) & grows fat & farmerlike.—I hope when I do arrive to find you all well, the old ones married, the new ones cherished, what can I say more?

yrs. very truly
BYRON

[TO FRANCIS HODGSON]   *Athens—January 20th. 1811*

My dear Hodgson,—In most of your letters, that is to say *two* the only ones I have received of yours, you complain of my silence, this complaint I presume to be removed by this time, as I have written frequently, but more particularly by H. who is of course long ago landed, and will amply gratify any further curiosity you may have beyond the limits of a letter.——I also wrote by the Black John, which however was taken off Algiers with the Capt. Moses Kennedy & several bags of long letters, but especially Hobhouse's intimates have to regret the capture of some enormous packets, which cost a world of pains at Constantinople in the Troad & elsewhere, as I can witness, & unless the French government publish them, I am afraid we have little chance of recovering these inestimable manuscripts.—But then to make amends to himself followed close on the heels of his letters (by the bye I fear *heels* of letters is a very incorrect metaphor) and will tell the world all how & about it, unless he also has been boarded & taken off Algiers.——Talking of taking, I was nearly taken myself six weeks ago by some Mainnote pirates (Lacedemonians & be damned to them) at Cape Colonna, but being well armed, & attended, the varlets were afraid, or they might have bagged us all with a little skirmishing.—I am still in Athens making little tours to Marathon,

Sunium, the top of Hymettus, & the Morea occasionally to diversify the season.—My Grand Giro finished with Constantinople & I shall not (I think) go further Eastward, but I am sure of nothing so little as my own intentions, and if I receive cash & comfortable news from home I shant trouble your foggy Island for amusement.—I am studying modern Greek with a Master, and my current tongue is Levant Italian, which I gabble perforce, my late dragoman spoke bad Latin, but having dismissed him, I am left to my resources which consist in tolerably fluent Lingua Franca, middling Romaic (modern Greek) and some variety of Ottoman oaths of great service with a stumbling horse, or a stupid servant.—I lately sent to England my only remaining Englishman with some papers about money matters, and am left d'ye see all by myself in these outlandish parts, and I don't find it *never* the *worser* for friends and servants that is to say fellow countrymen in those capacities are troublesome fellow travellers.—I have a variety of acquaintance, French, Danes, Germans Greek Italian & Turkish, and have contracted an alliance with Dr. Bronstedt of Copenhagen a pretty philosopher as you'd wish to see.[1]—Besides I am on good terms with some of my countrymen here, Messrs Grahame & Haygarth, & I have in pay a Bavarian Baron named "Lynch" (pronounce it Lyn*k*) who limns landscapes for the lucre of gain.[2]—Here also are Messrs Fiott, Cockerell & Foster[3] all of whom I know, and they are all vastly amiable & accomplished.—I am living in the Capuchin Convent, Hymettus before me, the Acropolis behind, the temple of Jove to my right, the Stadium in front, the town to the left, eh, Sir, there's a situation, there's your picturesque! nothing like that, Sir, in Lunnun, no not even the Mansion House. And I feed upon Woodcocks & red Mullet every day, & I have three horses (one a present from the Pacha of the Morea) and I ride to Piraeus, & Phalerum & Munychia,[4] which however dont look quite so magnificent after the harbours of Cadiz, Lisbon, Constantinople & Gibralter not forgetting Malta. I wish to be sure I had a few books, one's own works for instance, any damned nonsense on a long Evening.—I had a straggling number of the E[dinburgh] Review given me by a compassionate Capt. of a frigate

[1] Peter Oluf Brønsted (1780–1842) was an archaeologist from the University of Copenhagen.

[2] Jacob Linckh (1787–1841), a native of Cannstatt, had studied art in Rome before coming to Greece in September, 1810. He joined Cockerell, Foster, and Haller in the excavations of the site of the temple on Ægina in 1811.

[3] See Jan. 10, 1811, to Hobhouse, note 5; Nov. 26, 1810, note 7; [Nov., 1810?], note 1.

[4] Now called Turcolimano.

lately, it contains the reply to the Oxonian pamphlet, on the Strabonic controversy, the reviewer seems to be in a perilous passion & heaves out a deal of Slack-jaw as the Sailors call it.—You know to direct to Malta, whence my letters are or ought to be forwarded.—In two days I shall be twenty three, and on the 2d. above a year and a half out of England.—I suppose you & Drury sometimes drink one's health on a speechday, & I trust we shall meet merrily, and make a tour some summer to Wales or Scotland, it will be a great relaxation to me jaunting once more in a Chay.—I need not write at length as Hobby is brimful of remarks, and it would be cruel to curtail him of a syllable.— Tell him I have written to him frequently, as indeed I have to yourself and also to Drury & others, but this is a plaguy distance for a single sheet.—

Yours always
BYRON—

[TO JOHN HANSON (*a*)]   *Athens.—February 1st. 1811*

Sir,—As I have just received a firman enabling me to proceed to Ægypt & Syria, I shall not return to England before I have visited Jerusalem & Grand Cairo.—I have therefore to request, as by the return of my servant with the papers you will be enabled so to do; to remit immediately, as I have nearly finished my credit.—With my best remembrances to your family I remain

yrs. very truly
BYRON—

P.S.—Direct your letters to Malta, but let my credit be on Constantinople.—

[TO JOHN HANSON (*b*)]   *Athens February 1st. 1811*[1]

Dear Sir,—As I have received a firman from the Porte enabling me to visit Ægypt & Syria I shall not return to England before I have seen

---

[1] This letter is apparently a duplicate copy of the one of the same date to Hanson now in the Stark Library, University of Texas. Byron frequently repeated himself in letters to the same correspondents because of the uncertainty of the mails. But it is strange that he should have written two almost identical letters on the same day, which must have been sent by the same carrier. He did, however, add some details in the second letter about the Wymondham sale money and his refusal to sell Newstead.

Jerusalem & Grand Cairo.—I have therefore to request you will remit, my credit being nearly out, & I suppose the return of my servant with Mrs. B's Scotch papers will enable you so to do, even if you have not received the Wymondham purchase money.—You may sell Rochdale if you can but I will *not hear* of the sale of Newstead.—With my best remembrance to your house I remain

yrs. very truly
BYRON

P.S.—Direct your letters to Malta, but let my credit be on Constantinople.—

[TO JOHN CAM HOBHOUSE]   *Athens. February 1st. 1811*

Dear Cam,—My firman for Syria & Ægypt being arrived I am off in Spring for Mount Sion, Damascus, Tyre & Sidon, Cairo & Thebes.[1] —Pray whisper in Hanson's ear the word remittance, as I shall soon be run out if you dont urge that worthy but snail paced man.—I have written to you by various vessels, & for fear of accidents, a duplicate of this letter, or something like it.—

yours ever
BYRON

P.S.—Letters to Malta, but let the cash go on to Pera.—

[TO MRS. CATHERINE GORDON BYRON]   *Athens. February 2d. 1811*

Dear Mother,—Being enabled by a firman from the Porte to proceed to Jerusalem & Ægypt, I shall visit the Pyramids & Palestine before I return.—You will be good enough to remind Mr. Hanson of remittances & not allow him to leave me three thousand miles from England without cash or credit.—Fletcher being arrived by this time I

---

1 How serious Byron was about going to these places it is difficult to say. If the remittances had come from Hanson and if an agreeable travelling companion had joined him, it is probable he would have gone. But he was, as he himself recognized, moved chiefly by circumstances and moods.

say no more but send a duplicate of this letter; I have also written at intervals.——

yrs ever
BYRON

P.S.—Direct your letters to Malta, but let my money be sent to Constantinople.—

[TO [STRATFORD CANNING]]   *Athens. Febry. 26th. 1811*

Sir,—I have forwarded to the Caimacam of the Morea the letter which accompanied that of your Excellency, & it has produced a long apology from the Bey of Corinth, which is all that can be wished of Turk or Christian.[1]——I took the liberty of correcting a small mistake in the said remonstrance, & of exchanging the word *Coronna* & substituting that of *Corinth* in its stead, it being the Governor of the latter city of whom I had occasion to complain—I have now only to return my thanks to your Excellency for your interference which has had all the effect which could be desired, & have the honour to be your obliged

& very obedt. humble Servant
BYRON

[TO MRS. CATHERINE GORDON BYRON]   *Athens. February 28th. 1811*

Dear Madam,—As I have received a firman for Ægypt &c. I shall proceed to that quarter in the Spring, & I beg you will state to Mr. Hanson that it is necessary to [send] further remittances.—On the subject of Newstead I answer as before—*No.*—If it is necessary to sell, sell Rochdale.—Fletcher will have arrived by this time with my letters to that purport.—I will tell you fairly, I have in the first place no opinion of funded property.——If, by any particular circumstances I shall be led to adopt such a determination, I will at all events, pass my life abroad, as my only tie to England is Newstead, & that once gone neither interest or inclination lead me northward.—Competence in your country is ample Wealth in the East such is the difference in the value of money & the abundance of the necessaries of life, & I feel

[1] See Oct. 13, 1810, to Canning. Byron published a facsimile of this letter from the Bey of Corinth as a specimen of the Romaic in the first (quarto) edition of *Childe Harold* I–II.

myself so much a citizen of the world, that the spot where I can enjoy a delicious climate, & every luxury at a less expense than a common college life in England, will always be a country to me, and such are in fact the shores of the Archipelago.—This then is the alternative, if I preserve Newstead, I return, if I sell it, I stay away.——I have had no letters since yours of June, but I have written several times, & shall continue as usual on the same plan, believe me

yrs. ever
BYRON

P.S.—I shall most likely see you in the course of the summer but of course at such a distance I cannot specify any particular month.—

[TO JOHN HANSON]   *Athens February 28th. 1811*

Dear Sir,—An opportunity occurring I write to mention that having received a firman for Ægypt &c. I shall proceed to that quarter in the Spring.—You will if possible remit, as that is equally necessary for coming or going.—I beg leave to repeat my *negative* to your proposal about Newstead.—If we must sell, sell Rochdale.——I have no opinion of funded property, admitting that there were no other reasons against selling.— —One thing is certain, if I should ever be induced to sell N——I will pass my life abroad.—If I retain it, I return, if not, I stay where I am.—With my best remembrances to your family I remain yours ever

BYRON

[TO JOHN CAM HOBHOUSE]   *Athens—March 5th. 1811*

Dear Hobhouse,—Two English gentlemen after 7 years captivity in France having made their escape through Bosnia, and being arrived here on their way home I shall follow up my last letter with the present, which will be conveyed by these runaways whose names are Cazenove.[1] —I am this moment come out of the Turkish Bath, which is an immense luxury to me, though I am afraid it would not suit you at all, their[sic] being a great deal of rubbing, sweating, & *washing* (your aversion) to go through, which I indulge in every other day.— —I cannot sufficiently admire the punctuality & success with which you

---

[1] James Cazenove and his brother had escaped from France where they had been detained nearly eight years by Napoleon. Byron furnished them financial assistance to get back to England. See letter of July 23, 1815, to James Cazenove.

have written to me in reward for my numerous communications, the last of which must have arrived with the nincompoop Fletcher.— — Since my last letter 27 Ult. I have begun an Imitation of the "De Arte Poetica" of Horace (in rhyme of course) & have translated or rather varied about 200 lines and shall probably finish it for lack of other argument.[2]—The Horace I found in the convent where I have sojourned some months.— —Ever since my fever in the Morea in Septr. of which I wrote you an account, my health has been changing in the most tramontane way. I have been fat, & thin (as I am at present) a[nd?] had a cough & a catarrh & the piles and be damned to them, and I have had pains in my side & left off animal food, which last has done me some service, but I expect great things from the coming summer & if well & wealthy shall go to Jerusalem, for which I have a firman.— —Dun Hanson, & tell him, he wont persuade me to sell Newstead, unless something particular occurs.—If I sell it, I live abroad, if not, I come home, & I have no intention of selling it, but the contrary.—The English here & myself are on very good terms, we have balls & dinners frequently.—As I told you before, no letters have arrived from anybody, consequently I know nothing of you, or Matthews, or the Miscellany, I have seen English papers of October, which say little or nothing, but I have lately sent a Battello to Smyrna in hopes of hearing from my vagabond connections.—I don't think you will see me before July, and if things go on to my wish, not for another year.—I took it for granted all this time, that you are arrived in England, as the Salsette has returned these six months to Smyrna, but your silence makes me rather doubt it.—You see you were mistaken in your conjectures on the subject of my return, & I have remanded Fletcher, whom I by no means miss, unless it be by having less confusion than usual in my wardrobe & household. I got your Malta & Cagliari letters, but I expected you would have written from England, though I can excuse a little delay & drunkenness on your first arrival. I feel also interested in your plans, I want to know what you are doing, saying, & writing, whether your domestic affairs go on to your satisfaction, & having heard all this, I should be glad to be informed of Matthieu, who I suppose was pleased to see you again.— As for my own affairs I dont want to hear of them unless they shine a little brighter than in June last, when I received a jocose account of their inextricability from Mr. H[anson]—who might as well have kept his good things for a better opportunity.—If he remits a round sum I

---

[2] This was the beginning of Byron's "Hints from Horace".

will take that and his wit in good part, but I can't allow any waggery from Temple Bar without an adequate remuneration, particularly as three thousand miles (according to Fletcher's invariable calculation from the moment he *cleared* the *channel*) are too long for a repartee.— —I am at present out of spirits having just lost a particular friend, poor dear Dr. Bronstedt of Copenhagen (who lost half his rix dollars by our cursed bombardment) is lately gone to Constantinople, we used to tipple punch and talk politics; Sandford Graham is also gone, but then there are more coming.—Pray have you sent Mrs. Pigot a copy of the Miscellany?—Have you sent my letters to their proper places?—Have you fulfilled my commissions? And How dye do?

yrs. ever very truly
BYRON

[TO JOHN CAM HOBHOUSE]   *Athens. March 18th. 1811*

Dear Hobhouse—Though I neither know where you are or how you are, I write at a venture by way of Zante, as I have already done many times, indeed so often that I can't afford you more than this present sheet—I have just finished an imitation in English verse (rhyme of course) of Horace's "Art of Poetry" which I intend as a sequel to my "E[nglish] Bards," as I have adapted it entirely to our new school of Poetry, though always keeping pretty close to the original.—This poem I have addressed, & shall dedicate to you, in it you fill the same part that the "Pisones" do in Horace, & if published it must be with the Latin subjoined.—I am now at the "Limae[?] Labor" though I shant keep my piece nine years, indeed I question if Horace himself kept to his own precept.[1]—I am at present very fond of this bantling, as the youngest offspring of authors, like that of mothers, is generally most cherished, because 'tis the *weakest*.—Pray what are you doing? have you no literary projects in hand? can't you & Matthieu, & some of our wits, commence some literary journal, political, critical or or what not? I dont mean however like a common magazine or review, but some respectable novelty, which I recommend & leave to your own brilliant considerations.—You see my scribbling propensities though "expelled with a fork" are coming on again.—I am living here very amiably with English, French, Turks & Greeks, and tomorrow evening I give a supper to all the Franks in the place.—You know Athens so well, I shall say no more about it.— — — —As you have

[1] Horace, *Ars Poetica*, 388–89; see also Pope's advice to a Grub Street scribbler, *Arbuthnot*, I, 40.

been so sparing, and myself so liberal in late communications, I shall fold up this rag of paper, which I send tomorrow by a *snail* to Patras.— However it is more than you deserve from

Yours very angry
B.

P.S.—Have you sent Mrs. Pigot a copy of the Miscellany?— — — —

[TO JAMES CAWTHORN]   *Malta. May 9th. 1811*

Mr. Cawthorn,—I have seen here your third Edition of "E. B. & S. R." and observe that it is printed on the very type you rejected for the *second edition.*—Now why is the 3d. to be published in a worse form than the 2d.? which was more creditable to you & me.—I hope if the poem reaches a 4th. you will attend to what I have observed, and, if we *must change,* don't let it be for the worse.— — — —I shall soon probably be in England, if my health (which is very precarious) permit me, & I have a poem finished, which I designed for you to publish, but if you make these retrograde movements I must look elsewhere. If you see Mr. Dallas present my compts.

I am yr. obedt. Servt.
BYRON

[TO JOHN CAM HOBHOUSE]   *Malta. May 15th. 1811*

Dear Hobhouse,—Your last 2 letters of 1810 I have just received, they find me on my way homewards, in the beginning of June I sail in the Volage frigate with French prizes and other English ships of war in all I believe 6 or 7 frigates.— — —I must egotize a little.—I am in bad health & worse spirits, being afflicted in body with what Hostess Quickly in Henry 5th. calls a villainous *"Quotidian Tertian."* It killed Falstaff & may me. I had it first in the Morea last year, and it returned in Quarantine in this infernal oven, and the fit comes on every other day, reducing me first to the chattering penance of Harry Gill, and then mounting me up to a Vesuvian pitch of fever, lastly quitting me with sweats that render it necessary for me to have a man and horse all night to change my linen.— —Of course I am pulled down with a murrain, and as I hear nothing but croaking from H[anson] I am hastening homewards to adjust (if possible) my inadjustable affairs.—

He wants me to sell N[ewstead]—partly I believe because he thinks it might serve me, and partly I suspect because some of his clients want to purchase it.—I will see them d——d first. I told you I never would sell it in a former letter and I beg to repeat that Negative.— —I have told him fifty times to sell Rochdale & he evades and excuses in a very lawyerlike & laudable way.—Tell Davies it is with the greatest regret I see him in such a Situation from which he shall be at all events & at all expence relieved, for if money is not ready I will take the securities on *myself*.[1]—I have looked, asked, and raved after your marbles, and am still looking, asking, & raving, till people think they are my own.— Fletcher was my precursor.—Close, Lander, Mrs. D. have all been examined and declared "Ignoramus."[2]—And yet it is so odd that so many packages should have vanished that I shall (in the intervals of my malady) search the surface of the Island.—I am sorry to hear the stationary propensities of your "Miscellany" and attribute them— firstly—to the dead-weight of extraneous productions with which you loaded your own Pegasus, secondly—to the half guinea (one may buy an opera ticket for less at Hookham's)[3] and thirdly to that *"Walsh-ean"* preface from which you & Matttthews predicted such unutterable things.[4] Now what would I do?—cut away the lumber of Ld. Byron, the Honble. G. Lambe, Mr. Bent the Counsellor at Law, and the rest of your contributory friends,[5] castrate that Boccacian tale, expunge the *Walshean* preface (no offence to Matthieu) add some smart things of your own, change the title, and charge only seven & sixpence.— —I hear that Jeffrey has promised to review you, this will lift you into life, and seriously speaking, I think your own production would have done much better alone, and the "Imitations of Juvenal" are certainly as good in their kind as any in our language.— —I have completed an Imitation of Horace "De Arte Poetica" in which you perform the part of *both* the "Pisos." I have taken a good deal of pains with it, but wish you to see it before I print, particularly as it is addressed to you.—In one part (I deviate and adapt from the original) I have apostrophized

[1] Davies borrowed money in his own name and turned it over to Byron before the latter went abroad.

[2] Hobhouse had sent some specimens of ancient Greek sculpture home from Greece, but they had been mislaid in transhipping at Malta. Byron found them before leaving. See postscript to this letter.

[3] See Sept. 25, 1810, to Hobhouse, note 7.

[4] The preface to *Imitations and Translations* was an attempt at a sophisticated defence of publication by youthful poets and of the Swiftian use of "plain words" in some pieces.

[5] George Lamb, son of Lord Melbourne, was a minor literary figure. See *English Bards and Scotch Reviewers*, lines 55–58; 516–17. Mr. Bent is unidentified.

you as a lover of ("Vive la Bagatelle")[6] and it is curious that I should *afterwards* receive a letter from you on the subject of your projected society with that Motto.—I had written the lines without being at all aware of such an intention, and of course am pleased with the coincidence as well as your idea. But more of this in England.—I wish you would fill up your outline with your friends. I have nobody to recommend or to object against, but shall be happy to make a *joint* in the *tail* of your Comet!— —I have heard from Matthews, remember me to him most socially, he tells me you have thoughts of betaking shortly to Cambridge, surely this is better than the Militia,—why go abroad again? five and twenty is too late to *ring bells* and write *notes* for a Minister of legation? don't think of such a thing, *read, read, read,* and depend upon it in two years time Fortune or your Father will come round again.— — My picture of which you speak is gone to my mother, and if not, it was and is my intention *not* to be *shot* for a long time, and therefore Thou False and foul Insinuator! I repel your surmise, as "De Wilton" did the Adjuration of the voice from High Cross Edinburgh (see 4th, 5th, or 6th Canto of Marmion), and as it succeeded with him, I trust it will with me, you Unnatural (not Supernatural) Croaker! Avaunt thee Cam! I retort & repel your hint, and hope you yourself will be—shooter of a great many Ptarmigans (or men if you like it better), but don't draw me into your parties to shoot or be shotten! for I am determined to come off Conqueror on all such occasions.—I expect letters from you by next packet.—My fantastical adventures I reserve for you and Matthieu and a bottle of Champagne. I parted as I lived friends with all the English & French in Attica, and we had balls, dinners, and amours without number.—I bring you a letter from Cockerell.—Lusieri is also in Malta, and Nicolo whom you remember, who is gone to School here, he was very useful to me at Athens, and it is chiefly through him that I have acquired some knowledge of the Italian & Romaic languages. I was near bringing away Theresa but the mother asked *30 000* piastres!—I had a number of Greek and Turkish women, and I believe the rest of the English were equally lucky, for we were all *clapped*.—I am nearly well again of that distemper, & wish I was as well rid of my *"Quotidian Tertian"*— —I must go down to Newstead & Rochdale and my mother in a late letter tells me that my property is estimated at above a *hundred thousand pounds* even after all debts &c. are paid off.—And yet I am embarrassed and do not know where to raise a Shilling.— — —With regard to our acct. dont think of it or let your Father think of it, for I

[6] See *Hints from Horace*, lines 341–46.

will not hear of it till you are in a state to pay it as easily as so many shillings.—[7] I have fifty resources, & besides my person is parliamentary,—pay your tradesmen,—I am None.—I know your suspicions past & present, but they are ill founded.— —Will you meet me in London in July & go down to Rochdale & Notts by way of Cambridge to see Matthieu [?] Leave a direction at Ridgways.—Believe yours

indelibly
B.——

[On wrapper]
Malta, on [board? May] sixteenth, eighteen hundred & eleven
Li Marmi sono trovati;—dopo [cercando] tutta la Citta, furono [scoperti insie]me col'li al[tre   ?   .] Milordo [Elgin?] Li portaro al [T——vra?][8]

[**"FOUR OR FIVE REASONS IN FAVOUR OF A CHANGE"**]

B. Malta, May 22d. 1811

1st At twenty three the best of life is over and its bitters double. 2ndly I have seen mankind in various Countries and find them equally despicable, if anything the Balance is rather in favour of the Turks. 3dly I am sick at heart.

> "Me jam nec *faemina* . . .
> Nec *Spes animi credula mutui*
> Nec *certare* juvat *Mero*.[1]

4thly A man who is lame of one leg is in a state of bodily inferiority which increases with years and must render his old age more peevish & intolerable. Besides in another existence I expect to have *two* if not *four* legs by way of compensation.

---

[7] Hobhouse had quarrelled with his father before he left with Byron for the East, and he was not yet reconciled. Byron furnished him with the money for the voyage. When they parted, Hobhouse owed Byron £818. 3s. 4d.

[8] Part of this Italian note on the wrapper is torn out with the seal, but the important part is readable: "The marbles are found; after [searching] throughout the city, they were [discovered together] with the other [marbles of] Lord [Elgin?]. They will be carried to [?]."

[1] Byron was quoting from memory and somewhat inaccurately Horace's first ode of the fourth book ("To Venus"):

> Nor maid nor youth delights me now,
> Nor credulous dream of heart's exchange, nor hours
>   of challenged wine-bout, nor the brow
> Girt with a wreath of freshly gathered flowers.

5thly I grow selfish & misanthropical, something like the "jolly Miller" "I care for nobody no not I and Nobody cares for me."
6thly My affairs at home and abroad are gloomy enough.
7thly I have outlived all my appetites and most of my vanities aye even the vanity of authorship.[2]

[TO JOHN CAM HOBHOUSE]
Volage Frigate, at Sea. June 19th. 1811

My dear Hobhouse—In the gentle dullness of a Summer voyage I shall converse with you for half an hour.— —We left Malta on the 2d. with three other frigates, inclusive of the Lissa prizes, and are on our way, they to Glory, and I to what God pleases.—I am recovered from my Tertian, but neither my Health or my hitherto hoydenish Spirits, are so rampant as usual.—I received at Malta your letters, which I have answered, and I have succeeded in the discovery and embarkation of your memorable marbles, they shall be brought to town, or left in proper care at Portsmouth till you can arrange their removal.— —I am accompanied by two Greek servants[1] both middle aged men, & one is Demetrius your old misinterpreter.—I have letters for you from Cockerell whom I left well with other Franks, my own antiquities consist of four *tortoises*, and four *Skulls*, all taken out of ancient Sarcophagi. — —Our health is very lackadaisycal, I have a clap, & Sr. Demetrius a swoln testicle the fatal consequence of some forty "Sculamente".—I shall put off all account of my Winter in Athens, which was most social & fantastical, as also all my marchings and countermarchings, till our meeting, and indulge in speculation on my prospects in your Country. —I shall first endeavour to repair my irreparable affairs, and it seems I must set out for Lancashire, for I shall neither have coals or comfort till I visit Rochdale in person.—I wish you would meet me or tell me where to meet you, as I wish to consult you on various subjects, besides the pleasure I shall experience in your society.—With regard to all *Dross* business between us, dont think of it, till it is most perfectly convenient, I would rather you did not think of it at all, but as I know your Sentiments on the subject, I shall not annoy you by such a proposition.— —You tell me fine things—very fine things—on the

[2] This memorandum to himself should be considered as a journal entry rather than a letter.
[1] The Greek servants were Demetrius Zograffo and Spiro Saraci. Their names are given in a request for their passports to return to Greece, March 2, 1812. (Eg. 2611, f. 282.)

literary *"lay"* I suppose from your natural knowledge of our weak side, and with a view to set me *marble-hunting* by dint of compliment.—I have as I told you before, completed an Imitation of Horace "Ad Pisones" addressed to you, and to be published forthwith as you will readily conjecture.— —I hope the Miscellany mends in sale, it's failure must be attributed to that accursed "Walsh-ean" preface, which the Citoyen M[atthews] would recommend, and you see what it has come to.—M[atthe]ws has written to me, thank him, and say further, I shall have great pleasure in gratifying his curiosity, which however he must not raise too high.—You talk of the Militia,— Santissimi Coglioni! the Militia at five & twenty, Boys over your head, & brutes under you, Mess, Country quarters, Courts martial, and quelling of Riots.—If you will be mad or martial ('tis the same thing) go to Portugal again & I'll go with you (for I have some serious thoughts of it if matters are intricate at home) but don't waste your time in mere *holiday* soldiering as Major Sturgeon would call it.— — —I am writing all this time without knowing your address, however I shall send as usual to Ridgways who will forward my present as he has done the other letters.— —Fletcher must have arrived some time, I sent him off in November, he was useless and in the way, and in every respect, I did better without him.—How goes on "La Bagatelle"? have you met with any clubable persons with a sufficient tincture of Literature for your purpose?—You have not been in London it should seem, I shall proceed there from Portsmouth to Reddish's or Dorant's, for a few days, and afterwards to Newstead, and most probably abroad again as soon as my arrangements will admit.—Ld. Sligo is on his way home, I left him at Malta in Quarantine.—Bruce[2] is gone or going to Persia, he is a singular being, on the night he left Athens he made me a profession of Friendship, on the extremity of the Piraeus, the only one I ever received in my life, and certainly very unexpected, for I had done nothing to deserve it.— —Whitbread (in Peter Pindar's visit from George Guelph) says, he is too old for a *Knight*, and I am too old for a Friend, at least a new one, tell M[atthews] I have bade adieu to every species of affection, and may say with Horace "Me jam nec Fæmina" &c.—he will finish the lines.— — —Seriously I can't think for the soul of me, what possessed Michael, for like the Rovers "a sudden thought struck him" we had dined together so I know he was not drunk, but the truth is, he is a little chivalrous & romantic, and is smitten with unimaginable fantasies ever since his connection with Lady H. Stanhope.—However both her Ladyship & He were very

2 Michael Bruce, who was travelling with Lady Hester Stanhope.

polite, and asked me to go on with them a 2d. time to Constantinople, but having been there once, and preferring *philosophy* at Athens, I staid in my Convent.—Matthews tells me that Jeffrey means to review your Book, if he does, it will do you good one way or the other, but I think it probable he will praise you.—Have you nothing new for the Press?—Dont be discouraged by the Miscellany, but throw the blame on your friends, & the preface, and Matthews, & me, and the damned trash of your auxiliaries.— — —There is something very impudent in my offering this pert consolation, but I hope you will stand in no need of it, & begin to receive half guineas at a great rate, by the bye would not seven & sixpence have sold & sounded better?—M[atthews] has been advising you to philosophize at Cambridge, do, & I'll join you for a time, and we will tipple, and talk M. to death with our travels, and jest and squabble and be as insipid as the best of them.—*Bold* Webster (by way of keeping up that epithet I suppose) has married, and *bolder* still a Sister of Ld. V[iscoun]t Valentia, and *boldest* of all— has published letters to the Comm[ande]r in chief! Corpo de Caio Mario! what will the world come to? I take this to be one of the newest events "under the Sun".—Had he no friend, no relation, no pitying monitor to snatch the manuscript from one Devil to save it from the other? pray are the letters in prose or verse?— — —I have gossiped away till we are off Cape St. Vincent, and I am puzzled what to say next, or rather to ask, for my letter is a string of questions, quite forgetting you cant answer my Catechism. I am dull "dull as the last new Comedy" (vide Goldsmith's Goodnatured Man) though Capt. Hornby is a gentlemanly & pleasant man & a Salamander in his profession, fight anything, but as I have got all the particulars of his late action out of him, I don't know what to ask *him* next any more than *you*.— — —But we are infested in the Cabin by another passenger, a teller of tough stories, all about himself, I could laugh at him were there any body to laugh with, as it is, I yawn and swear to myself, & take refuge in the quarter Gallery, thank God he is now asleep, or I should be worried with impertinence.— —His name is Thomas and he is Staff or *Stuff* Apothecary to Genl. Oakes, who has rammed him down our throats for the voyage, and a bitter Bolus he is, that's the truth on't.— —But I long for land, and then for a post-chaise, and I believe my enjoyments will end there, for I have no other pleasure to expect, that I know of.— —We have had a tedious passage, all except the Straits where we had an Easterly Gale, and glided through the Gut like an oil Glyster.—Dear Hobby, you must excuse all this facetiousness which I should not have let loose, if I knew what the Devil to do, but I am so out of Spirits, & hopes, & humour, & pocket, & health, that you must bear with my merriment, my only resource against a Calenture.—Write to me, I am now going to patrole the melancholy deck, God be w'ye! yrs. alway,

B.—

P.S.—Take a mouthful of Salt-water poetry by a tar on the late Lissa Victory.—

> "If I had an Edication
> "I'd sing your praise *more large*,
> "But I'm only a common foremast Jack
> "On Board of *the Le Volage*!!!!!

[On cover]
Il Bastimento [torn out]nto part[illegible] dimane [per?] la C[torn out]l fiume (Nore) dunque an[torn out] alla Citta per [illegible] ricontrare Vol[illegible]

[TO MRS. CATHERINE GORDON BYRON]

Volage Frigate. At Sea.
June 25th. 1811

Dear Mother,—This letter which will be forwarded on our arrival at Portsmouth (probably about the 4th of July) is begun about 23 days after our departure from Malta.—I have just been two years (to a day on the 2d. of July) absent from England, and I return to it with much the same feelings which prevailed on my departure, viz. indifference, but within that apathy I certainly do not comprise yourself, as I will prove by every means in my power.—You will be good enough to get my apartments ready at Newstead, but don't disturb yourself on any account, particularly mine, nor consider me in any other light than as a visitor.—I must only inform you that for a long time I have been restricted to an entire vegetable diet neither fish or flesh coming within my regimen, so I expect a powerful stock of potatoes, greens, & biscuit, I drink no wine.— —I have two servants middle aged men, & both Greeks;—it is my intention to proceed first to town to see Mr. Hanson, & thence to Newstead on my way to Rochdale.—I have only to beg you will not forget my diet, which it is very necessary for me to observe.— —I am well in health, as I have generally been, with the exception of two agues, both of which I quickly got over.—My plans will so much depend on circumstances that I shall not venture to lay down an opinion on the subject.—My prospects are not very promising, but I suppose we shall wrestle through life like our Neighbours.— Indeed by H[anson]'s last advices I have some apprehensions of finding N———d dismantled by Messrs Brothers &c.[1] and he seems determined to force me into selling it, but he will be baffled.— —I dont suppose I shall be much pestered with visitors, but if I am, you must receive them, for I am determined to have nobody breaking in upon my retirement.—You know that I never was fond of society, & I am less so than before.—I have brought you a shawl, & a quantity of Ottar [sic] of Roses, but these I must smuggle if possible.—I trust to find my library in tolerable order, Fletcher is no doubt arrived, I shall separate the Mill from Mr. Bowman's farm (for his son is too "gay a deceiver" to inherit both) & place Fletcher in it, who has served me faithfully, & whose wife is a good woman. Besides, it is necessary to sober young Mr. Bowman,[2] or he will people the parish with bastards. —In a word, if he had seduced a dairy-maid, he might have found something like an apology, but the Girl is his equal, & in high life or low life, reparation is made in such circumstances.— —But I shall not interfere further (than like Buonaparte) by diminishing Mr. B's *kingdom*, and erecting part of it into a *principality* for Field Marshal Fletcher!—I hope you govern my little *empire* & it's sad load of national debt, with a wary hand.—To drop my metaphor, I beg leave to subscribe myself

yrs. ever
B.—

[On cover] This letter was written to be sent from Portsmouth but on arriving there the Squadron was ordered to the Nore, from whence I shall forward it, this I have not done before supposing you might be alarmed by the interval mentioned in the letter being longer than expected between our arrival in Port & my appearance at Newstead. B. July 14th 1811.

[TO ROBERT CHARLES DALLAS]   *Volage Frigate, at Sea*
June 28th, 1811

My dear Sir,—After two years' absence (to a day, on the 2d of July before which we shall not arrive at Portsmouth,) I am retracing my

[1] The upholsterer who refurbished Newstead and whose bill of £1,600 was still due.

[2] See June 28, 1810, to Mrs. Byron, note 2.

way to England. I have, as you know, spent the greater part of that period in Turkey, except two months in Spain and Portugal, which were then accessible. I have seen every thing most remarkable in Turkey, particularly the Troad, Greece, Constantinople, and Albania, into which last region very few have penetrated so high as Hobhouse and myself. I don't know that I have done any thing to distinguish me from other voyagers, unless you will reckon my swimming from Sestos to Abydos, on May 3d, 1810, a tolerable feat for a *modern*.

I am coming back with little prospect of pleasure at home, and with a body a little shaken by one or two smart fevers, but a spirit I hope yet unbroken. My affairs, it seems, are considerably involved, and much business must be done with lawyers, colliers, farmers, and creditors. Now this to a man who hates bustle as he hates a bishop, is a serious concern. But enough of my home department.

I find I have been scolding Cawthorn without a cause, as I found two parcels with two letters from you on my return to Malta. By these it appears you have not received a letter from Constantinople, addressed to Longman's, but it was of no consequence.

My Satire it seems is in a fourth edition, a success rather above the middling run, but not much for a production which, from its topics, must be temporary, and of course be successful at first, or not at all. At this period, when I can think and act more coolly, I regret that I have written it, though I shall probably find it forgotten by all except those whom it has offended. My friend **'s [Hobhouse's] Miscellany has not succeeded, but he himself writes so good-humouredly on the subject, I don't know whether to laugh or cry with him. He met with your son at Cadiz, of whom he speaks highly.

Your's and Pratt's protegé, Blackett the cobbler, is dead,[1] in spite of his rhymes, and is probably one of the instances where death has saved a man from damnation. You were the ruin of that poor fellow amongst you: had it not been for his patrons he might now have been in very good plight, shoe- (not verse-)making: but you have made him immortal with a vengeance. I write this, supposing poetry, patronage, and strong waters to have been the death of him. If you are in town in or about the beginning of July, you will find me at Dorant's, in Albemarle-street, glad to see you. I have an imitation of *Horace's Art of Poetry* ready for Cawthorn, but don't let that deter you, for I shan't

---

[1] Samuel Jackson Pratt, a miscellaneous writer and poet of the Della Cruscan school, was the discoverer and patron of the cobbler-poet, Joseph Blacket (1786–1810). Among those who befriended and patronized Blacket were Elliston, the actor, Dallas, and Miss Milbanke, afterward Lady Byron.

inflict it upon you. You know I never read my rhymes to visitors. I shall quit town in a few days for Notts, and thence to Rochdale. I shall send this the moment we arrive in harbour, that is a week hence.

Yours ever sincerely,
BYRON

[TO FRANCIS HODGSON]   *Volage Frigate At Sea June 29th. 1811*

My dear Hodgson—In a week with a fair wind we shall be in Portsmouth, & on the 2d. July I shall have completed (to a day) two years of peregrination, from which I am returning with as little emotion as I set out.—I think, upon the whole, I was more grieved at leaving Greece, than England, which I am impatient to see, simply because I am tired of a long voyage.—Indeed my prospects are not very pleasant, embarrassed in my private affairs, indifferent to public, solitary without the wish to be social, with a body a little enfeebled by a succession of fevers, but a spirit I trust yet unbroken, I am returning *home*, without a hope, & almost without a desire.— —The first thing I shall have to encounter, will be a Lawyer, the next a Creditor, then Colliers, farmers, surveyors, & all the agreeable attachments to Estates out of repair, & Contested Coalpits.—In short I am sick, & sorry, & when I have a little repaired my irreparable affairs, away I shall march, either to campaign in Spain, or back again to the East, where I can at least have cloudless skies, & a cessation from impertinence.— —I trust to meet, or see you in town, or at Newstead whenever you can make it Convenient, I suppose you are in Love, & in Poetry, as usual. That husband H. Drury, has never written to me, albeit I have sent him more than one letter, but I dare say the poor man has a family, & of course all his cares are confined to his circle

> "For children fresh expences yet
> "And Dickey now for school is fit.
> *Warton*

If you see him, tell him I have a letter for him from Tucker a regimental Chirurgeon & friend of his, who prescribed for me in a [two lines crossed out][1] & is a very worthy man, but too fond of hard words.— —I shall be too late for a speechday, or I should probably go down to Harrow.—Hobhouse is either abroad again, or in the Militia!!!

---

[1] The illnesses for which Tucker prescribed are described in July 7, 1811, to Drury.

so he writes, or perhaps at Cambridge, he has sent me a most humourous account of the failure of the Miscellany, which he attributes to Bawdry, but I always have said that if it fell, it must be owing to the preface, which Matthews swore was like Walsh. I regretted much in Greece, having omitted to carry the Anthology with me.— —I mean Bland & Merival[e]'s.—I trust something will weigh up H[obhouse]'s book again, I wish he had only asked *seven* shillings, I thought he would split on the odd three & sixpence.— —What has Sir Edgar done? & the Imitations and Translations? where are they? I suppose you don't mean to let the public off so easily, but charge them home with a Quarto.—For me, I am "sick of Fops, & Poesy, & Prate" & shall leave the "whole Castalian State" to Bufo or any body else, but you are a Sentimental & Sensibilitous person, & will rhyme to the end of the Chapter.—Howbeit I have written some 4000 lines of one kind or another on my travels.—I need not repeat that I shall be happy to see you, I shall be in town about the 8th. at Dorant's Hotel in Albemarle St. & proceed in a few days to Notts, & thence to Rochdale on business.—I am here, & there,

yrs. very sincerely
B.

[TO JOHN CAM HOBHOUSE]   *Volage Frigate—Bay of Biscay*
July 2d. 1811

My dear Hobhouse,—This very day two years we sailed from Inghilterra, so that I have completed the period I expected to be absent, though my wishes were originally more extensive. When we shall arrive, God knows! but till then I continue scribbling to you, for lack of other Argument.—My Situation is one you have been used to, so you will feel without further description, but I must do Capt. Hornby the Justice to say, he is one of the best Marine productions in my recollection. There is another Cabin passenger, an elderly, prosing, pestiferous, Staff Surgeon, of Oakes's, who has almost slain me with a thousand & one tales all about himself, & "Genl. This," and "Lord That," and "says Hes" & "says Is,"—& the worst of it is, I have no friend with me to laugh at the fellow, though he is too common a character for mirth.—Damn him,—I can make no more of him than a Hedgehog, he is too dull to be ridiculous.— —We have been beating about with hazy weather this last Fortnight, and today is foggy as the Isle of Man.— —I have been thinking again & again of a literary project we have at times started, to wit— —a periodical paper, something in the Spectator or Observer way. There certainly is no such thing at present.—Why not get one, Tuesdays & Saturdays.—You must be Editor, as you have more taste and diligence than either Matthews or myself (I beg M's pardon for lowering him to the same line with me) and I dont think we shall want other contributors if we set seriously about it.— —We must have for each day, one or two essays, miscellaneous, according to Circumstances, but now & then politics, and always a piece of poetry of one kind or other.—I give you these hints to digest the scheme at leisure,—it would be pleasant, and with success, in some degree profitable.—Above all we must be secret – at least at first.— —"Cosa pensate? Perpend, pronounce, Respond?— — We can call it "La Bagatelle" (according to your idea) or Lillibulero, if you like it, the name wont matter so that the Contents are palatable. — —But I am writing & projecting without knowing where you are, in Country or College Quarters, though I hope you have abandoned your Militia Scheme. Matthews gave me hopes that Arms would give way to the Gown, as you had visions of returning to Granta.—God keep bad port out of your Carcase! you would certainly fall a victim to Messing the very first Campaign. I have brought your marbles, which I shall leave at Portsmouth till you can settle where to put them. I shall be in town a very short time, meaning to proceed to Notts, & thence to Rochdale. I am tolerably well in Health, that is to say, instead of an *Ague*, & a *Clap*, and the *Piles*, all at once, I have only the two last. I wrote to you from Malta, during my Fever, my Terzana, or rather Quotidiana, for it was called intermittent "a *Non* Intermittendo." —I am as I say well, but in bitter bad spirits, skies foggy, head muzzy, Capt. sulky, ship lazy.—The accursed Pharmacopole is at present on deck,—the only pleasure I have had these three weeks. But I hope to tell you in person how truly I am yrs

B.

[TO JOHN HANSON]   *Volage Frigate. July 4th. 1811 Bay of Biscay*

Dear Sir,—Expecting to arrive in a day or two, & wishing to have a dispatch ready the moment of arrival I write to apprise you of my return.—On the 2d. Inst. (two days ago) I completed exactly two years of absence from England,—from London three weeks more.— —I wrote to you (by Wm. Fletcher) my determination with regard to Newstead, viz—*not* to sell it, by this I shall abide, Come what May!

nor shall I listen to an opinion on the subject.—My affairs, I must own, seem desperate enough, I shall adjust them as far as in my power, & (after procuring a recommendation & appointment on Ld. Wellingtons or Genl. Grahams supernumerary staff, which I am told I can easily obtain) I shall join one of the armies.— —In the mean time I am compelled to draw on you for 20 or 30 pounds to enable me to proceed from Port to London & pay the custom house duties.—There is a Bill of Miller's in Albemarle's which also must be paid immediately, on my arrival; I do not mean to reproach you, but I certainly thought there were funds to answer so small a draft when I left London, however it has remained in his hands *dishonoured* more than two years,— However when I consider the sums I owe you professionally, I have nothing further to observe, I have made up my mind to bear the ills of Poverty, Two years travel has tolerably seasoned me to privations.— —I have one question which must be resolved, is Rochdale mine, or not? can I not sell it? & why, if it will bring a sum to clear my debts is it not sold!—Newstead is out of the Question, & I do assure you, that if any other person had made such a proposal, I should have looked on it as an Insult.—The Annuities must be discussed, as they best can, at least I shall relieve my securities by taking them on myself, if other means of accommodation fail.— — —I enclose you Miller's bill, which I am most anxious to discharge, as he is a most respectable man independent of his profession, & if he were not, the affair of the draft is very disgraceful.—It shall be paid if I sell my watch, or strip myself of every sous to answer it, and also the two years interest.—Indeed he has behaved so well in the business, & his letters to me are so forbearing, that I shall never be easy till I settle the business.—I remain with my best respects to all yrs very truly

Byron

[TO JAMES CAWTHORN]   *Volage Frigate off Ushant July 7th. 1811*

Mr. Cawthorn,—I have been scolding you (like almost all Scolders) without a reason, for I found your two parcels, one at Athens, & the other at Malta on my way down.—In a few days on our arrival at Portsmouth, which we expect to make about the 10th. I shall send this off, however the date on the outside will apprise you of the day.—I shall thence proceed to town where I expect you to pay me a visit either at Dorant's or Reddish's Hotels in Albemarle or St. James's Street.—I hope the Satire has answered your purpose, & of course it has answered mine.—I have a poem in the same style, & much about the same length which I intend as a kind of Sequel to the former, it is ready for publication, but as my scrawl is impenetrable to Printers, & the Manuscript is a good deal blotted with Alterations &c. you must have an Amanuensis ready to copy it out fair on my arrival.—I suppose you have not lost by the last, but my only motive for asking is a wish that you *may not*, the present shall be yours for the risk of printing, as the last was.—But neither you nor I must suppose because the first has succeeded tolerably, a second will have the same fate, though it's style is similar, however, it will serve to make a tolerable volume with the other, with which it is in some degree connected.—The Nature of it I will explain more fully when I see you.—If you see Mr. Dallas or others of my acquaintance, you will present my Compts.—I remain

yr. obedt. Servt.

BYRON

P.S.—Accept my excuse for blaming you for what you did not deserve. I am sorry for it; the fault lay with my Maltese Correspondents.— — —

[TO HENRY DRURY] *Volage Frigate off Ushant. July 7th. 1811*

My dear Drury,—After two years absence (on the 2d.) & some odd days I am approaching your Country, the day of our arrival you will see by the outside date of my letter, at present we are becalmed comfortably close to Brest Harbour;—I have never been so near it since I left Duck Puddle.[1]—The enclosed letter is from a friend of yours Surgeon Tucker whom I met with in Greece, & so on to Malta, where he administered to me for three complaints viz. a *Gonorrhea* a *Tertian fever*, & the *Hemorrhoides*, *all* of which I literally had at once, though he assured me the *morbid* action of only one of these distempers could act at a time, which was a great comfort, though they relieved one another as regularly as Sentinels, & very nearly sent me back to Acheron, my old acquaintance which I left fine & flowing in Albania.— —We left Malta 34 days ago, & (except the Gut of Gibraltar which we passed with an Easterly wind as easy as an oil Glyster) we have had a tedious passage on't.—You have never written, this comes of Matrimony, Hodgson has,—so you see the Balance of Friendship is on

1 The swimming pool at Harrow.

the Batchelor's side.—I am at present well, that is, I have only two out of the three aforesaid complaints, & these I hope to be cured of, as they say one's Native fogs are vastly salubrious.— — —You will either see or hear from or of me soon after the receipt of this, as I pass through town to repair my irreparable affairs, & thence I must go to Nott's & raise rents, & to Lanc's, & sell collieries, & back to London, & pay debts, for it seems I shall neither have coals or comfort till I go down to Rochdale in person. I have brought home some marbles for Hobhouse;—& for myself, "Four ancient Athenian Skulls[''] [2] dug out of Sarcophagi, a "phial of Attic Hemlock," [3] ["]four live Tortoises" a Greyhound (died on the passage) two live Greek Servants one an *Athenian*, t'other a *Yaniote*, who can speak nothing but Romaic & Italian, & *myself*, as Moses in the "Vicar of Wakefield" says *slily*,[4] & I may say it too for I have as little cause to boast of my expedition as he of his to the Fair.—I wrote to you from the Cyanean Rocks, to tell you I had swum from Sestos to Abydos, have you received my letter?— — Hobhouse went to England to fish up his Miscellany, which foundered (so he tells me) in the Gulph of Lethe, I dare say it capsized with the vile goods of his contributory friends, for his own share was very portable.—However I hope he will either weigh up or set sail with a fresh Cargo, & a luckier vessel. Hodgson I suppose is four deep by this time, what would he give? to have seen like me the *real Parnassus*, where I robbed the Bishop of Chrisso of a book of Geography,[5] but this I only call plagiarism, as it was done within an hour's ride of Delphi.— —

Believe me yrs. ever
Byron

[to john cam hobhouse]   *Reddish's Hotel.—July 15th. 1811*

My dear Hobhouse,—The day after tomorrow (17th.) I will set out for Sittonbourne, to confabulate, I thank you for your advice, which I shall observe. My *Im*[itatio]*n* of *Hor*[a]*ce*, is now transcribing at Cawthorn's, so that I cannot bring the fair Copy, but the moment it is

---

[2] The Athenian skulls were later given to Walter Scott.
[3] Later given to John Murray.
[4] *Vicar of Wakefield*, Chapter XII.
[5] *Ancient and Modern Geography*, (Venice, 1728) by Meletius of Janina (1661–1714). Meletius was Archbishop of Athens, 1703–14. See July 15, 1811, to Hobhouse.

out of his hands you shall have it.—Your marbles are left at the Custom House, Sheerness, as I knew not where to send them, & to smuggle them was impracticable, you will get them on sending a cart or a letter.—I dine with Davies today, he came to me *drunk* last night, & was very friendly, & has got a new set of Jokes, but to you they are doubtless not new.—Drawings I have none, *ready*, but have an excellent Painter in pay in the Levant.—I have brought you *one* (from Cockerell) of Athens, & have in my possession a Romaic Lexicon in three Q[uart]o vols, two or three Greek plays, (i.e. translations from Metastasio & Goldoni) Meletius's Geography (we stole it from the Bishop of Chrysso) a Greek Grammar or two, two live Greeks (both between 30 & 40 yrs. of age & one of them your old Dragoman Demetrius) & some other Romaic publications (and a manuscript or two which you shall publish as they are very curious if you like) all of which with the owner are as usual very much at your service.—I will bring some of the books with me

yrs. ever
BYRON

[TO MRS. MASSINGBERD]   *Reddish's Hotel. July 16, 1811*

Madam,—It is with great concern I have just heard from Mr. Hanson the difficulty you have been under with regard to the annuities. —I have returned to England for the purpose of arranging the business, which shall be done as soon as I return from Lancashire where Mr. H. and myself in a short time proceed.—You are perhaps not aware of the illegality of the transaction, and if I hear that any further difficulty takes place, I shall be under the necessity of bringing the whole before a Court, but if Mr. Howard will remain quiet for a short time, and not compel us to such measures I shall make every effort to discharge you from your responsibility.—I shall certainly use my endeavour to prevent you from being further molested, and as I trust soon to be enabled to satisfy every body, it will be Mr. Howard's own fault if the business does not end quietly; and he must be perfectly aware of what I have already stated, and if *he* is not,—I am,—though I do not wish to rest my plea on such grounds, unless forced in your defence and mine so to do. I am Madam,

Yr. very obedt. Humble Svt.
BYRON

Reddish's Hotel. July 23d. 1811
St. James's Street London.

My dear Madam,—I am only detained by Mr. Hanson to sign some Copyhold papers, & will give you timely notice of my approach, it is with great reluctance I remain in town.— — —
I shall pay a short visit, as we go on to Lancashire on Rochdale business.—I shall attend to your directions of course & am with great respect

yrs. ever
BYRON

P.S.—You will consider Newstead as your house not mine, & me as only a visitor.— — — —

[TO JOHN CAM HOBHOUSE]   *Reddish's Hotel July 23d. 1811*

My dear Hobhouse,—I am just returned from Harrow.—The other day I called at Miller's, the moment he heard your name & Intention he expressed a wish in the handsomest manner to publish your work.— I wish you would think of it, Hodgson says he is the only eligible publisher.—As for C[awthor]n you may rely on it you will have some sneaking conduct before you get from his hands.[1]—Perpend, Pronounce.—In the mean time, Go on, there is every reason as far as I have heard to make you succeed, particularly if you anticipate Clarke.[2] — — —Command me as usual.—I shall not leave town for some ten days, being detained by cursed copyhold papers.—I shall be but too happy in employment, though I am a good deal dabbled with my own Ink.— — — —Remember I do not presume to advise, but recommend to your own judgement the Consideration of your publisher.—Much depends on him, & if the first men of the profession court your work, why deal with a vendor of lampoons?— —
Good morning, think of this when off Drill.

yrs. ever
BN.

[1] Hobhouse's *A Journey through Albania and Other Provinces of Turkey in Europe and Asia, to Constantinople, during the Years 1809 and 1810* was published by Cawthorn in 1813.
[2] E. D. Clarke, whose Eastern *Travels* appeared in successive volumes from 1810 to 1823.

Dear Sir,—I have been out of town some days & only returned last night.— —Thomas I have seen, he is tolerably quiet about the annuities, I have also written to Mrs. Massingberd.—Mrs. Byron writes that the papers are *all signed.*—On the 16th. I told Mr. Miller that in *fourteen* days he would receive his money, as I wish most particularly to have that arranged I hope & trust that he will not be put off again.—I have been much engaged, but the day after tomorrow I hope to have a quiet dinner at No. 6.—With my best respects to Mrs. H. I am

yrs. most truly
BYRON

[TO JOHN HANSON] *Reddish's Hotel. July 28th. 1811*

Dear Sir,—On the 30th Inst. Mr. Miller's draft (as I have already apprised you two or three times) will be presented & I do hope & trust it will not be again protested, if the remainder of the bill also could be settled at the same time (it is in your possession) it would remove a great weight from my mind, as the man has already been so scurvily used in the business, & at the same time has given me so little trouble.—Under the circumstances of the case, & the prospect of receiving the copyhold arrears, I trust you will not refuse my request.—

I am yrs. very truly
BYRON

[TO JAMES WEDDERBURN WEBSTER] *Reddish's Hotel. July 29th. 1811*

My dear Webster,—As this eternal Vis a vis seems to sit heavy on your soul,[1] I beg leave to apprise you that I have arranged with Godsall [Goodall?]; you are to give me the promised wheels, & the lining, with the box at Brighton, & I am to pay him the stipulated sum.— —I am obliged to you for your favorable opinion & trust that the happiness you talk so much of will be stationary, and not take those freaks to which the Felicity of common mortals is subject.—I do very sincerely wish you well, & am so convinced of the Justice of your matrimonial arguments, that I shall follow your example, when I can get a sufficient price for my Coronet.—In the mean [time] I should be happy to drill for my new Situation, under your auspices, but Business, inexorable Business, keeps me here—your letters are forwarded.—If I

[1] See July 31, 1811, to Webster, note 1.

can serve you in any way, command me, I will endeavour to fulfil your requests as awkwardly as another. I shall pay you a visit perhaps in the Autumn.—Believe [me] Dr. W.

yrs. *unintelligibly*
B.

[TO WILLIAM MILLER]   *Reddish's Hotel. July 30th. 1811*

Sir,—I am perfectly aware of the Justice of your remarks, & am convinced that if ever the poem is published the same objections will be made in much stronger terms.[1]—But as it was intended to be a poem on *Ariosto's plan* that *is* to *say* on *no plan* at all, & as is usual in similar cases having a predilection for the worst passages I shall retain those parts though I cannot venture to defend them.—Under these circumstances I regret that you decline the publication, on my own account, as I think the book would have been better in your hands, the pecuniary part you know I have nothing to do with.— —But I can perfectly conceive, & indeed *approve* your reasons, & assure you my sensations are not *Archiepiscopal* enough as yet to regard the rejection of my homilies.[2]

I am, Sir, your very obedt. humble Sert.
BYRON

[TO ——————]   [*Fragment—no date*] [*July 30, 1811?*][1]

. . . have been forthcoming amongst my posthumous M.S.S.?—In short you have lost them you say—or mislaid . . .

2. –discreet only—since you heard a bad motive attributed to me—and thought this the readiest way of repelling it.—But you should have asked my leave—this is but fair in such cases.—

[TO JAMES WEDDERBURN WEBSTER]   *Reddish's Hotel. July 31st. 1811*

My dear W. W.—I always understood that the *Lining* was to accompany the *Carriage*, if not, the *Carriage* may accompany the

---

[1] Byron submitted the manuscript of the first two cantos of *Childe Harold* to Miller before he allowed Dallas to take it to John Murray. Miller apparently was afraid of the unorthodox religious and political views expressed in it, and was reluctant to publish a poem that attacked Lord Elgin.

[2] An allusion to Gil Blas and the Bishop of Grenada. (Le Sage, *Gil Blas*, Bk. VII, Chap. 4.)

[1] These two fragments are in the Murray MSS. with the letter to William Miller of July 30, 1811.

Lining; for I will have neither one or the other.—In short to prevent squabbling, this is my determination, so decide;—if you leave it to my *feelings* (as you say) they are very strongly in favour of the said lining. —200 Gs. for a Carriage with ancient lining!!!¹ Rags & Rubbish! you must write another pamphlet my dear W. before—but pray do not waste your time & eloquence in expostulation, because it will do neither of us good, but Decide—Content or *not* content.— —The best thing you can do for the Tutor you speak of, will be to send him in your Vis (with the lining) to the U – niversity of Gottingen, how can you suppose (now that my own Bear is dead) that I have any situation for a German Genius of this kind till I get another, or some children.—I am infinitely obliged to you for your invitations, but I cant pay so high for a second hand chaise to make my friends a visit.—The Coronet will not *grace* the *"pretty Vis"* till your tattered lining ceases to dis*grace* it.— —Pray favour me with an answer, as we must finish the affair one way or another immediately before next week.—Believe me

yrs. very truly
BYRON

[TO JOHN CAM HOBHOUSE]   *Reddish's Hotel July 31st. 1811*

My dear H.— My Rochdale concerns not only wait but make me *wait* too, & (to [wiredraw?] the quibble a la Davies) will prevent my *waiting* upon your Cornish Minership.¹—This comes of soldiering—I say no more.—I would come down or go down but I really have not money to carry me to Dover and back, No, not by the long Coach, & what is more, I do not know when I shall have.—My affairs are in the most lackadaisical posture, & seem like Goldsmith's "young The." to get never the better for Age.²—Davies I see nothing of, though for aught I know he may be in town but this I cannot ascertain, having never entered a Coffee house since my return & meaning by the blessing of Reformation to keep out of them.—The Albanian vocabulary & every thing else is at a stand still with the Irish Expedition, Caw-

¹ Byron had ordered a *vis-à-vis* built by the carriage-maker Goodall (see July 29, 1811, to Webster). This he traded to his friend Webster for a carriage, who later repented of his bargain. Byron then arranged for Goodall to keep the *vis-à-vis* and undertook to buy the carriage from Webster.

¹ Hobhouse's regiment, the Cornish Miners, had been ordered to Ireland.

² Goldsmith's essay, "Serious Reflections on the Life and Death of the late Mr. T[heophilus] C[ibber]". ". . . his father was frequently heard to observe, that the young The——would be hanged".

thorn may swear (by the bye he will have to swear perhaps at Hewson Clarke's half a dozen trials, who is to be prosecuted by Mrs. B[yron] & myself for *libel, Scan. Mag. Breach* of *privilege* &c. &c. in fifty different actions next Novr. for buffooneries in the Scourge) [3] Cawthorn may swear, but his [face? force?] certainly discovered your work.—The "Scourge" is in the hands of the Attorney General, the foolish fellow of an Editor instead of something like the shadow of truth, has run aground upon charges of "Illegitimacy & Drunkenness["] against Mrs B[yron] ["]Descent from Murderers," & a variety of other phrases which will look lovely in an Indictment.— —So you will perceive in the Cork Chronicle, or the Munster Mercury, the scurrilous speeches which will doubtless be made on both sides, & all the trials; for Mrs. B's and mine are separate concerns, & mine again is a *separated* concern, as he has attacked my peerage & in short it will be a long & loud affair, & answer no purpose but punishing these poor devils, & making an advertisement to Cawthorn's book. I see nothing to prevent your publication, if you are serious, your friends can correct the proofs, but Cawthorn supplicates an Octavo your 16mo wont do, People love margin.—You need be under no alarm about your W. at B.[4] though I see no reason for you to be ashamed of it, yet there is little danger since only Cawthorns Customers are probably acquainted with the author at least I have not met myself above a dozen people besides, who guessed at him.— —Lord Elgin has been teazing to see me these last four days,[5] I wrote to him at his request all I knew about his robberies, & at last have written to say that as it is my intention to publish (in Childe Harold) on that topic, I thought proper since he

---

[3] In the March, 1811 number of *The Scourge* there was a scurrilously personal attack on Byron by his old enemy of *The Satirist*, Hewson Clarke, striking back for the aspersions on his lowly birth in the Postscript to the second edition of *English Bards and Scotch Reviewers*. He complained that Byron had released his lampoon only after he had left the shores of Britain, and continued: "It may be reasonably asked whether to be a denison of Berwick-upon-Tweed, be more disgraceful than to be the illegitimate descendant of a murderer . . . whether to be the offspring of parents whose only crime is their want of title, be not as honourable as to be the son of a profligate father, and a mother whose days and nights are spent in the delirium of drunkenness. . . ." (*The Scourge; or Monthly Expositor of Imposture and Folly*, Vol. I, p. 211.)

[4] Hobhouse had written an essay or pamphlet called "Weeks at Bath", perhaps a frank exposé of life at the watering place, which he had put in the hands of Cawthorn for publication, but he may have withdrawn it, for so far as is known it was never published. See Aug. 25, 1811, to Cawthorn.

[5] Byron had carried from Greece a letter from Lusieri, Lord Elgin's agent, and had sent it on to him after arriving. Elgin was no doubt eager to have first hand word of how Lusieri was proceeding, but since the death of Byron's mother called him to Newstead the next day it is unlikely that he ever saw Elgin.

insisted on seeing me to give him notice, that he might not have an opportunity of accusing me of double dealing afterwards.— —So you see how my matters stand, I believe we differ on Ld. E's subject,[6] or else he will be prettily trimmed among us i. e. Dr. Clarke,[7] you, & myself, prose & verse all rising in revenge of Minerva.— —Let me hear from you before your banishment, I am afraid I shall be abroad again before your return, but wherever I am you will reckon me amongst your friends, as for my little Circle of Friendship, Death & what is called *Life* have cut it to a Segment.—yours Alway.

BYRON

[TO JOHN HANSON (*a*)]   *July 31st. 1811*

Dear Sir,—I have called on you with Mr. Millers bill and I do again (as I repeatedly have done) beg you to enable me to settle it, I have used him so ill (God knows unintentionally) pray let him have the whole and speedily, & do not involve me in fresh disgrace in this instance.

yrs. very truly
BYRON

P.S.—Let me have your answer if possible *tonight*.

[TO JOHN HANSON (*b*)]   *July 31st. 1811—*

Dear Sir,—Pray favour me with an answer to my note of today if possible, I am so annoyed about Mr. M[iller]'s Bill & have been for some time, that till I have some news on the subject I shall be very ill at ease

yrs. truly
BYRON

---

[6] Hobhouse took a more favourable view of Elgin's work than did Byron, contending that preservation of the Greek marbles in London would benefit "an infinitely greater number of rising architects and sculptors". (*Journey*, I, 347n.) Byron's reply to this in his first letter on Bowles was: "I opposed, and will ever oppose, the robbery of ruins from Athens, to instruct the English in sculpture (who are as capable of sculpture as the Egyptians are of skating)."

[7] Edward Daniel Clarke, Professor of Mineralogy at Cambridge, had been in Greece before Byron, and in his *Travels* took a dim view of Elgin, but he himself brought home some marbles, including the Eleusinian Ceres, which are now in the Fitzwilliam Museum.

Dear Sir,—Mrs. Byron is in the greatest danger as Mrs. Hanson who saw the letter can apprise you.—To enable me to leave town I have been under the necessity of drawing on you for *forty pounds*, the occasion must excuse me

yrs. very truly
BYRON

[TO JOHN M. B. PIGOT] *Newport Pagnell, August 2, 1811*

My dear Doctor,—My poor mother died yesterday! and I am on my way from town to attend her to the family vault. I heard *one* day of her illness, the *next* of her death.—Thank God her last moments were most tranquil. I am told she was in little pain, and not aware of her situation.—I now feel the truth of Mr. Gray's observation, "That we can only have *one* mother." [1]—Peace be with her! I have to thank you for your expressions of regard, and as in six weeks I shall be in Lancashire on business, I may extend to Liverpool and Chester, [2]—at least I shall endeavour.

If it will be any satisfaction, I have to inform you that in November next the Editor of the Scourge will be tried for two different libels on the late Mrs. B[yron] and myself (the decease of Mrs. B. makes no difference in the proceedings), and as he is guilty, by his very foolish and unfounded assertion, of a breach of privilege, he will be prosecuted with the utmost rigour.

I inform of this, as you seem interested in the affair, which is now in the hands of the attorney-general. [3]

I shall remain at Newstead the greater part of this month, where I shall be happy to hear from you, after my two years' absence in the East.

I am, dear Pigot, yours very truly.
BYRON

[1] Gray to Nicholls, Aug. 26, 1766: ". . . I had discovered a thing very little known, which is, that in one's whole life one never can have more than a single mother."

[2] Pigot had finished his medical studies at Edinburgh and was practising in Chester.

[3] In the end, the Attorney-General, Sir Vicary Gibbs, gave his opinion against legal proceedings, on the ground of the time that had elapsed and the fact that Byron himself had provoked the attack.

My dear Sir,—The *Earl* of Huntley & the Lady *Jean* Stewart[1] daughter of James 1st. of Scotland were the progenitors of Mrs. Byron. I think it would be as well to be correct in the Statement.—Every thing is doing that can now be done plainly yet decently for the interment. — — —When you favour me with your company, be kind enough to bring down my carriage from Messrs Baxter's & Co Long Acre, I have written to them, & beg you will come down in it, as I cannot travel conveniently or properly without it.—I trust that the decease of Mrs. B[yron] will not interrupt the prosecution of the Editor of the Magazine, less for the mere punishment of the rascal, than to set the question at rest, which with the ignorant & weak minded might leave a wrong impression.—I will have no stain on the Memory of my Mother, with a very large portion of foibles & irritability, she was without a *Vice* (& in these days that is much) the laws of my country shall do her & me justice in the first instance, but if they were deficient, the laws of modern Honour should decide, cost what it may, Gold or blood, I will pursue to the last the cowardly calumniator of an absent man, & a defenseless woman.— — — —The effects of the deceased are sealed & untouched, I have sent for her agent Mr. Bolton, to ascertain the proper steps, & nothing shall be done precipitately.—I understand her jewels & clothes are of considerable value.—I shall write to you again soon, in the mean time, with my most particular remembrance to Mrs. Hanson, my regards to Charles, & my *respects* to the young Ladies I am Dear Sir

your very sincere & obliged servt.

BYRON

My dearest Davies,—Some curse hangs over me and mine. My mother lies a corpse in this house: one of my best friends is drowned in a ditch.[1] What can I say, or think, or do? I received a letter from him the day before yesterday. My dear Scrope, if you can spare a moment, do come down to me, I want a friend. Matthews's last letter was written on *Friday*,—on Saturday he was not. In ability, who was like

---

[1] Mrs. Byron traced her ancestry to the second Earl of Huntly and his second wife, Princess Annabella Stewart, daughter of James I of Scotland.

[1] Charles Skinner Matthews was drowned in the Cam in August 1811. For Byron's account of him see his letter of November 19, 1820, to John Murray.

Matthews? How did we all shrink before him? You do me but justice in saying, I would have risked my paltry existence to have preserved his. This very evening did I mean to write, inviting him, as I invite you, my very dear friend, to visit me. God forgive * * * for his apathy! What will our poor Hobhouse feel! His letters breathe but of Matthews. Come to me, Scrope, I am almost desolate—left almost alone in the world—I had but you and H[obhouse] and M[atthews] and let me enjoy the survivors whilst I can. Poor M. in his letter of Friday, speaks of his intended contest for Cambridge, and a speedy journey to London. Write or come, but come if you can, or one or both. Yours ever.

[TO JOHN CAM HOBHOUSE]   *Newstead Abbey. August 10th. 1811*

My dear Hobhouse,—From Davies I had already received the death of Matthews, & from *M.* a *letter* dated the *day* before his *death,*—In that letter he mentions you, & as it was perhaps the last he ever wrote, you will derive a poor consolation from hearing that he spoke of you with that affectionate familiarity, so much more pleasing from those we love, than the highest encomiums of the World.— —My dwelling, you already know, is the House of Mourning, & I am really so much bewildered with the different shocks I have sustained, that I can hardly reduce myself to reason by the most frivolous occupations. —My poor friend J. Wingfield,[1] my Mother, & your best friend, & (surely not the worst of mine) C[harles] S[kinner] M[atthews] have disappeared in one little month since *my return*, & without my seeing *either*, though I have *heard* from *All.*—There is to me something so incomprehensible in death, that I can neither speak or think on the subject.—Indeed when I looked on the Mass of Corruption, which was the being from whence I sprang, I doubted within myself whether I *was*, or She *was not.*—I have lost her who gave me being, & some of those who made that Being a blessing.—I have neither hopes nor fears beyond the Grave, yet if there is within us a "spark of that Celestial Fire"[2] M[atthews] has already "mingled with the Gods".— —In the room where I now write (flanked by the *Skulls* you have seen so often) did you & M. & myself pass some joyous unprofitable

---

[1] John Wingfield died at Coimbra before Byron returned from abroad, but he had not heard of it until the end of July.

[2] Probably a recollection of Pope's lines in the *Essay on Criticism* (line 195):

Oh, may some spark of your celestial fire,
The last, the meanest of your sons inspire

evenings, & here we will drink to his Memory, which though it cannot reach the dead, will soothe the Survivors, & to them only death can be an Evil.—I can neither receive or administer Consolation, Time will do it for us, in the Interim let me see or hear from you, if possible both.—I am very lonely, & should think myself miserable, were it not for a kind of hysterical merriment, which I can neither account for, or conquer, but, strange as it is, I do laugh & heartily, wondering at myself while I sustain it.—I have tried reading & boxing, & swimming, & writing, & rising early & sitting late, & water, & wine, with a number of ineffectual remedies, & here I am, wretched, but not "melancholy or gentlemanlike."—My dear *"Cam of the Cornish"* (M's *last* expression!!) may Man or God give you the happiness, which I wish rather than expect you may attain; believe me none living are more sincerely yours than BYRON.—

[TO ROBERT CHARLES DALLAS]   *Newstead Abbey Notts.*
                                              August 12th. 1811

My dear Sir,—Peace be with the Dead!—Regret cannot wake them, —with a sigh to the departed, let us resume the dull business of Life, in the certainty that we also shall have our Repose.—Besides her who gave me being, I have lost more than one who made that Being tolerable, the best friend of my friend Hobhouse (Matthews a Man of the first talents) & also not the worst of my narrow circle, has perished miserably in the muddy waves of the Cam, (always fatal to Genius) my poor Schoolfellow Wingfield at Coimbra—within a month, & whilst I had heard from *all three*, but *seen neither*; Matthews wrote to me the very day before his death, & though I feel for his fate I am still more anxious for Hobhouse who, I very much fear, will hardly retain his Senses, his letters to me since the event have been most incoherent.—But let this pass—we shall one day pass along with the rest, the world is too full of such things, & our very Sorrow is selfish.—I received a letter from you, which my late occupations prevented me from duly noticing,—I hope your friends & family will long hold together.— —I shall be glad to hear from you,—on business, or common place, or any thing, or nothing—but Death,—I am already too familiar with the Dead.—It is strange that I look on the skulls which stand beside me (I have always had *four* in my Study) without emotion, but I cannot strip the features of those I have known of their fleshly covering even in Idea without a hideous Sensation. But the

70

Worms are less ceremonious, surely the Romans did well when they
burned the Dead.— — — —
I shall be happy to hear from you & am yours very sincerely

BYRON

[TO SAMUEL BOLTON]   *Newstead Abbey, August 12th, 1811*

Sir,—I enclose a rough draft of my intended Will, which I beg to
have drawn up as soon as possible in the firmest manner. The alterations are principally made in consequence of the death of Mrs. Byron.
I have only to request that it may be got ready in a short time, and
have the honour to be,

Your most obedient, humble servant,

BYRON.

Newstead Abbey, Aug. 12th, 1811

DIRECTIONS FOR THE CONTENTS OF A WILL TO BE DRAWN UP IMMEDIATELY.[1]

The estate of Newstead to be entailed (subject to certain deductions)
on George Anson Byron, heir at law, or whoever may be the heir at
law on the death of Lord B. The Rochdale property to be sold in part
or the whole, according to the debts and legacies of the present Lord B.

To Nicolo Giraud of Athens, subject of France, but born in Greece,
the sum of seven thousand pounds sterling, to be paid from the sale of
such parts of Rochdale, Newstead, or elsewhere, as may enable the
said Nicolo Giraud (resident of Athens and Malta in the year 1810)
to receive the above sum on his attaining the age of twenty-one years.

To William Fletcher, Joseph Murray, and Demetrius Zograffo
(native of Greece), servants, the sum of fifty pounds pr. ann. each, for
their natural lives. To Wm. Fletcher, the Mill at Newstead, on condition that he payeth rent, but not subject to the caprice of the land-
lord. To Rt. Rushton the sum of fifty pounds per ann. for life, and a
further sum of one thousand pounds on attaining the age of twenty-
five years.

To Jn. Hanson, Esq. the sum of two thousand pounds sterling.

The claims of S. B. Davies, Esq. to be satisfied on proving the
amount of the same.

[1] The manuscript of this will, signed by Byron, is now in the Stark Library,
University of Texas.

The body of Lord B. to be buried in the vault of the garden of Newstead, without any ceremony or burial-service whatever, or any inscription, save his name and age. His dog not to be removed from the said vault.

My library and furniture of every description to my friends Jn. Cam Hobhouse, Esq., and S. B. Davies, Esq., my executors. In case of their decease, the Rev. J. Becher, of Southwell, Notts., and R. C. Dallas, Esq., of Mortlake, Surrey, to be executors.[2]

The produce of the sale of Wymondham in Norfolk, and the late Mrs. B's Scotch property,[3] to be appropriated in aid of the payment of debts and legacies.

[Comments added to Bolton's draft of the Will]

This is the last will and testament of me the Rt. Honble. George Gordon Lord Byron, Baron Byron of Rochdale in the county of Lancaster.—I desire that my body may be buried in the vault of the garden at Newstead without any ceremony or burial-service whatever, and that no inscription, save my name and age, be written on the tomb or tablet; and it is my will that my faithful dog may not be removed from the said vault. To the performance of this my particular desire, I rely on the attention of my executors hereinafter named.

[Bolton's comment] "It is submitted to Lord Byron whether this clause relative to the funeral had not better be omitted. The substance of it can be given in a letter from his lordship to the executors, and accompany the will; and the will may state that the funeral shall be performed in such manner as his lordship may by letter direct, and, in default of any such letter, then at the discretion of his executors."

It must stand.

B.

I do hereby specifically order and direct that all the claims of the said S. B. Davies upon me shall be fully paid and satisfied as soon as conveniently may be after my decease, on his proving ⟨by vouchers, or otherwise, to the satisfaction of my executors hereinafter named⟩ the amount thereof and the correctness of the same.

[Bolton's note] "If Mr. Davies has any unsettled claims upon Lord

---

[2] Bolton left blanks for the Christian names of the executors. Byron filled in all but that of Dallas and wrote in the margin: "I forget the Christian name of Dallas—cut him out."

[3] On Mrs. Byron's death, her Scotch property, consisting of £4,200, all that was left of the price of Gight, which had been invested for her, was paid over to Byron by her trustee.

Byron, that circumstance is a reason for his not being appointed executor; each executor having an opportunity of paying himself his own debt without consulting his co-executors."

So much the better—if possible, let him be an executor.

B.

[TO SAMUEL BOLTON]   *Newstead Abbey, August 16th, 1811*

Sir,—I have answered the queries on the margin. I wish Mr. Davies's claims to be most fully allowed, and, further, that he be one of my executors. I wish the will to be made in a manner to prevent all discussion, if possible, after my decease; and this I leave to you, as a professional gentleman.

With regard to the few and simple directions for the disposal of my *carcass*, I must have them implicitly fulfilled, as they will, at least, prevent trouble and expense;—and (what would be of little consequence to me, but may quiet the conscience of the survivors) the garden is *consecrated* ground. These directions are copied verbatim from my former will; the alterations in other parts have arisen from the death of Mrs. B.

I have the honour to be your most obedient, humble servant,

BYRON.

[TO SAMUEL BOLTON]   *Newstead Abbey, August 20, 1811*

Sir,—The witnesses shall be provided from amongst my tenants, and I shall be happy to see you on any day most convenient to yourself. I forgot to mention that it must be specified by codicil, or otherwise, that my body is on no account to be removed from the vault where I have directed it to be placed; and, in case any of my successors within the entail (from bigotry, or otherwise) might think proper to remove the carcass, such proceeding shall be attended by forfeiture of the estate, which, in such case, shall go to my sister, the Honble. Augusta Leigh and her heirs on similar conditions. I have the honour to be, sir,

Your very obedient, humble servant,

BYRON.

[TO JAMES CAWTHORN]   *Newstead Abbey Notts. Augst. 20th. 1811*

Mr. Cawthorn,—I have lately been too much occupied as you are aware to attend to any thing but the business immediately before me, but it is now time to ask you, if *your* & *my Amanuensis* delivered the Manuscript of the Im. of Horace to you according to my desire, & whether he has finished the copy of the Latin.—— —Will you be good enough to favour me with an answer that I may make some determination as to the manner of the publication viz. whether single, or at some future period in a joint volume with the Satire.—— —I am Sir

yr. very obedt. humble servt.

BYRON

P.S.—Mr. Hobhouse has sustained a very severe loss in his friend Mr. Matthews, which may perhaps interrupt his intention, have you heard from him on the Subject of his Travels?

[TO AUGUSTA LEIGH]   *Newstead Abbey. August 21st. 1811*

My dear Sister,—I ought to have answered your letter before, but when did I ever do anything that I ought?—I am losing my relatives & you are adding to the number of yours, but which is best God knows; —besides poor Mrs. Byron I have been deprived by death of two most particular friends within little more than a month, but as all observations on such subjects are superfluous & unavailing, I leave the dead to their rest, & return to the dull business of life, which however presents nothing very pleasant to me either in prospect or retrospection.— — —I hear you have been increasing his Majesty's Subjects, which in these times of War & tribulation is really patriotic, notwithstanding Malthus tells us that were it not for Battle, Murder, & Sudden death, we should be overstocked, I think we have latterly had a redundance of these national benefits, & therefore I give you all credit for your matronly behaviour.— —I believe you know that for upwards of two years I have been rambling round the Archipelago, & am returned just in time to know that I might as well have staid away for any good I ever have done, or am likely to do at home, & so, as soon as I have somewhat *repaired* my *irreparable* affairs I shall een go abroad again, for I am heartily sick of your climate & every thing it *rains* upon, always save & except *yourself* as in *duty bound*.—I should be glad to see you here (as I think you have never seen the place) if you could make it convenient. Murray is still like a Rock, & will probably outlast some six Lords Byron though in his 75th. Autumn.— —I took him with me to Portugal, & sent him round by sea to Gibraltar whilst I rode through the Interior of Spain which was then (1809) accessible.— —You say you have much to communicate to me, let us have it by all means, as I am utterly at a loss to guess; whatever it may be it will meet with due attention. Your trusty & well beloved cousin F. Howard[1] is married to a Miss Somebody, I wish him joy on your account, & on his own, though speaking generally I do not affect that Brood.— —By the bye *I* shall marry if I can find any thing inclined to barter money for rank, within six months; after which I shall return to my friends the Turks.—In the interim I am Dear Madam

[Signature cut out.]

[TO ROBERT CHARLES DALLAS]   *Newstead Abbey. Augst. 21st. 1811*

My dear Sir,—Your letter gives me credit for more acute feelings than I possess, for though I feel tolerably miserable, yet I am at the same time subject to a kind of hysterical merriment, or rather laughter without merriment, which I can neither account for nor conquer, & yet I do not feel relieved by it, but an indifferent person would think me in excellent Spirits.—"We must forget these things" & have recourse to our old selfish comforts, or rather——comfortable Selfishness.— I do not think I shall return to London immediately, & shall therefore accept freely what is offered courteously,—to wit—your mediation between me & Murray. I don't think my name will answer the purpose, & you must be aware that my plaguy Satire will bring the North & South Grubstreets down on the "Pilgrimage" but nevertheless if Murray makes a point of it, & you coincide with him, I will do it daringly, so let it be entitled by "the *Author of E[ngli]sh Bards & S[cot]ch R[eviewer]s*". My remarks on the Romaic &c. once intended to accompany the "*Hints from Horace*" shall go along with the other as being indeed more appropriate, also the smaller poems now in my possession, with a few selected from those published in H[obhouse]'s Miscellany.—I have found amongst my poor Mother's papers all my Letters from the East, & one in particular of some length from Albania, from this (if necessary) I can work up a note or two on that subject; as I kept no journal, the letters written on the Spot are the ne:t best.— — —But of this Anon—when we have definitely arranged, has Murray shown the work to any one?—he may—but I will have no traps for applause,—of course there are little things I would wish to alter, & perhaps the two Stanzas of a buffooning cast (on London's Sunday) are as well left out.[1]— —I much wish to avoid identifying

---

1 The Hon. Frederick Howard, third son of Lord Carlisle.
1 *Childe Harold*, I, 69–70. The stanzas were finally included.

Childe Harold's character with mine, & that in sooth is my second objection to my name on the T[itle] Page.—When you have made arrangements as to Time, size, type &c. favour me with a reply.—I am giving you an universe of trouble, which thanks cannot atone for.—I made a kind of prose apology for my Scepticism at the end of the MSS. which in recollection is so much more like an attack than a defence that haply it might better be omitted.—Perpend, Pronounce.— —After all I fear Murray will be in a Scrape with the Orthodox, but I cannot help it, though I wish well through it.—As for me "I have supped full of" Criticism, & I dont think that the most "dismal treatise" will stir & rouse my "fell of hair" till Birnam Wood do come to Dunsinane.— — —I shall continue to write at intervals & hope you will pay me in kind. —How does Pratt get on or rather get off Joe Blackett's posthumous Stock?[2]—You killed that poor man amongst you, in spite of your Ionian friend & myself who would have saved him from Pratt, Poetry, present poverty, & Posthumous oblivion.— —Cruel Patronage! to ruin a man in his calling, but then he is a divine subject for Subscription & Biography, & Pratt who makes the most of his dedications has inscribed the vol. to no less than five families of the first distinction. — —I am sorry you don't like Harry White,[3] with a great deal of Cant which in him was sincere (indeed it killed him as you killed Joe Blackett) certes there is Poesy & Genius, (I dont say this on account of my Simile & rhymes) but surely he was beyond all the Bloomfields[4] & Blacketts & their collateral coblers whom Lofft[5] & Pratt have or may kidnap from their calling into the service of "the *Trade.*" You must excuse my flippancy, for I am writing I know not what to escape from myself.—Hobhouse is gone to Ireland, Mr. Davies has been here on his way to Harrowgate, You did not know Matthews, he was a Man of the most astonishing powers as he sufficiently proved at Cambridge by carrying off more prizes & fellowships against the ablest candidates than any other Graduate on record, but a most decided Atheist, indeed noxiously so, for he proclaimed his principles in all Societies.—I knew him well, & feel a loss not easily to be supplied

[2] See June 28, 1811, to Dallas, note 1.
[3] Henry Kirke White, son of a Nottingham butcher, had been encouraged by Southey. Unlike Blacket, he had been at Cambridge. After he died in 1806, his poetic remains were published by Southey (1807). Byron praised White in *English Bards and Scotch Reviewers* (lines 831–48).
[4] Robert Bloomfield, a poet of humble origins, was a subject of Byron's irony in *English Bards* (777–98).
[5] Capell Lofft was a patron of Bloomfield and Blacket.

to myself,—to Hobhouse never.— —Let me hear from you & believe
me

always yours
BYRON

[TO FRANCIS HODGSON] *Newstead Abbey, August 22d, 1811*

You may have heard of the sudden death of my mother, and poor
Matthews, which, with that of Wingfield (of which I was not fully
aware till just before I left town, and indeed hardly believed it), has
made a sad chasm in my connexions. Indeed the blows followed each
other so rapidly that I am yet stupid from the shock, and though I do
eat and drink and talk, and even laugh, at times, yet I can hardly persuade myself that I am awake, did not every morning convince me
mournfully to the contrary.—I shall now wave the subject,—the dead
are at rest, and none but the dead can be so.

You will feel for poor Hobhouse,—Matthews was the "god of his
idolatry;" and if intellect could exalt a man above his fellows, no one
could refuse him pre-eminence. I knew him most intimately, and
valued him proportionably, but I am recurring—so let us talk of life
and the living.

If you should feel a disposition to come here, you will find "beef and
a sea-coal fire," and not ungenerous wine. Whether Otway's two
other requisites for an Englishman or not, I cannot tell, but probably
one of them.[1]—Let me know when I may expect you, that I may tell
you when I go and when return.—I have not yet been to Lancs. * * * *
* * * * * * * * * * * * * Davies has been here, and has invited me to
Cambridge for a week in October, so that, peradventure, we may encounter glass to glass. His gaiety (death cannot mar it) has done me
service; but, after all, ours was a hollow laughter.

You will write to me? I am solitary, and I never felt solitude irk-
some before. Your anxiety about the critique on * *'s[2] book is
amusing; as it was anonymous, certes it was of little consequence: I
wish it had produced a little more confusion, being a lover of literary
malice. Are you doing nothing? writing nothing? printing nothing?
why not your Satire on Methodism? the subject (supposing the public
to be blind to merit) would do wonders. Besides, it would be as well

---

[1] "Give but an Englishman his whore and ease,
   Beef and a sea-coal fire, he's yours for ever."
                    Venice Preserved, Act II, scene 3.
[2] Unidentified.

for a destined deacon to prove his orthodoxy.—It really would give me pleasure to see you properly appreciated. I say *really*, as, being an author, my humanity might be suspected. Believe me, dear H., yours always.

[TO JOHN MURRAY]   *Newstead Abbey. Notts. August 23d. 1811*

Sir,—A domestic calamity in the death of a near relation has hitherto prevented my addressing you on the subject of this letter.— My friend Mr. Dallas has placed in your hands a manuscript poem written by me in Greece, which he tells me you do not object to publishing.—But he also informed me in London that you wished to send the M.S. to Mr. Gifford.—Now, though no one would feel more gratified by the chance of obtaining his observations on a work than myself there is in such a proceeding, a kind of petition for praise, that neither my pride or—whatever you please to call it—will admit.—Mr. G. is not only the first Satirist of the day, but Editor of one of the principal Reviews.—As such, he is the last man whose censure (however eager to avoid it) I would deprecate by clandestine means.—You will therefore retain the M.S. in your own care, or if it must needs be shown, send it to another.—Though not very patient of Censure, I would fain obtain fairly any little praise my rhymes might deserve, at all events not by extortion & the humble solicitations of a bandied about M.S.— —I am sure a little consideration will convince you it would be wrong.— —If you determine on publication, I have some smaller poems (never published) a few notes, & a short dissertation on the Literature of the modern Greeks (written at Athens) which will come in at the end of the volume.— —And if the present poem should succeed, it is my intention at some subsequent period to publish some selections from my first work;—my Satire,—another nearly the same length, & a few other things, with the M.S. now in your hands, in two volumes.—But of these hereafter.—You will apprise me of your determination.—I am, Sir,

          your very obedt. humble Servt.
                BYRON

[TO JAMES WEDDERBURN WEBSTER]   *Newstead Abbey.*
                   August 24th. 1811

My dear W.— Conceiving your wrath to be somewhat evaporated, & your Dignity recovered from the *Hysterics* into which my innocent note from London had thrown it, I should feel happy to be informed how you have determined on the disposal of this accursed Coach,[1] which has driven us out of our Good humour & Good manners to a complete Standstill, from which I begin to apprehend that I am to lose altogether your valuable correspondence.— —Your angry letter arrived at a *moment*, to which I shall not allude further, as my happiness is best consulted in forgetting it.— —You have perhaps heard also of the death of poor Matthews, whom you recollect to have met at Newstead.—He was one whom his friends will find it difficult to replace, nor will Cambridge ever see his equal.—I trust you are on the point of adding to your relatives instead of losing them, and of *friends* a man of fortune will always have a plentiful stock—at his Table.— —I dare say now you are gay & connubial & popular so that in the next parliament we shall be having you a County Member.— But beware your Tutor, for I am sure he Germanized that sanguinary letter, you must not write such another to your Constituents; for myself (as the mildest of men) I shall say no more about it.— —Seriously —mio Caro W. if you can spare a moment from Matrimony, I shall be glad to hear that you have recovered from the pucker into which this *Vis* (one would think it had been a *Sulky*) has thrown you,—you know I wish you well—& if I have not inflicted my society upon you according to your own Invitation, it is only because I am not a social animal, & should feel sadly at a loss amongst Countesses & Maids of Honour, particularly being just come from a far Country, where Ladies are neither carved for, or fought for, or danced after, or mixed at all (publicly) with the Men-folks, so that you must make allowances for my natural diffidence & two years travel.—But (God and yourself willing) I shall certes pay my promised visit, as I shall be in town, if Parliament meets in October.— —In the mean time let me hear from you (without a privy Council) and believe me in sober sadness

yours very sincerely

BYRON

[TO ROBERT CHARLES DALLAS] *Newstead Abbey, August 25th, 1811*

My dear Sir,—Being fortunately enabled to frank, I do not spare scribbling, having sent you packets within the last ten days. I am passing solitary, and do not expect my agent to accompany me to

[1] See July 31, 1811, to Dallas, note 1.

Rochdale before the second week in September, a delay which perplexes me, as I wish the business over, and should at present welcome employment. I sent you exordiums, annotations, etc., for the forthcoming quarto, if quarto it is to be; and I also have written to Mr. Murray my objection to sending the MS. to Juvenal,[1] but allowing him to show it to any others of the calling. Hobhouse is amongst the types already; so, between his prose and my verse, the world will be decently drawn upon for its paper-money and patience. Besides all this, my "Imitation of Horace" is gasping for the press at Cawthorn's, but I am hesitating as to the *how* and the *when*, the single or the double, the present or the future. You must excuse all this, for I have nothing to say in this lone mansion but of myself, and yet I would willingly talk or think of aught else. What are you about to do? Do you think of perching in Cumberland, as you opined when I was in the metropolis? If you mean to retire, why not occupy Miss * * *'s [Milbanke's] "Cottage of Friendship" late the seat of Cobbler Joe, for whose death you and others are answerable? His "Orphan Daughter" (pathetic Pratt!) will, certes, turn out a shoe-making Sappho. Have you no remorse? I think that elegant address to Miss Dallas should be inscribed on the cenotaph which Miss * * * [Milbanke] means to stitch to his memory.[2] The newspapers seem much disappointed at his Majesty's not dying, or doing something better.[3] I presume it is almost over. If Parliament meets in October, I shall be in town to attend. I am also invited to Cambridge for the beginning of that month, but am first to jaunt to Rochdale. Now M * * [Matthews] is gone, and Hobhouse in Ireland, I have hardly one left there to bid me welcome, except my inviter. At three and twenty I am left alone, and what more can we be at seventy? It is true, I am young enough to begin again, but with whom can I retrace the laughing part of life? It is odd how few of my friends have died a quiet death; I mean in their beds. But a quiet life is of more consequence. Yet one loves squabbling and jostling better than yawning. This *last word* admonishes me to relieve you from

Yours very truly,
BYRON

---

[1] William Gifford, who published a translation of Juvenal (1802). See Aug. 23, 1811, to Murray.

[2] See June 28, 1811, to Dallas, note 1.

[3] The illness of the George III was mental. From this time forward he recovered his sanity only at intervals. Shortly after, the Prince of Wales was made Regent.

Sir,—I am in doubt what to do with the "Hints from Horace."—
Before it can be published I must have some friend in town, who understands the original thoroughly, to overlook the press, & I am inclined
to think it had better be delayed till the Satire is reprinted, & so come
out in the humbler light of an appendage to the aforesaid.—Besides I
have another thing in Mr. Murray's hands, and I dont like firing on
the Public with a *double Barrell* at least *one* had better be *discharged* at a
time, particularly as the *Captain's* prose being as it were connected
with my rhimes, & coming out at the same time, should make us
appear such pestilent scribblers, as this volley of Quarto's & Foolscap
Octavos certainly will.—Why, we shall want a press to ourselves, & if
we go on with "Weeks at Bath" & Travels, & Satires, & Imitations,
& poems descriptive & what not, your Neighbor Mr. Eyre the trunk-
maker will thrive prodigiously.— —I am very undecided, but in the
mean time the M. S. will do very well where it is, unless you send it to
Eyre's before it's time.—Capt. Hobhouse's book (not his "weeks at
Bath")[1] I shall be glad to hear of, & what arrangements he has made
as to the press, since poor Mr. M[atthews] was cut off one would
think on purpose to impede the coming Quarto.— —I am making out
an Albanian vocabulary for him, according to his wish, but what is to
be done with it? must it be sent to Cork?—I have not heard from Capt.
H. for some time.—On these topics you must communicate.—I am
Sir

your most obedt. very humble Servt.

BYRON

My dear Sir,—I was so sincere in my note on the late Charles S.
Matthews, & do feel myself so totally unable to do justice to his
talents, that the passage must stand for the very reason you bring
against it, to him all the Men I ever knew were pigmies, he was an
Intellectual Giant. It is true I loved W[ingfield] better, he was the
earliest & the dearest, & one of the few one could never repent of
having loved, but in ability—Ah—you did not know Matthews.—
"Childe Harold" may wait and welcome, works are never the worse
for delay in the publication. So you have got our Heir George Anson

---

[1] See July 31, 1811, to Hobhouse.

Byron & his sister the religious Julie,[1] poor Soul! why does not the pretty (& she is pretty) Muggletonian[2] get a spouse?—Failing in that I observe the Ladies transfer to God what Man has neglected, & become as lovingly religious as they would have been religiously loving. — —However I prefer piety to Cordials, the other resourse of the 'single blessed' though I think both are better exchanged for *Caudle* in these War-times.— —You may say what you please but you are one of the *Murderers* of Blackett; & yet you wont allow Harry White's Genius, setting aside his abominable Bigotry, he surely ranks next Chatterton.—It is astonishing how little he was known, & at Cambridge no one thought or heard of such a man, till his Death rendered all notice useless.—For my own part I should have been most proud of such an acquaintance, his very prejudices were respectable.— — There is a sucking Epic Poet at Granta, a Mr. Townsend[3] protegee of the late Cumberland,[4] did you ever hear of him & his "Armageddon?" I think his plan (the man I don't know) borders on the sublime, though perhaps the anticipation of the "Last Day" (according to you Nazarines) is a little too daring, at least it looks like telling the Lord what he's to do, & might remind an ill-natured person of the line

"For fools rush in where Angels fear to tread.["]

But I don't mean to cavil, only other folk will, & he may bring all the Lambs of Jacob Behman[5] about his ears.— —However I hope he will bring it to a Conclusion, though Milton is in his way.—Write to me, I doat on Gossip, & make a bow to Ju. & shake George by the hand for me, but take care for he has a sad sea-paw.—

Yrs. ever
B.—

P.S.—I would ask George here, but I don't know how to amuse him, all my horses were sold when I left England, and I have not had time

[1] George Anson Byron's father (who bore the same name) was a younger brother of Byron's father. He had married Henrietta Dallas, sister of R. C. Dallas, Byron's correspondent. The younger George Anson Byron's sister Julia later married the Rev. Robert Heath.

[2] The Muggletonian sect was founded about 1651 by Lodowicke Muggleton and John Reeve who claimed to be the "two witnesses" of Rev. xi, 3–6. Their eccentric views were not those of Julia probably, but Byron used the term to indicate facetiously her religious ardour.

[3] The Rev. George Townsend (1788–1857) of Trinity College published *Poems* in 1810, and eight books of his *Amageddon* in 1815. Byron has more to say of him in *Hints from Horace* lines 191–212, and in a note to line 191.

[4] Richard Cumberland, dramatist, novelist, essayist, over-praised Townsend's forthcoming poem in the *London Review*.

[5] The German mystic was the common butt of rationalist thinkers.

to replace them. Besides he would be meddling with the wenches.— Nevertheless if he will come down & shoot in Septr. he will be very welcome, but he must bring a Gun for I gave all mine to Aly Pacha & other Turks.—Dogs, a Keeper, & plenty of Game with a very large Manor I have.—A Lake, a boat, House room & *neat Wines*.—

[TO JAMES CAWTHORN]   *Newstead Abbey, August 30th. 1811*

. . . I don't see why you should suppose me dissatisfied with you because the other thing is published by Mr. Murray,[1] the subject being descriptive would have interfered too much with my friend C't H[obhouse]'s work, had they both been published by the same publisher. The "Hints" are mostly delayed by the difficulty of finding a friend to correct the press because he must understand the original perfectly and I have no one capable of doing it for me but Mr. Hodgson, who could adapt the Latin to the Imitation fully as well or better than myself, for in this instance the Corrector has two functions to perform, he must understand the original and make the copy understood. As to my name, I wished to be anonymous, but Mr. D[allas] teazed me out of it. You must not conceive me to be angry, neither is it of any consequence to you if I were so. I wish you success in every way.

yr. very obedt. humble servt.,

B.

[TO JOHN CAM HOBHOUSE]   *Newstead Abbey August 30th. 1811*

My dear Hobhouse,—Scrope Davies has been here & seemed as much affected by late events as could be expected from one who has lived so much in the world, his society was (as it is always wont to be) very reviving, but now he is gone & I am solitary & sullen.—-Not a scrap of paper has been found, at Cambridge, which is singular;—I can hardly agree with you in a wish to forget. I love to remember the dead, for we see only their virtues, & when our best friends are thus removed, we become reconciled to our own prospects & "long to be with them and at Rest."[1]— —I think when your mind is more calm, you ought to write his Epitaph, & we will erect to his memory a monument, in some appropriate place, I do not know any other who

---

[1] Cawthorn was apparently piqued because Byron had given *Childe Harold* to Murray and was dragging his feet on the publication of *Hints from Horace*.
[1] See *Samson Agonistes* 598 and *Psalms*, 55:6.

would do him justice, indeed it is *your right* & perhaps your *duty.*— Then "Give his fame to the winds, & let the Harp sigh over his narrow house" you are now in the land of Ossian.— — —In the poem which I wrote abroad, & is now in the hands of Murray the Bookseller for publication, at the close of the 1st. Canto which treats of Spain, I have two stanzas in commemoration of W[ingfield] who died at Coimbra, & in a note to these having occasion to mention the loss of three persons very dear to me in so very short a time, I have added a very short sentence or two on the subject of our friend, which though they can neither add to his credit or satisfaction, will at least shew my own pride in the acquaintance of such a man.— —Your book goes on well & I trust will answer your purpose & my expectations. Demetrius has made out a most formidable vocabulary, on which I wait for further orders.—I do not know who is your deputy in town, perhaps Baillie, or Shepherd.—I have had a letter from Bankes, of the patronizing kind, where I am invited to *"one* of *my places* in *Wales"*!!— —I am going to Lancs. & am in daily expectation of Hanson to back me, & I mean to marry, prudently if possible that is wealthily, I can't afford anything to Love.—I wish you were here, but you *will* be *here,* & we shall laugh again as usual & be very miserable dogs for all that.—My Sister writes me melancholy letters, things are not going on well there, but mismanagement is the hereditary epidemic of our Brood.— Hodgson is battening on "Lower Moor Herefordshire," Davies at Harrowgate.— —I am to visit him in Octr. at King's Coll.—Dallas is running to & from Mortlake with his pocket full of proofs of *all* his *friends* who are all Scribblers & make him a Packhorse.— —I am here boxing in a Turkish pelise to prevent obesity, & as usual very much yours

BYRON

[TO AUGUSTA LEIGH (*a*)]   *Newstead Abbey August 30th. 1811*

My dear Augusta,—The embarrassments you mention in your last letter I never heard of before, but that disease is epidemic in our family.— —Neither have I been apprised of any of the changes at which you hint, indeed how should I? on the borders of the Black Sea, we heard only of the Russians.—So you have much to tell, & all will be novelty.— —I don't know what Scrope Davies meant by telling you I liked Children, I abominate the sight of them so much that I have always had the greatest respect for the character of *Herod.*— —But as my house here is large enough for us all, we should go on very well, &

I need not tell you that I long to see *you.*— —I really do not perceive any thing so formidable in a Journey hither of two days, but all this comes of Matrimony, you have a Nurse & all the &cas. of a family. Well, I must marry to repair the ravages of myself & prodigal ancestry, but if I am ever so unfortunate as to be presented with an Heir, instead of a *Rattle,* he shall be provided with a *Gag.*— — —I shall perhaps be able to accept D[avies]'s invitation to Cambridge, but I fear my stay in Lancashire will be prolonged, I proceed there in the 2d. week of Septr. to arrange my coal concerns, & then if I can't persuade some wealthy dowdy to ennoble the dirty puddle of her mercantile Blood,—why—I shall leave England & all it's clouds for the East again,—I am very sick of it already.— —Joe[1] has been getting well of a disease that would have killed a troop of horse, he promises to bear away the palm of longevity from old Parr.—As you wont come, you will write, I long to hear all these unutterable things, being utterly unable to guess at any of them, unless they concern *your* relative the Thane of Carlisle,[2]—though I had great hopes we had done with him.—I have little to add that you do not already know, and being quite alone, have no great variety of incident to gossip with, I am but rarely pestered with visitors, & the few I have I get rid of as soon as possible.— —I will now take leave of you in the Jargon of 1794. "Health & *Fraternity!*"

Yrs. always
B.—

[TO AUGUSTA LEIGH (*b*)]   *Newstead Abbey Augst. 30th.* [31?] *1811*

My dear Augusta,—I wrote to you yesterday, & as you will not be very sorry to hear from me again, considering our long separation, I shall fill up this sheet before I go to bed.—I have heard something of a quarrel between your spouse & the Prince,[1] I don't wish pry into family secrets or to hear anything more of the matter, but I cant help regretting on your account that so long an intimacy should be dissolved at the very moment when your husband might have derived

---

[1] Joe Murray, servant at Newstead.

[2] Byron knew that Augusta was concerned about his quarrel with the Earl of Carlisle.

[1] Augusta's cousin-husband, Col. George Leigh, was equerry to the Prince of Wales. Byron's mother had written him on May 11, 1810: ". . . the cause of Col. Leigh's quarrel with the Prince is that he cheated him in selling a horse for him, as he *retained* for *himself* part of the purchase money". (Lytton Papers.)

some advantage from his R[oyal] H[ighness]'s friendship.—However, at all events, & in all Situations, you have a brother in me, & a home here.—I am led into this train of thinking by a part of your letter which hints at pecuniary losses.—I know how delicate one ought to be on such subjects, but you are probably the only being on Earth *now* interested in my welfare, certainly the only relative, & I should be very ungrateful if I did not feel the obligation.—You must excuse my being a little cynical, knowing how my *temper* was tried in Non-age, the manner in which I was brought up must necessarily have broken a meek Spirit, or rendered a fiery one ungovernable, the effect it has had on mine I need not state.— —However, buffeting with the World has brought me a little to reason, & two years travel in distant & barbarous countries has accustomed me to bear privations, & consequently to laugh at many things, which would have made me angry before.— — But I am wandering—in short I only want to assure you, that I love you, & that you must not think I am indifferent because I don't shew my affection in the usual way.— —Pray can't you contrive to pay me a visit between this & Xmas? or shall I carry you down with me from Cambridge, supposing it practicable for me to come.—You will do what you please, without our interfering with each other, the premises are so delightfully extensive, that two people might live together without ever seeing hearing or meeting,—but I can't feel the comfort of this till I marry.—In short it would be the most amiable matrimonial mansion, & *that* is another great inducement to my plan,—my wife & I shall be so happy,—one in each Wing.—If this description wont make you come, I cant tell what will, you must please yourself.—Good night, I have to walk half a mile to my Bedchamber

yrs. ever
Byron

[TO JAMES WEDDERBURN WEBSTER]   *Newstead Abbey. Notts.—*
Augst. 31st. 1811

My dear W.—I send you back your friend's letter, & though I dont agree with his Canons of Criticism, they are not the worse for that.— My friend Hodgson is not much honoured by the comparison to the "Pursuits of L" which is notoriously as far as the *poetry* goes the worst written of it's kind, the World has been long but of one opinion viz. that it's sole merit lies in the Notes, which are indisputably excellent. ——Had Hodgson's "alterative" been placed with the "Baviad" the compliment had been higher to both, for surely the Baviad is as much superior to H's poem, as I do firmly believe H's poem to be to the

"Pursuits of Literature.["]— — Your correspondent talks for talking's sake when he says Lady J. Gray is neither "Epic, dramatic, or legendary" who ever said it was *"epic"* or *"dramatic"*? he might as well say his letter was neither "epic or dramatic", the poem makes no pretensions to either character.—"Legendary" it certainly is, but what has that to do with it's merits? all stories of that kind founded on facts are in a certain degree legendary, but they may be well or ill written without the smallest alteration in that respect.—When Mr. Hare prattles about the "Economy" &c. he sinks sadly;—all such expressions are the mere cant of a schoolboy hovering round the Skirts of Criticism.—Hodgson's tale is one of the best efforts of his Muse, & Mr. H[are]'s approbation must be one of more consequence, before any body will reduce it to a "Scale," or be much affected by "the place" he "assigns" to the productions of a man like Hodgson.[1]—But I have said more than I intended & only beg you never to allow yourself to be imposed upon by such "common place" as the 6th. form letter you sent me.—Judge for yourself.— — —I know the Mr. Bankes[2] you mention though not to that *"extreme"* you seem to think, but I am flattered by his "boasting" on such a subject (as you say) for I never thought him likely to "boast" of anything which was not his own.— —I am not *"melancholick"* pray what *"folk"* dare to say any such thing? I must contradict them by being *merry* at their expence.—I shall invade you in the course of the winter, out of envy, as Lucifer looked at Adam & Eve.— —Pray be as *happy* as you can, & write to me that I may catch the infection   yrs. ever

BYRON

[TO JAMES CAWTHORN]   *Newstead. Augst. 31st. 1811*

Mr. Cawthorn.—I send you some alterations for the text & an additional note to the "Hints" which I request you will be good enough to arrange.—

yr. very obedt. Sert.
Bn.

[1] "Webster had sent Byron a letter from Naylor Hare, in which the latter criticised Hodgson's *Lady Jane Grey; and other Poems* (1809). . . . In the Volume (pp. 56–77) was printed his 'Gentle alterative prepared for the Reviewers,' which Hare apparently compared to *The Pleasures* [sic] [*Pursuits*] *of Literature* (1794–97), by T. J. Mathias. To this criticism Byron objected, saying that the 'alterative' might be more fairly compared to Gifford's *Baviad* (1794)." (Prothero's note, *LJ*, II, 14.)
[2] See Feb. 23, 1807, to Long, note 9.

My dear Augusta,—I wrote you a vastly dutiful letter since my answer to your second epistle, & I now write you a third for which you have to thank Silence & Solitude.—Mr. Hanson comes hither on the 14th. & I am going to Rochdale on business, but that need not prevent you from coming here, you will find Joe, & the house & the cellar & all therein very much at your Service.—As to a Lady B.— when I discover one rich enough to suit me & foolish enough to have me, I will give her leave to make me miserable if she can.—Money is the magnet, as to Women, one is as well as another, the older the better, we have than a chance of getting her to Heaven.—So, your Spouse does not like brats better than myself; now those who beget them have no right to find fault, but *I* may rail with great propriety.— My "Satire!"—I am glad it made you laugh for Somebody told me in Greece that you was angry, & I was sorry, as you were perhaps the only person whom I did *not* want to *make angry.*— — —But how you will make *me laugh* I don't know, for it is a vastly *serious* subject to me I assure you, therefore take care, or I shall hitch *you* into the next Edition to make up our family party.—Nothing so fretful, so despicable as a Scribbler, see what *I* am, & what a parcel of Scoundrels I have brought about my ears, & what language I have been obliged to treat them with to deal with them in their own way;—all this comes of Authorship, but now I am in for it, & shall be at war with Grubstreet, till I find some better amusement.— —You will write to me your Intentions & may almost depend on my being at Cambridge in October.— You say you mean to be &c. in the *Autumn*; I should be glad to know what you call the present Season, it would be Winter in every other Country which I have seen.— —If we meet in Octr. we will travel in my *Vis*.—& can have a cage for the children & a Cart for the Nurse.— Or perhaps we can forward them by the Canal.— —Do let us know all about it, your *"bright thought"* is a little clouded like the Moon in this preposterous climate.—Good even, Child.—

yrs. ever
B.—

My dear Hodgson,—I will have nothing to do with your immortality; we are miserable enough in this life, without the absurdity of speculating upon another. If men are to live, why die at all? and if they die, why disturb the sweet and sound sleep that "knows no waking"? "Post mortem nihil est, ipsaque Mors nihil . . . quæris quo jaceas post obitum loco? Quo *non* Nata jacent".[1]

As to revealed religion, Christ came to save men; but a good Pagan will go to heaven, and a bad Nazarene to hell; "Argal" (I argue like the gravedigger) why are not all men Christians? or why are any? If mankind may be saved who never heard or dreamt, at Timbuctoo, Otaheite, Terra Incognita, &c., of Galilee and its Prophet, Christianity is of no avail, if they cannot be saved without, why are not all orthodox? It is a little hard to send a man preaching to Judæa, and leave the rest of the world—Negers and what not—*dark* as their complexions, without a ray of light for so many years to lead them on high; and who will believe that God will damn men for not knowing what they were never taught? I hope I am sincere; I was so at least on a bed of sickness in a far distant country, when I had neither friend, nor comforter, nor hope, to sustain me. I looked to death as a relief from pain, without a wish for an after-life, but a confidence that the God who punishes in this existence had left that last asylum for the weary.

"Ον ὁ θεὸς ἀγαπάει ἀποθνήσκει νέος.[2]

I am no Platonist, I am nothing at all; but I would sooner be a Paulician, Manichean, Spinozist, Gentile, Pyrrhonian, Zoroastrian, than one of the seventy-two villainous sects who are tearing each other to pieces for the love of the Lord and hatred of each other. Talk of Galileeism? Show me the effects—are you better, wiser, kinder by your precepts? I will bring you ten Mussulmans shall shame you in all good-will towards men, prayer to God, and duty to their neighbours. And is there a Talapoin,[3] or a Bonze, who is not superior to a fox-hunting curate? But I will say no more on this endless theme; let me live, well if possible, and die without pain. The rest is with God, who assuredly, had He *come* or *sent*, would have made Himself manifest to nations, and intelligible to all.

I shall rejoice to see you. My present intention is to accept Scrope Davies's invitation; and then, if you accept mine, we shall meet *here* and *there*. Did you know poor Matthews? I shall miss him much at Cambridge.

[1] Seneca *Troades*, 397ff. "There is nothing after death, and death itself is nothing. You seek the place where one lies after death? Where those unborn lie."
[2] Whom the Gods love die young.
[3] A word used in the seventeenth century to designate the Buddhist monks of Ceylon and the Indo-Chinese countries. Byron may have taken it from Voltaire. (Dial. XXII, *André des Couches à Siam.*)

Mr. Cawthorn,—More notes for "the *Hints*"! you mistake me much by thinking me inattentive to this publication, if I had a friend willing & able to correct the press, it should be out with my good will immediately.—Pray attend to annexing the additional notes in their proper places, & let them be added immediately

yrs. &c.
BYRON

[TO ROBERT CHARLES DALLAS]   *Newstead Abbey. Septr. 4th. 1811*

My dear Sir,—I am at present anxious as Cawthorn seems to wish it, to have a small Edition of the "Hints from Horace" published immediately, but the Latin (the most difficult poem in the language) renders it necessary in the Correction of the press to be most particular not only in correcting the proofs with *Horace in his hand*, but in adapting the parallel passages of the Imitation in such places to the Original as may enable the Reader not to lose sight of the Allusion. — — —I don't know whether I ought to ask you to do this but I am too far off to do it for myself, & though it may be presumptuous in me to conjecture that you should be unacquainted with anything to which I myself make pretensions, perhaps your reading of late years has not lain among the Romans.— —If however you can condescend to my Schoolboy erudition, you will oblige me by setting this thing going, though you will smile at the importance I attach to it.—Believe me

ever yrs.
BYRON

[TO JOHN MURRAY]   *Newstead Abbey. Notts. Sept. 5th. 1811*

Sir,—The time seems to be past when (as Dr. Johnson said) a man was certain to "hear the truth from his Bookseller", for you have paid me so many compliments, that, if I was not the veriest scribbler on Earth, I should feel affronted.—As I accept your compliments, it is but fair I should give equal or greater credit to your objections, the more so as I believe them to be well founded.—— —With regard to the political & metaphysical parts, I am afraid I can alter nothing, but I have high authority for my Errors in that point, for even the *Æneid*

90

was a *political* poem & written for a *political* purpose, and as to my un-lucky opinions on Subjects of more importance, I am too sincere in them for recantation.[1]—On Spanish affairs I have said what I saw, & every day confirms me in that notion of the result formed on the Spot, & I rather think honest John Bull is beginning to come round again to that Sobriety which Massena's[2] retreat had begun to reel from it's Centre, the usual consequence of *un*usual success.— —So you perceive I cannot alter the Sentiments, but if there are any alterations in the structure of the versification you would wish to be made, I will tag rhymes, & turn Stanzas, as much as you please.—As for the *"Ortho-dox,"* let us hope they will buy on purpose to abuse, you will forgive the one if they will do the other.—You are aware that anything from my pen must expect no quarter on many accounts, & as the present publication is of a Nature very different from the former, we must not be sanguine.—You have given me no answer to my question—tell me fairly did you show the M.S. to some of your Corps?— —I sent an introductory Stanza to Mr. Dallas that it might be forwarded to you, the poem else will open too abruptly. The Stanzas had better be num-bered in Roman characters; there is a disquisition on the Literature of the modern Greeks, & some smaller poems to come in at the Close.— These are now at Newstead, but will be sent in time.—If Mr. D[allas] has lost the Stanza & note annexed to it, write & I will send it myself. —You tell me to add 2 Cantos, but I am about to visit my *Collieries* in Lancashire on the 15th. Inst. which is so *unpoetical* an employment that I need say no more. I am Sir

your most obedt. humble Servt.

B.

[TO ROBERT CHARLES DALLAS]   *Newstead Abbey, Sept. 7th, 1811*

My dear Sir,—As Gifford has been ever my "Magnus Apollo," any approbation such as you mention, would, of course, be more welcome than "all Bokara's vaunted gold, than all the gems of Samarkand."[1]

---

1 Murray had written that there were some expressions concerning Spain and Portugal that "do not harmonize with the general feeling" and that might inter-fere with the popularity of the poem. "I hope your Lordship's goodness will induce you to obviate them, and, with them, perhaps, some religious feelings which may deprive me of some customers amongst the *Orthodox*." (*LJ*, II, 25n.)

2 Massena's retreat into Spain had been interpreted as a victory for Wellington.

1 From Sir W. Jones's translation of a song by Hafiz (*Works* X, 251.) of which Byron wrote a parody called "The Barmaid" which was never published. The MS. is in the Murray collection.

But I am sorry the MS. was shown to him in such a manner, and had written to Murray to say as much, before I was aware that it was too late.

Your objection to the expression "central line," I can only meet by saying that, before Childe Harold left England, it was his full intention to traverse Persia, and return by India, which he could not have done without passing the equinoctial.

The other errors you mention I must correct in the progress through the press. I feel honoured by the wish of such men that the poem should be continued, but to do that, I must return to Greece and Asia; I must have a warm sun and a blue sky; I cannot describe scenes so dear to me by a sea-coal fire. I had projected an additional canto when I was in the Troad and Constantinople, and if I saw them again it would go on; but under existing circumstances and *sensations*, I have neither harp, "heart nor voice" to proceed. I feel that *you are all right* as to the metaphysical part, but I also feel that I am sincere, and that if I am only to write *"ad capitandum vulgus,"* I might as well edit a magazine at once, or spin canzonettas for Vauxhall.[2]

* * * * * * * * * * * * * * *
* * * * * * * * * * * * * * *

My work must make its way as well as it can; I know I have every thing against me, angry poets and prejudices; but if the poem is a *poem*, it will surmount these obstacles, and if *not*, it deserves its fate. Your friend's Ode I have read—it is no great compliment to pronounce it far superior to S * 's [Smyth's] on the same subject, or to the merits of the new chancellor. It is evidently the production of a man of taste, and a poet, though I should not be willing to say it was fully equal to what might be expected from the author of *"Horae Ionicae."*[3] I thank you for it, and that is more than I would do for any other Ode of the present day.

I am very sensible of your good wishes, and, indeed, I have need of them. My whole life has been at variance with propriety, not to say decency; my circumstances are become involved; my friends are dead or estranged, and my existence a dreary void. In M * * [Matthews] I have lost my "guide, philosopher, and friend;" in Wingfield a friend

[2] Vauxhall was then a resort for ballad singers.
[3] W. Smyth of Peterhouse, Professor of Modern History at Cambridge, composed an Ode for the installation of the Duke of Gloucester as Chancellor of Cambridge University on June 29, 1811. Dallas's friend who had composed the Ode which Byron thought superior was Walter Rodwell Wright.

only, but one whom I could have wished to have preceded in his long journey.

M * * [Matthews] was indeed an extraordinary man; it has not entered into the heart of a stranger to conceive such a man: there was the stamp of immortality in all he said or did; and now what is he? When we see such men pass away and be no more—men who seem created to display what the Creator *could make* his creatures gathered into corruption, before the maturity of minds that might have been the pride of posterity, what are we to conclude? For my own part I am bewildered. To me he was much, to Hobhouse every thing.—My poor Hobhouse doted on M * * [Matthews]. For me, I did not love quite so much as I honoured him; I was indeed so sensible of his infinite superiority, that though I did not envy, I stood in awe of it. He, Hobhouse, D * * [Davies], and myself, formed a coterie of our own at Cambridge and elsewhere. D * * [Davies] is a wit and man of the world, and feels as much as such a character can do; but not as Hobhouse has been affected. D * * [Davies], who is not a scribbler, has always beaten us all in the war of words, and by his colloquial powers at once delighted and kept us in order. H[obhouse] and myself always had the worst of it with the other two; and even M[atthews] yielded to the dashing vivacity of S * D * * [Scrope Davies]. But I am talking to you of men, or boys, as if you cared about such beings.

I expect mine agent down on the 14th to proceed to Lancashire, where, I hear from all quarters, I have a very valuable property in coals, &c. I then intend to accept an invitation to Cambridge in October, and shall, perhaps, run up to town. I have four invitations, to Wales, Dorset, Cambridge, and Chester; but I must be a man of business. I am quite alone, as these long letters sadly testify. I perceive, by referring to your letter, that the Ode is from the author; make my thanks acceptable to him. His Muse is worthy a nobler theme. You will write, as usual, I hope. I wish you a good evening, and am,

Yours ever,
BYRON

[TO AUGUSTA LEIGH]   *Newstead Abbey. Septr. 9th 1811*

My dear Augusta,—My Rochdale affairs are understood to be settled as far as the Law can settle them, & indeed I am told that the most valuable part is that which was never disputed, but I have never

reaped any advantage from them & God knows if I ever shall.—
Mr. H[anson] my agent is a good man & able, but the most dilatory
in the world.—I expect him down on the 14th to accompany me to
Rochdale, where something will be decided as to selling or working the
Collieries, I am Lord of the Manor (a most extensive one) & they
want to enclose which cannot be done without me, but I go there in the
worst humour possible & am afraid I shall do or say something not very
conciliatory.—In short all my affairs are going on as badly as possible,
& I have no hopes or plans to better them as I long ago pledged myself never to sell Newstead, which I mean to hold in defiance of the
Devil & Man.— —I am quite alone & never see strangers without
being sick, but I am nevertheless on good terms with my neighbours,
for I neither ride or shoot of move over my Garden walls, but I fence
& box & swim & run a good deal to keep me in exercise & get me to
sleep.— — —Poor Murray is ill again, & one of my Greek servants is
ill too, & my valet has got a pestilent cough, so that we are in a peck
of troubles, my family Surgeon sent an Emetic this evening for *one* of
them, I did not very well know *which*, but I swore *Somebody* should
take it, so after a deal of discussion the Greek swallowed it with tears
in his eyes, & by the blessing of it & the *Virgin* whom he invoked to
assist *it* & *him*, I suppose he'll be well tomorrow, if not, *another* shall
have the *next*.— —So your Spouse likes children, *that* is lucky as he
will have to bring them up, for my part (since I lost my Newfoundland
dog) I like nobody except his successor a Dutch Mastiff & three land
Tortoises brought with me from Greece.—I thank you for your letters,
& am always glad to hear from you, but if you wont come here before
Times I very much fear we shall not meet *here* at all, for I shall be off
somewhere or other very soon out of this land of Paper credit (or
rather no credit at all, for every body seems on the high road to Bank-
ruptcy) & if I quit it again I shall not be back in a hurry.— — — — —
However, I shall endeavour to see you somewhere, & make my bow
with decorum before I return to the Ottomans, I believe I shall turn
Mussulman in the end.—You ask after my health, I am in tolerable
leanness, which I promote by exercise & abstinence. I dont know that I
have acquired any thing by my travels but a smattering of two languages & a habit of chewing Tobacco.—

yrs ever
B.

Dear Hodgson,—I have been a good deal in your company lately, for I have been reading Juvenal & Lady Jane &ca.[1] for the first time since my return.—The 10th. Sat[ir]e has always been my favourite as I suppose indeed of every body's, it is the finest recipe for making one miserable with this life, & content to walk out of it, in any language.— I should think it might be redde with great effect to a man dying without much pain, in preference to all the stuff that ever was said or sung in churches. But you are a deacon, & I say no more. ah you will marry & become lethargic like poor Hal of Harrow,[2] who yawns at 10 o'nights, & orders caudle annually.—I wrote an answer to yours fully some days ago, & being quite alone & able to frank, you must excuse this sub- sequent epistle which will cost nothing but the trouble of decyphering. ——I am expectant of agents to accompany me to Rochdale, a journey not to be anticipated with pleasure; though I feel very restless where I am, & shall probably ship off for Greece again; what nonsense it is to talk of Soul, when a cloud makes it *melancholy*, & wine—*mad.*—Collet of *Staines* your "most kind Host" has lost that Girl you saw of his. She grew to five feet eleven & might have been God knows how high if it had pleased him to renew the race of Anak, but she fell by a Ptisick, a fresh proof of the folly of begetting children.——You knew Matthews, was he not an intellectual Giant?—I knew few better or more inti- mately, & none who deserved more admiration in point of Ability.— ——Scrope Davies has been here on his way to Harrowgate [sic], I am his Guest in October at King's, where we will "drink deep eer we depart".—"Wont you, Wont you, wont you, wont you, come Mr. Mug?"[3]—We did not amalgamate properly at Harrow, it was some- how rainy, & then a wife makes such a damp, but in a seat of celibacy I will have revenge.—Dont you hate helping Fish, & losing the wings of chicken? & then conversation is always flabby—oh in the East women are in their proper sphere, & one has—no conversation at all. —My house here is a delightful matrimonial mansion, when I wed, my spouse & I will be so happy!—one in each wing.— —I presume you are in motion from your Herefordshire station,[4] & Drury must be gone back to Gerund Grinding.— — —I have not been at Cambridge since

[1] Hodgson had published a translation of Juvenal in 1807, and *Lady Jane Grey, a Tale; and Other Poems in 1809.*

[2] Henry Drury.

[3] Possibly Matthew Mug, a character in Foote's *Mayor of Garratt.*

[4] Hodgson was staying with his uncle, the Rev. Richard Coke, of Lower Moor, Herefordshire.

I took my M. A. Degree in 1808. "Eheu fugaces"![5] I look forward to meeting you & Scrope there with the feelings of other times.— —Capt. Hobhouse is at Enniscorthy in Juverna.—I wish he was in England.

yrs. ever
B.

[TO ROBERT CHARLES DALLAS]   *Newstead Abbey. Notts.*
Septr. 10th. 1811

Dear Sir,—I rather think in one of the opening Stanzas of C[hild]e. H[arol]d. there is this line

"'Tis said at times the *sullen* tear would start,"

now a line or two after I have a repetition of the epithet "*sullen* reverie" so (if it be so) let us have "*speechless* reverie" or "*silent reverie*" but at all events do away the recurrence.

yrs. ever
B.

Perhaps as "Reverie" implies "*silence*" of itself, "wayward" "downcast" "gloomy" "wrinkling" "joyless" may be better epithets.[1]

[TO JOHN HANSON]   *Newstead Abbey Septr. 10th. 1811*

Dr. Sir,—Though you have not written lately I presume you will be here on the 14th. as my affairs draw rapidly to a crisis.— —I sent you the Duke of Devon's[1] letter to me, & as something must be *settled* or

---

[5] Eheu fugaces, Postume, Postume,
labuntur anni, nec pietas moram
rugis et instanti senectae
adferet indomitaeque morti.
         Horace, *Carmina*, XIV, 1
("Ah me, Postumus, Postumus, the fleeting years are slipping by, nor will piety give a moment's stay to wrinkles and hurrying old age and death the unconquerable.")
[1] "joyless" was finally adopted.
[1] William George Spencer Cavendish, Marquis of Hartington (1790–1858) succeeded his father as the sixth Duke of Devonshire in July 1811. The context of the letter to Hanson seems to indicate that he was dunning Byron for some debt. He had been at Trinity College in Byron's time. See July 5, 1807, to Elizabeth Pigot.

every thing *unsettled* very soon, I shall not I trust have to experience a
further delay so ruinous to my interest in every point of view.—I am

yrs very truly
BYRON

[TO FRANCIS HODGSON]   *Newstead Abbey, Sept. 13, 1811*

My dear Hodgson.—I thank you for your song, or, rather, your two
songs—your new song on love, and your *old song* on *religion*. I admire
the *first* sincerely, and in turn call upon you to *admire* the following on
Anacreon Moore's new operatic farce,[1] or farcical opera—call it which
you will:—

> Good plays are scarce,
> So Moore writes farce;
> Is fame like his so brittle?
> We knew before
> That "Little's" Moore,[2]
> But now '*tis Moore* that's *Little*.

I won't dispute with you on the arcana of your new calling; they are
bagatelles, like the King of Poland's rosary. One remark and I have
done: the basis of your religion is *injustice*; the *Son of God*, the *pure*,
the *immaculate*, the *innocent*, is sacrificed for the *guilty*. This proves *His*
heroism; but no more does away with *man's* guilt than a schoolboy's
volunteering to be flogged for another would exculpate the dunce from
negligence, or preserve him from the rod. You degrade the Creator,
in the first place, by making Him a begetter of children; and in the
next you convert Him into a tyrant over an immaculate and injured
Being, who is sent into existence to suffer death for the benefit of
some millions of scoundrels, who, after all, seem as likely to be damned
as ever. As to miracles, I agree with Hume that it is more probable
men should *lie* or be *deceived*, than that things out of the course of
nature should so happen. Mahomet wrought miracles, Brothers the
prophet had *proselytes*,[3] and so would Breslau the conjurer,[4] had he
lived in the time of Tiberius.

1 Thomas Moore's *M.P., or The Bluestocking* was played at the Lyceum on
September 9, 1811, but was not a success and was withdrawn.
2 Moore published his early erotic poems under the pseudonym of Thomas
Little.
3 Richard Brothers (1757–1824) believed that in the year 1795 he was to be revealed as Prince of the Hebrews and ruler of the world, but he was arrested and
confined as a lunatic.
4 See *Breslaw's Last Legacy; or, the Magical Companion*, 1784.

Besides, I trust that God is not a *Jew*, but the God of all mankind; and, as you allow that a virtuous Gentile may be saved, you do away the necessity of being a Jew or a Christian.

I do not believe in any revealed religion, because no religion is revealed; and if it pleases the Church to damn me for not allowing a *nonentity*, I throw myself on the mercy of the *"Great First Cause, least understood,"* who must do what is most proper; though I conceive He never made anything to be tortured in another life, whatever it may in this. I will neither read *pro* nor *con*. God would have made His will known without books, considering how very few could read them when Jesus of Nazareth lived, had it been His pleasure to ratify any peculiar mode of worship. As to your immortality, if people are to live, why die? And our carcases, which are to rise again, are they worth raising? I hope, if mine is, that I shall have a better *pair of legs* than I have moved on these two-and-twenty years, or I shall be sadly behind in the squeeze into Paradise. Did you ever read "Malthus on Population?" If he be right, war and pestilence are our best friends, to save us from being eaten alive, in this "best of all possible worlds."[5]

I will write, read, and think no more; indeed, I do not wish to shock your prejudices by saying all I do think. Let us make the most of life, and leave dreams to Emanuel Swedenborg.

Now to dreams of another genus—poesies. I like your song much; but I will say no more, for fear you should think I wanted to coax you into approbation of my past, present, or future acrostics. I shall not be at Cambridge before the middle of October; but, when I go, I should certes like to see you there before you are dubbed a deacon. Write to me, and I will rejoin.

Yours ever,
BYRON

[TO JOHN MURRAY]   *Newstead Abbey. Notts. Septr. 14th. 1811*

Sir,—Since your former letter, Mr. Dallas informs me that the M. S. has been submitted to the perusal of Mr. Gifford, most contrary to my wishes as Mr. D. could have explained, & as my own letter to you did in fact explain, with my motives for objecting to such a proceeding.— — —Some late domestic events, of which you are probably aware, prevented my letter from being sent before, indeed I hardly conceived you would have so hastily thrust my productions into

[5] *Candide*, Chapter XXX.

the hands of a Stranger, who could be as little pleased by receiving them, as their author is at their being offered in such a manner, & to such a Man.— —My address when I leave Newstead will be to "Rochdale, Lancashire," but I have not yet fixed the day of departure, & I will apprise you when ready to set off.— —You have placed me in a very ridiculous situation, but it is past, & nothing more is to be said on the subject.—You hinted to me that you wished some alterations to be made, if they have nothing to do with politics or religion, I will make them with great readiness.—I am Sir

yr. most obedt. humble Servt.

BYRON

[TO ROBERT CHARLES DALLAS]   *Newstead Abbey. Septr. 15th. 1811*

My dear Sir,—My agent will not be here for at least a week & even afterwards my letters will be forwarded to Rochdale. I am sorry that you & Murray should *groan* on my account, though *that* is better than the anticipation of applause, of which men & books are generally disappointed.—The Notes I sent are *merely matter* to be divided, arranged, & furbished *for notes* hereafter in proper places, at present I am too much occupied with earthly cares, to waste time or trouble upon Rhyme or it's modern indispensables—Annotations.— —Pray let me hear from you, when at leisure, I have written to abuse Murray for showing the M.S. to Mr. G[ifford]—who must certainly think it was done by my wish, though you know the contrary.—Believe me to be

yrs. ever

BN.

[TO JOHN HANSON]   *Newstead Abbey. Notts. Septr. 15th. 1811*

Sir,—As Mr. Smith has taken the liberty of drawing on me without the smallest advice, I will *not* accept his Bill, neither am I aware of the correctness of his Acct. as I have not the particulars.—In 1808 & 9, I settled his demands on me to some extent, till my return to England I was unacquainted with any further claim of his upon me, & certainly his manner of advancing it is (to me at least) a Novelty.—I am Sir

your most obedt. very humble Servt.

BYRON

Newstead Abbey Septr. 16th. 1811

Sir,—I return the proof, which I should wish to be shown to Mr. Dallas, who understands typographical arrangements much better than I can pretend to do.—The Printer may place the notes in his *own way*, or any *way*, so that they are out of *my way*; I care nothing about types or margins.— —If you have any communication to make, I shall be here at least a week or ten days longer. I am Sir your most obedt very humble Servt.

B.

[TO ROBERT CHARLES DALLAS] *Newstead Abbey*
September 16th, 1811

Dear Sir,—I send you a *motto*—

L'univers est une espèce de livre, dont on n'a lu que la première page quand on n'a vu que son pays. J'en ai feuilleté un assez grand nombre, que j'ai trouvé également mauvaises. Cet examen ne m'a point été infructueux. Je haïssais ma patrie. Toutes les impertinences des peuples divers, parmi lesquels j'ai vécu, m'ont réconcilié avec elle. Quand je n'aurais tiré d'autre bénéfice de mes voyages que celui-là, je n'en regretterais ni les frais, ni les fatigues.

Le Cosmopolite.[1]

If not too long, I think it will suit the book. The passage is from a little French volume, a great favourite with me, which I picked up in the Archipelago. I don't think it is well known in England; Monbron is the author; but it is a work sixty years old.

Good morning! I won't take up your time.

Yours ever,
BYRON

[TO ROBERT CHARLES DALLAS (a)] *Newstead Abbey*
September 17th, 1811

Dear Sir,—I can easily excuse your not writing, as you have, I hope, something better to do, and you must pardon my frequent invasions on

---

[1] Fougeret de Monbron published *Le Cosmopolite, ou le Citoyen du Monde* in 1750. Byron quoted the first paragraph of the edition of 1753 published in London. The sentiments expressed are not exactly those of *Childe Harold*, but Byron was pleased with the general cynical tone of the book.

your attention, because I have at this moment nothing to interpose between you and my epistles.

I cannot settle to any thing, and my days pass, with the exception of bodily exercise to some extent, with uniform indolence, and idle insipidity. I have been expecting, and still expect my agent, when I shall have enough to occupy my reflections in business of no very pleasant aspect. Before my journey to Rochdale, you shall have due notice where to address me. I believe at the post-office of that township. From Murray I received a second proof of the same pages, which I requested him to show you, that any thing which may have escaped my observation may be detected before the printer lays the corner-stone of an *errata* column.

I am now not quite alone, having an old acquaintance and school-fellow with me,[1] so *old*, indeed, that we have nothing *new* to say on any subject, and yawn at each other in a sort of *quiet inquietude*. I hear nothing from Cawthorn, or Captain Hobhouse, and *their quarto*—Lord have mercy on mankind! We come on like Cerberus with our triple publications. As for *myself*, by *myself*, I must be satisfied with a comparison to *Janus*. I am not at all pleased with Murray for showing the MS.; and I am certain Gifford must see it in the same light that I do. His praise is nothing to the purpose: what could he say? He could not spit in the face of one who had praised him in every possible way. I must own that I wish to have the impression removed from his mind, that I had any concern in such a paltry transaction. The more I think, the more it disquiets me; so I will say no more about it. It is bad enough to be a scribbler, without having recourse to such shifts to extort praise, or deprecate censure. It is anticipating, it is begging, kneeling, adulating—the devil! the devil! the devil! and all without my wish, and contrary to my desire. I wish Murray had been tied to *Payne's* neck when he jumped into the Paddington Canal,[2] and so tell him—*that* is the proper receptacle for publishers. You have thoughts of settling in the country, why not try Notts? I think there are places which would suit you in all points, and then you are nearer the metropolis. But of this anon.—I am,

Yours ever,
B——.

[1] John Claridge, one of Byron's favourites at Harrow.

[2] Payne, of the firm of Payne and Mackinlay, publishers of Hodgson's *Juvenal*, committed suicide by drowning himself in the Paddington Canal. Byron referred to the incident in a facetious note to *Hints from Horace* (line 657), using it as an excuse for ridiculing Southey.

Dear Sir,—I have just discovered some pages of observations on the modern Greeks, written at Athens, by me, under the title of "Noctes Atticæ." They will do to *cut up* into notes, and to be *cut up* afterwards, which is all that notes are generally good for. They were written at Athens, as you will see by the date.

Yours ever,

B.

My dear H[obhous]e—Our friend Scrope is a pleasant person, a "facetious companion," & "well respected by all who know him," he laughs with the living, though he dont weep with the dead, yet I believe he would do that also, could it do them good service, but good or bad we must endeavour to follow his example & return to the dull routine of business or pleasure, though I fear, the more we see of life, the more we shall regret those who have ceased to live.—We will speak of them no more.— —Demetrius has completed a copious specimen of the Arnaut dialect, which shall be sent tomorrow, the print might perhaps be improved by an elongation of the υποκαμισον[1] —as the drawers [descenders?] dont appear to advantage below it; altogether it is very characteristic.—I had a visit lately from Major (Capt.) Leake[2] "en passant" he talks of returning to Ali Pacha, & says the E[dinburgh] R[eview] knows nothing of Romaic;[3] he is grown less taciturn, better dressed, & more like an (English) man of this world than he was at Yanina.— —J[oh]n Claridge is here, improved in person a good deal, & amiable, but not amusing, now here is a good man, a handsome man, an honourable man, a most inoffensive man, a well informed man, and a *dull* man, & this last damned epithet undoes all the rest; there is S[crope] B[erdmore] D[avies] with perhaps no

[1] Literally "overshirt". In this context Byron probably meant the "ascenders", the parts of the letters that go above the line.

[2] Captain William Martin Leake was British emissary to the court of Ali Pasha when Byron was in Albania. See Nov. 12, 1809, to Mrs. Byron, note 4.

[3] In the *Edinburgh Review* for April, 1810, there was an article (as Byron said later, probably by Blomfield, a Greek scholar at Cambridge admired by Porson) in which in reviewing a French *Géographie de Strabon*, Traduite du Grèc en Français, the writer was severely critical of one of the translators, M. Coray, a Greek, native of Smyrna (Byron said of Scio), for his lack of knowledge of the modern Greek, or Romaic. Byron had seen the review and pointed out some of its errors in a long critique dated Athens, March 17, 1811, which he later published as a note to the second canto of *Childe Harold*. (See *Poetry*, II, 196–204.)

better intellects, & certes not half his sterling qualities, is the life & soul of me & every body else; but my old friend with the soul of honour & the zeal of friendship & a vast variety of inspid virtues, can't keep me or himself awake.—Alas *"Motley's the only wear."*—As for C. you cant even quarrel with him, & my life is as still as the Lake before the Abbey, till the North-wind disturbs the one, & Fletcher & my learned Thebans break my Pottery, or my tenants or Mr. H[anson] ruffle the other.— —I expect H. down daily to proceed to Rochdale or nothing will ever be settled.— — — —You are coming out in Quarto, & *I* am to be in *Quarto*, but I wish you to be *out* first, or at any rate *one* before the other; I am going to use you very shabbily, for I fear *that* Note is a "sine Qua non" to "C[hild]e *Harold"* had it been the *Horace,* you should have had it *all* to yourself.—As it is you shall have it to extract the essence long before it is published, & the information will be all the better for being in your own words, & if you are out first (as you most probably will be) I trust we shall answer both our purposes; in my notes to the poem I have assigned your publication as my excuse for saying very little about the Greeks, & referred my readers to *your* work for more interesting particulars of that people.— —You *must* have 6 plates at the *least,* indeed ten or 12 would be better, of course they are all at your service & the R[omai]c M.S.S. such as they are.— —I must contrive to meet you in the Spring or summer, & will bring Hodgson or D[avie]s with me. I am invited to Cambridge in Octr. to meet them & Dr. Clarke.—I don't know whether to be glad or sorry that you will not be *there,* if I am *glad* you will conceive it is on *your* account.—I shall write with Demetrius' Voc[abular]y

Dear H. Yours ever.

B.

[TO ROBERT CHARLES DALLAS] *Newstead Abbey. Septr. 21st. 1811*

My dear Sir,—I have shown my respect for your suggestions by adopting them.—But I have made many alterations in the *first* proof over & above.— —As for example

> "Oh Thou, in *Hellas* deemed of Heavenly birth
> "&c. &c.
> "Since *shamed full oft* by *later lyres* on Earth
> "Mine &c.
> "Yet there *Ive wandered* by the vaunted rill[1]

[1] *Childe Harold*, Canto I, stanza 1. This first stanza was written and sent to Dallas after Byron's return from Greece. See Sept. 5, 1811, to Murray.

and so on.— — —So I have got rid of "Dr. *Lowth*" & "*drunk*" to boot,[2] & very glad I am to say so.—I have also "*sullen*"*ised* the line as heretofore & in short have been quite conformable.——Pray write, you shall hear when I remove to Lancs.—I have brought you & my friend Juvenal Hodgson upon my back on the score of revelation, You are fervent, but he is quite *glowing*, & if he takes half the pains to save his own soul, which he risks to redeem mine, great will be his reward hereafter; I honour & thank you both but am convinced by neither.— —Now for Notes,—besides those I have sent, I shall send the observations on the E[dinburgh] R[eview]'s remarks on the Modern Greek,[3] an Albanian song in the Albanian (*not Greek*) language, specimens of *modern* Greek from, their New Testament, a comedy of Goldoni's translated (*one scene*) a prospectus of a friend's book, & perhaps a song or two, *all* in Romaic besides their Pater Noster, so there will be enough, if not too much with what I have already sent.[4] —Have you received the "Noctes Atticæ"?[5]—I sent also an annotation on Portugal.— —Hobhouse is also forthcoming[6]

yrs. ever

B

[TO ROBERT CHARLES DALLAS]   *Newstead Abbey Septr. 23d. 1811*

My dear Sir,—"Lisboa" is the Portuguese word, consequently the very best, Ulyssipon is pedantic, & (as I have "*Hellas*" & "*Eros*" not long before) looks like an Affectation of Greek terms, which I wish to avoid, since I shall have a perilous quantity of *modern* Greek in my notes as specimens of the tongue.—Therefore "Lisboa" may keep its place.— —I wont have Lisbo*n*a, *it* is neither English or any thing else. —You are right about the "Hints," they must not precede the "Romaunt," but Cawthorn will be savage if they don't, however keep *them back*, & *him* in *good humour* if we can, but don't let him publish.— — — —I have adopted I believe most of your suggestions, but "Lisboa" will be an exception to prove the rule.— —I have sent a quantity of notes, & shall continue, but pray let them be copied, no devil can read my hand.— —By the bye, I do not mean to exchange

---

[2] The first version read: ". . . drank the vaunted rill." Dallas may have pointed out some parallel passage in Dr. Robert Lowth (1710–1787).

[3] See Sept. 20, 1811, to Hobhouse, note 3.

[4] These were all meant for the notes to the second canto of *Childe Harold*.

[5] See Sept. 17, 1811, to Dallas.

[6] Hobhouse's *Journey through Albania* . . . (1813).

the 9th. verse of the "Good night" I have no reason to suppose my dog better than his brother brutes—mankind,[1] & *Argus* we know to be a fable.—The "Cosmopolite" was an acquisition abroad, I do not believe it is to be found in England, it is an amusing little vol. & full of French flippancy, I read though I do not speak the language.— —I *will* be *angry* with Murray, it was a bookselling, backshop, Paternoster Row, paltry proceeding, & if the experiment had turned out as it deserved, I would have raised all Fleetstreet, & borrowed the Giant's staff from St. Dunstan's church to immolate the betrayer of trust.— —I have written to him, as he never was written to before by an author I'll be sworn, & I hope you will amplify my wrath, till it has an effect upon him.— —You tell me always you have much to write,—write it, but let us drop metaphysics, there we shall never agree.—I am dull & drowsy as usual, doing *nothing*, & even *that nothing* a fatigue.—Adio! believe me

yrs. unfeignedly
B.

[TO FRANCIS HODGSON]   *Newstead Abbey, Sept. 25, 1811*

My dear Hodgson,—I fear that before the latest of October or the first of November, I shall hardly be able to make Cambridge. My everlasting agent puts off his coming like the accomplishment of a prophecy. However, finding me growing serious he hath promised to be here on Thursday, and about Monday we shall remove to Rochdale. I have only to give discharges to the tenantry here (it seems the poor creatures must be raised, though I wish it was not necessary), and arrange the receipt of sums, and the liquidation of some debts, and I shall be ready to enter upon new subjects of vexation. I intend to visit you in Granta, and hope to prevail on you to accompany me here or there or anywhere.

I am plucking up my spirits, and have begun to gather my little sensual comforts together. Lucy is extracted from Warwickshire;[1]

---

[1] In the ninth stanza of "Childe Harold's Good Night" in the first canto Byron wrote:

> Perhaps my Dog will whine in vain,
>   Till fed by stranger hands;
> But long ere I come back again,
>   He'd tear me where he stands.

[1] Lucy was the Newstead maid whom Byron had made pregnant before he left England. See Jan. 17, 1809, to Hanson, note 1.

some very bad faces have been warned off the premises, and more promising substituted in their stead; the partridges are plentiful, hares fairish, pheasants not quite so good, and Girls on the Manor * * * * Just as I had formed a tolerable establishment my travels commenced, and on my return I find all to do over again; my former flock were all scattered; some married, not before it was needful. As I am a great disciplinarian, I have just issued an edict for the abolition of caps; no hair to be cut on any pretext; stays permitted, but not too low before; full uniform always in the evening; Lucinda to be commander—*vice* the present, about to be wedded (*mem.* she is 35 with a flat face and a squeaking voice), of all the makers and unmakers of beds in the household.

My tortoises (all Athenians), my hedgehog, my mastiff and the other live Greek, are all purely. The tortoises lay eggs, and I have hired a hen to hatch them. I am writing notes for *my* quarto (Murray would have it a *quarto*), and Hobhouse is writing text for *his* quarto; if you call on Murray or Cawthorn you will hear news of either. I have attacked De Pauw, Thornton, Lord Elgin, Spain, Portugal, the *Edinburgh Review*,[2] travellers, Painters, Antiquarians, and others, so you see what a dish of Sour Crout Controversy I shall prepare for myself. It would not answer for me to give way, now; as I was forced into bitterness at the beginning, I will go through to the last. *Væ Victis!* If I fall, I shall fall gloriously, fighting against a host.

Felicissima Notte a Voss. Signoria,

B.

[TO ROBERT CHARLES DALLAS]   *Newstead Abbey. Septr. 26th. 1811*

My dear Sir,—In a Stanza towards the end of Canto 1st., there is as the concluding line

"Some bitter bubbles up and even on Roses *stings*"

I have altered it as follows,

"Full from the heart of Joy's delicious springs
Some Bitter oer the Flowers it's bubbling venom flings.["]"[1]

If you will point out the stanzas on Cintra which you wish recast I will send you mine answer.—Be good enough to address your letters here,

[2] See *Poetry*, II, 191, 194–96.
[1] *Childe Harold*, I, 82.

& they will either be forwarded or saved till my return.—My Agent comes tomorrow, & we shall set out immediately.—The press must not proceed of course without my seeing the proofs as I have much to do.—Pray do you think any alteration should be made in the Stanzas on *"Vathek"*?[2] I should be sorry to make any improper allusion, as I merely wish to adduce an example of wasted wealth, & the reflection which arose in surveying the most desolate mansion in the most beautiful spot I ever beheld.—Pray keep Cawthorn back, he was not to begin till Novr. & even that will be two months too soon.— —I am so sorry my hand is unintelligible, but I can neither deny your accusation or remove the cause of it.—It is a sad scrawl certes.—A perilous quantity of annotation hath been sent, I think about *enough* with the specimens of Romaic I mean to annex.— —I will have nothing to say to your metaphysics, & allegories of Rocks & Beaches, we shall all go to the bottom together, so "let us eat & drink for tomorrow" &c.—I am as comfortable in my creed as others, inasmuch as it is better to sleep than to be awake.— —I have heard nothing of Murray, I hope he is ashamed of himself.—He sent me a vastly complimentary epistle with a request to alter the two & finish another canto.—I sent him as civil an answer as if I had been engaged to translate by the sheet, declined altering anything in sentiment, but offered to tag rhymes & mend them as long as he liked.— —I will write from Rochdale, when I arrive, if my affairs allow me, but I shall be so busy & savage all the time with the whole set, that my letters will perhaps be as pettish as myself.—If so lay the blame on Coals & Coalheavers.—Very probably I may proceed to town by way of Newstead on my return from Lancs.—I mean to be at Cambridge in Novr. so that at all events we shall be nearer.—I will not apologize for the trouble I have given & do give you, though I ought to do so, but I have worn out my politest periods, & can only say that I am very much obliged to you.— —Believe me to be

yrs. alway
B.

[TO JAMES WEDDERBURN WEBSTER]   *Newstead Abbey*
Octr. 10th. 1811

Dear Webster,—I can hardly invite a gentleman to my house a second time who walked out of it the first in so singular a mood, but if

2 *Childe Harold*, I, 22–23.

you had thought proper to pay me a visit, you would have had a "Highland Welcome."—I am only just returned to it out of Lancashire where I have been on business to a Coal manor of mine near Rochdale, & shall leave it very shortly for Cambridge & London.— My companions or rather companion (for Claridge alone has been with me) have not been very amusing, & as to their *"Sincerity"* they are doubtless sincere enough for a man who will never put them to the trial.—Besides you talked so much of your conjugal happiness, that an invitation from home would have seemed like Sacrilege, & my rough Bachelor's Hall would have appeared to little advantage after the Bower of "Armida"[1] where you have been reposing.— —I cannot boast of my social powers at any time, & just at present they are more stagnant than ever.— —Your Brother in law[2] means to stand for Wexford, but I have reasons for thinking the Portsmouth interest will be against him, however I wish him success.— —Do *you* mean to stand for any place next election? what are your politics?—I hope Valentia's Lord is for the Catholics.— —You will find Hobhouse at Enniscorthy in the contested County.— —Pray what has seized you? your last letter is the only one in which you do not rave upon matrimony, are there no symptoms of a young W. W.? & shall I never be a Godfather?— —I believe I must be married myself soon, but it shall be a secret & a Surprise.— — However, knowing your exceeding discretion I shall probably entrust the secret to your silence at a proper period.—You have it is true invited me repeatedly to Dean's Court,[3] & now when it is probable I might adventure there, you wish to be off.—Be it so.— —If you address your letters to this place they will be forwarded wherever I sojourn.— —I am about to meet some friends at Cambridge and on to town in November.— —The papers are full of Dalrymple's Bigamy, (I know the man) what the Devil will he do with his *Spare-rib?*[4]— — —He is no beauty, but as lame as myself.—He has more ladies than legs, what comfort to a cripple!— —Sto sempre umilissimo servitore

BYRON

---

[1] The sorceress in Tasso's *Jerusalem Delivered* in whose house Rinaldo forgets his vow as a crusader. Byron was fond of the *Gerusalemme Liberata*. Four copies are listed in the catalogue of his books sold in April, 1816. He later likened himself and Lady Oxford to Rinaldo and Armida.

[2] George Annesley, Lord Valentia, afterward Earl of Mountnorris.

[3] Near Wimborne, Dorset.

[4] In a trial of July 16, 1811, Captain John William Henry Dalrymple was held to be married, by Scottish law, to Joanna Gordon, and his subsequent marriage to Miss Manners, sister of the Duchess of St. Albans, was declared illegal.

Dr. Sir,—Stanzas *24. 26. 29.* though *crossed* must *stand* with their *alterations*. The other *three* are cut out to meet your wishes.—We must however have a repetition of the proof, which is the first.—I will write soon.

yrs. ever

B.

P.S.—Yesterday I returned from Lancs.—

My dear Hodgson,—I have returned from Lancashire, where I went on *business*, but unluckily receiving an Invitation to a pleasant country seat near Rochdale full of the fair & fashionable sex, I left my affairs to my agent (who however managed better without me) never went within ken of a coalpit, & am returned with six new acquaintances but little topographical knowledge.—However the concern is more valuable than I expected, but plaguy troublesome, it has been surveyed &c. &c. & will no doubt benefit my heirs.— —Yours arrived this Even.—Your lines are some of the best you have ever written in that department, & as far as regards myself, extremely apropos, for I am just about to be connected with a very lucrative old Lady for the love of money.[1]—So you & Drury may drink my "Hymeneals" in good earnest, *anybody* may marry a young woman, *I* kindly take to the elderly for the sake of Humour, I shall have such pleasure in showing her to my friends, & then we shall be so happy in my house here, *one* in each *Wing*.—Prithee, set folks right about the title of my boke, a pize upon Murray's man I want you to see the thing, Murray *would* shew it to Mr. Gifford without my knowledge, before he undertook it, & the *Great* man, (unless much belied) gave an "Imprimatur."—
— —Cawthorn must keep back the *"Hints"* as we want the other out first, but dont let him into that secret lest he be savage; Hobhouse is anangered with him, so he writes from Enniscorthy, *his* Quarto with *cuts* from drawings *liberally* furnished by me, will be forth also.—I must send Drury some Game,—is Bland returned? what will become of his Dutch Parisioners![2]—Write unto me. I don't know that I shan't

---

[1] The "lucrative old lady" has not been identified. Since we do not hear of her again, it seems possible that she was a figment of Byron's facetious imagination.

[2] Hodgson's friend Robert Bland had been acting as English Chaplain in Holland.

soon be in London, but dont expect me.—Every thing about & concerning me wears a gloomy aspect, still I keep up my spirit, it may be broken but it shall never be bent.—I heard of a death the other day that shocked me more than any of the preceding, of one whom I once loved more than I ever loved a living thing, & one who I believe loved me to the last,[3] yet I had not a tear left for an event which five years ago would have bowed me to the dust; still it sits heavy on my heart & calls back what I wish to forget, in many a feverish dream.— —

yrs. ever

B.

[TO ROBERT CHARLES DALLAS] *Newstead Abbey*
October 11th. 1811

Dear Sir,—I have returned from Lancs, and ascertained that my property there may be made very valuable, but various circumstances very much circumscribe my exertions at present. I shall be in town on business in the beginning of November, and perhaps at Cambridge before the end of this month: but of my movements you shall be regularly apprized. Your objections I have in part done away by alterations, which I hope will suffice; and I have sent two or three additional stanzas for both "Fyttes." I have been again shocked with a *death*,[1] and have lost one very dear to me in happier times; but "I have almost forgot the taste of grief," and "supped full of horrors" till I have become callous, nor have I a tear left for an event which five years ago would have bowed down my head to the earth. It seems as though I were to experience in my youth the greatest misery of age. My friends fall around me, and I shall be left a lonely tree before I am withered. Other men can always take refuge in their families; I have no resource but my own reflections, and they present no prospect here or hereafter, except the selfish satisfaction of surviving my betters. I am indeed very wretched, and you will excuse my saying so, as you know I am not apt to cant of sensibility. Instead of tiring yourself with *my* concerns, I should be glad to hear *your* plans of retirement. I suppose you would not like to be wholly shut out of society; now I know a large village, or small town, about twelve miles off, where your family would have the advantage of very genteel society, without the hazard of being annoyed by mercantile affluence; where *you* would meet with men of

[3] John Edleston, the Cambridge choirboy, died in May, 1811. Byron had just heard the news from Edleston's sister.

[1] John Edleston. See Oct. 10, 1811, to Hodgson, note 3.

information and independence; and where I have friends to whom I should be proud to introduce you. There are, besides, a coffee-room, assemblies, etc. etc., which bring people together. My mother had a house there some years, and I am well acquainted with the economy of Southwell, the name of this little commonwealth. Lastly, you will not be very remote from me; and though I am the very worst companion for young people in the world, this objection would not apply to *you*, whom I could see frequently. Your expenses too would be such as best suit your inclinations, more or less, as you thought proper, but very little would be requisite to enable you to enter into all the gaieties of a country life. You could be as quiet or bustling as you liked, and certainly as well situated as on the lakes of Cumberland, unless you have a particular wish to be *picturesque*.

Pray is your Ionian friend in town?[2] You have promised me an introduction.—You mention having consulted some friends on the MSS. —Is not this contrary to our usual way? Instruct Mr. Murray not to allow his Shopman[3] to call the work—"Childe *of Harrow's* Pilgrimage"!!!!!!—as he has done to some of my astonished friends who wrote to inquire after my *Sanity* on the occasion as well they might.— —I have heard nothing of Murray whom I scolded heartily.—Must I write more Notes? are there not enough?— —Cawthorn must be kept back with the "Hints" I hope he is getting on with Hobhouse's Q[uart]o.— Good Even.

yrs. ever
B.

[TO FRANCIS HODGSON] *Newstead Abbey, Oct. 13th, 1811*

You will begin to deem me a most liberal correspondent; but as my letters are free, you will overlook their frequency. I have sent you answers in prose and verse to all your late communications, and though I am invading your ease again, I don't know why, or what to put down that you are not acquainted with already. I am growing *nervous* (how you will laugh!)—but it is true,—really, wretchedly, ridiculously, fine-ladically *nervous*. Your climate kills me; I can neither read, write, or amuse myself, or any one else. My days are listless, and my nights restless; I have very seldom any society, and when I have, I run out of it. At "this present writing" there are in the next room three *ladies*,

[2] Walter Rodwell Wright, had been Consul-General of the Seven Islands (Ionian Islands).

[3] The facsimile begins with this word and continues to the end of the letter.

and I have stolen away to write this grumbling letter.—I don't know that I sha'n't end with insanity, for I find a want of method in arranging my thoughts that perplexes me strangely; but this looks more like silliness than madness, as Scrope Davies would facetiously remark in his consoling manner. I must try the hartshorn of your company; and a session of Parliament would suit me well,—any thing to cure me of conjugating the accursed verb *"ennuyer."*

When shall you be at Cambridge? You have hinted, I think, that your friend Bland is returned from Holland. I have always had a great respect for his talents, and for all that I have heard of his character; but of me, I believe, he knows nothing, except that he heard my 6th form repetitions ten months together, at the average of two lines a morning, and those never perfect. I remembered him and his "Slaves" as I passed between Capes Matapan, St. Angelo, and his Isle of Ceriga, and I always bewailed the absence of the Anthology.[1] I suppose he will now translate Vondel, the Dutch Shakespeare, and "Gysbert van Amstel"[2] will easily be accommodated to our stage in its present state; and I presume he saw the Dutch poem, where the love of Pyramus and Thisbe is compared to the *passion of Christ*; also the love of *Lucifer* for Eve, and other varieties of Low Country literature. No doubt you will think me crazed to talk of such things, but they are all in black and white and good repute on the banks of every canal from Amsterdam to Alkmaar.

Yours ever,
B.

My Poesy is in the hands of its various publishers; but the "Hints from Horace" (to which I have subjoined some savage lines on Methodism,[3] and ferocious notes on the vanity of the triple Editory of the Edin. Annual Register),[4] my *"Hints,"* I say, stand still, and why? —I have not a friend in the world (but you and Drury) who can construe Horace's Latin, or my English, well enough to adjust them for the press, or to correct the proofs in a grammatical way. So that, unless you have bowels when you return to town (I am too far off to do it

[1] Robert Bland, who had been as assistant master at Harrow, had returned from Holland where he had been English Chaplain. He published *Four Slaves of Cythera* in 1809, and (with others) *Translations . . . from the Greek Anthology* (1806).

[2] Joost Van Vondel (1587–1679), an Anabaptist who became a Roman Catholic, wrote a number of tragedies on classical and religious subjects. *Gysbrecht van Amstel* appealed to Dutch patriotism, prophecying the future greatness of Amsterdam.

[3] *Hints from Horace*, lines 371–82.

[4] See *Hints from Horace*, note to line 657.

for myself), this ineffable work will be lost to the world for—I don't know how many *weeks*.

"Childe Harold's Pilgrimage" must wait till *Murray's* is finished. He is making a tour in Middlesex, and is to return soon, when high matter may be expected. He wants to have it in quarto, which is a cursed un-saleable size; but it is pestilent long, and one must obey one's book-seller. I trust Murray will pass the Paddington Canal without being seduced by Payne and Mackinlay's example,[5]—I say Payne and Mackinlay, supposing that the partnership held good. Drury, the villain, has not written to me; "I am never (as Mrs. Lumpkin says to Tony) to be gratified with the monster's dear wild notes."[6]

So you are going (going indeed!) into orders. You must make your peace with the Eclectic Reviewers—they accuse you of impiety, I fear, with injustice. Demetrius, the "Sieger of Cities," is here, with "Gilpin Horner."[7] The painter[8] is not necessary, as the portraits he already painted are (by anticipation) very like the new animals.—Write, and send me your "Love Song"—but I want "paulo majora" from you. Make a dash before you are a deacon, and try a *dry* publisher.

Yours always,

B.

Newstead Abbey. Octr. 13th. 1811

My dear Hobhouse,—Demetrius is laid up with a kick from a horse, so that for a few days he will be unserviceable to you or me.[1]—I sent the Voc[abular]y to Cawthorn to forward it in a parcel being too heavy for Franking.—The Letter of Ali Pacha shall be translated & returned or left at your Publishers as you think best.—Now for your Queries.— The Chimariots are *Arnauts*, what Greek they speak is acquired.— Some are Mussulmen indeed *most* of them, in Albania proper past Tepaleni except a few villages all are *Turks* (in religion) as far as *Bosnia*, where *all* are Mussulmen & the bravest of the Race.—The

---

[5] See Sept. 17, 1811, to Dallas, note 2.

[6] Mrs. Hardcastle (not Mrs. Lumpkin) in *She Stoops to Conquer* (Act II) says, "I'm never to be delighted with your agreeable wild notes, unfeeling monster!"

[7] Demetrius Zograffo, Byron's Greek servant, nicknamed for Demetrius Poliorcetes, and John Claridge, to whom he gives the name of Scott's legendary character.

[8] Byron had brought the painter Barber to Newstead to paint his wolf and his bear.

[1] Byron had put his Greek servant to work making an Albanian vocabulary for Hobhouse to append to his *Journey*.

Suliotes are Christians but wear the Camesa. Berat & Arnaut Beligrade are *one*,—12 hours from Tepaleni,—Ibrahim Pacha has nothing to do with Scutari, the Pacha of Scutari is a plaguy Troublesome fellow, *Ibrahim's* predecessor Giaffer Pacha was poisoned by *Ali's* order with a cup of coffee—in the bath at *Sophia*, Ali *lately* married his *daughter*;— *Coul* Pacha the Predecessor of Ali was a very formidable personage.— — —I will some day draw up an account of my reception by Veli Pacha in the Morea for your edification, but at present I am out of Sorts.— —I don't know *how* to send Meletius[2]—he is so *well bound*, & if we lose him!!—If you want any part consulted, refer me to the "Cap." but surely you will be in England before you come forth & can see the books yourself.—At present I am rather low, & dont know how to tell you the reason—you remember *E[dleston]* at Cambridge—he is *dead*— last May—his Sister sent me the account lately—now though I never should have seen him again, (& it is very proper that I should not) I have been more affected than I should care to own elsewhere; Death has been lately so occupied with every thing that was mine, that the dissolution of the most remote connection is like taking a crown from a Miser's last Guinea.— — — —You are exiled to Ireland, quite a military Swift!—we may now Swiftify & Popify as if we were wits of the last Century.—What shall we do with Davies? he is too facetious for a *Gay*, & not simple enough, the dog shall be a second hand St. John (chiefly on account of his irreligion) Hodgson shall be—what shall he be? Baillie, Dr. Arbuthnot,—Bold Webster—Earl of Peterborough "Almost as quickly as he *conquered Spain.*" *Cawthorn—Lintot*—and Dallas—the *Duchess* of Queensbury!—So we may play at wits, as children (no offence) at Soldiers. You will address here as usual.—I am about to join Davies at Cambridge, but your letters will be forwarded.—You shall have the Note when printed, but my publisher is in no hurry, nor am I.—do you get on. I hope we shant *contradict* one another. Dear H.,

yrs. ever
B.

[TO JOHN CAM HOBHOUSE] *Newstead Abbey. Octr. 14th 1811*

Dear Hobhouse,—In my last I answered your queries, & now I shall acquaint you with my movements according to your former request.— I have been down to Rochdale with H[anson]. the property there if I

---

[2] The copy of Meletius's *Geography* which Byron had acquired in Greece.

114

work the mines myself will produce about 4000 pr. Ann. but to do this I must lay out at least 10000 £ in et ce[ter]as, or if I chuse to *let* it without incurring such expenditure it will produce a rental of half the above sum, so we are to work the collieries ourselves of course.— Newstead is to be advanced immediately to 2100 pr. Ann. so that my income might be made about 6000 pr. Ann.—But here comes at least 20000 £ of Debt and I must mortgage for that & other expenses, so that altogether my situation is perplexing.—I believe the above statement to be nearly correct, & so ends the Chapter.—If I chose to turn out my old bad tenants & take monied men they say, Newstead would bear a few hundreds more from it's great extent, but this I shall hardly do.— —It contains 3800 Acres including the Forest land, the Rochdale Manor 8256 Acres of Lancashire, which are larger than ours.—So there you have my territories on the Earth & in "the Waters under the Earth" but I must marry some Heiress or I shall always be involved. — — —Now for higher matters.—My Boke is in ye. press, & proceeds leisurely, I have lately been sweating Notes, which I don't mean to be very voluminous, some remarks written at Athens & the flourish on Romaic which you have seen will constitute most of them.—The essence of that *"valuable information"* as you call it is at your service & shall be sent in time for your purpose.—I had also by accident detected in Athens a blunder of Thornton of a ludicrous nature in the *Turkish language* of which I mean to make some "pleasant mirth," in return for his abuse of the Greeks.—It is the passage about Pouqueville's story of the "Eater of Corrosive Sublimate."[1] By the bye, I rather suspect we shall be at right angles in our opinion of the Greeks, I have not quite made up my mind about them, but you I know are decisively inimical. —I will write to you from Cambridge or elsewhere.—Address to Newstead.—Claridge is gone after a lethargic visit of three perennial weeks.—How dull he is! I wish the dog had any *bad* qualities that one might not be ashamed of disliking him.—Adio! D. V. E. Umilissimo Servitore

B.—

[TO ROBERT CHARLES DALLAS (*a*)]   *October 14th, 1811*

Dear Sir,—Stanza 9th, for Canto 2d, somewhat altered, to avoid a recurrence in a former stanza.

---

[1] See *Childe Harold*, II, notes (*Poetry*, II, 194–96).

There, thou!—whose love and life together fled,
    Have left me here to love and live in vain:—
Twined with my heart, and can I deem thee dead,
    When busy Memory flashes o'er my brain?
Well—I will dream that we may meet again,
    And woo the vision to my vacant breast:
If aught of young Remembrance then remain,
    Be as it may
    What'er beside Futurity's behest;
or,   —Howe'er may be
For me 'twere bliss enough to see thy spirit blest!

I think it proper to state to you, that this stanza alludes to an event which has taken place since my arrival here, and not to the death of any *male* friend.[1]

[TO [ROBERT CHARLES DALLAS? (*b*)]]   *Newstead Abbey*
Octr. 14th. 1811

Dear Sir,—I send you three brace of birds two hares & a snipe, & apprise you before hand that you may neither be charged [for] the carriage or wronged by Mr. Draper

[TO ROBERT CHARLES DALLAS]   *Newstead Abbey. Octr. 16th. 1811*

Dear Sir,—I am on the wing for Cambridge.—Thence after a short stay to London.—Will you be good enough to keep an account of all the M.S.S. you receive for fear of omission.—Have you adopted the three *altered* stanzas of the latest proof? I can do nothing more with them.—I am glad you like the new ones, of the last of the *trio* I sent you a *new* edition.—Today a *fresh note*.—The lines of second [sheet?] I fear must stand, I will give you reasons when we meet.—Believe me
yrs. ever
BYRON

---

[1] This of course was not true. Having already told Dallas of the death of Edleston, Byron was trying to cover his tracks. This stanza and 95 and 96 of the second canto of *Childe Harold* were addressed to the Cambridge choirboy. In other poems to him, he gave the name of Thyrza, to encourage the public to think they were addressed to a girl.

P.S. We may have

"Which poets pave *in vain* with sands of Gold"

to remove the *strict* resemblance.—

[TO JOHN CAM HOBHOUSE] *King's Coll: C[ambridg]e*
Octr. 22d. 1811

My dear Hobhouse,—I write from Scrope's rooms, whom I have
just assisted to put to bed in a state of *outrageous* intoxication.—I think
I never saw him so bad before.—We dined at Mr. Caldwell's of Jesus
Coll: where we met Dr. Clarke[1] & others of the Gown, & Scrope
finished himself as usual.—He has been in a similar state every evening
since my arrival here a few days ago.—We are to dine at Dr. Clarke's
on Thursday.—I find he knows little of Romaic, so we shall have *that*
department entirely to ourselves, I tell you this that you need not fear
any competition, particularly so formidable a one as Dr. Clarke would
probably have been.—I like him much, though Scrope says *we* talked
so bitterly that he (the Said Scrope) lost his listeners.— I proceed hence
to town, where I shall enquire after your work which I am sorry to say
stands still for *"want of Copy"* to talk in Technicals.—I am very low-
spirited on many accounts, & wine, which however I do not quaff as
formerly, has lost it's power over me.—We all wish you here, & well
wherever you are, but surely better with us.—If you don't soon return, Scrope & I mean to visit you in quarters.—The event I mentioned
in my last[2] has had an effect on me, I am ashamed to think of, but there
is no arguing on these points. I could "have better spared a better
being."—Wherever I turn, particularly in this place, the idea goes
with me, I say all this at the risk of incurring your contempt, but you
cannot despise me more than I do myself.—I am indeed very wretched,
& like all complaining persons I can't help telling you so.— —The
Marquis Sligo[3] is in a great scrape, about his kidnapping the seamen.
I, who know him, do not think him so culpable as the Navy are determined to make him.—He is a good man.—I have been in Lancs.
Notts. but all places are alike, I cannot live under my present feelings,
I have lost my appetite, my rest, & can neither read write or act in

[1] Edward Daniel Clarke. Professor of Mineralogy at Cambridge, whose *Travels*
. . . appeared at intervals from 1810–1823.
[2] The death of John Edleston.
[3] See May 16, 1806, to Henry Angelo, note 4; July 20, 1810, to Mrs. Byron;
July 29, 1810, to Hobhouse; Aug. 23, 1810, to Hobhouse.

comfort.—Every body here is very polite & hospitable, my friend Scrope particularly. I wish to God he would grow sober, as I much fear no constitution can long support his excesses.—If I lose him & you, what am I?— —Hodgson is not here but expected soon.—Newstead is my regular address.—Demetrius is here much pleased with ye. place. Ld. Sligo is about to send back his Arnaouts.—Excuse this dirty paper, it is of Scrope's best.—Good night'

ever yrs.
BYRON

[TO ROBERT CHARLES DALLAS]   *Cambridge Oct. 25th. 1811*

Dear Sir,—I send you a conclusion to the *whole*—in a stanza towards the end of C[ant]o 1st. in the line "Oh known the earliest & *beloved* the most," I shall alter the epithet to "*esteemed* the most".[1]—The present stanzas are for the end of C[ant]o 2d.—In the beginning of ye. week I shall be at No. *8* my old lodgings in St. James's Street where I hope to have the pleasure of seeing you.

yrs. ever
B

[TO THOMAS MOORE]   *Cambridge, October 27th, 1811*

Sir,—Your letter followed me from Notts. to this place, which will account for the delay of my reply. Your former letter I never had the honour to receive;[1]—be assured, in whatever part of the world it had found me, I should have deemed it my duty to return and answer it in person.

The advertisement you mention, I know nothing of.—At the time of your meeting with Mr. Jeffrey, I had recently entered College, and remember to have heard and read a number of squibs on the occasion, and from the recollection of these I derived all my knowledge on the subject, without the slightest idea of "giving the lie" to an address which I never beheld. When I put my name to the production, which

---

[1] *Childe Harold*, I, 92, a tribute to his school friend John Wingfield, who died at Coimbra.

[1] Moore had sent Byron a letter on January 1, 1810, which Hodgson had held and not sent to him, sensing it to be a challenge. Moore had taken offence at some derisive lines in *English Bards and Scotch Reviewers* (2nd ed., lines 458–61) referring to his part in a farcical duel with Francis Jeffrey, editor of the *Edinburgh Review*. Though aimed at Jeffrey, the gibe put Moore in a ridiculous light.

has occasioned this correspondence, I became responsible to all whom it might concern,—to explain where it requires explanation, and, where insufficiently or too sufficiently explicit, at all events to satisfy. My situation leaves me no choice; it rests with the injured and the angry to obtain reparation in their own way.

With regard to the passage in question, *you* were certainly *not* the person towards whom I felt personally hostile. On the contrary, my whole thoughts were engrossed by one, whom I had reason to consider as my worst literary enemy, nor could I foresee that his former antagonist was about to become his champion. You do not specify what you would wish to have done: I can neither retract nor apologize for a charge of falsehood which I never advanced.

In the beginning of the week, I shall be at No. 8, St. James's-street. —Neither the letter or the friend to whom you stated your intention ever made their appearance.

Your friend Mr. Rogers,[2] or any other gentleman delegated by you, will find me most ready to adopt any conciliatory proposition which shall not compromise my own honour,—or, failing in that, to make the atonement you deem it necessary to require.

I have the honour to be, sir your most obedient, humble servant,

BYRON

[TO MRS. MARGARET PIGOT]   *Cambridge, Octr. 28th. 1811*

Dear Madam,—I am about to write to you on a silly subject & yet I cannot well do otherwise.—You may remember a *cornelian* which some years ago I consigned to Miss Pigot, indeed *gave* to her, & now I am going to make the most selfish & rude of requests.— —The person who gave it to me, when I was very young, is *dead*,[1] & though a long time has elapsed since we ever met, as it was the only memorial ⟨almost⟩ I possessed of that person (in whom I was once much interested) it has acquired a value by this event, I could have wished it never to have borne in my eyes.—If therefore Miss P[igot] should have preserved it, I must under these circumstances beg her to excuse my requesting it to be transmitted to me at No. 8 St. James's Street London & I will replace it by something she may remember me by equally well.— —As she was always so kind as to feel interested in the fate of [those?] that formed the subject of our conversations, you may

---

[2] Samuel Rogers, the banker poet. See Biographical sketch in Appendix.
[1] See "The Cornelian" in *Fugitive Pieces*. John Edleston had given Byron the Cornelian.

tell her, that the Giver of that Cornelian died in May last of a consumption at the age of twenty one, making the *sixth* within four months of friends & relatives that I have lost between May & the end of August![2]
—Believe [me] Dear Madam

yrs. very sincerely
BYRON

P.S.—I go to London tomorrow.

[TO ROBERT CHARLES DALLAS]   8, *St. James's-street*
29th October, 1811

Dear Sir,—I arrived in town last night, and shall be very glad to see you when convenient.

Yours very truly,
BYRON

[TO THOMAS MOORE]   8, *St. James's-street, October 29th, 1811*

Sir,—Soon after my return to England, my friend, Mr. Hodgson, apprized me that a letter for me was in his possession; but a domestic event hurrying me from London, immediately after, the letter (which may most probably be your own) is still *unopened in his keeping*.[1] If, on examination of the address, the similarity of the handwriting should lead to such a conclusion, it shall be opened in your presence, for the satisfaction of all parties. Mr. H[odgson] is at present out of town;— on Friday I shall see him, and request him to forward it to my address.

With regard to the latter part of both your letters, until the principal point was discussed between us, I felt myself at a loss in what manner to reply. Was I to anticipate friendship from one, who conceived me to have charged him with falsehood? Were not *advances*, under such circumstances, to be misconstrued,—not, perhaps, by the person to whom they were addressed, but by others? In *my* case, such a step was impracticable. If you, who conceived yourself to be the offended person, are satisfied that you had no cause for offence, it will not be difficult to convince me of it. My situation, as I have before

2 Five of these were his mother, Matthews, Wingfield, Hargreaves Hanson, and Edleston. Byron did not elsewhere mention a sixth.
1 See Oct. 27, 1811, to Moore, note 1.

stated, leaves me no choice. I should have felt proud of your acquaintance, had it commenced under other circumstances; but it must rest with you to determine how far it may proceed after so *auspicious* a beginning.

I have the honour to be, &c.

8, St. James's-street, October 30th, 1811

Sir,—You must excuse my troubling you once more upon this very unpleasant subject. It would be a satisfaction to me, and I should think, to yourself, that the unopened letter in Mr. Hodgson's possession (supposing it to prove your own) should be returned "in statu quo" to the writer; particularly as you expressed yourself "not quite easy under the manner in which I had dwelt on its miscarriage."

A few words more, and I shall not trouble you further. I felt, and still feel, very much flattered by those parts of your correspondence, which held out the prospect of our becoming acquainted. If I did not meet them, in the first instance, as perhaps I ought, let the situation in which I was placed be my defence. You have *now* declared yourself *satisfied*, and on that point we are no longer at issue. If, therefore, you still retain any wish to do me the honour you hinted at, I shall be most happy to meet you, when, where, and how you please, and I presume you will not attribute my saying thus much to any unworthy motive.

I have the honour to remain, &c.

8, St. James's-street
October 31st, 1811

Dear Sir,—I have already taken up so much of your time that there needs no excuse on your part, but a great many on mine, for the present interruption. I have altered the passages according to your wish. With this note I send a few stanzas on a subject which has lately occupied much of my thoughts. They refer to the death of one to whose name you are a *stranger*, and, consequently, cannot be interested.[1] I mean them to complete the present volume. They relate to the same person I have mentioned in canto 2d, and at the conclusion of the poem.

[1] Stanzas 95 and 96 of the second canto of *Childe Harold* were addressed to Edleston.

I by no means intend to identify myself with *Harold*, but to *deny* all connexion with him. If in parts I may be thought to have drawn from myself, believe me it is but in parts, and I shall not own even to that.[2] As to the *"Monastic dome,"* etc., I thought those circumstances would suit him as well as any other, and I could describe what I had seen better than I could invent. I would not be such a fellow as I have made my hero for the world.

Yours ever,
B.

[TO MISS HODGSON[1]] *[Nov., 1811? or in 1812?]*

Ld. Byron presents his Compliments to Miss Hodgson & would have been most happy to avail himself of her invitation had not a prior engagement with a [part of MS. missing] for the obliging mark of attention & trusts that he shall be permitted to make his acknowledgements in person.—

[TO THOMAS MOORE] *8, St. James's-street, November 1st, 1811*

Sir,—As I should be very sorry to interrupt your Sunday's engagement, if Monday, or any other day of the ensuing week, would be equally convenient to yourself and friend, I will then have the honour of accepting his invitation. Of the professions of esteem with which Mr. Rogers has honoured me, I cannot but feel proud, though undeserving. I should be wanting to myself, if insensible to the praise of such a man; and, should my approaching interview with him and his friend lead to any degree of intimacy with both or either, I shall regard our past correspondence as one of the happiest events of my life. I have the honour to be,

Your very sincere and obedient servant,
BYRON

[TO JOHN HANSON] *Nov. 1st. 1811*

Dear Sir,—I send ye. enclosed from Mrs. Massingberd, by which you will see something must be done, as to *her* annuities we can more

---

[2] Byron stated in his Preface that Harold was a "fictitious character".
[1] Unidentified. A sister or other relation of Francis Hodgson?

easily manage, (but I do not wish to commit my friend D[avies?]'s name) do pray contrive something.[1]

yrs. ever
BYRON

[TO JOHN CAM HOBHOUSE]   *8 St. James's Street Novr. 2d. 1811*

Dear Hobhouse,—I never meant to confound the Bosnians & Arnaouts but merely to say that *all* the Bosnians & most of ye. *upper Albanians* were Mussulmen. The Suliotes are villainous Romans & speak little Illyric. I am full of news & business—to the which— Firstly I have been engaged in a correspondence with *Anacreon Moore*,[1] who requested me to *retract* or *atone* for a "charge of falsehood" *he* supposed me to have made against an address to the public which he published, God knows when, on his duel with Jeffrey.—I neither *retracted* nor would *apologize*, never having seen ye. address in question, & told him in answer to his *demi-hostile semi-amicable* epistle, (for it began with a complaint & ended with a hope that *we* should be "*intimate*") that I was willing "to adopt any conciliatory proposition that should not compromise my own honour, or failing in *that* to give him satisfaction."—This being done under the auspices of Scrope, who was to have enacted as second in case of need, Mr. M[oore] was *satisfied*, & on Monday next we are to meet at the house of "Pleasures of Memory" Rogers, who is M[oore]'s friend & has behaved very well in ye. business.— —So as dinners are preferable to duels, & nothing has been conceded on my part, further than the truth viz, that I knew nothing of said address [2] (did you ever see it? & what was it about?) & consequently could not give the lie to what I never beheld, & as the Bard has been graciously pleased to talk about his "sincere respect for my talents" & "good will" &c. why—I shall be glad to know what you think of the matter.—You will remember that the first hint towards acquaintance came from Moore, & coldly enough I met it, as I fairly told him till the principal point was discussed between us, I could not reply to the other part of his letter, but now that is settled, Mr. R[ogers] (whom I never saw) has sent me an invitation to meet the Irish Melodist on Monday. However you shall see all the letters &

---

[1] Scrope Davies seems to have borrowed money from the usurers for Byron, either as co-signer or in his own name. See May 15, 1811, to Hobhouse, note 1.

[1] Moore's Odes translated from Anacreon, dedicated to the Prince of Wales, appeared in 1800, and gave him entrée to the houses of the Whig Aristocracy.

[2] Moore's public statement regarding his duel with Jeffrey.

copies of mine when we come together again.— — —Yesterday Hodgson dined with me, & muddled himself so much, that at the play, he was with difficulty kept in order.—Bold Webster dropped in after dinner & managed to annoy Hodgson with his absurdity, he talked of H[odgson]'s satire & particularly his address to the *"Electric!!!"* (Eclectic) critics, and Porson's edition of *Phocion*!!![3] and finished by asking H[odgson] if he had ever redde his (W's) *pamphlet*!!—He made one cursed speech which put me into a fever, about ἕνα παιδί[4] & made Hodgson nearly sink into the earth, who unluckily recollected our telling him the "two hundred a year" proffer pro ιακίνθος.[5]—He then to mend matters entered into a long defence of his brother in law,[6] without any occasion as nobody had mentioned his name, persisted in spite of all endeavours to make him change ye. subject, & concluded by saying that Ld. Courtney[7] was "called Cousin by the King of Prussia!!!" Now all this is verbatim conversation of Bold W[ebster].— You will think me Banksizing but it is fact Per Dio!— —Cawthorn has Ali's letter[8] but I will send it if you please in a few days, pray what are become of *all* my *Greek* epistles?—they are not with the prints.— —The Note you shall have but it is not in the press yet, & lies in Dallas's possession. Demetrius is better of the Excalcitration & is at his wit's end to answer yr. Queries.—Dr. Clarke was highly polite to him & me & offered me his journals &c.—I admire him much.—Scrope is at Newmarket.—I was well enough treated at Cambridge, but glad to leave it, it made me *"lemancholy"* for many reasons, & some d——d bad ones.—

yrs. ever
Μπαιρων

[TO JOHN CAM HOBHOUSE]   *8 St. James's Street Novr. 3d. 1811*

Dear Hobhouse,—I wrote yesterday but as usual expatiated more on my own concerns than yours & owe you a second letter.—I shall

[3] Richard Porson, Fellow of Trinity College and Professor of Greek at Cambridge, edited four plays of Euripides, *Hecuba, Orestes, Phaenissae*, and *Medea*. Webster probably intended to refer to Porson's transcript of "The Lexicon of Photius", a manuscript given to Trinity College.

[4] a boy

[5] Hyacinth. See June 22, 1809, to Matthews, and Aug. 23, 1810, to Hobhouse.

[6] George Annesley, Lord Valentia, brother of Webster's wife.

[7] See June 25, 1809, to Hodgson, note 2.

[8] Ali Pasha's letter to Byron has not been found. Byron received another letter from Ali in 1813, brought by Dr. Henry Holland, the traveller (see letter of Sept. 8, 1813, to Moore). But that letter was written in Latin.

order a transcript of ye. note & send it to you forthwith, as it will not be in *my* press for some time.—Ibrahim Pacha is 'nown brother to Coul the obnoxious, *no*—I am wrong—*brother* to *Giaffer* the victim of Ali, the Pacha of Scutari's name I forget, & never heard of *Ochrida* as a Pachalik.—As to boundaries I always thought dear Delvinachi was the frontier.—Adam Bey whom we met going to Libochabo, is *dead* in spite of Seculario & Frank, he was nephew to Ali as you know.—He was twenty three years of age.—Do come to England, & copy Meletius in person, if you can't it will then devolve on your humble Servitor. —I will fac-similize if it be requisite.—I do take much interest in your Q[uart]o & have no doubt of it's success, Albania is untrodden ground.[1] —I don't know that a traveller has much to do with "likes or dislikes" but you see Dr. Clarke's "Dislikes" have answered very well.—My own mind is not very well made up as to ye. Greeks, but I have no patience with the absurd extremes into which their panegyrists & detractors have equally run.—I believe the No. of the *E[dinburgh] R[eview]* with all that stuff on the Romaics was written by Bloomfield,[2] Leake agreed with me that it was very sad, & you know *he* is well qualified to judge.— —This is a *secret*, & Dr. Clarke told it me, knowing *your* discretion to be similar to mine, or at least that there is nobody at *Enniscorthy* who will be much edified by it, I send it over St. George's Channel.— —I find I am a member of ye. Alfred Club,[3] & consequently a pot companion of your amiable progenitor, Ld. Valentia, the Archbishop of Canterbury, & such cattle, I believe Ward[4] is also one.— —Bold Webster is in a scrape with the Morning Post, Morning Chronicle, & all the Posts Morning & Evening, about some letters on politics with which he has lately been tying Cannisters to his tail, they charged him ten pounds for inserting one of these precious billets, & if they had asked a hundred the disgrace to the paper was honestly worth it.—It is in vain that *Wife, relations, friends* & *enemies* have risen up in fierce opposition to his malady, nothing but a thumbscrew or a whitloe on the itching finger can quell his scribbling. —He has exposed himself, nay hurt himself, for he was soliciting a Scotch place, & wrote a defence of Ld. Fingal by way of ingratiating

---

[1] Byron was supplying information for Hobhouse's *Journey through Albania.*

[2] See Sept. 20, 1811, to Hobhouse, note 3.

[3] The Alfred Club at 23 Albemarle Street had among its members Sir James Mackintosh, William Gifford, and Sir William Drummond. See Byron's comment on it in his "Detached Thoughts" (No. 30). Byron was elected to membership while he was abroad.

[4] John William Ward (afterward Lord Dudley). See July 13, 1809, to Hanson, note 1.

himself with Ministers!!! & the worst of it is that every body knew this devil of a defence to be his, though sans signature, & for fear they should not be told it unto all men.—His wife is very pretty,[5] & I am much mistaken if five years hence, she don't give him reason to think so.—Knowing the man, one is apt to fancy these things, but I really thought, she treated him even already with a due portion of conjugal contempt, but I dare say this was only the megrim of a Misogynist.— — —At present he is the happiest of men, & has asked me to go with them to a tragedy to see his *wife cry*!— —Just before I left Malta, I wrote during my Ague, a copy of Hudibrastics as an Adieu to La Valette,[6] which I gave to Com[mander] Fraser because it contained a compliment to Mrs. F[raser][7] without intending the thing to be bandied about. No sooner were we sailed than they were set in circulation, & I am told by a lately arrived traveller, that they are all, but particularly *Oakes*,[8] in a pucker, and yet I am sure there is nothing to annoy any body, or a single personal allusion throughout, as far as I remember, for I kept no copy.—So pray be quiet at Enniscorthy, or you may get a reprimand like Capt. P. Hunter, Ensign Y. & Lt. J. for lampooning ye. burghers.— —When you write, address to Cawthorn's, & he will forward your epistles, as I don't know where I am going, or what I am about to do.—You cant conceive how I miss you, much more than I did after your departure in the Archipelago, for there we were but two, but here there are so many things we should laugh at together, & support each other, when laughed at ourselves, that I yearn for you prodigiously.—Sir J. Debathe[9] hath called upon me, he is a good deal improved in every thing but person, and I think may live a Session or two longer on his good behaviour.— —Claridge[10] my *dearest* friend (for he cost me much more than *fifteen* shillings) is indeed dull, as to his "attachment", will attachment keep one awake? or say pleasant things? or even soar beyond an execrable Oxonian pun? and at our time of life, to talk of "attachment!" when one has left

[5] Webster had married, in 1810, Lady Frances Caroline Annesley, daughter of Arthur, first Earl of Mountnorris and eighth Viscount Valentia.
[6] Byron's "Farewell to Malta", written on May 26, 1811, while he was in Valleta on his way home, was first published in the sixth edition of *Poems on his Domestic Circumstances* (W. Hone, 1816.)
[7] It was at Mrs. Fraser's house that Byron first met Mrs. Constance Spencer Smith.
[8] Major General Hildebrand Oakes was then His Majesty's Commissioner for the Affairs of Malta.
[9] James De Bathe, one of Byron's younger friends at Harrow.
[10] John Claridge, another school friend, who had bored Byron during his visit to Newstead Abbey.

School, aye and College too, Sdeath, one would think you were like Euripides who admired the Autumn of Agatho.—When I was a child, I thought as a Child, (saith St. Paul & so say I) but now give me a man of Calibre, a little sense, a sprinkling of information, and as for "attachment" I leave it with other trifles,

> "To those who trifle with more grace & care
> Whose trifling pleases, & whom trifles please.["]¹¹

I believe my Rochdale Statement was pretty correct, with this proviso, that if I could afford to lay out twenty or thirty thousand pounds on it, the Income would probably be double the utmost I mentioned.— Davies also saw at Harrowgate several Lancashire gentry who told him the same thing, & I suppose he speaks truth on this occasion, having no motive to the contrary.— —But you know I always was, & always shall be an embarrassed man, & I must een fight my way through between the files of ruined nobles, & broken shopkeepers, which increase daily.— —I must marry, you know I hate women, & for fear I should ever change that opinion, I *shall* marry.—My Satire is going into a fifth Edition, to which will be added the "Hints from Horace.".—Hodgson tells me your tale from Boccace is much liked with all it's indecency.—Bland is come back from France.—

yrs ever
Bn.——

[TO FRANCIS HODGSON]   *8. St. James's Street Novr. 4th. 1811*

Dear Hodgson,—Dine with me on Saturday next & meet *Rogers, Campbell,* & *Moore* whom I have just left, & who spoke highly of *you* & *yours.*—Do pray contrive to meet me at Dorant's on that day as I think they are men you would not dislike to know.

yrs. ever
BYRON

[TO MR. DEIGHTON]   *8 St. James's Street Novr. 7th. 1811*

Sir,—The Draft I sent you, should have been drawn on a *stamp*, of this I was not aware till lately, as the regulation took place subsequent to my leaving England.—To avoid a penalty which would equally affect

¹¹ Unidentified.

you & myself it must be returned to me, & I will send you a draft for the same sum on a *proper stamp.* I am Sir,

yr. very obedt. Servt.

BYRON

[TO JOHN CAM HOBHOUSE] 8 *St. James's Street. Novr. 9th 1811*

My dear Hobhouse.—I have lately been leading a most *poetical* life with Messrs Rogers Moore & Campbell,[1] the latter indeed I have only seen once at dinner at Mr. R[ogers]'s, but that *once* was enough to make me wish to see him again.—He was to have dined with me today, but is laid up at Sydenham, however I shall see him next week.— R[oger]s & Moore are very pleasing, & not priggish as poetical personages are apt to be. Campbell is not at all what you would suppose him from his writings, but agreeable nonetheless.— —I have also seen a good deal of Ward[2] the eloquent, who meets me today with R[oger]s M[oor]e & our Hodgson to dinner.— —I am very glad to have been *elected* at the Alfred, not only because it is a difficult thing, but I have met there several old acquaintances particularly Peele[3] the Secretary sub Secretario.—I saw there Sotheby[4] the scribbler who is a disagreeable dog, with rhyme written in every feature of his wrinkled Physiognomy.—I have also received indirectly a kind of pacific overture from Ld. Holland, so you see, people are very civil when one dont deserve it.—All Webster's connections are at their Wits' end to cure him of his malady, they have applied to me to talk to him seriously on ye. subject, & I *have* talked, but to no purpose, for he lost his temper, & invited me to a *controversy* in the *Newspapers*!!! —Valentia is vastly annoyed, & so is W[ebster]'s spouse, but nothing will do, he persists in his laudable design of becoming ridiculous.— — —Cawthorn is at a stand still for Lack of Copy, *Copy, Copy!*—Will you come here at Xmas & bring or send my Romaic M.S.S.? or I will put you into Fosbrooke's "Gloster Journal,"[5] so I will.— —Do write soon,

---

[1] Thomas Campbell, along with Samuel Rogers, was one of the few contemporary poets praised by Byron in *English Bards and Scotch Reviewers.*

[2] For John William Ward, see July 13, 1809, to Hanson, note 1.

[3] Robert Peel, later distinguished as a statesman, was at Harrow with Byron.

[4] William Sotheby (1757–1833) had achieved a literary reputation with the publication of *Oberon* (1798) and his *Georgics* (1800). See *English Bards and Scotch Reviewers*, line 818. Byron found him "a good man . . . but . . . a bore". ("Detached Thoughts", No. 50). He later ridiculed Sotheby as a "Bustling Botherby" (*Beppo*, stanza 72) and in *Don Juan* (Canto I, stanza 206).

[5] Thomas Dudley Fosbroke (1770–1842), an antiquary, published "Abstracts of Records and MSS. respecting the County of Gloucester" in 1807.

I am obliged to conclude on acct. of the Post.— —Baillie & Kinnaird[6] I saw yesterday, K[innaird] with his Piece, she is pretty & but pretty, perhaps only prettyish.—Believe me

yrs ever

Μπαιρῶν

[TO FRANCIS HODGSON]   *London, Nov. 15, 1811*
Send a certain letter.[1]

B.

[TO JOHN CAM HOBHOUSE]   *8 St. James's Street. Novr. 16th. 1811*

My dear H.—That is a most *impudent* simile & incorrect, for the *"vomit"* came to the *"dog"* & not the *"dog"* to the *"vomit"* & if you will teach me how to spit in any body's face without offence, I will shake off these gentlemen with the greatest good-will, however I have never *called* on either, so am not to blame for the slightest degree of good manners.— —I send you Demo's[1] traduzione, & make the most of it, you must orthographize it in both languages as you will perceive. Why have you omitted the earthquake in the night at Libochabo? I will give up the *flatulent* Secretary, but do let us have the Terramoto.— I dine today with Ward to meet the Lord knows whom.—Moore & I are on the best of terms, I answered his letters in an explanatory way, but of course conceded nothing in the shape of an apology, indeed his own letters were an odd mixture of complaint, & a desire of amicable discussion.—Rogers said his behaviour was rather Irish, & that mine was candid & manly, I hope it was at *least* the latter.—I consulted Scrope before I sent off my letter, but now the matter is completely adjusted, as R[ogers] said "honourably" to Both. Sotheby, whom I abused in my last, improves, his face is rather against him, & his manner abrupt & dogmatic, but I believe him to be much more amiable than I thought him.—Rogers is a most excellent & unassuming Soul, & Moore an Epitome of all that's delightful, I asked them & Hodgson to dinner. H[odgson] of course was drunk & Sensibilitous.— —Bland (the *Revd*) has been *challenging* an officer of Dragoons, about a *whore*,

6 Douglas Kinnaird, a Cambridge friend of Byron, who later became his banker and business and literary agent. See Biographical sketch in Appendix.
1 Moore's original challenge, which Hodgson had withheld. Byron was eager for Moore to see that it had not been opened.
1 Demetrius Zograffo, Byron's Greek servant, was translating Greek passages for Hobhouse's travel book.

& my assistance being required, I interfered in time to prevent him from losing his *life* or his *Living*.—The man is mad, Sir, mad, frightful as a Mandrake, & lean as a rutting Stag, & all about a bitch not worth a Bank token.—She is a common Strumpet as his Antagonist assured me, yet he means to marry her, Hodgson meant to marry her, the officer meant to marry her, her first Seducer (seventeen years ago) meant to marry her, and all this is owing to the *Comet!*— —During Bland's absence, H[odgso]n was her Dragon, & left his own Oyster wench to offer her his hand, which she *refused*.—Bland comes home in Hysterics, finds her in keeping (not by H[odgso]n however) & loses his wits.— Hodgson gets drunk & cries, & he & Bland (who have been berhyming each other as you know these six past Olympiads) are now the Antipodes of each other.—I saw this *wonder*, & set her down at seven shilling's worth.— —Here is gossip for you! as you know some of the parties.—As to self, I am ill with a cough, Demo has tumbled down stairs, scalded his leg, been kicked by a horse, hurt his kidneys, got a terrible "catchcold" (as he calls it) & now suffers under these accumulated mischances.—Fletcher is fat & facetious.—

yrs. ever
Μπαιρῶν

[TO JOHN CAM HOBHOUSE]   *8 St. James's Street. Novr. 17th. 1811*

Dear H.—I wrote you a gossiping letter yesterday, & shall do as much today, being partly confined with a cough which prevented me from dining with Ward according to Invitation.—Demo's decipherings and paraphrases I sent off at the same time & trust they will put you in good humour.—But I want my Romaic M.S.S. being in labour of "Childe Harold" who is coming costively into the World, after having undergone the Ordeal of Gifford's & Campbell's inspection, not that I am indebted to either for a single alteration, for the same reason that Lady Mary refused Pope with a "No touching" &c.— However, they have been pleased to say very pleasant things if I may trust the word of others for Gifford, & Campbell's own for himself.— The thing was shown by Murray, (as you know I never was in the habit of bandying M.S.S. of my own) & against my privity or concurrence, however it has by good luck turned out well, or I should have been "feroce" with the Bookseller & very deservedly.—Good paper, clear type, & vast margin as usual.—I have been sweating Notes to a large amount, so that ye. "Body of ye. Book" will be

bulky.—Sixty five stanzas of ye. first Canto are printed.—Cawthorn is
also at work with a fifth Edition of E[nglish] B[ard]s[;] this & the
H[int]s from Horace, with a thing on Ld. Elgin, called the ''Curse of
Minerva'' which you have never seen, will constitute Master Lintot's
department, and make a monstrous vol. of Crown Octavo.—You are
very slow with *copy*, & will delay till the *Season* is over, your book will
not come in before Green peas, surely you don't intend it for Summer
Reading.— —The few pages of today's proof are all I have redde; as
Cawthorn is shy of showing me your work, Lord knows why.— —He
had an MS. offered (I am not at Liberty to mention names) through
the medium of Hodgson who is not the Author however, which he rejected, though backed by your humble Servitor.—Not that I much
admired the said MS. which abused all my acquaintances, but I wished
to oblige Hodgson.— —I am living as quietly as you can be, & have
long left off Wine entirely, & never enter a coffee house of any
description, my meal is generally at ye. Alfred, where I munch my
vegetables in peace.—Town is empty but I stay on business, to get
rid of these damned annuities.— —Webster is vanished with his
Wife,—Ward, Peele, Rogers, Moore, Sotheby, Sir W. Ingilby[1] are
the few I have lately seen most of, with Ld. Valentia, in whom I see
nothing very ''cat[t]ivo,'' and as every body speaks to him, one can't
very well avoid it.——Ellice called yesterday, & certain travellers
whom I knew after your return.—W[ebste]r will be a noble subject for
Cuckoldom in three years, though he has managed to impregnate her
Ladyship, which consequently can be no very difficult task.—She is
certainly very pretty, & if not a dunce, must despise her ''Bud''
heartily.—She is not exactly to my taste, but I dare say Dragoons
would like her.—Sir W.[2] with whom you are so wrothfully displeased,
is gone to Edinbug—burgh, I tell you, he is not what you take him
for, but is going to be married, reformed and *all that*.—My Establishment at Newstead improves, I have Lucy, Susan[3] a very pretty Welsh
Girl, & a third of the Nott's breed, whom you never saw, all under age,
and very ornamental. But my diet is so low that I can carry on nothing
carnal.—I wish you would come over before Xmas, & go down to
Notts with me. All the fathers on the Earth & under it should never
keep me at Enniscorthy.—I give you joy of your dinner with the

1 Sir William Ingilby was the son of Sir John Amcotts-Ingilby. The baronetcy
was created in 1642, but lapsed in 1772; it was revived in 1781 after Sir John, an
illegitimate son of the last baronet, married an heiress of the Amcotts family.
2 Unidentified.
3 Susan Vaughan.

Bishop of *Ferns*.—Was not "Atherton"[4] a Bishop? what says the Dean?—What a proper Scoundrel that same Serving man must have been, I thought better of the Irish.— —Mrs. Fraser's[5] Adair's Antipathy is in town, surely she is agreeable, & Bob a coxcomb to find fault with her phantasies.—Consider *it* is a woman, & what can be expected!— Peacock is come home, & dangling after her secondo al' suo Solito.— Ld. Sligo is in Ireland & a scrape, his Arnaouts are going back to Rumelia, Government would not allow them to go to Ireland,—Why?— nor further than ten miles from London—Wherefore? Dallas is bringing out a farce, his last did not succeed bitterly, but has merit.— Pratt has put Joe Blackett into two volumes as bad as Purgatory, poor Joe, killed first, & published afterwards, if the thing had been reversed the wonder had been less, but the cruelty equal.—I have heard nothing of Miss Milbanke's posthumous buffooneries, but here is Miss Seward[6] with 6 tomes of the most disgusting trash, sailing over Styx with a Foolscap over her periwig as complacent as can be.—Of all Bitches dead or alive a scribbling woman is the most canine.—Scott is her Editor, I suppose because she lards him in every page.

yrs. aye

Mπαιρων

[TO FRANCIS HODGSON]   8, *St. James's Street, November 17, 1811*

Dear Hodgson,—I have been waiting for the *letter*, which was to have been sent by you *immediately*, and must again jog your memory on the subject. I believe I wrote you a full and true account of poor ——'s [Bland's][1] proceedings. Since his reunion to —— I have heard nothing further from him. What a pity! a man of talent, past the heyday of life, and a clergyman, to fall into such imbecility. I have heard from Hobhouse, who has at last sent more copy to Cawthorn for his *Travels*. I franked an enormous cover for you yesterday, seemingly to convey at least twelve cantos on any given subject. I fear the aspect of it was too *epic* for the post. From this and other co-

4 John Atherton (1598-1640), Bishop of Waterford and Lismore, was found guilty of an unnatural crime, degraded and hanged at Dublin in 1640.

5 Wife of an officer at Malta. It was at her home that Byron first met Mrs. Spencer Smith.

6 Anna Seward (1747-1809), authoress known as the "Swan of Lichfield", had been a friend of Boswell, Dr. Johnson, Dr. Darwin, and others. Walter Scott edited six volumes of her letters in 1811.

1 See Nov. 16, 1811, to Hobhouse. Hodgson inked out the names.

incidences I augur a publication on your part, but what, or when, or how much, you must disclose immediately.

I don't know what to say about coming down to Cambridge at present, but live in hopes. I am so completely superannuated there, and besides feel it something brazen in me to wear my magisterial habit, after all my buffooneries, that I hardly think I shall venture again. And being now an ἄριστον μεν ὑδωρ[2] disciple I won't come within wine-shot of such determined topers as your collegiates. I have not yet subscribed to Bowen.[3] I mean to cut Harrow *"enim unquam"* as somebody classically said for a farewell sentence. I am superannuated there too, and, in short, as old at twenty-three as many men at seventy.

Do write and send this letter that hath been so long in your custody. It is important that Moore should be certain that I never received it, if it be *his*. Are you drowned in a bottle of Port? or a Kilderkin of Ale? that I have never heard from you, or are you fallen into a fit of perplexity? Cawthorn has declined, and the MS. is returned to him. This is all at present from yours in the faith,

Μπαιρῶν

[TO JOHN HANSON]   *8 St. James's Street Novr. 18th. 1811*

Dear Sir,—It is proper that the Newstead tenants should be made aware of the amount of the intended rental immediately, so pray, let the proportion of each be made out & sent down forthwith.—Believe me

yrs. truly
BYRON

P.S.—Have you heard from Scotland?[1]

[TO THE REV. DR. VALPY][1]   *8 St. James's Street. Novr. 19th. 1811*

Sir,—The Evening before I left Notts. I had the honour of a letter from you, which remained unanswered, as I had left the letter amongst

2 The Greek phrase means "Water [is] best".
3 Perhaps the Bowen, Sr. listed by E. N. Long as among the boys at Harrow at the time he arrived just before Byron?
1 From the Trustees of Mrs. Byron's estate.
1 There were several Valpys, but this was probably the Rev. Dr. Richard Valpy (1754–1836), Fellow of the Society of Antiquaries and Headmaster of Reading School. He published classical and other school books.

133

other papers, & had forgotten the address.—In reply to it, I shall have great pleasure in subscribing to the work of which it was the subject.— —With regard to my *influence*, which you requested, I cannot offer what is not worth acceptance, in fact I possess *none*.— Your second letter I received last night and have to thank you for the present by which it was accompanied.—My researches, such as they were, when in the East, were more diverted to the language & the inhabitants than to Antiquities.— —The few remarks I made on the modern Greeks & their Literature, with several Romaic Books & M.S.S. I have for the present lent to a friend who is about to publish his travels in those countries.—With the exception of one inscription at [Scrippo?] (the ancient Orchomenos) which is in excellent preservation, I brought away nothing worth notice, & that is given more accurately in Meletius' Geography (a Romaic work in my possession) than could be done in writing.—I do not know that we discovered anything worthy of remark in the Levant, except an Amphitheatre about three hours ride from Yanina in Epirus,[2] and even of that discovery the merit belongs to *Major Leake* the English Minister in Albania, who first investigated it with Mr. Lusieri Ld. Elgin's agent.—With the exception of these two Gentlemen I question whether it had been seen by previous travellers to ourselves.—The Amphitheatre in question is in Sr. Lusieri's opinion the largest and most perfect in the Levant or Italy, & far superior to a similar ruin at Epidaurus.—No trace remains of the city to which it belonged, nor does Strabo throw any light on the subject.— Every other ruin in Greece or the adjacent countries has already been fully investigated.—I beg leave once more to thank you for your letter & present & have the honour to be

yr. most obedt. very humble Servt.

BYRON

[TO JOHN HANSON]   *20th Novr. 1811*

Dr. Sir,—I send the enclosed from Mrs. M[assingberd].—I shall want cash tomorrow being about to go down to Cambridge on Friday. —I will call tomorrow.

yrs.

B

[2] The amphitheatre was identified as that of Dodona by excavations carried out by Constantin Carapanos of Arta in 1876. Byron was unaware of the identity of the ruins. In *Childe Harold* he wrote: "Oh! where, Dodona! is thine aged Grove,/ Prophetic Font, and Oracle divine?" (Canto II, stanza 53).

Cambridge. Novr. 26th 1811

Dear Sir—I shall be in town on Saturday at furthest, so that it will be loss of time to send a proof here. I have merely time to write you this much & beg you to believe me

yrs. ever very sincerely

BYRON

[TO JOHN CAM HOBHOUSE] *8. St. James's Street Decr. 3d. 1811*

My dear H.— All the MSS are arrived but your letter is dissatisfactory.—I mean to annex some Specimens of Romaic but by no means to enter into details for Which I have neither time nor talent.—But supposing such to have been my intention, is not the field wide enough for both? I declare to you most sincerely that I would rather throw up my publication entirely than be the means of curtailing a page of yours.— —There is a most formidable serious puff about you & your work in the last No. of the Critical review, & we have all great expectations from it, and I am convinced that the more you say on Romaic the better.—My thing shall be sent off to you the moment it is finished & before it is with the public; & so far from impeding you I did hope that it would be a stepping stone instead of a stumbling block in your way.—My notes will not be extensive, nor the specimens numerous, nor shall I say one word on the grammar or minutiae of ye. language.—So don't give up an idea on my account and as to contradicting me, you will only do it where I am wrong, & I shall forgive you & so will the World.—Indeed I have assigned in my notes as a reason for saying so little, that *you* have much more to say on the subject.—So don't make me lie in that respect at least.—Why not translate the Drama, I certainly shall *not*, but insert a trans. in verse of the "Δευτε"[1] song &c.—Besides *you* have the Albanian Voc[ular]y & *I* merely two Albanian songs with a bald translation in prose.—The extracts & specimens I leave to the learned to construe, but I think you should insert them with a translation.— The Devil's in it, if there is not a field for both.—By the bye why not publish a Romaic Lexicon? I have an excellent one, it is only translating the Italian into English, & prefacing & editing, & such a work is sure to sell & much wanted.—I wish you to undertake this & will put the three quartos into your

---

[1] Byron's translation of the Greek war song, Δευτε παιδες by Riga, "Sons of the Greeks, arise!", appeared at the end of the volume containing the first two cantos of *Childe Harold* in 1812.

hands if you will think of it.—I am just returned from Cambridge, where I have been visiting Hodgson & Harness an old Harrow friend whom you don't know.—Do pray come to England, & be my guest during your stay both in town & Notts?— —Hodgson & Harness are to be in Notts at Xmas.—come & join us.—I wish your damned regiment was disbanded,— —Sdeath why don't you desert? Every body enquires after you & what answer can I give?—

yrs. ever
B.

[TO FRANCIS HODGSON]   *8 St. James's Street: December 4, 1811.*

My dear Hodgson,— I have seen Miller, who will see Bland, but I have no great hopes of his obtaining the translation from the crowd of candidates.[1] Yesterday I wrote to Harness, who will probably tell you what I said on the subject. Hobhouse has sent me my Romaic MSS. and I shall require your aid in correcting the press, as your Greek eye is more correct than mine. But these will not come to type this month, I dare say. I have put some soft lines on ye Scotch in the "Curse of Minerva," take them:

Yet Caledonia claims some native worth, &c.[2]

If you are not content now, I must say with the Irish drummer to the deserter who called out, "Flog high, flog low"—"The de'il burn ye, there's no pleasing you, flog where one will." Have you given up wine, even British wine?

I have read Watson to Gibbon.[3] He proves nothing, so I am where I was, verging towards Spinoza; and yet it is a gloomy Creed, and I want a better, but there is something Pagan in me that I cannot shake off. In short, I deny nothing, but doubt everything. The post brings me to a conclusion. Bland has just been here.

Yours ever,
Bn.

[1] Byron was trying to get for Hodgson's friend Bland the job of translating Lucien Bonaparte's poem *Charlemagne*, but was unsuccessful. It was finally translated by Dr. Butler (head-master of Shrewsbury) and Hodgson, and was published in 1815.

[2] Lines 149–56.

[3] Richard Watson, Professor of Divinity at Cambridge, afterward Bishop of Llandaff. published in 1776 *An Apology for Christianity, in a Series of Letters to Edward Gibbon, Esq.*

My dearest William.—I write again, but don't suppose I mean to lay such a tax on your pen & patience as to expect regular replies, when you feel inclined, write, when silent I shall have the consolation of knowing that you are much better employed. Yesterday Bland & I called on Mr. Miller who being then out will call on B[land] today or tomorrow.— —I shall certainly endeavour to bring them together, but you wrong my best of Booksellers Miller,[1] he is rich but not ignorant or assuming, on the contrary he is the most *genteel* of his profession & very well informed & well bred.—You are very censorious, Child, when you are a little older you will learn to dislike every body but abuse nobody.—With regard to the person of whom you speak, your own Good sense must direct you, I never pretend to advise being an implicit believer in the old Proverb.— In the present *frost* I sincerely sympathize with you it is the first I have felt these three years, though I longed for one in the Oriental Summer, where no such thing is to be had unless I had gone to the top of Hymettus for it.—I thank you most truly for the concluding part of your letter, I have been of late not much accustomed to kindness from any quarter, & I am not the less pleased to meet with it again from one where I had known it earliest.—Be assured I have not changed, in all my ramblings, Harrow & of course *yourself* never left me, and the

—"dulces reminiscitur Argos"[2]

attended me to the very spot to which that semi-line alludes in the mind of the fallen Argive.— —I fix no date to our Intimacy for it commenced before I began to date at all, & it rests with you to continue it till the hour which must number it & me with the things that *were*.— —And now don't give way to your imaginations & the balancing of "words" & "looks" (to use your own expression) I cant say much for either of mine, but if ever they seem cold to you believe them at variance with my heart, which is as much yours as it was in the fourth form.— —You read, don't you? I should think X plus Y at least as amusing as the "Curse of Kehama" & much more intelligible. —Master Southey's poems *are* in fact what parallel lines *might* be viz. prolonged ad infinitum, without ever meeting anything half so absurd as themselves.—

[1] See Dec. 4, 1811, to Hodgson, note 1.
[2] Virgil, Æneid, Book X, line 781, said of the dying Antores, an Argive companion of Hercules: *Dulces moriens reminiscitur Argos* ("dying remembers sweet Argos").

"What news, what news Queen Orraca?
What news of the Scribblers five?
Southey, Wordsworth Coleridge Lloyd & Lambe
All damned, though yet alive![''][3]

Coleridge is lecturing,[4] "many an old fool" (said Hannibal to some such Lecturer) have I heard "but such as this never."—[5] Good morrow, my dearest William

ever yrs. most affectionately
BYRON

[TO JAMES WEDDERBURN WEBSTER]   8. *St. James's St.*
Decr. 7th. 1811

My dear W.—I was out of town during the arrival of your letters, but forwarded all on my return.—I hope you are going on to your satisfaction, & that her Ladyship is about to produce an heir with all his mother's Graces & all his Sire's good qualities.—You know I am to be a Godfather, Byron Webster! a most heroic name, say what you please.—Don't be alarmed, my *"caprice"* wont lead me into Dorset, no, *Bachelors* for me, I consider you as dead to us, & all my future devoirs are but tributes of respect to your *Memory*.— Poor fellow, he was a facetious companion & well respected by all who knew him, but he is gone, sooner or later we must all come to it.—I see nothing of you in the *papers*, the only place where I dont wish to see you, but you will be in town in the Winter.—What dost thou do? shoot, hunt, & "wind up ye. Clock" as Caleb Quotem says,[1] thou art vastly happy I doubt not.— —I see your brother in law at times, & like him much, but we miss you much; I shall leave town in a fortnight to pass my Xmas in Notts.—Good afternoon Dear W. believe me

yrs ever most truly
B.

---

[3] Byron is parodying a stanza in Southey's "Queen Orraca and the Five Martyrs of Morocco".

[4] Coleridge began a course of lectures on Shakespeare on November 18, 1811. Later Byron attended at least one of his lectures with Rogers.

[5] Taken to hear a peripatetic philosopher named Phormio, Hannibal, when asked his opinion of the lecturer, replied: "I have seen many old fools often, but such an old fool as Phormio, never." (Cicero, *De Oratore*, II, 18.)

[1] Caleb Quotem's song is in *The Review, or Wags of Windsor* (Act II, Scene 2), by George Colman the Younger.

Dear Sir,—We must come to the point. If your friend cannot furnish ye. sum Mrs. M[assingberd]'s Norwich Gentleman will procure it in a fortnight. Pray let us determine, I am harrassed with this business beyond bearing.—Have the Scotch begun their instalments, the sooner the better. I must leave town next week.

yrs truly
BYRON

[TO FRANCIS HODGSON]   *London. Decr. 8th. 1811*

Dear Hodgson—I sent you a sad tale of three Friars the other day, & now take a dose in another style.—I wrote it a day or two ago on hearing a song of former days—

[1]

Away, Away ye notes of Woe,
  Be silent thou once soothing strain,
Or I must flee from hence, for oh!
  I dare not trust those sounds again,
To me they speak of brighter days,
  But lull the chords, for now, Alas!
I must not think, I may not gaze
  On what I *am*—on what I *was*.

[2]

The voice that made those sounds more sweet
  Is hushed, and all their charms are fled
  And now their softest notes repeat
  A dirge, an Anthem on the dead,
Yes, Thyrza,[1] yes, they breathe of thee,
  Beloved dust, since dust thou art,
And all that once was Harmony
  Is hideous discord to my heart.

[3]

'Tis silent all—but on my ear
  The well remembered Echoes thrill,
I hear a voice I would not hear,
  A voice that now might well be still,

---

[1] Byron's poetic name for John Edleston.

Yet oft my doubting Soul 'twill shake,
  Ev'n Slumber owns it's gentle tone,
Till Consciousness will vainly wake
  To listen, though the Dream be gone.

[4]

Sweet Thyrza waking as in sleep,
  Thou art but now a lovely dream,
A Star, that trembled oer the deep,
  Then turned from Earth its tender beam,
But he that through Life's dreary way
  Must pass, when Heaven is veiled in wrath,
Will long lament the vanquished Ray,
  That scattered Gladness oer his path.

I have gotten a book by Sir W. Drummond (printed, but not published), entitled *Œdipus Judaicus*,[2] in which he attempts to prove the greater part of the Old Testament an allegory, particularly Genesis and Joshua. He professes himself a theist in the preface, and handles the literal interpretation very roughly. I wish I could see it. Mr. Ward[3] has lent it me, and I confess to me it is worth fifty Watsons.[4]

You and Harness must fix on the time for your visit to Newstead; I can command mine at your wish, unless any thing particular occurs in the interim. Master William Harness and I have recommenced a most fiery correspondence; I like him as Euripides liked Agatho, or Darby admired Joan, as much for the past as the present. Bland dines with me on Tuesday to meet Moore. Coleridge has attacked the *Pleasures of Hope*,[5] and all other pleasures whatsoever. Mr. Rogers was present, and heard himself indirectly *rowed* by the lecturer. We are going in a party to hear the new Art of Poetry by this reformed

---

[2] Sir William Drummond (1770–1828) held various diplomatic posts until 1809, when he retired and devoted himself to literature. Byron, who met him at Gibraltar and probably again at the Alfred Club, admired his Voltairian skepticism. His *Ædipus Judaicus* (1811) attempted to explain many parts of the Old Testament as astronomical allegories.

[3] See July 13, 1809, to Hanson, note 1.

[4] See Dec. 4, 1811, to Hodgson, note 3.

[5] Coleridge in his lecture of Dec. 5, 1811, the sixth of his series on Shakespeare, according to Henry Crabb Robinson, rambled widely from his subject. This may be the lecture in which he referred to Campbell's "Pleasures of Hope" and indirectly attacked Rogers. (*Henry Crabb Robinson on Books and their Writers*, ed. by Edith J. Morley, I, 53.)

schismatic;[6] and were I one of these poetical luminaries, or of sufficient consequence to be noticed by the man of lectures, I should not hear him without an answer. For you know, "an a man will be beaten with brains, he shall never keep a clean doublet."[7] Campbell will be desperately annoyed. I never saw a man (and of him I have seen very little) so sensitive;—what a happy temperament! I am sorry for it; what can *he* fear from criticism? I don't know if Bland has seen Miller, who was to call on him yesterday.[8]

To-day is the Sabbath,—a day I never pass pleasantly, but at Cambridge; and, even there, the organ is a sad remembrancer.[9] Things are stagnant enough in town; as long as they don't retrograde, 'tis all very well. Hobhouse writes and writes, and writes, and is an author. I do nothing but eschew[10] tobacco. I wish parliament were assembled, that I may hear, and perhaps some day be heard;—but on this point I am not very sanguine. I have many plans;—sometimes I think of the East again, and dearly beloved Greece. I am well, but weakly Yesterday Kinnaird told me I looked very ill, and sent me home happy.

You will never give up wine. See what it is to be thirty! if you were six years younger, you might leave off anything. You drink and re-pent; you repent and drink.

Is Scrope still interesting and invalid? And how does Hinde with his cursed chemistry? To Harness I have written, and he has written, and we have all written, and have nothing now to do but write again, till Death splits up the pen and the scribbler.

The Alfred has three hundred and fifty-four candidates for six vacancies. The cook has run away and left us liable, which makes our committee very plaintive. Master Brook, our head serving-man, has the gout, and our new cook is none of the best. I speak from report,—for what is cookery to a leguminous-eating Ascetic? So now you know as much of the matter as I do. Books and quiet are still there, and they may dress their dishes in their own way for me. Let me know your determination as to Newstead, and believe me,

Yours ever,

Μπαιρῶν

[6] Byron told Hobhouse on Dec. 15, 1811: "Tomorrow I dine with Rogers and go to Coleridge's Lecture."

[7] *Much Ado About Nothing*, Act V, scene 4, inaccurately quoted.

[8] Concerning the translation of Lucien Bonaparte's *Charlemagne*. See Dec. 4, 1811, to Hodgson, note 1.

[9] It reminded him of Edleston, the Cambridge choirboy.

[10] Whether from ignorance or facetiousness, Byron several times used "eschew" for "chew". See *Don Juan*, Canto XII, stanza 43.

My dearest William.—Behold a most formidable sheet without gilt or black edging, & consequently very vulgar & indecorous particularly to one of your precision, but this being Sunday I can procure no better, & will atone for its length by *not* filling it.—Bland I have not seen since your last letter, but on Tuesday he dines with me & will meet Moore the Epitome of all that is exquisite in poetical or personal accomplishments.—How Bland has settled with Miller I know not, I have very little interest with either, & they must arrange their concerns according to their own Gusto, I have done my endeavours at ⟨Hodgson's⟩ your request to bring them together & hope they may agree to their mutual advantage.—Coleridge has been lecturing against Campbell, Rogers was present, & from him I derive the information, we are going to make a party to hear this Manichean of Poesy.[1]—Pole is to marry Miss Long,[2] & will be a very miserable dog for all that; the present Ministers are to *continue* and his Majesty *does continue* in ye. same state.[3] So, there's Folly & Madness for you both in a breath.— —I never heard but of one man truly fortunate, & he was Beaumarchais (the French author of Figaro) who buried two wives & gained three lawsuits before he was thirty.—[4]Now, Child, what art thou doing? *reading I trust.* I want to see you take a degree, remember this is the most important period of your life, & don't disappoint your Papa & your Aunts & all your kin, besides myself, don't you know that all male children were begotten for the express purpose of being Graduates? & that even *I* am an M. A. though how I became so the public Orator only can resolve.—Besides you are to be a priest, & to confute Sir Wm. Drummond's late book about the Bible[5] (printed but not published) & all other infidels whatsoever.— —Now, leave Master Horsley's gig & Mr. S's suppers & become as immortal as Cambridge can make you.—You see, mio Carissimo Amico, what a pestilent correspondent I am likely to become, and that your auguries are to be resolved by contraries.—But then you shall be as quiet at Newstead as you please, & I wont disturb you as I do now.—When do you fix the day? that I may take you up according to compact.—

[1] See Dec. 6, 1811, to Hanson, note 4; and Dec. 8, 1811, to Hodgson, note 6.

[2] William Pole Wellesley (1788–1857), a nephew of the Duke of Wellington, married in March, 1812, Catherine, daughter of Sir James Tylney Long and added his wife's double name to his own.

[3] A reference to the continuing Tory ministry and to the madness of George III.

[4] Byron was inaccurate. Beaumarchais had married twice, but his second wife died when he was 38; he won two lawsuits, the second long after he was thirty.

[5] See Dec. 8, 1811, to Hodgson, note 2.

Hodgson talks of making a third in our journey, but we can't stow him inside at least, positively you shall go with me, as was agreed, & dont let me have any of your politesse to H[odgson] on the occasion.—I shall manage both with a little contrivance.— —I wish H[odgso]n was not quite so fat, & we should pack better.—Has he left off vinous liquors? he is an excellent soul, but I don't think water would improve him at least *in*ternally.—You will want to know what I am doing — chewing Tobacco.—You see nothing of my allies Scrope Davies and Matthews, they dont suit you, & how does it happen that I (who am a pipkin of the same pottery) continue in your good graces?— —Good night—I will go on in the Morning.— —Decr. 9th.— —1811. In a morning I am always sullen & this day is as sombre as myself.— — Rain & Mist are worse than a Sirocco particularly in a beef eating & beerdrinking Country.— —I think Master Betty taught you to drink ale, a mathematical but not dramatic beverage.— — My Bookseller (Cawthorne) has just left me, & tells me with a most important face that he is in treaty for a novel of Madame D'Arblay's (the *Miss Burney*)[6] for which 1000 Gs. are asked!—He wants me to read the M. S. (if he obtains it) which I shall do with pleasure, but I should be very cautious in venturing an opinion on her whose "Cecelia" Dr. Johnson superintended.—If he sends it to me I shall put it in ye. hands of Rogers & Moore who are truly Men of Taste.— —I have filled the sheet & beg your pardon, I will not do it again.— —I shall perhaps write again, but if not, believe, silent or scribbling that I love you most entirely & am my dearest Wm.

ever m[os]t Affectionately yrs.

Bn.

[TO JOHN CAM HOBHOUSE]   *8. St. James's Street. Decr. 9th. 1811*

My dear Hobhouse.—At length I am your rival in Good fortune. I this night saw *Robert Coates* perform Lothario at the Haymarket,[1] the house crammed, but bribery (a bank token) procured an excellent place near the Stage.—Before the curtain drew up a performer (all Gemmen) came forward and thus addressed the house, Ladies &c. "A melancholy accident has happened to the Gentleman who undertook the part of Altamont,—(here a dead stop—then—) this accident

---

[6] *The Wanderer, or Female Difficulties*, Madame d'Arblay's fourth and last novel, was finally published in 1814 by Longman, Hurst, Rees, Orme, and Browne. She was to receive £1,500 in three instalments.

[1] Robert Coates (1772–1848) appeared at the Haymarket on December 9, 1811, as "Lothario" in Rowe's *Fair Penitent*.

has *happened* to *his brother* who fell this afternoon through a *loop hole* into the *London Dock,* & was taken up dead, Altamont has just entered the house *distractedly,* is—now dressing!!! & will appear in 5 minutes!!!"—Such were verbatim the words of the Apologist, they were followed by a roar of laughter & Altamont himself, who did not fall short of Coates in absurdity.—Damn me, if ever I saw such a scene in my life, the play was closed in 3d. act, after Bob's demise nobody would hear a syllable, he was interrupted several times before, & made speeches, every soul was in hysterics, & all the actors on his own model.—You can't conceive how I longed for *you,* your taste for the ridiculous would have been gratified to surfeit. A farce followed in dumb show, after Bob had been hooted from the stage for a bawdy address he attempted to deliver between play & farce.—"Love a la mode" was damned, Coates was damned, every thing was damned & damnable.—His enacting I need not describe, you have seen him at Bath.—But never did you see the *others,* never did you hear the *apology,* never did you behold the "distracted" survivor of a "brother" neckbroken through a *"loop-hole* in ye. *London Dock"*!!—Like George Faulkner[2] these fellows defied burlesque.—Oh Captain! eye hath not seen, ear hath not heard, nor can the heart of man conceive tonight's performance.—Baron Geramb was in the Stage box, & Coates in his address *nailed* the *Baron* to the infinite amusement of the audience, & the discomfiture of Geramb,[3] who grew very wroth indeed.—I meant to write on other topics but I must postpone, I can think talk & dream only of these buffoons.—"Tis done, tis numbered with the things that were, would would it were to come."[4] & you by my side to see it.—Heigh ho! Good night.—yrs ever

B

[TO JOHN HANSON] *8. St. James's St. Decr. 10th. 1811*

Dear Sir,—I have thrice written without receiving any answer, which I again request as the comfort of so many persons depends on our

---

[2] George Faulkner (1699?–1775) was a Dublin bookseller, who had made himself ridiculous by entering into a newspaper squabble about the pirating of Richardson's novels. He figured under the name of Peter Paragraph in Samuel Foote's play *The Orators,* first produced at the Haymarket in 1762.

[3] Francois Ferdinand, Baron de Geramb (1772–1848), a title he held in the Holy Roman Empire, was an adventurer who later (in 1817) became a Trappist monk. Byron wrote of him in a letter of February 5, 1822, to the editor of *The Courier* that "Baron Gerambe was at one time a guest and especial favourite of Carlton palace".

[4] Unidentified.

144

speedy determination.—I presume that the new Rental has been sent to Notts, where I propose to proceed on Monday next.—If you wish to see me I will call at any given time.—

yrs. truly
BYRON

[TO THOMAS MOORE]   *December 11th, 1811.*

My dear Moore,—If you please, we will drop our formal monosyllables, and adhere to the appellations sanctioned by our godfathers and godmothers. If you make it a point, I will withdraw your name; at the same time there is no occasion, as I have this day postponed your election "sine die," [1] till it shall suit your wishes to be amongst us. I do not say this from any awkwardness the erasure of your proposal would occasion to *me*, but simply such is the state of the case; and, indeed, the longer your name is up, the stronger will become the probability of success, and your voters more numerous. Of course you will decide—your wish shall be my law. If my zeal has already outrun discretion, pardon me, and attribute my officiousness to an excusable motive.

I wish you would go down with me to Newstead. Hodgson will be there, and a young friend, named Harness, the earliest and dearest I ever had from the third form at Harrow to this hour. I can promise you good wine, and, if you like shooting, a manor of 4000 acres, fires, books, your own free will, and my own very indifferent company. "Balnea, vina * *" * * * [2]

Hodgson will plague you, I fear with verse;—for my own part, I will conclude, with Martial, "nil recitabo tibi;" [3] and surely the last inducement is not the least. Ponder on my proposition, and believe me, my dear Moore,

Yours ever,
BYRON.

[TO FRANCIS HODGSON]   *8. St. J[ames]'s Street. Decr. 12th. 1811.*

Why Hodgson I fear you have left off wine & me at the same time, I have written & written & written & no answer!—My dear Sir Edgar,[1]

---

[1] Byron had proposed Moore's name for membership in the Alfred Club.
[2] "Balnea, vina, Venus corrumpunt corpora nostra," Gruter, *Corpus Inscriptionum* (1603), p. 912. (*LJ*, II, 88n.)
[3] Martial (XI. lii, 16) *Ad Julium Cerealem*: "Plus ego polliceor: nil recitabo tibi."
[1] Hodgson published *Sir Edgar, a Tale* in 1810.

water disagrees with you, drink sack, & write.—Bland did not come to his appointment, being unwell, but Moore supplied all other vacancies most delectably.—I have hopes of his joining us at Newstead, I am sure you would like him more & more as he developes, at least *I* do.—How Miller & Bland go on I don't know [line cut out and crossed out: I have Pd. * * * his trouble?] Cawthorn talks of being in treaty for a novel of Me. D'Arblay's,[2] & if he obtains it (at 1000 Gs.!!) wishes me to see the M.S. this I should read with pleasure, not that I should ever dare to venture a criticism on her whose writings Dr. Johnson once revised, but for the pleasure of the thing; if my worthy publisher wanted a sound opinion I should send the M. S. to Rogers & Moore, as men most alive to true taste.— — — —I have had frequent letters from Wm. Harness, & *you* are silent, certes you are not a schoolboy.—However I have ye. consolation of knowing that you are better employed, viz. reviewing.— —You dont deserve that I should add another syllable, & I wont.

yrs ever
B

P.S.—I only wait for yr. answer to fix our meeting.—

[TO ROBERT CHARLES DALLAS]   [*Dec. 13, 1811?*]

Dear Sir,—I have only this *scrubby* paper to write on.—Excuse it.— I am certain that I sent some more notes on Spain & Portugal, particularly one on the latter, pray rummage, & dont mind my *politics.*—I believe I leave town next week.—Are you better, I hope so

yrs. ever
B

[TO JOHN HANSON]   *Decr. 13th. 1811*

Dear Sir,—I am sorry that I cannot accompany you to Farleigh[1] as I have settled to go down to Newstead next week, but I shall be very happy to see you at Newstead in January to settle ye. business of the tenantry.—I wish your friend could give some positive answer,[2] as my situation becomes more critical daily.—If he does not, or some one

---

2 See Dec. 8, 1811, to Harness, note 6.
1 Hanson's farm in Hampshire.
2 Concerning a loan or a mortgage which would extricate him from the usurers.

else, I must take the securities on myself at all hazards.—I shall call tomorrow [morn?]ing. believe me

yrs. ever
BYRON

[TO JOHN HANSON]   *Decr. 15th. 1811*

Dear Sir,—I have enclosed a letter of Mrs. Massingberd's who is in the usual dilemma.—In short I must take the securities on myself, & request you will arrange with the Jews on ye. subject.—There is nothing else left for it, I cannot allow people to go to Gaol on my account, it is better they should tear my property to pieces, than make me a scoundrel.—The remedy is desperate but so is the disease.—I wish to see you & have called for that purpose.—I will call tomorrow Morning.—

yrs. ever
BYRON

P.S.—Cannot Mrs. M. resist on legal grounds? do see & do something for the poor old Soul immediately.—

[TO JOHN CAM HOBHOUSE]   *8. St. James's Street: Decr. 15th. 1811*

My dear Hobhouse.—You are silent —I suppose for ye. same reason that George Lambe's Wit in ye. farce said nothing.—But this awful pause gives me hopes of seeing & hearing you in "these parts."—I have been living quietly, reading Sir W. Drummond's book on the bible, & seeing Kemble & Mrs. Siddons.[1]—Yesterday Moore went over with me to Sydenham, but did not find Campbell at home.[2]— M[oore] said he was probably at home but "nefariously dirty" & would not be seen in a poetical pickle.—I think you would like Moore, and I should have great pleasure in bringing you together.—Tomorrow I dine with Rogers & go to Coleridge's Lecture.[3] Coleridge has attacked the "Pleasures of Hope" & all other pleasures whatsoever.—Cawthorn rises in ye. world, he talks of getting a novel of Me. D'Arblay's for 1000 Gs!![4]—You & I must hide our diminished

[1] John Kemble played a number of Shakespearean parts with his sister, Mrs. Siddons.

[2] Thomas Campbell lived at Sydenham from 1804 to 1820.

[3] This would suggest that Byron heard at least two of Coleridge's lectures, for Crabb Robinson recorded in his diary seeing him there on January 20, 1812.

[4] See Dec. 8, 1811, to Harness, note 6.

heads.— —What are you doing?—Dallas is ill, Hodgson going crazy, (I had a woeful letter from him yesterday, full of Phantasmagoria) Bland is half killed by his faithless Trulla, & Scrope at Cambridge, full of pleasant Mirth.—Hodgson passes his Xmas at Newstead, so does Harness, *him* you dont know, he is a *Harrow* man, that will be *enough* for you.—Sir Wm. Ingilby[5] I have frequently seen lately & other returned voyagers.—Bold Webster is preparing Caudle for his spouse, & I am to be a Godfather.—Ward has left town, & Ld. Valentia gone with his son to Arley hall, is there not a *letter* or *two* wanting in the name of his place?—The Alfred does well, but our Cook has absconded in debt & be damned to him, which has thrown the managing Committee into Hysterics.—I presume ye. papers have told of ye. Riots in Notts, breaking of frames & heads, & out-maneouvreing the military.[6]—Joe Murray has been frightened by dreams & Ghosts, it is singular that he never superstitized for seventy six years before.—All my affairs are going on very badly, & I must rebel too if they don't amend—I shall return to London for the meeting of Parliament—Cambridge stands where it did, but all our acquaintances are gone or superannuated. I have now exhausted my Gossip, & will spare you for the present, believe me

yrs. ever most truly

Μπαιρῶν

[TO WILLIAM HARNESS]   8. *St. James's Street. Decr. 15th. 1811.*

My dearest William.—I wrote you an answer to your last, which on reflection pleases me as little as it probably has pleased yourself.—I shall not wait for your rejoinder, but proceed to tell you that I had just then been greeted with an epistle of Hodgson's full of his petty grievances, and this at the moment when (from circumstances it is not necessary to enter upon) I was bearing up against recollections, to which *his* imaginary sufferings are as a Scratch to a Cancer. These things combined put me out of humour with him & all mankind.—The latter part of my life has been a perpetual struggle against affections which embittered the earlier portion, & though I flatter myself I have in a great measure conquered them, yet there are moments (and this was one) when I am as foolish as formerly.—I never said so much

---

[5] See Nov. 17, 1811, to Hobhouse, note 1.

[6] The weavers of Nottingham were in revolt against the use of machines that put them out of work. Byron's first speech in the House of Lords (Feb. 27, 1812) was in defence of them against Tory measures of repression.

before, nor had I said this now if I did not suspect myself of having
been rather savage in my letter, & wish to inform you thus much of ye.
cause.—You know I am not one of your dolorous Gentlemen so now let
us laugh again. Yesterday I went with Moore to Sydenham to visit
your *"costive"* Campbell (as you call him) he was not visible.[1]—
M[oor]e Said he was probably within, but *"nefariously dirty"* & did not
like to be seen in so poetical a plight.—So, we jogged homewards
merrily enough.—Tomorrow, I dine with Rogers & am to hear
Coleridge,[2] who is a kind of rage at present.—Last night I saw Kemble
in Coriolanus,[3] he was glorious & exerted himself wonderfully.—By
Good luck I got an excellent place in ye. best part of ye. house which
was more than overflowing. Clare & Delawarr who were there on ye.
same speculation were less fortunate.—I saw them by accident, we
were not together. I wished for you to gratify your dramatic propensities in their fullest extent. Last week I saw an exhibition of a different
kind in a Mr. Coates at ye. Haymarket who performed Lothario in a
damned & damnable manner.—[4] Bland is ill of a Gonorrhea, a clerical
& creditable distemper, particularly to a despairing Corydon.—
Hodgson I should conjecture to have a Syphilis at least, if I may judge
by his querulous letter.—So much for these Sentimentalites who console themselves in the stews for the loss, the never to be recovered loss,
the despair, of the refined attachment of a brace of Drabs!—When I
compare myself with these men my Elders & my Betters, I really begin
to conceive myself a monument of prudence, a walking statue without
feeling or failing.—And yet the World in general hath given me a
proud preeminence over them in profligacy.—Yet I like the men, &
God knows, ought not to condemn their aberrations, but I own I feel
provoked when they dignify all this with ye. name of love, & deify
their common Strumpets.—Romantic attachments for things marketable at a dollar!—Their Ladies may be averaged at a token each, I
believe they have been bought cheaper.

Decr. 16th.—

I have just received your letter my dearest William, & feel your kindness very deeply.—The foregoing part of my letter written yesterday
will, I hope, account for the tone of my former though it cannot excuse
it. I *do* like to hear from you, more than *like*; next to seeing you I have

[1] See Dec. 15, 1811, to Hobhouse, note 2.
[2] See Dec. 6, 1811, to Harness; Dec. 8, 1811, to Hodgson; Dec. 8, 1811, to
Harness; and Dec. 15, 1811, to Hobhouse.
[3] See Dec. 15, 1811, to Hobhouse, note 1.
[4] See Dec. 9, 1811, to Hobhouse.

149

no greater satisfaction. But you have other duties & greater pleasures, & I should regret to take a moment from either.—Hodgson was to call today but I have not seen him.—The circumstance you mention at ye. close of your letter is another proof in favour of my opinion of mankind, such you will always find them, selfish & distrustful, I except none.—The cause of this is the state of Society, in the World every one is to steer for himself, it is useless, perhaps selfish to expect any thing from his neighbour; but I do not think we are born of this disposition, for you find friendship as a schoolboy, & Love enough before twenty.—I want to see Hodgson, he keeps me in town, where I dont wish to be at present, he is a good man but totally without conduct.—And now my dearest William I must wish you Goodmorrow, notwithstanding your Veto. I must still sign myself *"sincerely"* but ever most affectionately yrs.

BYRON

P.S.—I shall write the moment I have been able to fix the day.—

φίλτατε χαῖρε![5]

[TO JOHN CAM HOBHOUSE]   8. *St. James's Street. Decr. 17th. 1811*

My dear H.— Pray translate the drama. I shall print it without any translation whatever.—I thought you had sent me your copies of the MS. and meant to keep the originals for I am in need of one of the two.—Sr. Demetrius is posed with your queries, & I would not advise you to depend on him for correctness, your notes have been regularly put into his hands, & I will press him about an answer. You are devilish despondent, & I am not much better, but in a state of tolerable apathy as to the fate of my scribblings.—Other things affect me just at present. There is an omission in the answer of the *"πραγματευτης"*.[1] as to your verbal queries I can say nothing, Murray has the M.S. queries & all.— —I leave town tomorrow (19th) for Notts. where the weavers are in arms & breaking of frames,[2] Hodgson thinks *his frame* will be broken amongst the rest.—I hope not.—The moment

[5] A common Greek greeting, especially in letters; it means "Rejoice dearest [friend]".

[1] Πραγματευτης = Tradesman (the publisher).

[2] Because of slackness of trade a number of stocking-weavers had lost their opportunity to work. Discontent among the weavers in Nottingham was increased by the introduction of a wide frame which would make production more efficient and reduce the demand for their labour. In November, 1811, the weavers began to break into houses and destroy the frames. The rioting became worse when a thousand infantrymen were sent to Nottingham in November and December.

my Note has passed the press you shall have the original, Cawthorn sent you a proof yesterday, I read part of it, & like it much, so did Hodgson.—There was one Sentence we did not understand & I put as much in the margin.—I am perplexed with a thousand cares, all worldly, but shall return to town about the 10th. of January.—I am going to Notts to be sulky for a fortnight.— — —From the little my notes will say, you can take freely, & improve on them, as I shall be out first.— —I begin to be rather alarmed as the moment of publication approaches, but must man myself.—I assure you it is by no means smooth water.—If you come to England in February you will find me here very quiet & glad to see you.— —Sir Wm. Drummond has printed a profane book on the bible, but not published it for fear of Clerical hysterics.[3]—It is all Hebrew & Chaldaic & what not.—I must fold up this scrawl.

yrs. ever

B

[TO ROBERT CHARLES DALLAS]   *Dec. 17, 1811*

I send you an addition to the catalogue of authors, at the close of the vol. in a kind of appendix, we will have the MSS. and extracts printed, but I leave to you to determine whether the lighter pieces in rhyme had better be printed before or after the Romaic . . . you have omitted the last stanza but one, if you please we will have it inserted as I have directed the printer. In the song also it should be "Chimari" instead of "Chimora," . . . .

[TO JOHN CAM HOBHOUSE]   [*Newstead Abbey, Dec. 25, 1811*]

My dear H[obhous]e—After Hodgson's verse take a mouthful of my Prose, such as it is, we are here "and want but you, & want but you."—I am at present principally occupied with a fresh face & a very pretty one too, as H[odgson] will tell you, a Welsh Girl[1] whom I lately added to the bevy, and of whom I am tolerably enamoured for the present. But of this by the way, I shall most probably be cool enough before you return from Ireland.—I have written to you frequently from town & expect reprisals. Believe me

yrs. ever

B.

[3] See Dec. 8, 1811, to Hodgson, note 2.
[1] Susan Vaughan.

[TO SAMUEL ROGERS. (*a*)]   [*1812?*]

Dear Rogers—I am not in force to join you at dinner today—but I wish much to see you when convenient—as I have found the pre-correspondence between M[oore] & myself with copies of my answers which if you like to see you shall.—[1]

yrs. ever
B

[TO SAMUEL ROGERS. (*b*)]   [*1812?*]

Dear Rogers—Are you *sole* or going out this Evening—if so—you will tell me—if not and I should not really disturb you—I will come & sit with you for half an hour.—

ever yrs. most truly
B

[TO SAMUEL ROGERS. (*c*)]   *11 on ye. Clock.* [*1812?*]

Dear Rogers—I have called for you according to compact — & hope you have by this time digested your ducal dinner[.]

yrs ever
[$\mu\pi$ = B][1]

[TO JOHN HANSON]   [*1812?*]

Sir,—If you will advance the sum of three hundred & thirty odd pounds to Mrs. Massingberd tomorrow on my *note* for a few days till we can arrange for other security, I will accede to your proposal of [arranging?] the annuities at five pr. cent.— I remain

yr. obedt. Servt.
BYRON

---

1 Byron was eager for Rogers to see the correspondence between him and Moore to show that he had not played a cowardly part in the negotiations which avoided a duel between the two and led to a friendly meeting. He also offered to show the correspondence to Hobhouse.

1 Byron frequently used this monogram signature made of the two Greek letters that give the sound of "B" in that language.

J[anuar]y 4th. 1812

Sir,—If it is the same thing to Mr. Throll, I shall wish the bill to be drawn on *me*, which I will accept payable at 6. Chancery Lane; will you have ye. goodness to forward it to [me] through Mealey of ye. Hutt tomorrow. I remain

> yr most obedt. humle. Servt.
> BYRON

[TO JOHN HANSON] *Newstead Abbey. January 4th. 1812*

Dear Sir,—I have been in daily expectation of hearing from you.— Mrs. M[assingber]d tells me that Mr. Blake had written to you, you yourself also mentioned before I left town, that some person was in negociation on the subject of ye. Mortgage, and I am very anxious to know ye. result.—The Creditors are extremely pressing, I mean these exclusive of ye. annuities, & I trust the Scotch money is forthcoming.— I shall be in town on the 10th. but will order things to be ready for you and Mr. Neale when you arrive.—¹ If you are in town, pray answer this letter & believe me

> yrs very truly
> BYRON

[TO JOHN HANSON] *January. 14th. 1812*

Dear Sir,—Will you allow one of your clerks to accompany my foreign servant to the Alien Office to procure a license and explain that the reason of his not appearing before was my ignorance of the regulation.—There is another at Newstead they are both *Greeks*,¹ and subjects of a power at peace with Britain.—Pray let this be done, or we shall be in a scrape.—

> yrs. ever
> B

---

¹ Perhaps a Nottingham tradesman.
¹ Hanson was coming to Newstead on Estate business, to reappraise the farms and raise the rents. Mr. Neale may have been his clerk, or a surveyor.
¹ Byron's two Greek servants were Demetrius Zograffo and Andreas Saraci. Later in this year he sent them back to Greece at their request.

Lord Byron to the best of his knowledge and recollection in Decr. 1805 January 1806 applied to *King* in consequence of an advertisement in ye. papers who acquainted Ld. B. *that his minority* prevented all money transactions without the security of competent persons; *through Mr. K.* he became acquainted with a Mr. Dellvalley another of the tribes of Israel, and *subsequently* with a Mr. *Howard* of Golden Square.—After many delays during which Ld. B. had interviews with Howard, once he thinks in Golden Square, but more frequently in Piccadilly, Mrs. M[assingberd] agreed to become security jointly with her daughter.—Ld. B. knows Howard's person perfectly well, has not seen him subsequent to the transaction, but recollects Howard's mentioning to him that He Ld. B. was acting imprudently, stating that he made it a rule to advise young men against such proceedings.—Ld. B. recollects on *the day on which the money was paid* at Mrs. M[assingberd]'s house, *that he remained* in the next room, till the papers were signed, Mrs. M. having stated that the parties wished him to be kept out of sight during the business *and wished to avoid even mentioning his name.*—Mrs. M. deducted the interest for two years & a half and 100 £ for Howards papers.—The second annuity was *settled at Worthing.* Ld. B. thinks Mrs. M. has some letters of Ld. B's at that time written. —Ld. B. was not present.—In 1807. Ld. B. through the means of a Mr. Carpentiere or Carpenter then living at Dorant's hotel as manager of the York under Dorant, was made acquainted with Messrs Thomas & Riley *who declined advancing money on* Mrs. & Miss M[assingberd]'s security without the addition of another. —Mr. D[orant?] on *Ld. B's application* consented to lend his name. —The papers were signed by Mr. D[orant?] in *Ld. B's presence* at *Mr Thomas's* in Hanover Street, *Ld. B. received* [two words illegible] *paid for the papers after some dispute* on the exorbitancy of the charges, and lodged certain sums with Mr. D[orant?] for the payment of Interest.[1]—Afterwards *proceeded* to the Insurance office in

---

[1] The first loan was for £1,800. It was completed in February, 1806. The second loan for £1,500 went through in August, 1806, and the third in 1807. After all the deductions for interest and charges, Byron could not have retained more than two thirds of the amount. Another transaction with the money lenders is not mentioned here. On June 19, 1809, Byron wrote to Hanson: "I have been under the necessity of giving Thomas an annuity for his bond, and taking up further monies on annuity at seven years purchase to the *tune* of four hundred per annum altogether including T's bond."

the Strand.—Ld. B. has frequently seen Messrs Thomas & Riley before & since the transaction, at their house, at Brompton, & in St. James's Street.—They perfectly understood at the time, the annuities were taken up by him.—Recollects Riley pointed out *one of the parties* at Mr. T[homas]' saying with a smile, "this man wishes to see how his money is paid himself."—

[TO JOHN CAM HOBHOUSE]   *8. St. James's Street. January 16th. 1812*

My dear Hobhouse.—Swinburne prates of the *Dalmatians*,[1] Demo has not found a single parallel in our Albanian dialect nor understood a syllable of Mr. S[winburne]'s similarities except in the English he has lately acquired.—I have ordered Demo to write you the longest of letters.— —We are just returned from Newstead, half wild about these damned annuities, we are going to law, Hanson says they are quashable, so we have all to make affidavits.—Hodgson was with me at Newstead & a Mr. Harness of Harrow a mighty friend of mine, but I am sick of Harrow things.—I have gotten a very pretty Cambrian girl there of whom I grew foolishly fond,[2] & Lucy[3] & Bess became very greeneyed on the occasion.—Hodgson & myself longed for you and drank your health daily, & I always threatened Harness with *you* (when he misbehaved) as a particular enemy to fine feelings & *sentimental* friendships.—Hodgson is ruined, Harry Drury ruined, Butler ruined, and Harrow not rising.—Nottingham is in a sad state, London as usual.—*Do* leave Ireland, I fear your Catholics will find work for you, surely *you* wont fight against them.—Will you? I went down to the house & resumed my seat yesterday, I mean to try a speech but have not yet determined on my subject.—I have told Cawthorn the contents of your letter, at least that part which regards the man of paper.—As for your compliments in the preface, I thank you, I have gotten a tribute to you in my notes, already printed.—All this is laughable, but never mind they can only call us Noodle &

1 Henry Swinburne in his *Travels in the Two Sicilies*, 1783 (vol. I, pp. 351–352) listed forty common English words which he said had been incorporated in the language of the Albanians settled in Calabria. On the basis of what Demetrius Zograffo, Byron's Albanian servant, told him, Hobhouse took exception to this statement in an appendix on the Albanian language in his *Journey through Albania* (p. 1125).

2 Her name was Susan Vaughan. See Jan. 21, 1812, to Rushton; [Jan. 28, 1812], to Hodgson; and Jan. 28, 1812, to Susan Vaughan.

3 Lucy was Byron's favourite before he went abroad. See Jan. 17, 1809, to Hanson and Feb. 4, 1809, to Hanson.

Doodle as they called Bland & Hodgson.— —I have been reviewing in the Monthly,[4] Galt is in England, has published, & is to send me his book.—I think the Monthly & Quarterly will be kind to you & very likely the Edin[burgh].—For myself I am perplexed with weightier cares than Authorship.—My affairs are disordered in no small degree, but as those of every body else seem no better, one has the consolation of being embarrassed in very good company.—I am dunning in Scotland for my mother's money, & it has not yet been paid, I have been into Lancashire to no great purpose, but Newstead is to be doubled in rent directly.— —If these annuities are set aside & H[anson] has little doubt, it will be a great relief.—In the mean time I am dear H.

yrs ever most affectly
B.—

[TO EDWARD DANIEL CLARKE]   *8 St. James's Street*
January 19th. 1812

My dear Sir,—Your very kind letter, which I received at Newstead, deserved a less tardy acknowledgment, but I have lately been so much occupied with business of no very pleasing nature, that I have been unable to offer those thanks which I now most sincerely beg you to accept.— —Attribute my silence to anything but disrespect, or the want of a due sense of the obligation conferred upon me.—I am no stranger to the character of Lord Aberdeen, and feel highly flattered by what his lordship has been pleased to say on a very unworthy subject.—But before he does me the honour of proposing my name in the Athenian club,[1] it is proper that I should mention to you a circumstance that might perhaps render it unpleasant.—In the notes to a thing of mine now passing through the press, there is some notice taken of an agent of Lord A[berdeen]'s in the Levant, *Grossius* by name, & a few remarks on Ld. Elgin, Lusieri &c. & their pursuits, which may render the writer not very acceptable to a zealous Anti-

[4] Byron's reviews in *The Monthly Review* included *Poems*, by W. R. Spencer (Vol. 67, 1812, pp. 54–60); and *Neglected Genius*, by W. H. Ireland (Vol. 70, 1813, pp. 203–205).

[1] George Hamilton Gordon, Earl of Aberdeen, was a grandson of the man who had bought Mrs. Byron's estate of Gight. On his return from a tour of Greece (1801–1803), he founded the Athenian Society, and later became President of the Society of Antiquaries. Byron had mentioned him as one of the pilferers of Greece in *Childe Harold* (in a suppressed stanza following stanza 13 of Canto II). Byron did not become a member of the Athenian Society.

quarian.—Ld. A's [name] is not mentioned or alluded to in any manner personally disrespectful, but Ld. Elgin is spoken of according to the writer's decided opinion of *him* & *his.*—Pray excuse all this tirade about *me* & *mine*, I cannot here avoid the most noxious egotism; but I wish to act fairly & openly, & not creep into the society of men who may regret my admission.—Still less do I wish to involve one for whom I entertain so high a respect as Dr. Clarke in my petty scribbling squabbles.—It would fall upon you,—"Dr. C[larke] has done this! *he* has brought amongst us a fellow who has no respect for cameos, who does not know a Gorgon from a Grace, or the Parthenon from the Pantheon!["]—Truth is, I am sadly deficient in gusto, and have little of the antique spirit, except a wish to immolate Ld. Elgin to Minerva & Nemesis. But should these omissions & offences be got over, I should feel truly happy in being one of the Elect.—At all events your kind endeavours have laid me under great obligations.—I have further to thank you for your poetical notice of my poor friend Matthews, a circumstance no less gratifying to Hodgson (who was with me) on account of the mention made of Whittington.—²We were both delighted.—Believe me to be, my dear Sir,

your much obliged & very sincere & obedt. Servt.

BYRON

[TO ROBERT RUSHTON]   *8 St. James's Street January 21st. 1812*

Though I have no objection to your refusal to carry *letters* to Mealey's,¹ you will take care that the letters are taken by *Spero*² at the proper time.—I have also to observe that Susan³ is to be treated with civility, and not *insulted* by any person over whom I have the smallest controul, or indeed by anyone whatever, while I have the power to protect her.—I am truly sorry to have any subject of complaint against *you*, I have too good an opinion of you to think I shall have occasion to repeat it, after the care I have taken of you, and my favourable intentions in your behalf.—I see no occasion for any communication whatever between *you* & the *women*, & wish you to occupy yourself in preparing for the situation in which you will be placed.—If a common sense of decency cannot prevent you from conducting yourself towards them with rudeness, I should at least hope that your *own interest.* &

² Unidentified.
¹ Owen Mealey, Newstead steward, who lived in the Hut, or gatehouse.
² Spiro Saraci, one of Byron's Greek servants.
³ Susan Vaughan, the Welsh maid, with whom Byron was then enamoured.

regard for a Master who has *never* treated you with unkindness, will have some weight.—

yrs. &c.

BYRON

P.S.—I wish you to attend to your Arithmetic, to occupy yourself in surveying, measuring, and making yourself acquainted with every particular relative to the *land* of Newstead; and you will *write* to me *one letter every week*, that I may know how you go on.—

[TO ROBERT RUSHTON]   *8, St. James's Street, January 25, 1812*

Your refusal to carry the letter was not a subject of remonstrance: it was not a part of your business; but the language you used to the girl was (as *she* stated it) highly improper.

You say, that you also have something to complain of; then state it to me immediately; it would be very unfair, and very contrary to my disposition, not to hear both sides of the question.

If any thing has passed between you *before* or since my last visit to Newstead, do not be afraid to mention it. I am sure *you* would not deceive me, though *she* would. Whatever it is, *you* shall be forgiven. I have not been without some suspicions on the subject, and am certain that, at your time of life, the blame could not attach to you. You will not *consult* any one as to your answer, but write to me immediately. I shall be more ready to hear what you have to advance, as I do not remember ever to have heard a word from you before *against* any human being, which convinces me you would not maliciously assert an untruth. There is not any one who can do the least injury to you, while you conduct yourself properly. I shall expect your answer immediately.

Yours, etc.,

BYRON

[TO JOHN GALT]   *8 St. James's Street Jy 27th. 1812*

Dear Sir—On *friday* next a division is expected in the house, & I must be present during the question.[1]— Will you excuse then my postponing the pleasure of seeing you till *Sunday?* or any other day on

---

[1] This was written just as Byron was beginning to take an active interest in Parliamentary affairs, and was thinking about his maiden speech, though he had not yet determined the topic.

which you will honour me with your company? Pray favour me with an answer, whether Sunday will suit you, or on what other day you will meet me at the St. Albans.— Believe me

> your obliged & very sincere St.
>
> BYRON

[TO FRANCIS HODGSON]   [*January 28, 1812.*]

. . . I do not blame her, but my own vanity in fancying that such a thing as I am could ever be beloved. . . .[1]

[TO SUSAN VAUGHAN]   *8. St. James's Street January 28th. 1812*

I write to bid you farewell, not to reproach you.—The enclosed papers, *one* in *your own handwriting* will explain every thing.—I will not deny that I have been attached to you, & I am now heartily ashamed of my weakness. —You may also enjoy the satisfaction of having deceived me most completely, & rendered me for the present sufficiently wretched.—From the first I told you that the continuance of our connection depended on your own conduct.— —All is over.—I have little to condemn on my own part, but credulity; you threw yourself in my way, I received you, loved you, till you have become worthless, & now I part from you with some regret, & without resentment.— —I wish you well, do not forget that your own misconduct has bereaved you of a friend, of whom nothing else could have deprived you.—Do not attempt explanation, it is useless, I am *determined*, you cannot deny your handwriting; return to your relations, you shall be furnished with the means, but *him*, who now addresses you for the last time, you will never see again.—

> BYRON

God bless you!

[TO THOMAS MOORE]   *January 29th, 1812*

My dear Moore,—I wish very much I could have seen you; I am in a state of ludicrous tribulation.

* * * * * * * * * * * * * *

---

[1] This sentence (the only one quoted from the letter in the Hodgson *Memoir*) refers to Susan Vaughan.

Why do you say that I dislike your poesy? I have expressed no such opinion, either in *print* or elsewhere. In scribbling myself, it was necessary for me to find fault, and I fixed upon the trite charge of immorality,[1] because I could discover no other, and was so perfectly qualified, in the innocence of my heart, to "pluck that mote from my neighbour's eye."

I feel very, very much obliged by your approbation; but, at *this moment*, praise, even *your* praise, passes by me like "the idle wind." I meant and mean to send you a copy the moment of publication; but now, I can think of nothing but damned, deceitful,—delightful woman, as Mr. Liston says in the Knight of Snowdon.[2]

Believe me, my dear Moore, ever yours, most affectionately,

BYRON

[TO FRANCIS HODGSON]   *8, St. James's Street, Feb. 1, 1812*

My dear Hodgson,—. . . I could not have withstood the "silent eloquence of grief," but the rage of a Welsh woman makes me laugh, and cures me at once. . . .[1]

I am rather unwell with a vile cold, caught in the House of Lords last night. Lord Sligo and myself, being tired, *paired off*, being of opposite sides, so that nothing was gained or lost by *our* votes. I did not speak: but I might as well, for nothing could have been inferior to the Duke of Devonshire, Marquis of Downshire, and the Earl of Fitzwilliam. The Catholic Question comes on this month, and perhaps I may then commence. I must "screw my courage to the sticking place," and we'll *not* fail.

Yours ever,

B.

[TO SAMUEL ROGERS]   *February 4th. 1812*

My dear Sir,—With my best acknowledgements to Lord Holland, I have to offer my perfect concurrence in the propriety of ye. question previously to be put to Ministers.—If their answer is in ye. negative, I shall with his Lordship's approbation, give notice of a motion for a

[1] See *English Bards and Scotch Reviewers*, lines 283–94.

[2] See Jan. 28, 1812, to Susan Vaughan. Macleod, played by Liston, in Thomas Morton's "The Knight of Snowdon" (Act III, sc. 3) exclaimed: "Oh woman! woman! deceitful, damnable,—(*changing into a half smile*) delightful woman!"

[1] This first sentence is quoted in the Sotheby catalogue, March 2, 1885.

committee of enquiry.—I would also gladly avail myself of his most able advice, & any information in documents with which he might be pleased to entrust me, to bear me out in the statement of facts it may be necessary to submit to the house.[1]—From all that fell under my own observation during my Xmas visit to Newstead, I feel convinced that if *conciliatory* measures are not very soon adopted, the most unhappy consequences may be apprehended.—Nightly outrage & daily depredation are already at their height, & not only the masters of frames who are obnoxious on account of their occupation, but persons in no degree connected with the malcontents or their oppressors, are liable to insult & pillage.— —I am very much obliged to you for the trouble you have taken on my account, and beg you to believe me ever your obliged

& sincere f[rien]d
BYRON

[TO JOHN CAM HOBHOUSE]   8. *St. James's Street February 10th. 1812*

Dear Hobhouse,—I have just recovered from an attack of the *Stone* in the *kidney*, an agreeable disease which promises to be periodically permanent. The very unpromising state of my worldly affairs compels me to recur to a subject upon which I have not often touched & which I shall now dispatch as quick as possible.—In case of any accident befalling yourself or me, you are aware that I possess no *document note* or *memorial* of the money transactions between us beyond the mention of the sum in one or two of your letters, & I should, if you have no particular objection, like to have your note of hand for the amount.[1]—Of this you will hardly suspect that I shall take any advantage, I wish it merely as an acknowledgement in case of accidents. —Now to change the theme.—Your M.S.S. are found.—I have been most painfully ill, cupped on the loins, glystered, purged & vomited., secundum artem, & am condemned to the strictest regimen, & the most durable of disorders for the residue of my life.—I have been

---

[1] Byron was already thinking of making his maiden speech in the House of Lords against repressive measures then being discussed in Parliament to put down the Nottingham frame-breakers. He sought Lord Holland's advice because he was leader of the Whig Opposition, and because he, as Recorder of Nottingham, had a special interest and special knowledge of the situation.

[1] On March 17, 1812, Hobhouse's father repaid Byron the money advanced to his son for his trip abroad. When they parted, Hobhouse owed Byron £818 3s. 4d. The sum repaid, with accrued interest added, was £1,323.

voting for the Catholics.—I am about to sell off my furniture &c. at Newstead.—I have almost arranged ye. annuity business with Scrope Davies,[2] who has behaved very well indeed, much better than he has been treated, though that was not my fault.—I have dismissed my Seraglio for squabbles & infidelities.— Now for you.—I regret that your work has met with so many obstructions I have told Demo to write 150 times, but he either dont or wont understand me, if you were on the spot, all this could be easily arranged, as it is, I see no remedy. —Your letters have all been put into his hands, God knows I wish you every success, that a man in great bodily pain & mental uneasiness can wish any thing of any body's, I assure you I have lately suffered very severely from kidneys within & Creditors without, my two great *bodily* comforters are Wm. Bankes & Mrs. Hanson, one tells me his Grandfather died of the *Stone*, & the other that her father was killed by the *Gravel!*—For my part I am *kilt* (you will understand that phrase by this time) by what a methodist would call a congregation, a bookseller a compilation, and a quack a complication of disorders.

yrs ever
B.

[TO JOHN COWELL[1]] *8, St. James's-street, February 12th, 1812*

My dear John,—You have probably long ago forgotten the writer of these lines, who would, perhaps, be unable to recognize *yourself*, from the difference which must naturally have taken place in your stature and appearance since he saw you last. I have been rambling through Portugal, Spain, Greece, &c. &c. for some years, and have found so many changes on my return, that it would be very unfair not to expect that you should have had your share of alteration and improvement with the rest. I write to request a favour of you: a little boy of eleven years, the son of Mr * * [Hanson], my particular friend, is about to become an Etonian, and I should esteem any act of protection or kindness to him an obligation to myself; let me beg of you then to take some little notice of him at first, till he is able to shift for himself.

I was happy to hear a very favourable account of you from a schoolfellow a few weeks ago, and should be glad to learn that your family

[2] See May 15, 1811, to Hobhouse, note 1.

[1] Byron had met Cowell at Brighton in 1808, had asked Henry Drury's brother, a master at Eton, to look after him, and saw him again at Hastings in 1814. For his account of his relations with Byron, see Moore, *Memoir*, V, 302–303.

are as well as I wish them to be. I presume you are in the upper school;—as[2] an *Etonian*, you will look down upon a *Harrow* man, but I never even in my boyish days disputed your superiority, which I once experienced in a Cricket match where I had the honour of making one of eleven, who were beaten to their hearts' content by your College in *one Innings*.—

Believe me to be with great truth very faithfully yrs

BYRON

[TO FRANCIS HODGSON]   *8, St. James's Street, February 16, 1812*

Dear Hodgson,—I send you a proof. Last week I was very ill and confined to bed with stone in the kidney, but I am now quite recovered. The women are gone to their relatives, after many attempts to explain what was already too clear. If the stone had got into my heart instead of my kidneys, it would have been all the better. However, I have quite recovered *that* also, and only wonder at my folly in excepting my own strumpets from the general corruption,—albeit a two months' weakness is better than ten years. I have one request to make, which is, never to mention a woman again in any letter to me, or even allude to the existence of the sex. I won't even read a word of the feminine gender;—it must all be *propria quae maribus*.

In the spring of 1813 I shall leave England for ever. Every thing in my affairs tends to this, and my inclinations and health do not discourage it. Neither my habits nor constitution are improved by your customs or your climate. I shall find employment in making myself a good Oriental scholar. I shall retain a mansion in one of the fairest islands, and retrace, at intervals, the most interesting portions of the East. In the mean time, I am adjusting my concerns, which will (when arranged) leave me with wealth sufficient even for home, but enough for a principality in Turkey. At present they are involved, but I hope, by taking some necessary but unpleasant steps, to clear every thing. Hobhouse is expected daily in London: we shall be very glad to see him; and, perhaps, you will come up and "drink deep ere he depart," if not, "Mahomet must come to the mountain;"—but Cambridge will bring sad recollections to him, and worse to me, though for very different reasons. I believe the only human being, that ever loved me in truth and entirely, was of, or belonging to, Cambridge, and, in that,

---

[2] The facsimile starts with this word and continues to the end of the letter.

no change can now take place. There is one consolation in death—where he sets his seal, the impression can neither be melted nor broken, but endureth for ever.[1]

Yours always,
B.

P.S.—I almost rejoice when one I love dies young, for I could never bear to see them old or altered.

[TO FRANCIS HODGSON]   *London, February 21, 1812*

My dear Hodgson,—There is a book entituled "Galt, his Travels in ye Archipelago,"[1] daintily printed by Cadell and Davies, ye which I could desiderate might be criticised by you, inasmuch as ye author is a well-respected esquire of mine acquaintance, but I fear will meet with little mercy as a writer, unless a friend passeth judgment. Truth to say, ye boke is ye boke of a cock-brained man, and is full of devices crude and conceitede, but peradventure for my sake this grace may be vouchsafed unto him. Review him myself I can not, will not, and if you are likewise hard of heart, woe unto ye boke, ye which is a comely quarto.

Now then! I have no objection to review if it pleases Griffiths[2] to send books, or rather *you*, for you know the sort of things I like to play with. You will find what I say very serious as to my intentions. I have every reason to induce me to return to Ionia. Believe me,

Yours always,
B.

[TO JOHN COWELL]   *8 St. James's Street F[ebruar]y 21, 1812*

My dear John,—I will just trouble you with my thanks for your readiness to patronize the son of my friend Mr. Hanson.[1]—Of the boy himself I know little or nothing but you will soon discover his disposition & treat him accordingly, he will hardly be sent before Easter.

---

[1] Byron expressed this sentiment about Edleston in one of the Thyrza poems: "And thou art dead, as young and fair."

[1] John Galt published in 1812 his *Voyages and Travels in the Years 1809, 1810, and 1811.* He had met Byron on the voyage from Gibraltar to Malta and had seen him again in Athens. Hodgson reviewed frequently for the *Monthly Review.*

[2] George Edward Griffiths was owner and publisher of the *Monthly Review.*

[1] See Feb. 12, 1812, to Cowell, note 1.

—I need not say that I shall be very glad to see you here or elsewhere, & when you have nothing better to do, to hear from you.—Believe me

yrs ever
BYRON

[TO LORD HOLLAND]   *8 St. James's Street February 25th. 1812*

My Lord,—With my best thanks I have the honour to return the Notts letter to your Lordship.—I have read it with attention, but do not think I shall venture to avail myself of it's contents, as my view of the question differs in some measure from Mr. Coldham's.—I hope I do not wrong him, but *his* objections to ye. bill appear to me to be founded on certain apprehensions that he & his coadjutors might be mistaken for the *"original advisers"* (to quote him) of the measure.— —For my own part, I consider the manufacturers[1] as a much injured body of men sacrificed to ye. views of certain individuals who have enriched themselves by those practices which have deprived the frame workers of employment.—For instance;—by the adoption of a certain kind of frame 1 man performs ye. work of 7—6 are thus thrown out of business.—But it is to be observed that ye. work thus done is far inferior in quality, hardly marketable at home, & hurried over with a view to exportation.—Surely, my Lord, however we may rejoice in any improvement in ye. arts which may be beneficial to mankind; we must not allow mankind to be sacrificed to improvements in Mechanism. The maintenance & well doing of ye. industrious poor is an object of greater consequence to ye. community than ye. enrichment of a few monopolists by any improvement in ye. implements of trade, which deprives ye workman of his bread, & renders ye. labourer "unworthy of his hire."—My own motive for opposing ye. bill is founded on it's palpable injustice, & it's certain inefficacy.—[2] —I have seen the state of these miserable men, & it is a disgrace to a civilized country.—Their excesses may be condemned, but cannot be subject of wonder.— The effect of ye. present bill would be to drive them into actual rebellion.—The few words I shall venture to offer on Thursday will be founded upon these opinions formed from my own observations on ye. spot.—By previous enquiry I am convinced these men would have been restored to employment & ye. county to tranquillity.—It is perhaps not yet too late & is surely worth the trial. It can never be too late to

[1] *i.e.* factory workers.
[2] This is the line of argument in Byron's maiden speech in the House of Lords on February 27, 1812, against the Bill making frame-breaking a capital offence.

employ force in such circumstances.— —I believe your Lordship does not coincide with me entirely on this subject, & most cheerfully & sincerely shall I submit to your superior judgment & experience, & take some other line of argument against ye. bill, or be silent altogether, should you deem it more adviseable.— —Condemning, as every one must condemn the conduct of these wretches, I believe in ye. existence of grievances which call rather for pity than punishment.— —I have ye honour to be with great respect, my Lord, yr. Lordship's

most obedt. & obliged Servt.

BYRON

P.S.—I am a little apprehensive that your Lordship will think me too lenient towards these men, & *half* a *framebreaker myself*.

[TO JOHN HANSON]   F[ebruar]y 28th. 1812

Dear Sir,—In the report of my speech (which by the bye is given very incorrectly) in the M[orning] *Herald, Day,* & B[ritis]h *Press,* they state that I mentioned *Bristol*—a place I never saw in my life & know nothing of whatever, nor *mentioned* at all last night.— —Will you be good enough to send to these *papers immediately* & have the mistake corrected, or I shall get into a scrape with the Bristol people.— I am yrs. very truly

B.

[TO JAMES PERRY[1]]   8, *St. James's Street, Sunday, March 1st, 1812*

Sir,—I take the liberty of sending an alteration of the two last lines of Stanza 2d which I wish to run as follows,

"Gibbets on Sherwood will *heighten* the Scenery
Showing how Commerce, *how* Liberty thrives!"[2]

I wish you could insert it tomorrow for a particular reason; but I feel much obliged by your inserting it at all. Of course, do *not* put *my name* to the thing. Believe me,

Your obliged and very obedt. Servt.,

BYRON

[1] Editor of the *Morning Chronicle.*

[2] Byron had sent Perry "An Ode to the Framers of the Frame Bill", which was saucy and personal beyond anything he had said in his speech. It expressed the hope that "the frames of the fools may be first to be *broken,/* Who, when asked for a *remedy,* sent down a *rope."* It was published anonymously in the *Morning Chronicle* on March 2, 1812.

[TO JOHN HANSON]   *2d. March 1812*

Pray Send the bearers Demetrius & Spero for their passports to the
Alien office that they may leave the country[1]

                                                              yrs.
                                                              B.

[TO FRANCIS HODGSON]   *8. St. James's Street March 5th. 1812*

My dear Hodgson,—*We* are not answerable for reports of speeches
in the papers, they are always given incorrectly, & on this occasion
more so than usual from the Debate in the Com[mon]s on the same
night.—The M[ornin]g P[o]st should have said 18 *years.*—However
you will find the speech as spoken in the Parliamentary Register,
when it comes out.—Lds. Holland & Grenville,[1] particularly the
latter paid some high compts. in the course of their speeches as you
may have seen in the papers, & Ld. Eldon & Harrowby[2] answered
me.— —I have had many marvelous eulogies repeated to me since in
person & by proxy from divers persons *ministerial—yea ministerial*! as
well as oppositionists, of them I shall only mention Sir F. Burdetts.—
He says it is the best speech by a *Lord* since the "Lord knows when"
probably from a fellow feeling in ye. sentiments.—Ld. H[olland] tells
me I shall beat them all if I persevere,[3] & Ld. G[renville] remarked
that the construction of some of my periods are very like *Burke's*!!—
And so much for vanity.— —I spoke very violent sentences with a
sort of modest impudence, abused every thing & every body, & put
the Ld. Chancellor very much out of humour, & if I may believe what I
hear, have not lost any character by the experiment.—As to my
delivery, loud & fluent enough, perhaps a little theatrical.— —I
could not recognize myself or any one else in the Newspapers.— —I
hire myself unto Griffiths,[4] & my poem comes out on Saturday.[5]
—Hobhouse is here, I shall tell him to write.—My Stone is gone for

---

[1] Demetrius Zograffo and Spiro Saraci were Byron's Greek servants.

[1] William Wyndham, Baron Grenville (1759–1834), a leader with Lord Grey
and Lord Holland of the Moderate Whigs.

[2] Dudley Ryder, first Earl of Harrowby (1762–1847), was President of the
Council. He was a Tory supporter of the Bill.

[3] Lord Holland was glad to support a new Opposition member of the House, but
he was more candid in his *Memoirs*: "His [Byron's] speech was full of fancy, wit,
and invective, but not exempt from affectation nor well reasoned, nor at all suited
to our common notions of Parliamentary eloquence." (Holland, *Memoirs*, p. 123.)

[4] Griffiths was owner and publisher of the *Monthly Review* to which Hodgson
contributed.

[5] *Childe Harold*, Cantos I and II, was advertised for publication on March 1, but
did not actually reach the public until March 10, 1812.

the present, but I fear is part of my habit.— —We *all* talk of a visit to Cambridge.

yrs. ever

B.

[TO LORD HOLLAND]   *St. James's-street, March 5th, 1812*

My Lord,—May I request your lordship to accept a copy of the thing which accompanies this note?[1] You have already so fully proved the truth of the first line of Pope's couplet,

"Forgiveness to the injured doth belong,"[2]

that I long for an opportunity to give the lie to the verse that follows. If I were not perfectly convinced that any thing I may have formerly uttered in the boyish rashness of my misplaced resentment had made as little impression as it deserved to make, I should hardly have the confidence—perhaps your lordship may give it a stronger and more appropriate appellation—to send you a quarto of the same scribbler. But your lordship, I am sorry to observe to-day, is troubled with the gout: if my book can produce a *laugh* against itself or the author, it will be of some service. If it can set you to *sleep*, the benefit will be yet greater; and as some facetious personage observed half a century ago, that "poetry is a mere drug," I offer you mine as a humble assistant to the "eau médecinale." I trust you will forgive this and all my other buffooneries, and believe me to be, with great respect,

Your lordship's obliged and sincere servant,

BYRON

[TO COL. GREVILLE [SENT TO THOMAS MOORE]]   [*March, 1812?*]

With regard to the passage on Mr. Way's loss no unfair play was hinted at as may be seen by referring to the book[1] & it is expressly added that the *Managers were ignorant* of that transaction.—Of the prevalence of play at the Argyle it cannot be denied that there were

---

[1] *Childe Harold's Pilgrimage*, Cantos I and II.

[2] The quotation is from Dryden, not Pope. The next line reads: "But they ne'er pardon, who have done the wrong." (Dryden, *Conquest of Grenada*, Part II, Act 1, Scene 2.) Byron referred to the wrong he had done Lord Holland in his accusations in *English Bards and Scotch Reviewers*, where he called the *Edinburgh* reviewers "Holland's hirelings" (line 521).

[1] In *English Bards and Scotch Reviewers* Byron referred to Colonel Greville, Manager of the Argyle Institution, as "Our arbiter of pleasure and of play!"(See lines 638–667). The matter was amicably settled by Moore and G. F. Leckie, who acted for Byron and Greville. (Moore, I, 349.)

billiards & *dice* Ld. B. has been a *witness* to the use of both in the Argyle Rooms.—These it is presumed come under the denomination of play.—If play be allowed the President of the institution can hardly complain of being termed the "Arbiter of play" or what becomes of his authority?—Ld. B. has no personal enmity to Col. Greville[;] a *public* institution to which he himself was a subscriber, he considered himself to have a right to notice *publicly*,—Of that Institution Col. G[reville] was the avowed director it is too late to enter into the discussion of its merits or demerits.—Ld. B. must leave the discussion of the reparation for the real or supposed injury to Col. G[reville]'s friend & Mr. Moore the friend of Ld. B. begging them to recollect that while they consider Col. G[reville]'s honour Ld. B. must also maintain his own.—If the business can be settled amicably Ld. B. will do as much as can & ought to be done by a man of honour towards conciliation, if not he must satisfy Col. G[reville] in the manner most conducive to his further wishes.—

[TO EDWARD DANIEL CLARKE]   *March 8th. 1812*

Dear Sir—I beg your acceptance of the volume which accompanies this note[1]—It will be delivered by my friend Mr. Davies. Believe me

Yr. obliged & faithful St.

BYRON

[TO ROBERT CHARLES DALLAS]   [*March 11? 1812*]

I wish you to answer me *sincerely* if the enclosed letter is not from *one* of *your family?*

Yours,

B.

[TO THOMAS MOORE]   *March 25th, 1812*

Know all men by these presents, that you, Thomas Moore, stand indicted—no—invited, by special and particular solicitation, to Lady C[aroline] L * *'s [Lamb's][1] to-morrow even, at half-past nine

---

[1] Byron sent E. D. Clarke a copy of his newly published *Childe Harold*. Clarke wrote that he "was never so much affected by any poem". (*LJ*, II, 130n.)

[1] Lady Caroline Lamb had read an early copy of *Childe Harold* and wished to meet the author. She wrote him an anonymous letter, but waited for a propitious moment when other women were not surrounding him to be introduced. See the biographical sketch in the Appendix.

o'clock, where you will meet with a civil reception and decent entertainment. Pray, come—I was so examined after you this morning, that I entreat you to answer in person.

Believe me, &c.

[TO THOMAS MOORE]   *Friday Noon [April 3, 1812?]*

My dear Moore—I should have answered your note but I expected to meet you at Ly. Glenbervies.[1]—Ye. Correspondents have done very well but I wonder you should think it necessary to talk of apologies to me as if I were an elderly Lady instead of a middle aged gentleman. —I was glad to hear that your wound was trifling & apprehensions groundless. Can you come & visit a man confined to the house by a dose of *Salts*, I *dare* not venture to you.—

yrs. ever affectly
B.

[TO LADY CAROLINE LAMB]   *Sy. Even [April, 1812?]*

I never supposed you artful, we are *all* selfish, nature did that for us, but even when you attempt deceit occasionally, you cannot maintain it, which is all the better, want of success will curb the tendency.— — Every word you utter, every line you write proves you to be either *sincere* or a *fool*, now as I know you are not the one I must believe you the other. I never knew a woman with greater or more pleasing talents, *general* as in a woman they should be, something of every thing, & too much of nothing, but these are unfortunately coupled with a total want of common conduct.—For instance the *note* to your *page*, do you suppose I delivered it? or did you mean that I should? I did not of course.—Then your heart—my poor Caro, what a little volcano! that pours *lava* through your veins, & yet I cannot wish it a bit colder, to make a *marble slab* of, as you sometimes see (to understand my foolish metaphor) brought in vases tables &c. from Vesuvius when hardened after an eruption.—To drop my detestable tropes & figures you know I have always thought you the cleverest most agree-

1 Sylvester Douglas (1743–1823), created in 1800 Baron Glenbervie, married in 1789 Catherine, eldest daughter of Lord North, Prime Minister under George III. Mary Berry, the friend and editor of Horace Walpole, mentioned in her journal having met Byron at Lord Glenbervie's on Thursday, April 2, 1812. (*Journal and Correspondence of Miss Berry*, II, 496–97.)

able, absurd, amiable, perplexing, dangerous fascinating little being that lives now or ought to have lived 2000 years ago.— —I wont talk to you of beauty, I am no judge, but our *beauties* cease to be so when near you, and therefore you have either some or something better. And now, Caro, this nonsense is the first & last compliment (if it be such) I ever paid you, you have often reproached me as wanting in that respect, but *others* will make up the deficiency.—Come to Ly. Grey's,[1] at least do not let me keep you away.—All that you so often *say*, I *feel*, can more be said or felt?— —This same prudence is tiresome enough but one *must* maintain it, or what can we do to be saved?—Keep to it.—
[written on cover]
If you write at all, write as usual—but do as you please, only as I never see you — Basta!

[TO LADY MELBOURNE. (*a*)]   [*April–July, 1812?*]

Dear Ly. M.—I have just written to you a long note—& will wait on you at 1/2 past nine exactly

                                                            ever yrs.—

[TO LADY MELBOURNE. (*b*)]   *Friday* [*April–July, 1812?*]

Dear Lady Melbourne—At two or perhaps a little later I shall have the honour of waiting upon you, as indeed I would have done before had I imagined that you wished it. Believe me respectfully

                                                            yr. obliged Servt.
                                                            BYRON.—

[TO EDWARD DANIEL CLARKE]   8. *St. James's Street*
                                                            April 5th. 1812

My dear Sir,—I cannot express to you how much I feel gratified by your approbation & that of your friend Mr. Mathias.[1] I can only beg

---

[1] Wife of the second Earl Grey, one of the leading Whig statesmen.
[1] T. J. Mathias, author of *Pursuits of Literature* and *The Shade of Alexander Pope.* Clarke wrote to Byron that he had said to Mathias: "Surely Lord Byron, at his time of life, cannot have experienced such keen anguish as those exquisite allusions to what older men *may* have felt seem to denote!" And Mathias replied: "*I fear he has—he could not else have written such a poem.*" (*LJ,* II, 130n.)

you to accept my warmest acknowledgements.—The extract from your letter I shall certainly reduce into a note & with your leave state my authority.[2]—Whatever coincidence of opinion comes from such a quarter will add tenfold value to my observations in the *public* mind & in my own.—I never read the passage in Petrarca to which you allude, but I am not sorry for the involuntary plagiarism, as I ought to be; but rather rejoice that a single drop of Petrarch's vial should have fallen by accident into mine.—I could not thank you the other day as I should have done, & have not at this moment time to thank you enough, but I beg that you will believe me

ever yr. obliged & affecte. Servt.

BYRON

[TO WILLIAM BANKES (*a*)]   [*April, 1812?*]

My dear Bankes,—My eagerness to come to an explanation has, I trust, convinced you that whatever my unlucky manner might inadvertantly be, the change was as unintentional as (if intended) it would have been ungrateful. I really was not aware that, while we were together, I had evinced such caprices; that we were not so much in each other's company as I could have wished, I well know, but I think so *acute* an *observer* as yourself must have perceived enough to *explain this*, without supposing any slight to one in whose society I have pride and pleasure. Recollect that I do not allude here to "extended" or "extending" acquaintances, but to circumstances you will understand, I think, on a little reflection.

And now, my dear Bankes, do not distress me by supposing that I can think of you, or you of me, otherwise than I trust we have long thought. You told me not long ago that my temper was improved, and I should be sorry that opinion should be revoked. Believe me, your friendship is of more account to me than all those absurd vanities in which, I fear, you conceive me to take too much interest. I have never disputed your superiority, or doubted (seriously) your good will, and

[2] The extract was this: "When the last of the Metopes was taken from the Parthenon, and in moving it, great part of the superstructure with one of the triglyphs, was thrown down by the workmen whom Lord Elgin employed, the Disdar, who beheld the mischief done to the building, took his pipe out of his mouth, dropped a tear, and, in a supplicating tone of voice, said to Lusieri [Elgin's agent]—τελος![‘The end’]'' Byron quoted this in a note to subsequent editions of *Childe Harold*. (*Poetry*, II, 172.)

no one shall ever "make mischief between us" without the sincere regret on the part of your ever affectionate, &c.

P.S.—I shall see you, I hope, at Lady Jersey's.[1] Hobhouse goes also.

[TO WILLIAM BANKES (*b*)]   *Sunday Even. [April, 1812?]*

My dear Bankes,—I am engaged at ten, but can't you come at 8? I want very much to see you & hear all your treacheries.—I have been & still am laughing at parts of yr. note, you certainly are the best of companions & (I *wont say*) the worst of friends, in me you find the reverse.—yrs ever most affectly.

BYRON

[TO WILLIAM BANKES]   *April 20th. 1812*

My dear Bankes—I feel rather hurt (not savagely) at the speech you made to me last night & my hope is that it was only one of your *profane* jests.—I should be very sorry that any part of my behaviour should give you cause to suppose that I think higher of myself or otherwise of you than I have always done.—I can assure you that I am as much the humblest of your servants as at Trin. Coll: & if I have not been at home when you favoured me with a call the loss was more mine than yours.—In the bustle of buzzing parties there is there can be no rational conversation, but when I can enjoy it there is nobody's I can prefer to your own.—Believe me ever faithfully

& most affectly. yrs.

BYRON

[TO THOMAS MOORE]   *Friday, noon. [April, 1812?]*

I should have answered your note yesterday, but I hoped to have seen you this morning. I must consult with you about the day we dine

---

[1] Lady Sarah Sophia Fane, eldest daughter of John, tenth Earl of Westmorland, married in 1804 George Childe-Villiers, who the following year succeeded his father as the fifth Earl of Jersey. Lady Jersey, who was the reigning beauty and wit of aristocratic society, took a liking to Byron and was one of the few high society ladies who remained loyal to him after the scandal and rumours of the separation from his wife in 1816.

with Sir Francis.[1] I suppose we shall meet at Lady Spencer's[2] to-night. I did not know that you were at Miss Berry's[3] the other night, or I should have certainly gone there.

As usual, I am in all sorts of scrapes, though none, at present, of a martial description. Believe me, &c.

[TO JOHN MURRAY. (*a*)]   *Monday Eve. [May. 1812?]*

Sir—I am told that *we* are in the E[dinburgh] R[evie]w & as this is intelligence of some consequence to me & *more* to you, I should be glad to know if you can inform me of what tenor the criticism is supposed to be, & whether you have seen it or heard the report.—I am your well wisher

& obedt. Sert.
BYRON

[TO JOHN MURRAY. (*b*)]   *[May, 1812?]*

Dr. Sir—Can you send me the Brit[ish] Crit[ic].[1]—I don't mean for any review of *us*—but there is a *Church article* I want to see in it— The Edin[burgh] is very polite[2]—& I of course very grateful—

yrs.
B.

---

[1] Probably Sir Francis Burdett.

[2] Wife of John, first Earl Spencer. Her daughter, Lady Bessborough, was the mother of Lady Caroline Lamb.

[3] Miss Mary Berry, a literary "blue-stocking", whose Journal recorded meetings with all the notable people of her day.

[1] *The British Critic* for April, 1812 (Vol. 39, pp. 325–333) had an article on *Church Union* by Edward Davies, another on *Theological Works* of the Late John Skinner, Episcopal Clergyman in Longside, Aberdeenshire (pp. 334–339), and a third on "Remarks on two Particulars in a Refutation of Calvinism" (pp. 393–408). Perhaps Byron was interested in the second because of the Aberdeenshire connection. He may have known Skinner, who was also a poet. The *British Critic* for May, 1812 (Vol. 39, pp. 478–482) gave high praise to *Childe Harold*.

[2] The *Edinburgh Review* (Dated February, 1812; issued May, 1812, XIX, 466–477) praised *Childe Harold* judiciously but fairly. The review was written by Francis Jeffrey, the editor, whom Byron had wrongly supposed to be the caustic reviewer of his *Hours of Idleness* in 1808, and whom he had satirized as the hanging "Judge Jeffreys" of literature in *English Bards and Scotch Reviewers*.

Dr. Sir/—Could you send me a copy of ye British Rev[iew] & send it here—it is or is to be sent?

yrs. ever

B

Pray is the *North* B[ritish] out?—if it is send it to me—if not when it appears you need not *trouble* yourself at any rate to answer.—

[TO LADY CAROLINE LAMB] *May 1st. 1812*

My dear Lady Caroline,—I have read over the few poems of Miss Milbank[1] with attention.—They display fancy, feeling, & a little practice would very soon induce facility of expression.—Though I have an abhorrence of Blank verse, I like the lines on Dermody[2] so much that I wish they were in rhyme.—The lines in the cave at Seaham[3] have a turn of thought which I cannot sufficiently commend & here I am at least candid as my own opinions differ upon such subjects.—The first stanza is very good indeed, & the others with a few slight alterations might be rendered equally excellent.—The last are smooth & pretty.—But these are all, has she no others?— —She certainly is a very extraordinary girl, who would imagine so much strength & variety of thought under that placid countenance?— —It is not necessary for Miss M. to be an authoress, indeed I do not think publishing at all creditable either to men or women, and (though you will not believe me) very often feel ashamed of it myself, but I have no hesitation in saying that she has talents, which were it proper or requisite to indulge, would have led to distinction.—A friend of mine (fifty years old & an author but not *Rogers*)[4] has just been here, as there is no name to the M.S.S. I shewed them to him, & he was much more enthusiastic in his praises than I have been.—He thinks them beautiful; I shall content myself with observing that they are better much better than anything of Miss M's protegee Blacket.[5] You will

---

[1] Annabella Milbanke, cousin of Caroline's Husband, William Lamb. See biographical sketch in Appendix.
[2] Thomas Dermody, a precocious Irish poet who died young. His posthumous *Harp of Erin* was published in 1806; his collected poems in 1807.
[3] The Milbanke home near Durham.
[4] Probably Dallas.
[5] See June 28, 1811, to Dallas.

say as much of this to Miss M. as you think proper.—I say all this very sincerely, I have no desire to be better acquainted with Miss Milbank, she is too good for a fallen spirit to know or wish to know, & I should like her more if she were less perfect.—

Believe me yrs. ever most truly

B.

May 8th, 1812

I am too proud of being your friend to care with whom I am linked in your estimation, and, God knows, I want friends more at this time than at any other. I am "taking care of myself" to no great purpose. If you knew my situation in every point of view, you would excuse apparent and unintentional neglect. * * * * * * * * I shall leave town, I think; but do not you leave it without seeing me. I wish you, from my soul, every happiness you can wish yourself; and I think you have taken the road to secure it. Peace be with you! I fear she has abandoned me.[1] Ever, &c.

[TO THOMAS JAMES MATHIAS[1]] *Sunday. May 10, 1812*

Dear Sir,—Amongst some testimonies of approval from those whose opinions are worth having, believe none have been or can be more flattering to my vanity & agreeable to a better feeling I trust than vanity, than that with which you have honoured me.—I must still regret that you should be too much devoted to a foreign Muse, & hope that some national *Pursuit* will enable us again to claim you more entirely our own.—I will not however insult you with my praise but beg you to believe me most respectfully

yr. obliged & faithful St.

BYRON

[TO LADY CAROLINE LAMB] *Tuesday [May 19, 1812?]*

You should answer the note for the writer seems unhappy.—And when we are so a slight is doubly felt.— —I shall go at 12, but you must send me a ticket which I shall religiously pay for. I shall not call

---

[1] Byron was in the throes of his love affair with Lady Caroline Lamb.
[1] See April 5, 1812, to E. D. Clarke, note 1.

because I do not see that we are at all improved by it, why did you send your boy? I was out, & am always so occupied in a morning that I could not have seen him as I wished had I been at home. I have seen Moore's wife, she is beautiful, with the darkest eyes, they have left town.—M[oore] is in great distress about us, & indeed people talk as if there were no other pair of absurdities in London.—It is hard to bear all this without cause, but worse to give cause for it.—Our folly has had the effect of a fault.—I conformed & could conform, if you would lend your aid, but I can't bear to see you look unhappy, & am always on the watch to observe if you are trying to make me so.—We must make an effort, this dream this delirium of two months must pass away, we in fact do not know one another, a month's absence would make us rational, you do not think so, I know it, we have both had 1000 previous fancies of the same kind, & shall get the better of this & be as ashamed of it according to the maxim of Rochefoucault.—[1] But it is better that I should leave town than you, & I will make a tour, or go to Cambridge or Edinburgh.—Now dont abuse me, or think me altered, it is because I am not, cannot alter, that I shall do this, and cease to make fools talk, friends grieve, and the wise pity.—Ever most affectionately & sincerely yrs.

B.

[TO THOMAS MOORE]   *May 20th, 1812*

On Monday, after sitting up all night, I saw Bellingham[1] launched into eternity, and at three the same day I saw * * * [Lady Caroline Lamb] launched into the country. * * * * * * *

I believe, in the beginning of June, I shall be down for a few days in Notts. If so, I shall beat you up "en passant" with Hobhouse, who is endeavouring, like you and every body else, to keep me out of scrapes.

I meant to have written you a long letter, but I find I cannot. If any thing remarkable occurs, you will hear it from me—if good; if *bad*, there are plenty to tell it. In the mean time, do you be happy.

Ever yours, &c.

[1] La Rochefoucault in his 71st "Maxime" wrote: "Il n'y a guère de gens qui ne soient honteux de s'être aimés quand ils ne s'aiment plus." ("There are few people who are not ashamed of having loved when they no longer love.")

[1] John Bellingham, who conceived that he had a grievance against the government, shot and killed Spencer Perceval, First Lord of the Treasury and Chancellor of the Exchequer, in the House of Commons on May 11, 1812. Bellingham was hanged in front of Newgate on May 18. Byron rented a window from which to watch the execution. (See Moore, I, 357.)

P.S.—My best wishes and respects to Mrs. * * [Moore];—she is beautiful. I may say so even to you, for I never was more struck with a countenance.

[TO ——————]   *May 20th. 1812*

Sir—You have my consent to insert any part of the *Notes* or *Appendix* or Romaic *extracts* which may tend to advance the objects of pursuit in your work.—

                                                        I am yr. obedt. St.
                                                                BYRON

[TO EDWARD DANIEL CLARKE]   *8. St. James's Street May 27th. 1812*

My dear Sir,—I must appear very ungrateful in not having answered your very kind letter before but I shall not attempt apologies, for I trust you will forgive me without.—I have availed myself in ye. 2d. En. of your permission to quote you in a note,[1] & most happy I was in your concurrence, it makes "assurance double sure".—I have printed 8 copies of a certain thing one of which shall be yours.—To you and Mathias & one or two more *such* I am indebted for a much higher gratification than the praises of women & children & Reviews, though Jeffrey has behaved most handsomely.—[2] I am in a *Portuguese review* would you like to see it? Latin & Italian help as to the meaning.— Believe me

                                                        ever most truly yrs.
                                                                BYRON

P.S.—I trust Mrs. Clarke is well and all "the little Clarkes" like those in George Colman's song.—

[TO BERNARD BARTON[1]]   *8. St. James's Street June 1st. 1812*

Sir—The most satisfactory answer to the concluding part of your letter is that Mr. Murray will republish your volume if you still retain

[1] See April 5, 1812, to Clarke, note 2.
[2] See [May, 1812?], to Murray (*b*), note 2.
[1] Bernard Barton (1784–1849) was a Quaker poet and friend of Charles Lamb. His *Metrical Effusions* was published in 1812. He was a clerk in a bank in Woodbridge, Suffolk. Lamb's advice to him was similar to Byron's: "Keep to your bank, and the bank will keep you." (Letter of Jan. 9, 1823.)

your inclination for the experiment which I trust will be successful.—Some weeks ago my friend Mr. Rogers showed me some of the stanzas in M.S. & I then expressed my opinion of their merit which a further perusal of the printed volume has given me no reason to revoke. I mention this as it may not be disagreeable to you to learn that I entertained a very favourable opinion of your powers before I was aware that such sentiments were reciprocal.———Wa[i]ving your obliging expressions as to my own productions for which I thank you very sincerely & assure you that I think not lightly of the praise of one whose approbation is valuable, will you allow me to talk to you candidly not critically on the subject of yours?—You will not suspect me of a wish to discourage, since I pointed out to the publisher the propriety of complying with your wishes.—I think more highly of your poetical talents than it would perhaps gratify you to hear expressed, for I believe from what I observe of your mind that you are above flattery.—To come to the point—you deserve success, but we know before Addison wrote his Cato, that desert does not always command it.—But suppose it attained

> "You know what ills the author's life assail,
> Toil, envy, want, the *patron*, & the Jail,[2]

do not renounce writing, but never trust entirely to Authorship.—If you have a profession, retain it, it will be like Prior's fellowship,[3] a last & sure resource.—Compare Mr. Rogers with other authors of the day, assuredly he is amongst the first of living poets, but is it to that he owes his station in society & his intimacy in the best circles? no, it is to his prudence & respectability, the world (a bad one I own) courts him because he has no occasion to court it.—He is a poet, nor is he less so because he was something more.—I am not sorry to hear that you are not tempted by the vicinity of Capel Lofft Esqre.[4] though if he had done for you what he has for the Bloomfields I should never have laughed at his rage for patronizing.—But a truly constituted mind will ever be independent.—That you may be so is my very sincere wish & if others think as well of your poetry as I do, you will have no cause to complain of your readers.— Believe me

yr obliged & obedt. Sert.
BYRON

---

[2] Slightly misquoted from Johnson's *Vanity of Human Wishes*, lines 158–59.

[3] Matthew Prior became a Fellow of St. John's College in 1688.

[4] For Capell Lofft and the Bloomfields, see Aug. 21, 1811, to Dallas, notes 4 and 5.

My dear Lord,—I must appear very ungrateful & have indeed been very negligent, but till last night I was not apprized of Lady Holland's situation & shall call tomorrow to have the satisfaction I trust of hearing that she is well.—I hope that neither Politics nor Gout have assailed your Lordship since I last saw you & that you also are "as well as could be expected".—The other night at a Ball I was presented by order to our gracious Regent, who honoured me with some conversation & professed a predilection for Poesy.—[1] I confess it was a most unexpected honour, & I thought of poor Bankes's adventure with some apprehensions of a similar blunder.—I have now great hopes in the event of Mr. Pye's decease, of "warbling truth at Court" like Mr. Mallet[2] of indifferent memory.—Consider, 100 marks a year! besides the wine & the disgrace,[3] but then remorse would make me drown myself in my own Butt before the year's end, or the finishing of my first dythyrambic.—So that after all I shall not meditate our Laureat's death by pen or poison.—Will you present my best respects to Lady Holland & believe me hers

> & yrs very sincerely & obliged
> BYRON

My dear Sir,—Will you accept my very sincere congratulations on your second volume[1] wherein I have retraced some of my old paths adorned by you so beautifully that they afford me double delight.— The part which pleases me best after all is the preface, because it tells me you have not yet closed labours to yourself not unprofitable nor without gratification for what is so pleasing as to give pleasure?—I

---

[1] At a ball at Miss Johnson's, the Prince Regent, hearing that Byron was present, expressed a desire to meet him. Byron was impressed by the Prince's conversation on Walter Scott, but he tried to make light of it to Lord Holland, leader of the Whig Opposition. The word "predilection" is taken from a letter of February 13, 1812, from the Regent to the Duke of York repudiating his Whig friends.

[2] David Mallet (originally Malloch) (1705?–65), poet and miscellaneous writer, who for his political writing was awarded a sinecure under the Tory Prime Minister Lord Bute. With James Thomson he wrote a masque, *Alfred* (1740) in which *Rule Britannia* first appeared. In 1812 Henry James Pye was Poet Laureate, and was noted for his fawning and sycophantic verses to the Royal family.

[3] A butt of wine was a traditional stipend paid to the Poet Laureate.

[1] Clarke's *Travels in Various Countries of Europe, Asia, and Africa* appeared at intervals, in six volumes, from 1810 to 1823.

have sent my copy to Sir Sydney Smith, who will derive much gratification from your anecdotes of Djezzar his "energetic old man"[2] I doat upon the *Druses,* but who the deuce are they with their Pantheism? I shall never be easy till I ask *them* the question. How much you have traversed!—I must resume my seven leagued boots & journey to Palestine, which your description mortifies me not to have seen more than ever.— —I still sigh for the Ægean? shall not you always love it's bluest of all waves & brightest of all skies?—You have awakened all the Gipsy in me, I long to be restless again & wandering—see what mischief you do, you wont allow gentlemen to settle quietly at home.— I will not wish you success & fame for you have both, but all the happiness which even these cannot always give, believe me you cannot deserve more than is desired in your behalf by

yr. ever obliged & faithful Servt.

Byron

[TO MR. LONGMAN]   *June 30, 1812*

Ld. Byron presents his compliments to Mr. Longman & requests that he will do Ld. B. the favour to transmit his best thanks to the Conductor of the B[ritis]h Review for the present of that work & for the very gratifying critique contained in the last number.[1]

[TO LADY MELBOURNE]   *Saturday Even. [July–Dec., 1812?]*

Dear Lady Melbourne,—If you would permit me to see you for a very few minutes tomorrow at your own hour I think I could convince you by something like proof how far the *"perversion* of *principle"* which is indeed the "unkindest cut of all" has been justly brought forward.—I cannot much boast of my religious or moral code but my opinions in conversation I generally keep to myself, & in this instance

---

[2] Sir Sydney Smith had defended Acre against Napoleon in 1799. Djezzar Pasha had fortified Acre in 1775. Accounts of these exploits are in Clarke's *Travels* (Part II, sec. i, chap. 12, "Greece, Egypt, and the Holy Land").

[1] *The British Review, and London Critical Journal* (published by Longman), June, 1812, pp. 275–302, attempted to give a balanced judgement of *Childe Harold,* praising the beauty of some parts but deprecating the melancholy; it concluded with "a sincere declaration of our respect for his genius and talents". This was rather generous praise from an Evangelical periodical. William Roberts of Corpus Christi College, Oxford, editor of the *British Review* from 1811 to 1822, later became the butt of Byron's jesting in *Don Juan,* when he referred to Roberts as the editor of "My Grandmother's Review". (See *Don Juan,* I, 209–210.)

I cannot plead guilty.—I really feel very [sincerely?] your kindness on this occasion, and I will not again intrude upon it, or even *now* if I trouble you too much.—It is singular enough that one whose whole life has been spent in open opposition to received opinions should be charged with hypocrisy.—

ever yrs.
B.

[TO WALTER SCOTT[1]]   *St. James's Street July sixth 1812*

Sir,—I have just been honoured with your letter.—I feel sorry that you should have thought it worth while to notice the "evil works of my nonage" as the thing is suppressed *voluntarily* & your explanation is too kind not to give me pain.—The satire was written when I was very young & very angry, & fully bent on displaying my wrath & my wit, & now I am haunted by the ghosts of my wholesale Assertions. —I cannot sufficiently thank you for your praise and now wa[i]ving myself let me talk to you of the Prince R[egen]t's.[2] He ordered me to be presented to him at a ball, & after some sayings peculiarly pleasing from royal lips, as to my own attempts; he talked to me of you & your immortalities; he preferred you to every bard past & present, & asked which of your works pleased me most, it was a difficult question—I answered, I thought the "Lay" he said his own opinion was nearly similar; in speaking of the others I told him that I thought you more particularly the poet of *Princes*, as *they* never appeared more fascinating than in Marmion & the Lady of the Lake, he was pleased to coincide & to dwell on the description of your James's no less royal than poetical. —He spoke alternately of Homer & yourself & seemed well acquainted with both, so that (with the exception of the Turks[3] & your humble servant) you were in very good company.—I defy Murray to have exaggerated his R[oyal] H[ighness]'s opinion of your powers, nor can I pretend to enumerate all he said on the subject, but it may give you pleasure to hear that it was conveyed in language which would only suffer by my attempting to transcribe it, & with a tone &

<hr>

[1] Byron had told Murray about the Prince Regent's admiration for Scott, and Murray relayed the account to Scott, who then wrote Byron praising *Childe Harold*, and explaining that his motive for writing *Marmion* had not been mercenary (which was the subject of part of Byron's attack in *English Bards*—see lines 165–184).

[2] See June 25, 1812, to Lord Holland, note 1.

[3] The Turkish Ambassador and his suite were at the ball.

taste which gave me a very high idea of his abilities & accomplishments, which I had hitherto considered as confined to *manners*, certainly superior to those of any living *gentleman.*— —This interview was accidental;—I never went to the levee, for having seen the courts of Mussulman & Catholic sovereigns, my curiosity was sufficiently allayed, & my politics being as perverse as my rhymes, I had in fact "no business there."[4]—To be thus praised by your Sovereign must be gratifying to you, & if the gratification is not allayed by the communication being made through me, the bearer of it will consider himself very fortunately & sincerely

yr obliged & obedt. Servt.

BYRON

P.S.—Excuse this scrawl scratched in a great hurry & just after a journey.—

[TO MISS MERCER ELPHINSTONE[1]]   *July 29th 1812.—*

St. James's Street

Dear Miss Mercer—In compliance with your request I send the frank which you will find on the outside, & in compliance with no request at all, but I believe in defiance of the etiquette established between single ladies & all gentlemen whatsoever plural or singular, I annex a few lines to keep the cover in countenance. London is very dull & I am still duller than London.—Now I am at a stand still— what shall I say next?—I must have recourse to hoping—this then "comes hoping"—that you survived the dust of your Journey, & the fatigue of *not* dancing at Ly. Clonmell's the night before;—that Mrs. Lamb bears her widowhood like the matron—of Ephesus, & that all Tunbridge [Wells] is at this moment waltzing or warbling it's best in honour of you both.— —I hope moreover that you will not gladden

---

[4] Byron had already written his "Sympathetic Address to a Young Lady" on the tears of the Princess Charlotte when her father refused to call in the Whig ministry on assuming the Regency. (Published anonymously in the *Morning Chronicle,* March 7, 1812.)

[1] Miss Margaret Mercer Elphinstone, a wealthy heiress, was one of the young ladies casting eyes at Byron when Annabella Milbanke first saw him at Melbourne House. Byron was attracted to her calm good nature in contrast to the tempestuousness of Caroline Lamb. She later invited him to visit her at Tunbridge Wells, where she had gone with Mrs. George Lamb (Caroline's sister-in-law). But he was too entangled with Caroline to escape. Miss Mercer married, in 1817, the Comte de Flahault.

the eyes & break the hearts of the royal corps of Marines at Plymouth for some time to come, & that—that—I am come to the end of all I can say upon nothing.— Pray forgive the inside of this for the sake of the *out*, & believe me if you had not done me the honour to require the one I should never have troubled you with the other.—I am (to talk diplomatically) with the very highest consideration

yr. sincere & most obedt. Sert.

B.

P.S.—I am not sure that I have not been guilty of considerable impertinence in sending a word beyond the superscription—if so— let my offence & apology go together with my best respects to Mrs. Lamb, & tell her I wish the circuit well over.

[TO LADY MELBOURNE (*a*)]   [*August, 1812?*]

Dear Ly. M.—That I am not trifling with you but have *sincere* business of some consequence the enclosed note from my solicitor will convince you[1]—which though a *secret*—I would tell you if my life depended on it rather than you should *doubt me* under the circumstances in which poor Ly.B.[2] is placed.— —The moment I can arrange this, & I will not wait in the hope of further or better proposals, I shall leave town.—[3]

yrs. ever

P.S.—You can have the goodness to state the real fact to Ly. B[essborough] & C[aroline]— —I do assure you I have Ly. B's comfort more at heart than my own convenience even in this a cast of some moment.—You will return me the note at your own leisure.—

[TO LADY MELBOURNE (*b*)]   [*August, 1812?*]

My dear Ly. M.—In answer to Ly. B[essborough] I have only to observe that if she will abide by the consequences, I will *not* see C. at

---

[1] Newstead Abbey was being put up for auction on August 14th.

[2] Lady Bessborough, Caroline Lamb's mother.

[3] A near elopement with Caroline on July 29th, and Caroline's uncontrollable conduct, had caused Lady Melbourne, her mother-in-law, to ask Byron to leave town.

all—& it was with the greatest reluctance & something of *disgust* that I ever consented with which I beg she may be made acquainted.—I regret very much that I shall not have the pleasure of seeing you at Ly. Ossulstone's[1] this Evening to whom I must request you to furnish me with a *proper* excuse.—The fact is I have made a resolution (*weak* to the extent of Ly. Blarney's[2] anathema) not to go anywhere but—no matter you will plead a sudden cold in my behalf which will shine in your description.—Believe me dear Ly. M.

ever yrs.

B.

[TO LADY CAROLINE LAMB]   *[August, 1812?]*[1]

My dearest Caroline—If tears, which you saw & know I am not apt to shed, if the agitation in which I parted from you, agitation which you must have perceived through the *whole* of this most nervous *nervous* affair, did not commence till the moment of leaving you approached, if all that I have said & done, & am still but too ready to say & do, have not sufficiently proved what my real feelings are & must be ever towards you, my love, I have no other proof to offer; God knows I wish you happy, & when I quit you, or rather when you from a sense of duty to your husband & mother quit me, you shall acknowledge the truth of what I again promise & vow, that no other in word or deed shall ever hold the place in my affection which is & shall be most sacred to you, till I am nothing I never knew till *that moment*, the *madness* of—my dearest & most beloved friend—I cannot express myself—this is no time for words—but I shall have a pride, a melancholy pleasure, in suffering what you yourself can hardly conceive—for you do not know me.—I am now about to go out with a heavy heart, because—my appearing this Evening will stop any absurd story which the events of today might give rise to—do you

---

[1] Charles Augustus (Bennet), Earl of Tankerville, styled Lord Ossulston till 1822, married in 1806 Corisande Armandine Sophie Leonice Hélène, daughter of the Duc de Gramont. She was said to possess great charm and to write letters in very pure French, but Lord Melbourne in 1839 told Queen Victoria that she was "a frivolous little woman, who doesn't know what she is about". (*The Complete Peerage*, XII, 635.)

[2] Byron's nickname for Lady Bessborough, Caroline's mother, borrowed from the ridiculous society lady in Goldsmith's *Vicar of Wakefield*.

[1] This lithographic facsimile has been questioned, but the handwriting is undoubtedly Byron's. There are several copies at John Murray's. Caroline wrote to Medwin in 1824: "I have had one of his letters copied in the stone press for you; one just before we parted." (*LJ*, II, 452.)

think *now* that I am *cold* & *stern*, & *artful*—will even *others* think so, will your *mother* even—that mother to whom we must indeed sacrifice much, *more* much more on my part, than she shall ever know or can imagine.—"Promises not to love you" ah Caroline it is past promising—but I shall attribute all concessions to the proper motive—& never cease to feel all that you have already witnessed—& more than can ever be known but to my own heart—perhaps to yours—May God protect forgive & bless you—ever & even more than ever

yr. most attached
Byron

P.S.—These taunts which have driven you to this—my dearest Caroline—were it not for your mother & the kindness of all your connections, is there anything on earth or heaven would have made me so happy as to have made you mine long ago? & not less *now* than *then*, but *more* than ever at this time—you know I would with pleasure give up all here & all beyond the grave for you—& in refraining from this—must my motives be misunderstood—? I care not who knows this—what use is made of it—it is to *you* & to *you* only that they owe yourself, I was and am *yours*, freely & most entirely, to obey, to honour, love—& fly with you when, where, & how you yourself *might* & *may* determine.

[TO MISS MERCER ELPHINSTONE]   *St. James's Street*
August 3d. 1812

Dear Miss Mercer—The reply with which you have honoured me has dispelled certain qualms which followed my presumption, for if right I am rejoiced to be so for once in my life, & if wrong—you have been good enough to forgive, though so speedy a repetition of the offence can hardly lay claim to further patience or future pardon.—"Sans phrase" then I have so great a dread of Mrs. L[amb]'s wrath, & am so fully convinced of her most sincere wish to see me—not at Tunbridge or in her awful presence, but there or anywhere else so that I am not in London at this very *unwholesome* season of the year, that I shall in a few days with the greatest reluctance forthwith proceed to do penance at her feet, & listen to the very appropriate *parables*, which she selects for the edification of the *penitent*.—If you will have the goodness to submit to her inspection the above sentence, she will probably understand it without my troubling you or her with further comment.—I should be so sorry to see her "quite angry" that though I am well aware it is not the exquisite pleasure of seeing me, but of preventing *me* from *seeing* that induces her kind request, I shall comply with it & set out for Mecca or Tunbridge on Wednesday next.[1]——But why will she grow fat? and you too? that additional wing (with a bit of the breast superadded I dare say) is worse than waltzing.—But as I actually dined yesterday myself, I must bear these trespasses, & you must bear my impertinence in repeating an offence less pardonable.— —I have been out & about amongst the select & benevolent few still left in London & we console ourselves with regretting the absentees.—I doubt if any of us are equally fortunate. I shall not much embarrass myself with the brilliant society at Tunbridge, but I shall do honour to your [not "Derby"] cavalcade in which I may most appropriately join.—Ever since school & my sojourn at Cintra, I have delighted in asses like a Sandman.—My apology for this second intrusion will not I fear be better received for being delivered in person, but it will at all events prevent any further trouble from the pen ink & paper of your

obliged & sincere St.
BYRON

P.S.—I am somewhat ashamed of the above hieroglyphics, but you cannot say that I am ignorant of what Pope calls the "last great art" of writing—"the *art* to *blot*" after casting your eye over the scratches on the present page.

[TO LADY MELBOURNE]   [*August 12, 1812?*]

Dear Lady M.—I trust that Ly. C[aroline] has by this time reappeared or that her mother is better acquainted than I am, God knows, where she is.[1]—If this be the case I hope you will favour me with one line, because in the interim my situation is by no means a *sinecure*, although I did not chuse to add to *your* perplexities this morning by joining in a *duet* with Ly. B[essborough].—As I am one of the principal performers in this unfortunate drama. I should be glad to

[1] Mrs. George Lamb had been eager to get Byron away from London and his dangerous liaison with Caroline Lamb. There is no evidence, however, that he went to Tunbridge, though he probably wanted to.

[1] On August 12, 1812, Lady Caroline Lamb, reproached for her conduct by Lord Melbourne, ran away. Lady Melbourne and her mother, Lady Bessborough, thought she had gone to Byron. Later he found her and took her home.

know what my part requires next?—seriously I am extremely uneasy on account of Ly C[aroline] & others, as for myself—it is of little consequence—I shall bear & forbear as much as I can—but I must not shrink now from anything.—

6 o clock
Thus much I had written when I receive yours—not a word *of* or *from* her—what is the cause of all this, I mean the *immediate* circumstance which has led to it? I thought every thing was well & quiet in the morning till the Apparition of Ly. B[essborough].—if I see or hear from her Ly. *B* shall be informed, if *you*—pray tell me, I am apprehensive for her personal safety, for her state of mind,—here I sit alone, & however I might *appear* to you, in the most painful suspense.—

ever yrs

𝕭

[TO LADY MELBOURNE]   [*August, 14 1812?*][1]

Dear Ly. M.—In justice to Ly. C[aroline] I must declare that she mentioned no names nor had I reason to believe that she alluded to you —but I wrote so fast & my ideas were so confused that God knows what I said, or meant, except that she never did nor can deserve a single reproach which must not fall with double justice & truth upon myself, who am much much more to blame in every respect, nor shall I in the least hesitate in declaring this to any of her family who may think proper to come forward—no one has a right to interfere with *her* but yourself & Mr. L[amb].—with me the case is different—to them *I* will answer—& if she is to be persecuted for my faults—to be reproached with the consequences of a misplaced affection but too well returned—by any but *you* & *yours* (who have acted so differently with a kindness which I did not believe to exist in human nature) I cannot & will not bear it, without at least taking my own just share of the consequences.—In the mean time, command me—& dear Ly. M. comfort & be kind to her, you *have been*, she owns it with the greatest gratitude, in every thing of this kind the *man* is—& must be most to

---

[1] The date is conjectured from the reference in the postscript to "auctioneers". Newstead Abbey came up for auction on August 14, 1812, but on Hanson's advice was bought in because no bid was high enough. But the next day Thomas Claughton of Haydock Lodge near Warrington in Lancashire offered £140,000 for it, and the offer was accepted a few days later.

blame, & I am sure not less so in this instance than every other.—
—Act with me as you think proper—I seek no excuse—no evasion—I
have given you my *word* it shall be observed—& I am sure Ly.
C[aroline] will be the last to make me break it.—

yrs. ever

P.S.—Forgive this scrawl—I have been so hurried with Lawyers,
auctioneers—buyers & sellers this morn., besides *this* agreeable
accompaniment—that I hardly know what I am about.— — —

[TO JOHN HANSON]   *17th Augt. 1812*

Dear Sir—I shall not be able to be with you before 1—but I will
be punctual to that hour.—I will leave to your discretion—such
[points?] as do not appear of very great importance.—

yrs. ever—

[TO JOHN HANSON]   *Cheltenham August 23d. 1812*[1]

Dear Sir—When the mortgage is secured on Newstead—I wish to
know whether the titled deeds will not remain in *our* hands as is usual
in all well secured mortgages *not* in *Register Counties*.——If you have
any information—pray tell me—I hope you are better.—

yrs. ever
B.

[TO JOHN HANSON]   *Cheltenham August 31st. 1812*

Dear Sir—I think of remaining here at least a week longer if the
tenants' discharges must be signed before that time they had better be
sent.—If you have any intention of coming here I do not think the
difficulty of procuring lodgings would be great though the place is
full.—If I can serve you in this, command me.—Mr. Claughton must

1 At the end of August, after Lady Caroline Lamb had left for Ireland with her
mother and husband, Byron went to Cheltenham where a number of his friends had
gathered at the fashionable watering place.

keep to the contract[2]—I have already complimented him with a *cup* which I highly valued, & this must content him—amongst the plate there is a vase of silver worth nearly three hundred guineas with which & my sabres &c. I would not part to please a *Caliph*.—The agreement is so specified—*"it is not in his bond"* the things may remain at Newstead for the present but he must on no account have *anything like possession* till all is fulfilled.—I have no wish to raise obstacles—but let him keep to the Contract—so will I.—Poor Birch[3]—his gross habit did this—there are none like your *ailing* people—they always complain & always outlive the healthy.—Best compts to Mrs. H. & all the family—

> yrs. ever sincerely
> *B.*

[TO THE REV. ROBERT WALPOLE[1]]   [*Sept.*, *1812*]

. . . very much at your service, if you think them worth your attention, there is a Lexicon & a Meletius[2] amongst them, the rest except the grammars & Testament, are not worth a Para.—My inclination points very strongly towards Greece, & I trust next Spring to revisit Athens, where *your* memory is by no means faded.—I think Ld. Aberdeen & yourself are more frequently spoken of than any other Frank travellers.— —So if you are as emulous of the approbation of the Athenians as Alexander was, you may enjoy it to the full.—I wish you every success & have the honour to be

> yr, obliged & sincere S[ervan]t
> BYRON

[TO JOHN MURRAY]   *High Street. Cheltenham Septr. 5th. 1812*

Dear Sir,—Pray have the goodness to send these dispatches & a No. of the E[dinburgh] R[eview] with the rest.—I hope you have written to Mr. Thompson, thanked him in my name for his present & told him that I shall be truly happy to comply with his request—How do

---

[2] After signing the contract for the purchase of Newstead, Claughton apparently repented of his bargain and for more than two years tried to get out of his obligation to complete the purchase. He finally forfeited £25,000 of his down payment of £28,000, and withdrew.

[3] J. Birch was Hanson's law partner.

[1] The Rev. Robert Walpole (1781–1856) was a classical scholar who had travelled in Greece.

[2] See July 7, 1811, to Drury, note 5; and July 15, 1811, to Hobhouse.

you go on? & when is the graven image "with *bays* & *wicked rhyme upon't*" to grace or disgrace some of our tardy editions? Send me "*Rokeby*" who the deuce is he?[1] no matter—he has good connections, & will be well introduced.—I thank you for your enquiries, I am so so—but my thermometer is sadly below the poetical point. What will you give *me* or *mine* for a poem of 6 Cantos (*when complete—no* rhyme—*no* recompence) as like the last 2 as I can make them?— —I have some ideas which one day may be embodied & till winter I shall have much leisure.—Believe me

> *yrs very sincerely*
> BYRON

P.S.—My last question is in the true style of Grub Street, but like *Jeremy Diddler* I only "ask for information"[2] Send me Adair on Diet & regimen just republished by Ridgway.[3]

[TO LORD HOLLAND]   *Cheltenham Septr. 10th. 1812*

My dear Lord—The lines which I sketched off on your hint *are* still or rather *were* in an unfinished state for I have just committed them to a flame more decisive than that of Drury.[1]— —Under all the circumstances I should hardly risk a contest with Philodrama— Philodrury—Asbestos—Horace Twiss[2]——and all the anonymes & synonymes of the Committee candidates.—Seriously I think you have a chance of something much better, for prologuising is not my forte, & at all events either my pride or my modesty won't let me incur the hazard of having my rhymes buried in next month's magazine under

---

1 Walter Scott's poem *Rokeby* was published in 1812.

2 In Kenney's *Raising the Wind*, Act I, scene 1, Diddler asks Sam, "you haven't got such a thing as tenpence about you, have you?" Sam: "Yes, And I mean to keep it about me, see." Diddler replies: "Oh, aye, certainly. I only asked for information."

3 James MacKittrick, under the name of Adair, published in 1804 *An Essay on Diet and Regimen*.

1 Fire destroyed Drury Lane Theatre on February 24, 1809. For the opening of the new Drury Lane, scheduled for October 10, 1812, the Committee of Management had offered a competition for a poetical Address to be spoken on the opening night. Lord Holland had asked Byron to submit an Address. He wrote one but changed his mind about entering it in the competition. After the Committee found none of the Addresses submitted acceptable, Lord Holland on behalf of the Committee asked Byron to write one, and he then consented.

2 Horace Twiss (1787–1849), a contributor of squibs to the newspapers, whose literary pretensions made him the butt of ridicule.

essays on the murder of Mr. Perceval[3] & "cures for the bite of the mad dog" as poor Goldsmith complained on the fate of far superior performances.[4]— —I am still sufficiently interested to wish to know the successful Candidate—& amongst so many—I have no doubt— some will be excellent, particularly in an age when writing verse is the easiest of all attainments.— —I cannot answer your intelligence with the "like comfort" unless as you are deeply theatrical you may wish to hear of Mr. Betty,[5] whose acting is I fear utterly inadequate to the London engagement into which the Managers of C[ovent] G[arden] have lately entered.—His figure is fat, his features flat, his voice unmanageable, his action ungraceful, & as Diggory says "I defy him to *ex*tort that d——d muffin face of his into madness"—[6] I was very sorry to see him in the character of the "Elephant on the slack rope" for when I last saw him I was in raptures with his performance, but then I was sixteen—an age to which all London then condescended to subside—after all much better judges have admired & may again— but I venture to "prognosticate a prophecy" (see the Courier) that he will not succeed.—So poor dear Rogers has stuck fast on "the brow of the mighty Helvellyn"[7] I hope not forever.—My best respects to Ly. H[olland].—her departure with that of my other friends was a sad event for me now reduced to a state of the most cynical solitude.— "By the waters of Cheltenham I sate down & *drank,* when I remem- bered thee oh Georgiana Cottage!—as for our *harps* we hanged them up, upon the willows that grow thereby—then they said sing us a song of Drury Lane &c."—but I am dumb & dreary as the Israelites. —The waters have disordered me to my heart's content, you were *right,* as you always are.—Believe me

ever yr. obliged & affecte. Servt.

BYRON

[TO LADY MELBOURNE]   *Cheltenham Septr. 10th. 1812*

Dear Ly. Melbourne—I presume you have heard & will not be sorry to hear *again* that *they* are safely deposited in Ireland[1] & that the

---

[3] See May 20, 1812, to Moore, note 1.
[4] See *Vicar of Wakefield*, chapter 20.
[5] See April 25, 1805, to Augusta, notes 2 and 3.
[6] One of Liston's parts in Jackman's *All the World's a Stage*, Act I, scene 2.
[7] Rogers had gone on a tour to the north of England. The quotation is from Scott's poem *Helvellyn*.
[1] Lady Caroline Lamb and her mother and husband had gone to Ireland.

sea rolls between you and *one* of your torments; the other you see is still at your elbow.— —Now (if you are as sincere as I sometimes almost dream) you will not regret to hear that I wish this to end, & it certainly shall not be renewed on my part.—It is not that I love another, but loving at all is quite out of my way; I am tired of being a fool, & when I look back on the waste of time, & the destruction of all my plans last winter by this last romance, I am—what I ought to have been long ago.—It is true from early habit, one must make love mechanically as one swims, I was once very fond of both, but now as I never swim unless I tumble into the water, I don't make love till almost obliged, though I fear *that* is not the shortest way out of the troubled waves with which in such accidents we must struggle.—But I will say no more on this topic, as I am not sure of my ground, and you can easily outwit me as you always hitherto have done.—Today I have had a letter from Ld. Holland wishing me to write for the Opening Theatre, but as all Grubstreet seems engaged in the Contest, I have no ambition to enter the lists, & have thrown my few ideas into the fire—I never risk *rivalry* in any thing, you see the very *lowest*—as in this case discourages me from a sort of mixed feeling, I don't know if it be *pride*, but *you* will say it certainly is not *modesty*.— —I suppose your friend Twiss[2] will be *one*—I hear there are five hundred—& I wish him success—I really think he would do it well; but few men who have any character to lose would risk it in an anonymous scramble, for the sake of their own feelings.— I have written to Ld. H[olland] to thank him & decline the chance.—Betty[3] is performing here, I fear, very ill, his figure is that of a hippopotamus, his face like the Bull and *mouth* on the pannels of a heavy coach, his arms are fins fattened out of shape, his voice the gargling of an Alderman with the quinsey, and his acting altogether ought to be natural, for it certainly is like nothing that *Art* has ever yet exhibited on the stage.—Will you honour me with a line at your leisure? on the most *indifferent* subject you please & believe me

ever yrs very affectly

B.

[TO LADY MELBOURNE]   *Cheltenham Septr. 13th. 1812*

My dear Lady M.—The end of Ly. B[essborough]'s letter shall be the beginning of mine "for Heaven's sake do not lose your hold on

2 See Sept. 10, 1812, to Lord Holland, note 2.
3 See April 25, 1805, to Augusta Byron, notes 2 and 3.

him" pray don't—*I* repeat,—& assure you it is a very firm one "but the yoke is easy & the burthen is light" to use one of my scriptural phrases.—So far from being ashamed of being governed like Lord Delacour[1] or any *other Lord* or *master*, I am always but too happy to find one to regulate or misregulate me, & I am as docile as a Dromedary & can bear almost as much.—Will you undertake me? If you are sincere (which I still a little hesitate in believing) give me but time, let *hers* retain her in Ireland—the *"gayer"* the better, I want her just to be sufficiently gay that I may have enough to bear me out on my own part, grant me but till Decr. & if I do not disenchant the Dulcinea & Don *Quichotte* both,—then I must attack the Windmills, & leave the land in quest of adventures.—In the mean time I must & do write the greatest absurdities to keep her "gay" & the more so because ye. last epistle informed me that "8 guineas a mail & a packet *could* soon bring her to London" a threat which immediately called forth a letter worthy of the Grand Cyrus or the Duke of York, or any other hero of Madame Scudery or Mrs. Clarke.[2]— —Poor Ly. B[essborough]! with her hopes & her fears; in fact it is no jest for her —or indeed any of us; I must let you into one little secret, *her* folly half did this, at ye. commencement she piqued that "vanity" (which it would be the *vainest* thing on earth to deny) by telling me she was certain "I was not beloved," that I was only led on for the sake of &c. &c." this raised a devil between us which now will only be laid I do really believe in the *Red* sea, I made no answer, but determined— not to *pursue*, for pursuit it was not —but to *sit* still, and in a week after I was convinced—not that———[Caroline] loved me—for I do not believe in the existence of what is called Love—but that any other man in my situation would have believed that he *was* loved.— Now my dear Ly. M. you are all out as to my real sentiments—I was, am, & shall be I fear attached to another, one to whom I have never said much, but have never lost sight of, & the whole of this interlude has been the result of circumstances which it may be too late to regret. — —Do you suppose that at my *time* of *life*, were I so very *far* gone, that I should not be in *Ireland* or at least have followed into Wales, as

[1] Lord Delacour is a character in Maria Edgeworth's novel *Belinda* (1801). See letter of May 15, 1813, to Lady Davy, where Byron indicates that he is familiar with Miss Edgeworth's novels and is awed at the prospect of meeting her.

[2] Mrs. Mary Ann Clarke, mistress of the Duke of York, was supposed to have influenced military patronage controlled by the Duke. In January, 1809, Col. Gwyllym Wardle brought forward a motion for a Parliamentary inquiry into the matter. *Artamène, ou le Grand Cyrus* was a lengthy novel in which Madame Scudery painted herself as the heroine Sappho.

it was hinted was *expected* — now they have crossed the channel I feel anything but regret, I told you in my two last, that I did not "like any other &c. &c." I deceived you & myself in saying so, there was & is one whom I wished to marry, had not this affair intervened, or had not some occurrences rather discouraged me.—When our Drama was "rising" (I'll be d———d if it falls off I may say with Sir Fretful) in the 5th act, it was no time to hesitate, I had made up my mind, to bear ye. consequences of my own folly; honour pity, & a kind of affection all forbade me to shrink, but now if I can *honorably* be off, if *you* are not deceiving me, & if she does not take some accursed step to precipitate her own inevitable fall (if not with me, with some less lucky successor) if these impossibilities can be got over, all will be well.—If not,—she will travel.———As I have said so much I may as well say all—the woman I mean is Miss Milbank—I know nothing of her fortune, & I am told that her father is ruined, but my own will when my Rochdale arrangements are closed, be sufficient for both, my debts are not 25000 p[oun]ds & the deuce is in it, if with R[ochdale] & the surplus of N[ewstead] I could not contrive to be as independent as half the peerage.—But I know little of her, & have not the most distant reason to suppose that I am at all a favourite in that quarter, but I never saw a woman whom I *esteemed* so much.—But that chance is gone—and there's an end.—Now—my dear Ly. M. I am completely in your power, I have not deceived you; as to———[Caroline] I hope you will not deem it vanity—when I soberly say—that it would have been want of Gallantry—though the acme of virtue—if I had played the Scipio on this occasion.—If through your means, or any means, I can be free, or at least change my fetters, my regard & admiration would not be increased, but my gratitude would, in the mean time it is by no means unfelt for what you have already done.—To Ly. B[essborough] I could not say all this, for she would with the best intentions, make the most absurd use of it; what a miserable picture does her letter present of this daughter? she seems afraid to know her, & blind herself writes in such a manner as to open the eyes of all others.—I am still here, in Holland's house, quiet & alone without any wish to add to my acquaintances, your departure was I assure you much more regretted than that of any of your lineals or collaterals, so do not you go to Ireland or I shall follow you oer "flood and fen" a complete Ignis fatuus—that is *I* the *epithet* will not apply to you, so we will divide the expression you would be the *light* & I the *fool*.—I send you back the letter, & this fearful ream of my own.—C[aroline] is suspicious about our counter plots, & I am obliged to be as treacherous as

Tallyrand, but remember *that treachery* is *truth* to you; I write as rarely as I can, but when I do, I must lie like George Rose,[3] your name I never mention when I can help it; & all my amatory tropes & figures are exhausted—I have a glimmering of hope, I *had* lost it, it is renewed—all depends on it, her worst enemy could not wish her such a fate as *now* to be thrown back upon me.—

yrs. ever most truly

P.S.—Dear Ly. M.—Dont think me careless, my correspondence since I was sixteen has not been of a nature to allow of any trust except to a Lock & key, & I have of late been doubly guarded—the few letters of yrs. & all others in case of the worst shall be sent back or burnt, surely after returning the one with Mr. *L[amb]'s message*, you will hardly suspect me of wishing to take any advantage, *that* was the only important one in behalf of my own interests;—think me bad if you please, but not *meanly* so. Ly. B[essborough]'s under another cover accompanies this.

[TO JOHN MURRAY]   *Cheltenham Septr. 14th. 1812*

Dear Sir,—The parcels contained some letters & verses all (but one) anonymous & complimentary and very anxious for my conversion from certain infidelities into which my goodnatured correspondents conceive me to have fallen.—The Books were presents of a *convertible* kind also, "Christian Knowledge" & the "Bioscope"[1] a religious dial of life explained, to the author of the former (Cadell publisher) I beg you will forward my best thanks for his letter, his presents, & above all, his good intentions.—The "Bioscope" contained an M.S.S. copy of very excellent verses, from whom I know not, but evidently the composition of some one in the habit of writing & of

---

[3] George Rose, father of William Stewart Rose, translator of French and Italian romances and legendary lays, was a political figure in the Duke of Portland's government. He was the butt of a political satire:

> No rogue that goes
> Is like that Rose
> Or scatters such deceit.

Byron was willing to think the worst of him as a spokesman for the lying Tory Government.

[1] Granville Penn, *The Bioscope, or Dial of Life Explained*. The "Christian Knowledge" was probably Penn's *Christian's Survey of all the Primary Events and Periods of the World*, a second edition of which was published in 1812.

writing well, I do not know if he be ye. author of the "Bioscope" which accompanied them, but whoever he is if you can discover him, thank him from me most heartily.—The other letters came from Ladies, who are welcome to convert me when they please, & if I can discover them & they be young as they say they are, I could convince them perhaps of my devotion.—I had also a letter from Mr. Walpole[2] on matters of this world which I have answered.—So you are Lucien's publisher,[3] I am promised an interview with him, & think I shall ask *you* for a letter of introduction, as "the Gods have made him poetical" from whom could it come with a better grace than *his* publisher & mine?—Is it not somewhat treasonable in you to have to do with a relative of the "direful foe" as the Morning Post calls his brother?— But my book on "Diet & regimen" where is it? I thirst for Scott's Rokeby let me have ye. first begotten copy.—The Antijacobin Review is all very well, & not a bit worse than the Quarterly,[4] & at least less harmless [harmful?].—By the bye have you secured my books? I want all the Reviews, at least the Critiques, quarterly monthly &c. Portuguese & English extracted & bound up in one vol. for my *old age*; & pray send my Romaic books, & get the vols. lent to Mr. Hobhouse?— he has had them now a long time.—If any thing occurs you will favour me with a line, & in winter we shall be nearer neighbours.—

yrs. very truly
BYRON

P.S.—I was applied to, to write ye. address for Drury Lane, but the moment I heard of the contest I gave up the idea of contending against all Grubstreet & threw a few thoughts on the subject into the fire.—I did this out of respect to you being sure you would have turned off any of your authors who had entered the lists with such scurvy competitors; to triumph would have been no glory, & to have been defeated— Sdeath—I would have choaked myself like Otway with a quartern loaf[5]—so—remember I had & have nothing to do with it upon *my Honour!*—

2 See [Sept., 1812?], to Walpole.

3 Lucien Buonaparte, brother of Napoleon, was an exile in England. His epic poem *Charlemagne*, translated by Dr. Butler of Shrewsbury and Francis Hodgson, was published in 1815.

4 The *Anti-Jacobin Review* published a critique of *Childe Harold* in August, 1812; The *Quarterly* review appeared in March, 1812.

5 Otway's death at the age of thirty-three was said by Theophilus Cibber (*Lives of the Poets*, ed. 1853, Vol. II, pp. 333–34) to have been caused by his choking on a roll.

My dear Ly. M.—"If I were looking in your face entre les deux yeux" I know not whether I should find "frankness or truth"—but certainly something which looks quite as well if not better than either, & whatever it may be I would not have it changed for any other expression; as it has defied Time, no wonder it should perplex *me.*— "*Manage* her"!—it is impossible—& as to friendship—no—it must be broken off at once, & all I have left is to take some step which will make her hate me effectually, for she must be in extremes.—What you state however is to be dreaded, besides—she presumes upon the weakness & affection of all about her, and the very confidence & kindness which would break or reclaim a good heart, merely lead her own farther from deserving them.—Were this but secure, you would find yourself mistaken in me; I speak from experience; except in one solitary instance, three months have ever cured me, take an example.— In the autumn of 1809 in the Mediterranean I was seized with an *everlasting* passion considerably more violent on my part than this has ever been—[1] every thing was settled—& *we* (the *we's* of that day) were to set off for the Friuli; but lo! the Peace spoilt every thing, by putting this in possession of the French, & some particular occurrences in the interim determined me to go on to Constantinople.—However we were to meet next year at a certain time, though I told my amica there was no time like the present, & that I could not answer for the future.—She trusted to her power, & I at the moment had certainly much greater doubts of her than myself.—A year sped & on my return downwards, I found at Smyrna & Athens dispatches, requiring the performance of this "bon billet qu'a la Chatre" & telling me that one of us had returned to the spot on purpose.—But things had altered as I foresaw, & I proceeded very leisurely, not arriving till some months after, pretty sure that in the interim my Idol was in no want of Worshippers.—But she *was* there, & we met—at the Palace & the Governor[2] (ye. most accomodating of all possible chief Magistrates) was kind enough to leave us to come to the most diabolical of explanations.—It was in the Dogdays, during a Sirocco—(I almost perspire now with the thoughts of it) during the intervals of an intermittent fever (my love had also intermitted with my malady) and I certainly feared the Ague & my Passion would both return in full

[1] See Sept. 15, 1809, to Mrs. Byron, note 1. This is an account, long after the event, of Byron's love affair at Malta with Mrs. Spencer Smith.

[2] Major General Hildebrand Oakes was then "his Majesty's Commissioner for the Affairs of Malta".

force.—I however got the better of both, & she sailed up the Adriatic & I down to the Straits.— —I had certes a great deal to contend against, for the Lady (who was a *select* friend of the Queen of Naples) had something to gain in a few points, & nothing to lose in *reputation*, & was a woman perfectly mistress of herself & every art of intrigue personal or political, not at all in love, but very able to persuade me that she was so, & sure that I should make a most *convenient* & complaisant fellow traveller.— —She is now I am told writing her Memoirs at Vienna, in which I shall cut a very indifferent figure; & nothing survives of this most ambrosial amour, which made me on one occasion risk my life, & on another almost drove me mad, but a few Duke of York*ish* letters, & certain baubles which I dare swear by this time have decorated the hands of half Hungary, & all Bohemia.—Cosi finiva la Musica.—

[TO LADY MELBOURNE]   *Cheltenham Septr 18th. 1812*

My dear Ly. Melbourne—I only wish you thought your influence worth a *"boast"* I should look upon it as the highest compliment paid to myself.—To you it would be none, for (besides the little value of the thing) you have seen enough to convince you how easily I am governed by anyone's *presence*, but *you* would be obeyed even in absence.—All persons in this situation are so from having too much *heart* or too little *head*, one or both, set mine down according to your own calculations. You & yours seem to me much the same as the Ottoman family to the faithful, they frequently change their rulers, but never the reigning race; I am perfectly convinced that if I fell in love with a woman of Thibet she would turn out an *emigré cousin* of some of you.—You ask "am *I* sure of myself?" I answer—no—but *you* are, which I take to be a much better thing.—Miss M[ilbanke] I admire because she is a clever woman, an amiable woman & of high blood, for I have still a few Norman & Scotch inherited prejudices on the last score, were I to marry.—As to *Love*, that is done in a week, (provided the Lady has a reasonable share) besides marriage goes on better with esteem & confidence than romance, & she is quite pretty enough to be loved by her husband, without being so glaringly beautiful as to attract too many rivals.—She always reminds me of "Emma" in the modern Griselda, & whomever I may marry, that is the woman I would wish to *have married*.—It is odd enough that my acquaintance with C———[Caroline] commenced with a confidence on my part about your Niece, C[aroline] herself (as I have often told her) was *then* not at all to my taste, nor I, (& I may believe her) to hers, & we shall end probably as we begun.—However, if after all "it is decreed on high" that, like James the Fatalist, I *must* be hers, she shall be *mine* as long as it pleases her, & the circumstances under which she becomes so, will at least make me devote my life to the vain attempt of reconciling her to herself, wretched as it would render me, she should never know it; the sentence once past, I could never restore that which she had lost, but all the reparation I could make should be made, & the cup drained to the very dregs by myself so that it's bitterness passed from her.—In the mean time, till it *is* irrevocable, I must & may fairly endeavour to extricate both from a situation, which from our total want of all but selfish considerations has brought us to the brink of the gulph, before I sink I will at least have a *swim* for it, though I wish with all my heart it was the *Hellespont* instead, or that I could cross *this* as easily as I did ye. other.— One reproach I cannot escape, whatever happens hereafter *she* will charge it on me & so shall I, & I fear that

> "The first step of error none e'er could recall
> And the woman once fallen forever must fall,
> Pursue to the last the career she begun,
> And be *false* unto *many*, as *faithless* to *one*." [1]

Forgive one stanza of my own sad rhymes, you know I never did inflict any upon you before, nor will again.—What think you of Ly. B[essborough]'s last? she is losing those brilliant hopes expressed in the former epistle.—I have written 3 letters to Ireland, & cannot compass more, the last to Ly. B[essborough] herself in which I never mentioned Ly. C[aroline]'s name nor yours (if I recollect aright) nor alluded to either.— —It is an odd thing to say, but I am sure Ly. B[essborough] will be a little provoked, if *I* am the *first* to change, for like the Governor of Tilbury fort, although "the *Countess* is resolved" the *mother intenerisce un poco*, & doubtless will expect her daughter to be adored (like an Irish Lease) for a term of 99 years.—I say it again, that happy as she must & will be to have it broken off *anyhow*, she will *hate* me if *I* don't break my heart; now is it not so?—laugh—but answer me truly?— —I am not sorry that C[aroline] sends you extracts from my epistles, I deserve it for the passage I shewed once to

---

[1] This stanza was never published, but Byron used two lines of it in the last stanza of his poem to Lady Frances Webster in 1816. This last stanza was not published until the present century. See Marchand, *Byron: A Biography*, II, 581.

you, but remember that was in the *outset* & when every thing said or sung was exculpatory, & innocent & what not—Moreover recollect what absurdities a man must write to his Idol, & that "garbled extracts" prove nothing without the context; for my own part I declare that I recollect no such proposal of an *epistolary truce*, & the Gambols at divers houses of entertainment with ye. express &c. tend ye. rather to confirm my statement. But I cannot be sure, or answerable for all I have said or unsaid since "*Jove* himself (some with Mrs. Malaprop would read *Job*) has forgotten to "laugh at our perjuries" I am certain that I tremble for the trunkfuls of my contradictions, since like a Minister or a woman she may one day exhibit them in some magazine or some quartos of villainous memoirs written in her 7000th love fit.— Now dear Ly. M. my *paper* spares you—Believe me with great regard yrs ever,

ß

P.S.—In your last you say you are "surrounded by fools"—why then "Motley's the only wear"

"Oh that I were a fool a motley fool
I am ambitious of a motley coat"

well will you answer "thou shalt have one"

Chi va piano va sano
e chi va sano va lontano

My progress has been "lontano" but alas ye "sano" & "piano" are past praying for.—

[TO JOHN HANSON]   [*Sept. 19, 1812.*]

Sent—with *carte blanche* as to Rochdale at the same [time?] recommending *emphatic measures* with *Sr. Dearden*,[1] & *good discretion* on the *Tithe* business—Best compts. to Mrs. H[anson] & Miss E. H[anson] & a good Journey

yrs.

ß

Address to No. 8 St. James's Street in case I should have left C[heltenha]m it will be forwarded.

[1] James Dearden held the lease on the coal mines at Rochdale, which Hanson was trying to break for Byron. He finally bought Rochdale just before Byron's death.

Miss M[ilbanke] I admire, & as I said in my last could love if she would let me, still I cannot believe what you say, that she is not engaged to E[den].[1] I have been assured of the contrary, by such good authority. *Aunts* are not trusted on such subjects. . . . Whatever you may think, I assure you I have a very domestick turn, & should wish to be married to a Woman whom I could love & esteem & in whom I could place the greatest confidence. . . . .[2]

[TO LADY MELBOURNE]   *Cheltenham Septr. 21st. 1812*

Dear Lady M.—I have had at last a letter offering a kind of release, & demanding an answer to a curious question viz—"whether I could live without her"? I began an answer particularly as I have not written these 3 weeks, but bewildering myself in the course of the first sentence, threw it into the fire,—& shall write no more.—They, & she in particular have been extremely gay, to which I can have no objection whatever, the best proof of which is that I have not expressed any; Ly. B[essborough] I rather think will encourage some other connection or connections, as a temporary expedient, poor soul, her *remedy* would yield me *eventually* ample revenge if I felt any resentment against her which indeed I do not.—I think my dear Ly. M. you must agree with me that————[Caroline?] will fulfil ye. prophecy in my last & would, had the present object of your fears never existed.—I have not written, because it would only lead to endless recapitulation, recrimination, *bother*ation (take a Kilkenny phrase) accusation, & all -ations but *salv*ation.—Before I become candidate for the distinguished honour of *Nepotism* to your Ladyship, it will be as well for me to know that your Niece is not already disposed of to a better bidder, if not I should like it of all things, were it only for the pleasure of calling you *Aunt*! & soliciting your benediction.— My only objection (supposing of course that ye. Lady's was got over) would be to my *Mamma*, from whom I have already by instinct imbibed a mortal aversion.—I am sadly out of practice in this sort of *suit*, & shall make some villainous

---

[1] Miss Milbanke had been wooed by George Eden, Lord Auckland's heir, and she continued to be friendly with him though she rejected his offer of marriage. Later, she let Byron think that she was engaged, and then was embarrassed as to how to undeceive him without admitting to a lie.

[2] The text of this letter is perhaps unreliable, since sentences (often inaccurate) from other letters, of which the manuscripts are extant, are mingled with it. I have given here only the parts of the letters not in other extant ones.

blunder; but I will try & if this fails, anything else.—Your letter arrived just in time to prevent me from setting off for Rochdale, where I am going to purchase the great Tythes of 12000 acres of waste which cannot be enclosed without my permission, & as enclosure alone makes the said tithes valuable, & the Archbishop wishes to sell them, & I have hitherto held out against enclosing with the view of obtaining them, my Agent is gone instead, which will do quite as well, & save me a tiresome journey. C[aroline's] last letter is full of reproaches, which I don't feel at all disposed to controvert, nor to recriminate; but how could anything of this kind be carried without 10000 perfidies, particularly one so vilely perplexed in all its branches! —I cannot write, I would not seem jealous, & it would be under *all circumstances*, improper to appear indifferent and—and—Oh I am in a diabolical dilemma—my great hope rests in the Kilkenny theatricals, some hero of the Sock, some Gracioso of the buskin will perhaps electrify poor Ly. B[essborough]—& transfer her alarms to an Irish Roscius.—If I marry, positively it must be in three weeks; in the mean time I am falling in love as much as I can with a new Juliet, who sets off for London in the long Coach tomorrow to appear on (not in) Covent Garden, with an Italian songstress, with a Welsh [Sempstress?] with my Agent's wife & daughter, & a picture of Buonaparte's Empress who looks as fair & foolish as he is dark & diabolical.— —Now my dear Ly. M. if I could not frank my letters I should feel for you, as it is, if they *wake* you in the morning it is good for yr. health, & if they make you sleep at night — still better.—

ever yrs most affectly. & truly

P.S.—A letter of mine to you (before the voyage) was found by her Heaven knows where, & on this she has again expatiated— n'importe—but *who* was careless? ma tante—methinks that reproach was somewhat misplaced.—If you left it in ye. way on purpose —it had a blessed effect—it is but adding another *winding* to our *Labyrinth,*—she quotes from it passages which I recollect—how could you Lady M—how could you "wear a pocket with a hole [in it]"?—

[TO LORD HOLLAND] *Septr. 22d.* [*1812*]

My dear Lord—In a day or two I will send you something which you will still have the liberty to reject if you dislike it, I should like to have had more time but will do my best, but too happy if I can oblige *you* though I may offend 100 Scribblers & the discerning public.—[1]

ever yrs.

B.

Best respects to Ly. H[olland]. Keep *my name* a *secret* or I shall be beset by all the rejected, & perhaps damned by a party.

[TO CHARLES HANSON]   *Cheltenham Septr. 22d. 1812*

Dear Charles,—I will thank you to send me by return of post the sum of two hundred & fifty pds. previously taking the number of the *notes* & all precautions.—

Believe me yrs. ever

BYRON

P.S.—I have particular occasion for this sum.—Your Father is gone to Newstead & so on to Rochdale.—

[TO LORD HOLLAND]   *Cheltenham Septr. 23d. 1812*

My dear Lord—Ecco!—I have marked some passages with *double readings*—chuse between them—*cut*—*add*—*reject*—or *destroy*—do with it as you will—I leave it to you—& the *Committee*—you cannot say so called—a "non *commitendo*["]—what will they do (& I do) with the hundred & one rejected troubadours?[1]—"With trumpets yea—& with shawms" will you be assailed in the most diabolical doggerel—I wish my name not to transpire, till the day is decided—I shall not be in town so it wont much matter—but let me have a good *deliverer*—I think Elliston[2] should be the man—or Pope[3]—not

---

[1] This was the first draft of Byron's Drury Lane Address, which he had promised Lord Holland.

[1] Actually 112 addresses had been submitted. In November, 1812, an enterprising bookseller, B. McMillan, of Bow Street, Covent Garden, published 42 of them as *The Genuine Rejected Addresses presented to the Committee of Management for Drury Lane Theatre; preceded by that written by Lord Byron and adopted by the Committee.*

[2] Robert William Elliston (1774–1831), a leading actor at Drury Lane at the time, spoke Byron's prologue.

[3] Alexander Pope (1763–1835) was for some years a principal tragedian at Covent Garden. He was noted for the "mellow richness" of his voice.

Raymond[4] I implore you by the Love of *Rythmus*! The passages with words marked thus ≡ ≡ above & below are for you to chuse between epithets & such like poetical furnitures. Pray write me a line & believe me ever yrs.

B.

My best remembrances to Ly. H. Will you be good enough to decide between the various readings *marked* & erase the others—or our *Deliverer* will be as puzzled as a Commentator, & belike repeat both—. If these *versicles* wont do—I will hammer out some more endecasyllables.—

Tell Ly. H[olland] I have had sad work to keep out the Phenix—[5] I mean the *fire office* of that name—it has *insured* the theatre & why not the address!— —

[Following the poem]: This had perhaps better be recopied—if sent to my Publisher it will save your Lordship any further trouble on that score—but I wish *you* to decide first on the different readings.—

If "stormed" appears to[o] strong a word remember Johnson

"And unresisted Passion *stormed* the heart".[6]

[TO LORD HOLLAND (*a*)]   *Septr. 24.* [*1812*]

My dear Lord—I send a recast of the four first lines of the concluding paragraph

> "This greeting oer—the ancient rule obeyed,
> The Drama's homage by her Herald paid,
> Receive *our Welcome too*, whose every Tone
> Springs from our hearts, & fain would win your own,
> The Curtain rises &c. &c.["]

And do forgive all the trouble;—see what it is to have [to] do even with the *genteelest* of us!—

ever yrs.
B.

---

[4] Stage manager at Drury Lane and occasional actor. He played the Ghost in the cast of *Hamlet*, with which Drury Lane reopened.

[5] Sixty-nine of the competitors had in one way or another invoked the Phoenix. Byron studiously avoided it.

[6] Johnson's Drury Lane Prologue, line 8: "And unresisted passion stormed the breast."

My dear Lord—I must bore you still further with alterations as they rise.—[Perhaps?] these couplets—

> "Here too when tragic tears forget to flow
> "The vein of wit shall chase the sounds of woe

had better run thus—

> "Shall *Congreve's Wit* succeed to *Otway's Woe*—

and another

> "Friends of the Stage—for whom our voice we raise

had better be—

> "Friends of the stage—to whom both players & play
> "Must sue in turn for pardon or for praise

Churchill has *Player* as a monosyllable frequently—Propound—pronounce, & excuse all this, which will show you that I am anxious to do the little I can as desirably as Time & the Cheltenham waters will allow—to say nothing of my want of practice in this line of rhyming—

ever yrs.
B.

"*livid* wave" may be "glowing wave" *burning—blazing—fiery*—oh Lord—even "sulphurous" are all *bespoke* "purple" "crimson" are too *feeble*—if you think of some [hugeous?] *epithet*—in with it instead.—

My dear Lord—I believe this is the third scrawl since yesterday all about *epithets*.—I think the epithet "intellectual" must convey the meaning I intend & though I hate compounds for the present I will try (col permesso) the word—"Genius-gifted patriarchs of our line" instead—Johnson has our "many-coloured life" a compound but they are always best avoided—however it is the only one in 90 lines, but will be happy to give way to a better.—I am ashamed to intrude any more remembrances on Ly. H. or letters upon you; but you are fortunately for me gifted with patience already too often tried by your obliged & sincere St.

BYRON

My dear Lord,—Still "more matter for a May morning,"[1] having patched the middle & end of the address I send one more couplet for a part of the beginning—which if not too turgid you will have the goodness to add.—After that flagrant image of the *Thames* (I hope no unlucky wag will say I have set it on fire, though Dryden in his Annus Mirabilis & Churchill in his "Times"[2] did it *before* me), I mean to insert this

"As flashing far the new Volcano shone

"And swept the skies with $\begin{cases} \text{meteors} \\ \text{Lightnings} \end{cases}$ not their own,

"*While thousands thronged around* the burning dome

&c. &c.

I think "thousands" less flat than "crowds collected," but don't let me plunge into the Bathos, or rise into Nat Lee's *bedlam* metaphors.[3]— By the bye the best view of the said fire, (which I myself saw from a House-top in C[ovent] Garden) was at W[estminster] Bridge from the reflection on the Thames.— —Perhaps the present couplet had better come in after "trembled for their home" the two lines after, as otherwise the image certainly *sinks* & it will run just as well.—The lines themselves perhaps may be better thus—chuse or refuse—but please *yourself* & don't mind "*Sir Fretful*"—[4]

"As flashed the volumed blaze, and $\begin{cases} \text{sadly} \\ \textit{ghastly} \end{cases}$ shone

"The skies with lightnings awful as their own,

The last *runs smoothest*—& I think best, but you know *better* than best.—"*Lurid*" is *also* a less *indistinct* epithet than "*livid* wave" & if you think so—a dash of the pen will do.—I expected one line this

---

1 *Twelfth Night*, Act III, scene 4.

2 Dryden, *Annus Mirabilis*, stanza 231; Churchill, *Times*, lines 701–702.

3 Nathaniel Lee (1653?–92), a dramatist who collaborated with Dryden. His dramas were full of extravagance and bombast. He finally lost his mind and was confined in Bethelehem Hospital for the insane, where he is said to have written a tragedy in 25 acts.

4 In Sheridan's *The Critic* (Act I, scene 1) Sneer says of Sir Fretful Plagiary, ". . . the insidious humility with which he seduces you to give a free opinion on any of his works can be exceeded only by the petulant arrogance with which he is sure to reject your observations."

morning—in the mean time I shall remodel & condense & if I do not hear from you, shall send another copy.—

I am ever yr. obliged & sincere

B.

My dear Ly. M.—It would answer no purpose to write a syllable on any subject whatever & neither accelerate nor retard what we wish to prevent, she must be left to Chance; conjugal affection and the Kilkenny Theatricals are equally in your favour—for my part it is an accursed business *towards* nor *from* which I shall not move a single step; if she throws herself upon me "cosi finiva" if not, the sooner it is over the better—from this moment I have done with it, only before she returns allow me to know that I may act accordingly; but there will be nothing to fear before that time, as if a woman & a selfish woman also, would not fill up the vacancy with the first comer?—As to Annabella she requires time & all the cardinal virtues, & in the interim I am a little verging towards one who demands neither, & saves me besides the trouble of marrying by being married already.— —She besides does not speak English, & to me nothing but Italian, a great point, for from certain coincidences the very sound of that language is Music to me, & she has black eyes & *not* a very white skin, & reminds me of many in the Archipelago I wished to forget, & makes me forget what I ought to remember, all which are against me.—I only wish she did not swallow so much supper, chicken wings—sweetbreads,—custards —peaches & *Port* wine—a woman should never be seen eating or drinking, unless it be *lobster sallad* & *Champagne*, the only truly feminine & becoming viands.—I recollect imploring one Lady not to eat more than a fowl at a sitting without effect; & have never yet made a single proselyte to Pythagoras.—Now a word to yourself—a much more pleasing topic than any of the preceding.—I have no very high opinion of your sex, but when I do see a woman superior not only to all her own but to most of ours I worship her in proportion as I despise the rest.—And when I know that men of the first judgment & the most distinguished abilities have entertained & do entertain an opinion which my own humble observation without any great effort of discernment has enabled me to confirm on the same subject, you will not blame me for following the example of my elders & betters & admiring you certainly as much as you ever were admired.— My only regret is that the very awkward circumstances in which we are placed prevents & will prevent the improvement of an acquaintance which I now almost regret having made—but recollect whatever happens that the loss of it must give me more pain than even the *precious* [*previous?*] *acquisition* (& this is saying *much*) which will occasion that loss. Ld. Jersey has reinvited me to M[iddleton] for the 4 Octr. & I will be there if possible, in the mean time whatever step you take to break off this affair has my full concurrence— but *what* you wished me to write would be a little too indifferent; and *that* now would be an insult, & I am much more unwilling to hurt her feelings now than ever, (not from the mere apprehension of a disclosure in her wrath) but I have always felt that one who has given up much, has a claim upon *me* (at least—whatever she deserve from others) for every respect that she may not feel her own degradation, & this is the reason that I have not written at all lately, lest some expression might be misconstrued by her.—When the Lady herself begins the quarrel & adopts a new "Cortejo" then my Conscience is comforted.—She has not written to me for some days, which is either a very bad or very good omen.—

yrs. ever

I observe that C[aroline] in her late epistles, lays peculiar stress upon her powers of attraction, upon W[illiam]'s attachment &c. & by way of enhancing the extreme value of her regards, tells me, that she "could make any one in love with her" an amiable accomplishment— but unfortunately a little too general to be valuable, for was there ever yet a woman, not absolutely disgusting, who could not say or do the same thing? any woman can *make* a man in *love* with her, show me her who can *keep* him so?—*You* perhaps *can* show me such a woman but I have not seen her for these—*three weeks.*—

[TO LORD HOLLAND]   *Septr. 26th.*[*–27th.*] *1812*

My dear Lord—You will think there is no end to my villainous emendations.—5 & 6th. lines I think to alter thus—

oh Sight admired & mourned
"Ye who beheld—⟨and who forgets the sight⟩
When Radiance mocked the Ruin it adorned
⟨"When burst the radiant Ruin into light?⟩

because "*night*" is repeated the next line but one, & as it now stands

209

the conclusion of the paragraph "worthy him (Shakespeare) & *you*" appears to apply the *"you"* to those only who were out of bed & in Covent Garden market on the night of the Conflagration, instead of the Audience or the discerning public at large *all* of whom are intended to be comprised in that comprehensive & I hope comprehensible pronoun.—By the bye—one of my corrections in the fair copy sent yesterday has dived into the Bathos some sixty fathom

"When Garrick died—& Brinsley ceased to write["], ceasing to *live* is a much more serious concern, & ought not to be first therefore—I will let the old couplet stand—with it's half rhymes *"sought"* & *"wrote"* second thoughts in every thing are best, but in rhyme third & fourth don't come amiss—I am very anxious in this business & I do hope that the [sorry?] trouble I occasion you will plead it's own excuse, & that it will tend to shew my endeavour to make the most of the time allotted. I wish I had known it months ago, for in that case I had not left one line standing on another.—I always scrawl in this way, and smoothe as much as I can but never sufficiently, & latterly I can weave a nine line stanza faster than a couplet, for which measure I have not the cunning.—When I began "Ch[ild]e Harold" I had never tried Spenser's measure, & now I cannot scribble in any other.— After all, my dear Lord, if you can get a decent address elsewhere, dont hesitate to put this aside; why did you not trust your own Muse? I am very sure she would have been triumphant, & saved the Committee their trouble, "tis a joyful one" to me but I fear I shall not satisfy even myself.—After the account you sent me tis no compliment to say, you would have beaten your candidates, but I mean that in that case there would have been no occasion for their being beaten at all.—There are but two decent prologues in our tongue—Pope's to Cato—[1] Johnson's to Drury Lane,[2] this with the Epilogue to the "Distrest Mother"[3] & I think one of Goldsmith's,[4] and a prologue of Old Colman's to Beaumont & Fletcher's Philaster[5] are the best things of the kind we have.—

My homage to Ly. H.——& best thanks for her kind remembrances

[1] Pope wrote the Prologue to Addison's *Cato* when it was acted at Drury Lane, April 13, 1713.

[2] Johnson wrote the Prologue when Garrick opened Drury Lane, September 15, 1747, with the *Merchant of Venice*.

[3] Addison is supposed to have written the epilogue to Ambrose Philips's adaptation of Racine's *The Distrest Mother*, which was presented at Drury Lane, March 17, 1712.

[4] It is not certain to which of Goldsmith's epilogues Byron refers.

[5] George Colman the Elder wrote the Prologue for the production of *Philaster* at Drury Lane, October 8, 1763.

My dear Lord—I have just received your very kind letters, & hope you have met with a second copy corrected & addressed to H[olland] H[ouse] with some omissions & this new couplet

> "as glared each rising flash & ghastly shone
> The skies with lightnings awful as their own.["]

As to remarks I can only say I will alter & acquiesce in anything.— With regard to the part which W[hitbread][6] wishes to omit I believe the address will go off *quicker* without it though like the agility of the Hottentot at the expence of *one* testicle.[7]—I leave to *your* choice entirely the different specimens of *stucco work*, & a *brick* of your own will also much improve my Babylonish turret.— —I should like Elliston[8] to have it with your leave.— "Adorn" & "mourn" are lawful rhymes in Pope's Death of the unfortunate Lady;—Gray has *"forlorn"* & *"mourn"*—& "torn and mourn" are in Smollet's famous "tears of Scotland"[9]— —As there will probably be an outcry amongst the rejected—I hope the Committee will testify (if it be needful) that I sent in nothing to the Congress whatever with or without my name as your Lordship well knows.—All I have to do with it is with & through you, & though I of course wish to satisfy the audience—I do assure you my first object is to comply with your request, & in so doing shew the sense I have of the many obligations you have conferred upon me.

yrs. ever
B.—

[TO JOHN MURRAY]   *Cheltenham Septr. 27th. 1812*

Dear Sir,—I sent in no address whatever to the Committee, but out of nearly one hundred (this is *confidential*) none have been deemed worth acceptance, & in consequence of their *subsequent* application to *me*, I have written a prologue which *has* been received & will be

---

[6] Samuel Whitbread, son of a wealthy brewer, was married to the sister of the second Earl Grey, the Whig statesman. He entered Parliament as an independent Whig. He was a Foxite and an advocate of peace with France. As manager of Drury Lane, he joined with Lord Holland in requesting Byron to write the Drury Lane address for the opening of the new theatre.

[7] In Raynal's *History of the Indies*, translated by Justamond, 1776, (London ed. 1783, I, 807), is this statement, which Byron may have read: "It is very certain, and has often been observed that the Hottentot men have but one testicle."

[8] See Sept. 23, 1812, to Lord Holland, note 2.

[9] Gray, "The Bard", lines 101–102; Smollet, "The Tears of Scotland", lines 1–2.

spoken.—The MS. is now in the hands of Ld. Holland.—I write this merely to say that (however it is received by the audience) you will publish it in the next Edition of C[hilde] H[arol]d & I only beg you at present to keep my name secret till you hear further from me, & as soon as possible I wish you to have a correct copy to do with as you think proper.—

I am yrs. very truly

BYRON

P.S.—I should wish a few copies printed off *before* that the News-paper copies may be correct *after* the *delivery*.—

[TO LORD HOLLAND (a)]   *Septr. 28th. 1812*—

My dear Lord—Will this do better?—the metaphor is more complete

"Till slowly ebbed the $\begin{Bmatrix} \textit{Lava of the} \\ \textit{spent volcanic} \end{Bmatrix}$ wave

"And blackening Ashes marked the Muse's grave

if not we will say "burning" wave, & instead of "*burning* clime" in the line some couplets back have "glowing".—Is Whitbread determined to *castrate* all my *cavalry* lines?[1] I dont see why t'other house should be spared, besides it is the public who ought to know better, & you recollect Johnson's was against similar buffooneries of Rich's but certes I am not Johnson.—[2] Instead of "effects" say "labours"

---

[1] Whitbread objected to the strength of the indictment of the public taste in these lines, which Byron finally acquiesced in omitting:

Nay, lower still, the Drama yet deplores
That late she deigned to crawl upon all-fours.
When Richard roars in Bosworth for a horse,
If you command, the steed must come in course.
If you decree, the Stage must condescend
To soothe the sickly taste we dare not mend. . . .

In 1811 a troop of horses had been brought on the stage at Covent Garden in *Bluebeard*, and again in Lewis's *Timour the Tartar*. And later a live elephant appeared. The Drury Lane Company had ridiculed this tendency in a burlesque, *Quadrupeds, or the Manager's Last Kick*, in which tailors were mounted on asses and mules. The prologue would perhaps have been better if Byron's lines had remained.

[2] Johnson in his prologue had attacked the "buffooneries" of John Rich, who introduced pantomime in England.

"degenerate" will do——will it?—Mr. Betty is no longer a *babe* therefore the lines cannot be personal.—Would this do?

> "Till ebbed the Lava of $\begin{cases} \text{the burning} \\ \text{that molten} \end{cases}$ wave"

with "glowing dome" in case you prefer "burning" added to this "wave" metaphorical.—The word "fiery pillar" was suggested by the "pillar of fire" in the book of Exodus which went before the Israelites through the red Sea.—I once thought of saying "Like Israel's pillar" & making it a simile but I did not know—the great temptation was leaving the epithet "fiery" for the supplementary wave.—I want to work up that passage—as it is the only new ground a prologuizer can go upon.—

> "This is the place where if a poet
> "Shined in description he might show it."

If I part with the possibility of a future conflagration we lessen the compliment to Shakespeare, however we will een mend it thus—

> "Yes it shall be—the Magic of that Name
> "That scorns the scythe of Time, the torch of Flame,
> "On the same spot &c.

there—the deuce is in it, if that is not an improvement to W[hit-bread]'s content.—Recollect, it is the *"name"* & not the *magic* that has a noble contempt for those same weapons, if it were the "Magic"— my metaphor would be somewhat of the maddest, so the "name" is the antecedent.—But my dear Lord—your patience is not quite so immortal, therefore—with many & sincere thanks I am

yrs. ever most affectly.
BYRON

P.S.—I foresee there will be charges of partiality in the papers— but you know I sent in no address—& glad both you & I must be that I did not—for in that case their plea had been plausible.—I doubt the Pit will be testy—but conscious Innocence a novel & pleasing sensation makes me bold.—

[TO LORD HOLLAND (*b*)]   *Septr. 28th. 1812*

My dear Lord—I have altered the 3d line & *middle* couplet so as I hope partly to do away W[hitbread]'s objection; I do think in the present state of the Stage, it had been unpardonable to pass over the horses & Miss *Mudie* &c.[1]—as Betty is no longer a boy—how can this be applied to him?—he is now to be judged as a man—if he acts still like a boy—the public will but be more ashamed of their blunder. —I have, you see, *now* taken it for *granted* that these things are reformed—I confess I wish that part of the address to stand—but if W[hitbread] is inexorable een let it go—I have also new cast the lines & softened the hint of future combustion.—and sent them off this morning.—Will you have the Goodness to add or insert the *"approved"* alterations as they *arrive.*—They "come like Shadows so depart"[2] occupy me, & I fear disturb you.— Do not let Mr. W[hitbread] put the address into Elliston's hands till you have settled on these alterations.—I may think of more—but I have about done.— E[lliston] will think it *too long*—much depends on the speaking—I fear it will not bear much curtailing without *chasms* in the sense.—It is certainly too long in the reading, but if E[lliston] exerts himself— such a favourite with the public will not be thought tedious.—*I* should think it so—if *he* were not to speak it.—

yrs. ever my dear Ld. most obliged

P.S. On looking again I doubt my idea of having obviated W[hitbread]'s objection to the other house allusion is a "non sequitur" but I wish to plead for this part, because the thing really is not to be passed over.—Many afterpieces in the Lyceum by the *same company* have already attacked this "Augean *Stable*"—& Johnson in his prologue against ["*Lun?*"] (the Harlequin manager Rich) "Hunt—"*Mahomet*",[3] &c. is surely a fair precedent

[TO WILLIAM BANKES]   *Cheltenham Septr. 28th. 1812*

Dear Bankes—When you point out to me how people can be intimate at the distance of some seventy leagues I will plead guilty to your charge & accept your farewell, but not *wittingly* till you give me

---

[1] For the horses see Sept. 28, 1812, to Lord Holland (*a*), note 1. Miss Mudie was a girl actress with whom Covent Garden's manager had hoped to rival the success of Betty, the "Young Roscius", but she was hissed from the stage when she appeared on November 23, 1805, as "Peggy" in *The Country Girl.*

[2] *Macbeth*, Act IV, scene 1.

[3] For Rich, see Sept. 28, 1812, to Lord Holland (*a*). Hunt was a stage boxer; Mahomet a rope-dancer.

some better reason than my silence which merely proceeded from a notion founded on your own declaration of *old* that you hated writing & receiving letters.—Besides how was I to find out a man of many residences? if I had addressed you *now* it had been to your Borough where I must have conjectured you were amongst your constituents. So now in despite of Mr. N & Ly. W. you shall be as "much better" as the Hexham Post-office will allow me to make you; I do assure you I am much indebted to you for thinking of me at all, & can't spare you even from amongst the superabundance of friends with whom you suppose me surrounded.—You heard that N[ewstead] is sold—the sum *£140.000* sixty to remain in Mortgage on the Estate for 3 years paying interest of course.[1]—Rochdale is also likely to do well.—So my worldly matters are mending.— — —I have been here sometime drinking the waters, simply because there are waters to drink, & they are very medicinal & sufficiently disgusting. In a few days I set out for Ld. Jersey's but return here, where I am quite alone, go out very little & enjoy in it's fullest extent the "dolce far niente".— What are you about I cannot guess even from your date, not dancing to the sound of the Gitourney, in the Halls of the Lowthers?[2] one of whom is here, ill, poor thing, with a Ptisich.—I heard that you passed through here (at the sordid Inn where I first alighted) the very day before I arrived in these parts.—We had a very pleasant set here at first ye. Jerseys Melbournes Cowpers & Hollands,[3] but all gone,—& the only persons I know are the Rawdon's[4] & Oxfords[5] with some later acquaintances of less brilliant descent.—But I do not trouble them much, & as for your rooms & your assemblies "they are not dreamed of in our philosophy".— —Did you read of a sad accident in the Wye t'other day? a dozen drowned, & Mr. Rossoe[6] a corpulent

[1] For the sale of Newstead see Aug. 31, 1812, to Hanson, note 2.

[2] William Lowther (1757–1844), first Earl of Lonsdale, was a patron of Wordsworth. His son William was at Harrow and Trinity College, and received his M.A. in 1808, the same year as did Byron.

[3] For Lady Jersey, see [April, 1812], to Bankes, note 1. Byron commented on his stay at Middleton (Lord Jersey's) in his "Detached Thoughts" (No. 92). For the Melbournes, see biographical sketches in Appendix. Peter, fifth Earl of Cowper, married in 1805 Emily Mary Lamb, daughter of Lord and Lady Melbourne.

[4] Francis Rawdon, created Baron Rawdon in 1783, had married the Countess of Loudoun in 1804. He succeeded as the second Earl of Moira (Irish Peerage) in 1793. He had been a general in the American and Napoleonic wars, and was an active supporter of the Prince of Wales.

[5] For the Oxfords, see the biographical sketch in the Appendix.

[6] The *Annual Register* for Sept. 21, 1812, gives an account of the event. Of a party of ten people, three were saved, among them a Mr. Rothery, not Rossoe, as Byron says.

gentleman preserved by a boathook or an eelspear begged when he heard that his wife was saved—no—*lost*—to be thrown in again!!—as if he could not have thrown himself in had he wished it—but this passes for a trait of sensibility.—What strange beings men are in & out of the Wye.—I have to ask you a thousand pardons for not fulfilling some orders before I left town; but if you knew all the cursed entanglements I *had* to wade through, it would be unnecessary to beg your forgiveness.—When will Parliament (the new one) meet? in sixty days on account of Ireland I presume, the Irish election will demand a longer period for completion than the Constitutional allotment.—Yours of course is safe, & all your side of the question, Salamanca[7] is the ministerial watchword & will go well with you.—I hope you will speak more frequently, I am sure at least you *ought*—& it will be expected.— —I see Portman[8] means to stand again.—Good night. Believe me dear Bankes

> ever yrs. most affectly.
> Μπαίρων

[TO LADY MELBOURNE]   *Septr. 28th. 1812*

My dear Lady M.—The *non*-mention of Miss R[awdon] certainly looks very suspicious but your correspondent has fallen into a mistake in which I am sure neither ye. lady nor myself could possibly join.— Since your departure I have hardly entered a single house, the Rawdons & the Oxfords & a family named Macleod are the only persons I know; Ly. C. Rawdon gave me a general retainer to her box at the theatre, where I generally go, which has probably produced the surmise you mention.—Miss R[awdon][1] has always been a mighty favourite with me, because she is unaffected, very accomplished, & lived amongst the Greeks of Venice & Trieste consequently well versed in many topics which are common to her & me & would be very stupid to any one else; I moreover think her very pretty though not at all in the style of beauty which I most admire; but she *waltzes*, & is for many reasons the very last woman on earth I should covet (unless she

---

[7] The battle of Salamanca, July 22, 1812, marked a decisive victory in the Peninsular War. Wellington's defeat of Marmont opened the way for the capture of Madrid. The Tory government took it as a justification of their policies in the war.

[8] Edward Berkeley Portman was first elected for Dorset in 1806. He was reelected in 1807, and retained his seat in 1812.

[1] See Sept. 28, 1812, to Bankes, note 4.

were "my neighbor's wife" & then the breaking a commandment would go far in her behalf) nor do I think that our acquaintance has extended even to a common flirtation, besides *her* views are in another quarter, & so most assuredly are mine.—I never heard of the report Ly. M[ilbanke?] *starts* from, & I am sure you will do me the justice to believe, I never dreamed of such a thing, & had I heard it should have disbelieved such nonsense as I do now;—I am not at all ashamed of my own bias towards your niece, nor should have the least objection to it's being posted up in Charing Cross, though I should never wish to hazard a refusal.— —I certainly did wish to cultivate her acquaintance, but C[aroline] told me she was engaged to Eden,[2] so did several others, Mrs. L[amb?], *her* great friend, was of opinion (& upon my honour I believed her) that she neither did could nor ought to *like* me, & was moreover certain that E[den] would be the *best husband* in the world & I it's *Antithesis*, & certainly *her* word deserved to be taken for *one* of us.—Under all these circumstances, & others I need not recapitulate, was I to hazard my heart with a woman I was very much inclined to like, but at the same time sure could be nothing to me?—& then you know my unfortunate manner which always leads me to talk too much to some particular person or not at all.—At present as I told you in my last I am rather captivated with a woman not very beautiful, but very much in the style I like, dark & lively, & neither more nor less than "La Pucilla" [Pulcella?] of the Opera, whom I see sometimes at Col. Macleod's & whenever Italian is spoken I always strive to repair ye. inroads want of practice make in my memory of that dearest of all languages.— —She is very fond of her husband, which is all the better, as thus, if a woman is attached to her husband how much more will she naturally like one who is *not* her husband—in the same manner as a woman does not always dislike a man who is violently in love with another, arguing says Fielding in this way, "if Mr.——loves Mrs. or Miss so *much*, how much more will he love *me* who am so far the superior not only of Mrs. or Miss but of all other Mistresses or Misses whatsoever?"— —You can hardly say I do not trust you when I tell you all these fooleries— —AT THIS *moment*, another *express* from Ireland!!! more Scenes!—this woman will never rest till she has made us all—what she & I at least deserve.—I must now write to her—I wrote Ly. B[essborough] a letter, which she was fool enough to shew her, though I addressed it under cover to Ld. B.—that she might not—*her* name

[2] See Sept. 19, 1812, to Lady Melbourne, note 1.

was not mentioned in it, but it was easy to discern by the contents, that I was not eager for their return.—

6. o Clock.

So—having now remanded Mr. O Brien (the Irish Cupid on whose wings this despatch was wafted) back to Waterford—I resume merely to say that I see nothing but marriage & a *speedy one* can save me; if your Niece is attainable I should prefer her—if not—the very first woman who does not look as if she would spit in my face, amongst the variety of spouses provided for me by your *correspondents* &c. I am infinitely amused with my Cameriero's[3] (who has lived with me since I was ten years old & been over the Mediterranean a prey to all the Mosquitoes & Siroccos in the Levant in my service) he is eternally sounding the praises of a *Dutch Widow* now here of great riches & rotundity, & very pretty withal; whose Abigail has made a conquest of him (a married man) & they have agreed how infinitely convenient it would be that as *they* can't marry, their master & mistress should.— We shall meet at Middleton I hope mia carissima *Zia*—I wish my Nepotism was well over—I do not care at all about Sir R[alph]'s involvements,[4] for I think that with the command of floating capital which my late N[ewstead] Business has put in my power, some arrangements might be made with *him* that might be advantageous to both—supposing this marriage could be effected.—When they come here I don't see how we are to meet for I go no-where—Does Annabella *waltz?*—it is an odd question—but a very essential point with me.—I wish somebody would say at once that I wish to propose to her—but I have great doubts of *her*—it rests with *herself* entirely. —Believe me

dear Ly. M. *ever* yrs. most affectly.

P.S.—I have written you the vilest & most Egotistical letter that ever was scribbled but Caro's courier made me feel *selfish* & you will pardon my catching the infection.—Your apology for Ly. M's[5] appellation was needless—though all my rhymes have got for me is a villainous nickname.—I know her, but latterly we *cut*—I suppose upon this most stupid rumour. I don't know how I shall manage this

[3] Byron's valet William Fletcher.
[4] Sir Ralph Milbanke, Annabella's father, had overspent himself in electioneering for Parliament.
[5] Lady Milbanke.

same wooing—I shall be like Comus & the Lady; I am sadly out of practice lately, except for a few sighs to a Gentlewoman at supper who was too much occupied with ye. *fourth* wing of her *second* chicken to mind anything that was not material.

[TO LORD HOLLAND] *Septr. 29th.* [*1812*]

My dear Lord—Shakespeare certainly ceased to reign in *one* of his Kingdoms, as George 3d did in America, & George 4th may in Ireland.—now we have nothing to do out of our own realms, and when the monarchy was gone, his majesty had but a barren sceptre— I have *cut away* you will see, & altered, but make it what you please— only I do implore for my *own* gratification one lash on those *accursed quadrupeds*[1]—a "long shot Sir Lucius if you love me."[2] I have altered *wave* &c. & the *fire* & so forth for the timid.— —Let me hear from you when convenient & believe me

ever yr. obliged

B.

P.S.—Do let *that* stand—& cut out elsewhere.—I shall choak if we must overlook their d——d menagerie.—

[TO CHARLES HANSON] *Septr. 29th. 1812*

Dear Charles—I acknowledge the receipt of two hundred & fifty pds. on acct. & thank you most sincerely for your promptitude of remittance. Believe me ever yrs. most truly

BYRON

[TO LORD HOLLAND (*a*)] *Septr. 30th. 1812*

My dear Lord.—I send you the most I can make of it—for I am not so well as I was—& find I "pull in resolution."[1]—I wish much to see you, & will be at Tetbury by 12 on Saturday, & from thence I go on to Ld. Jersey's—It is impossible not to allude to the degraded state of the Stage, but I have lightened *it*—and endeavoured to obviate your *other* objections—there is a new couplet for Sheridan allusive to his

[1] See Sept. 28, 1812, to Lord Holland (*a*), note 1.
[2] Bob Acres in *The Rivals* (Act V, scene 3).
[1] *Macbeth*, Act V, scene 5.

monody[2]—all the alter[ations] I have marked thus / and you will see
by comparison with the other copy.—I have cudgelled my brains with
the greatest willingness—& only wish I had more time to have done
better—You will find a sort of clap-trap laudatory couplet altered for
the quiet of the Committee & I have added towards the end, the couplet
you were pleased to *like*. The whole address is 73 lines.—still perhaps
too long—but if shortened you will save time, but I fear a little of what
I meant for sense also.—With myriads of thanks—I am ever yrs.

B.

My sixteenth Edition of respects to Ly. H.—How she must laugh at
all this.—I wish Murray my publisher to print off some copies as soon
as your Lordship returns to town—it will ensure correctness in the
papers afterwards.— — —

[TO LORD HOLLAND (*b*)]   *Septr. 30th. 1812*

> Far be from him that hour which asks in vain
> Tears such as flow for Garrick in his Strain!
> or
> Far be that hour that vainly asks in turn
> Such verse for him as $\begin{Bmatrix} \textit{crowned his} \\ \textit{wept oer } \text{Garrick's} \end{Bmatrix}$ Urn!

My dear Lord—Will you chuse between these added to the lines on
Sheridan, or "cherish or reject".[1]—I think they will wind up the
panegyric & agree with the train of thought preceding them.—Now
one word as to the committee, how could they resolve on a rough copy
of an address never sent in? unless you had been good enough to retain
in Memory or on paper the thing they have been good enough to adopt.
—By the bye the circumstances of the case should render the committee
less "avidus gloriae" for all praise of them would look plaguy suspicious—if necessary to be stated at all the simple facts bear them
out—they had surely a right to act as they pleased—my sole object
is one I trust which my whole conduct has shown—viz—that I did
nothing insidious—sent in *no address whatever*—but *when* applied to
did my best for them & myself—but above all that there was no undue
partiality—which will be what the rejected will endeavour to make
out—fortunately—most fortunately—I sent in no lines on the

---

[2] Sheridan's *Monody on Garrick.*
[1] The added lines were not retained.

occasion—for I am sure that had they in that case been preferred—it would have been asserted that *I* was known & owed the preference to private friendship.—This is what we shall probably have to en- counter, but if once spoken & approved, we shan't be much em- barrassed by their brilliant conjectures, & as to Criticism, an *old* author like an old Bull grows cooler (or ought) at every baiting.— — The only thing would be to avoid a party on the night of delivery, afterwards the more the better; & the whole transaction inevitably *leads* to a good deal of discussion.—Murray tells me there are myriads of ironical addresses ready—*some* in *imitation* of what is called *my style*—[2] if they are as good as the Probationary odes[3] or Hawkins' Pipe of Tobacco,[4] it will not be bad *fun* even for the *imitated.*

ever yrs. my dear Ld.

B—

in Tetbury on *Saturday* between 12 & 1.—

[TO LORD HOLLAND (*c*)]   *Septr. 30th.* [*1812*]

My dear Lord—I am just recovering from a smart attack of the stone (what a pleasing posthumous hope for a man to be able to have his monument carved out of his kidneys) & will meet you at Tetbury (before *12* I hope) on Saturday morning.—I go on next day to Ld. Jersey's but I wish to see you *first* & will bring a *recast* of the prologue with more alterations still.—

ever yrs obliged & sincerely

B.

P.S.—Shakespeare ceased to reign with a vengeance when D[rury] L[ane] was burnt for C[ovent] G[arden] was not then *rebuilt*—

P.S.—As I have now "*Tears such*["] &c. or "Such Verse" &c.—the next paragraph beginning also "such were the times" had better be "These were the days &" or "*Though* past the days"—& perhaps instead of "The *trophied names*" "*Triumphant*" or "*immortal*" will be preferable.—I am diluted to the throat with medicine for the Stone, &

---

[2] James and Horace Smith published in 1812 *Rejected Addresses*, parodying the styles of some of the writers of the day who supposedly wrote addresses for the opening of Drury Lane. The parody of Byron, "Cui Bono", imitates the style of *Childe Harold.*

[3] The *Probationary Odes*, a part of the *Rolliad* (1794) were satirical poems re- cording the result of an imaginary contest for the laureateship. They were inspired by Warton's Ode in honour of George III's birthday, 1785.

[4] *In Praise of a Pipe of Tobacco* (1736), by Isaac Hawkins Browne, was an ode in imitation of Swift, Pope, Thomson, and other contemporary poets.

[Boisragen?] wants me to try a [warm?] climate for the winter—but I wont.—

[TO LADY MELBOURNE]   [*September 30?, 1812?*]

It is not *I* who am to be feared now,[1] but *her* with her *Pique*; I need not repeat that I lay no stress upon attachment, *two* balls & *one* admirer will settle the last to her heart's content.—I do not at all know how to deal with her, because she is unlike every one else.—My letters have not reached her in Ireland, & she complains on that acct. the fault is not mine, I have written twice but the Post has been negligent, or *Ly. B*[essborough] *diligent*, & they will make her do some silly thing.——If we are not enemies before their return, you will inform me when they are expected, & I will be out of the way, unless something occurs to make that unnecessary.—I shall not write any more to Ireland, if I can avoid it, in fact I have said & unsaid & resaid till I am exhausted—& *you* will think that I have transferred my tediousness & my letters from her to you.—I would marry before they return, this would settle it at once, but I am new to that business, never having made a proposal in my life (though I was brought up till sixteen to be married to one who was older than myself & could not *wait*) & never married except by the *month* in the Levant where I was divorced twenty times from those who have been divorced twenty times before & since & are now widowed again I dare say.—Besides I do not know a single gentlewoman who would venture upon me, but that seems the only rational outlet from this adventure.— —I admired your niece, but she is engaged to Eden— —Besides she deserves a better heart than mine.— What shall I do—shall I *advertise*?—I thank you so much for your letters, on all topics *different* or indifferent they are most welcome.— Cheltenham is a desart, nothing but the Waters detain me here.—One word to break the monotony of my days with delight

ever yrs. most truly

[TO LADY CAROLINE LAMB]   [*October, 1812?*]

. . . correct yr. vanity which is ridiculous & proverbial, exert yr. Caprices on your new conquests & leave me in peace, yrs. Byron.[1]

[1] The beginning of this letter is missing.
[1] See letters of [Nov., 1812?], to Caroline Lamb.

My dear Lord,—I hope you have received *another* copy since 29th addressed to [Bowood?], on the 30th. with some additions omissions & alterations.—In case you have not I will write it out at Tetbury to-morrow where I wish to meet you about 12 or 1, if convenient, at all events *I* will be there, do not *you* come on to Cirencester, you have had quite trouble enough already—Many & sincere thanks to Ld. L[ans-downe?] for his invitation which I fear I cannot accept,[1] but *that* I will answer more certainly tomorrow.—I write in a great hurry from Lady Oxfords in a room full of people—pardon therefore this *address*, & believe me in the hope of meeting you at T[etbury] tomorrow Noon.—

ever yr. obliged
B.

P.S.—My last copy of the address is 73 lines, with the additional couplet on Sheridan.—

My dear Lord—A copy of this *still altered* is sent by the post but this will arrive first—It must be "humbler" *yet aspiring* does away the *modesty*, & after all *truth* is *truth*—besides there is a *puff* direct altered to please your *plaguy* [masters?] [on purpose?] *next* page – 6th couplet.—I shall be at *Tetbury* by 12 or 1 but send this for you to ponder over, there are several little things marked thus / altered for your perusal.— —I have dismounted the Cavalry—& I hope arranged to your *general* satisfaction.—

ever yrs.
B.

At Tetbury by *Noon*—I hope after it is sent there will be no more *elisions*—it is not now so long, 73 lines—two less than allotted.—I will allow all Committee objections, but I hope you won't permit Elliston to have any *voice* whatever except in *speaking* it.—Best compts. to Ly. H., Ld. & Ly L[ansdowne?]

---

[1] Lord Holland had been at Bowood Park, Lord Lansdowne's home near Calne in Wiltshire.

My dear Lord—As a "sudden thought strikes me" I send it (& may
more) to complete my patchwork—You will perceive by a comparison
of the passages here & on the M.S.S. that I have *interstitched* two more
couplets.—If it will do—let it stand—if not—"una [litura?]",[1] & spare
not the sponge.—

yrs. ever

B.

[TO LORD HOLLAND]   *Octr. 9th. 1812*

My dear Lord—I have only time to say thus—

> *Vain* of our ancestry &c.
> While thus Remembrance borrows Banquo's glass
> To claim the sceptred &c.
> And *we* the mirror $\begin{cases} \text{hold} \\ \text{show} \end{cases}$ whose $\begin{cases} \text{distant} \\ \text{imaged shine} \end{cases}$
> Immortal &c.

or

> And *we* that magic mirror $\begin{cases} \text{hold where shine} \\ show \end{cases}$

or any epithet but it must not be a *common one* such as *bright* & so
forth.—Do not talk of *your* regrets but think of Ld. & Ly. J's & our
own.—Best r[espec]ts to Ly. H.—

Ever yrs.

B.

[TO JOHN MURRAY]   *Cheltenham Octr. 12th. 1812*

Dear Sir,—I have a *very strong objection* to the engraving of the
portrait & request that it may on no account be prefixed, but let *all* the
proofs be burnt, & the plate broken.[1]—I will be at the expence which
has been incurred, it is but fair that *I* should, since I cannot permit the
publication.—I beg as a particular favour that you will lose no time in
having this done for which I have reasons that I will state when I see

---

[1] A "litura", now given in Italian dictionaries as obsolete, is a cancellation.

[1] The portrait was a miniature by Sanders. Murray had intended to use it as a
frontispiece to a new edition of *Childe Harold*. It seems that Byron objected to the
engraving rather than to the portrait.

you. Forgive all the trouble I have occasioned you.—I have received no account of the reception of the address, but see it is vituperated in the papers, which does not much embarrass an *old author.*—I leave it to your own judgment to add it or not to your next edition when required.—Pray comply *strictly* with my wishes as to the engraving & believe me

yrs very truly
Byron

P.S.—Favour me with an answer, as I shall not be easy till I hear that the *proofs* &c. are destroyed.— —I hear that the *Satirist* has reviewed C[hilde] H[arold] in what manner I need not ask, but I wish to know if the old personalities are revived.—I have a better reason for asking this than any that merely concerns *myself,* but in publications of that kind others particularly female names are sometimes introduced.—[2]

[TO LORD HOLLAND]   *Cheltenham Octr. 14th 1812*

My dear Lord,—I perceive that the papers yea even Perry's are somewhat ruffled at the injudicious preference of the committee; my friend Perry has indeed *"et tu Brute"* 'd me rather scurvily[1] for which I will send him for ye. M[orning] C[hronicle] the next epigram I scribble as a token of my full forgiveness.— —Do the Committee mean to enter into no explanation of their proceedings? you must see there is a leaning towards a charge of partiality.— You will at least acquit me of any great anxiety to push myself before so many elder & better anonymous to whom the 20 gs. (which I take to be about two thousand pds. *Bank* currency) & the—Honour would have been equally welcome.—*"Honour"* I see hath no *"skill in paragraph*

[2] Byron perhaps feared that his affair with Lady Caroline Lamb would be mentioned. The *Satirist* review (Oct. 1, 1812, Vol. 11, pp. 344–358; continued Dec. 1, 1812, Vol. II, pp. 542–550) was, however, very laudatory on the whole. The critic said that *Childe Harold* "contains many passages which would do honour to any poet, of any period, in any country". But he took the author to task for his melancholy tone and for his "unpatriotic" anti-war stanzas. The reviewer, who could not have been his old enemy of the earlier *Satirist* attacks, Hewson Clarke, was delighted with the descriptions of Greece: "This is exquisite poetry."

[1] James Perry's *Morning Chronicle,* October 12, 1812, said in part of Byron's Drury Lane Address: "We cannot suppose that it was selected as the most poetical composition. . . . But, perhaps by its tenor, by its allusions to the fire, to Garrick, to Siddons, and to Sheridan, it was thought most applicable to the occasion, notwithstanding its being in parts unmusical, and in general tame."

writing".—I wish to know how it went off at the second reading, & whether anyone has had the grace to give it a glance of approbation.— I have seen no paper but Perry's & two Sunday ones, Perry is severe & the others silent.—If however you & your Committee are not now dissatisfied with your own judgment, I shall not much embarrass myself about the brilliant remarks of the journals.— —My own opinion upon it is what it always was, perhaps, pretty near that of the public.— Believe me my dear Ld.

ever yrs most obliged & sincerely
B.

P.S.—My best respects to Ly. H. whose smiles will be very consolatory even at this distance.—

[TO CHARLES HANSON]   *Cheltenham Octr. 15th. 1812*

Dear Charles—It is very odd that I hear nothing from or of yr. father, where is he & what is he about—pray be so good as to write instantly.

ever yrs
B.

[TO LADY MELBOURNE]   *Cheltenham Octr. 17th. 1812*

"*Cut* her!" My dear Ly. M. marry—Mahomet forbid!—I am sure we shall be better friends than before & if I am not embarrassed by all this I cannot see for the soul of me why *she* should [1]—assure *her* con tutto rispetto that The subject shall never be renewed in any shape whatever, & assure yourself my carissima (not *Zia* what then shall it be? chuse your *own* name) that were it not for this embarras with C[aroline] I would much rather remain as I am.— — I have had so very little intercourse with the fair Philosopher that if when we meet I should endeavour to improve our acquaintance she must not *mistake* me, & assure her I never shall mistake her.—I *never did* you will allow;—& God knows whether I am right or not, but I do think I am not very apt to think myself encouraged.—She is perfectly right in every point of view, & during the slight suspense I felt something very like remorse for sundry reasons not at all connected with C[aroline] nor with any occurrences since I knew you or her or hers; finding I must

---

[1] Lady Melbourne had sounded out her niece, Annabella Milbanke, with Byron's marriage proposal and had received an involved negative.

marry however on *that* score, I should have preferred a woman of birth & talents, but such a woman was not at all to blame for not preferring me; my *heart* never had an opportunity of being much interested in the business, further than that I should have very much liked to be *your relation.*—And now to conclude like Ld. Foppington, "I have lost a thousand women in my time but never had the ill manners to quarrel with them for such a trifle." [2]—Talking of addresses put me in mind of my *address* which has been murdered (I *hear*) in the delivery & mauled (I *see*) in the newspapers, & you don't tell me whether you heard it recited, I almost wish you may not, if this be the case.—I am asked to Ld. O[xford]'s & Ld. Harrowby's [3] & am wavering between the two.—I cannot sufficiently thank you for all the trouble you have taken on my account, the interest with which you honour me would amply repay for fifty vexations even if I felt any & perhaps I do without knowing it; but I can't tell how it is, but I think C[aroline] may be managed now as well as if the whole had taken place if she has either *pride* or *principle*, because she *may* now be convinced with a *little* dexterity at *her return* that I am most anxious to end every thing— added to which the present *denial* [4] will lessen me in her estimation as an *article* of *value*, & her Vanity will help marvellously to her conversion. — —You talk of my "religion" *that* rests between Man & his Maker & to *him* only can my feelings be known, for A[nnabella] it had been sufficient not to find me an *"infidel"* in anything else.—I must now conclude for I am pressed by the post—pray let me hear from you often & believe me ever my dear Ly. M.

> yrs. most affectly.
> *B.*

[TO JOHN MURRAY (*a*)]   *Cheltenham Octr.* [*17th.?*] *1812*

Dear Sir—Will you have the goodness to get this parody of a peculiar kind (for all the first lines are *Busby's* entire) inserted in

[2] This is an instance of Byron's familiarity with 18th-century plays and his retentive memory of quotable lines that caught his fancy or amused him. In Colley Cibber's *The Careless Husband* (Act V) Lord Foppington says to Lady Betty Modish: "I have lost a thousand women in my time, but never had the ill manners to be out of humour with any one for refusing me, since I was born."

[3] For the Oxfords see the biographical sketch in the Appendix. The first Earl of Harrowby held various ministerial posts. He had been Foreign Secretary under Pitt.

[4] The rejection of Byron's proposal by Annabella Milbanke.

several of the papers *correctly* & copied *correctly* (*my hand* is difficult) particularly the M[orning] Chronicle.[1]— Tell Mr. Perry I forgive him all he has said & may say against *my address*, but he will allow me to deal with the Doctor, *"Audi alteram partem"* & not *betray* me—I cannot think what has befallen Mr. P[erry] for of yore we were very good friends—but no matter—only get this inserted—I have a poem on Waltz for *you*, of which I make *you* a present, but it must be anonymous.[2]—It is in the old style of E. B. & S. R.

ever yrs.

B.

P.S.—With the next E[dition] of C[hilde] H[arold] you may print the first 50 or 100 opening lines of "The Curse of Minerva" down to the couplet—beginning "Mortal twas thus she spake" &c.[3] of course the moment the *Satire* begins there you will stop & the opening is the best part.—

[TO JOHN MURRAY (*b*)]   *Octr. 17th. 1812*

Dear Sir,—Many thanks but I *must* pay the *damage*—& will thank you to tell me the moment for the engraving.[1]—I think the "rejected addresses"[2] by far the best thing of the kind since the Rolliad & wish *you* had published them.—Tell the author "I *forgive* him were he twenty times our satirist," & think his imitations not at all inferior to the famous ones of Hawkins Browne.[3] He must be a man of very lively wit, & much less scurrilous than Wits often are, altogether I very much admire the performance & wish it all success.—The S[atiris]t has taken a *new* tone as you will see,[4] we have now I think

---

[1] Byron's *"Parenthetical Address*, by Dr. Plagiary" was printed in the *Morning Chronicle* on October 23, 1812. It was a parody (embodying quotations from the original) of one of the Addresses rejected by the Committee, written by Dr. Thomas Busby, a musical composer and parliamentary reporter. On October 14th his son forced his way on to the stage and tried to recite his father's Address but was stopped. The original was published in the *Genuine Rejected Addresses* and parodied in *Rejected Addresses* ("Architectural Atoms"). (See *LJ.*, II, 176n.)

[2] *The Waltz* was published anonymously in the spring of 1813.

[3] Byron finally published the opening lines of *The Curse of Minerva* (since he decided not to publish that poem) at the beginning of the third canto of *The Corsair* (1814).

[1] See Oct. 12, 1812, to Murray.

[2] *Rejected Addresses*, by James and Horace Smith. See Sept. 30, 1812, to Lord Holland (*b*), note 2.

[3] See Sept. 30, 1812, to Lord Holland (*b*), note 4.

[4] See Oct. 12, 1812, to Murray, note 2.

finished with C[hilde] H[arold]'s critics.—I have in *hand* a *satire* on *Waltzing* which you must publish anonymously, it is not long, not quite 200 lines, but will make a very small boarded pamphlet—in a few days you shall have it.—

ever yrs
B.

P.S.—The Editor of the S[atirist] almost ought to be thanked for his revocation it is done handsomely after five years warfare.—

[TO LADY MELBOURNE] *Octr. 18th. 1812*

My dear Lady M.— —Of A[nnabella] I have little to add, but I do not regret what has passed; the report alluded to had hurt her feelings, & she has now regained her tranquillity by the refutation to her own satisfaction without disturbing mine.—This was but fair—and was not unexpected by me, all things considered perhaps it could not have been better.—I think of her nearly as I did, the specimen you send me is more favourable to her talents than her discernment,[1] & much *too indulgent* to the subject she has chosen, in some points the resemblance is very exact, but you have not sent me the whole (I imagine) by the abruptness of both beginning & end.—I am glad that your opinion coincides with mine on the subject of her abilities & her excellent qualities, in both these points she is singularly fortunate.—Still there is something of the *woman* about her; her *preferring* that the letter to you should be sent forward to *me per esempio* appears as if though she would not encourage, she was not disgusted with being admired.—I also may hazard a conjecture that an *answer* addressed to *herself* might not have been displeasing, but of this you are the best judge from actual observation.—I cannot however see the necessity of it's being forwarded unless I was either to admire the composition or reply to ye. contents.—*One* I certainly do, the other would merely lead to mutual compliments very sincere but somewhat tedious.—By the bye, what two famous letters *your own* are, I never saw such traits of discernment, observation of character, knowledge of your *own sex.* & *sly concealment* of your *knowledge* of the *foibles* of *ours,* than in these epistles, & so that I preserve you *always* as a friend & *sometimes* as a correspondent (the oftener the better) believe me my dear Ly. M. I shall regret nothing but—the week we passed at Middleton till I can

[1] This was probably Annabella's "Character" of Byron which she had written on October 8th, but had not finished.

enjoy such another.—Now for C[aroline]—your name was never mentioned or hinted at—the passage was nearly as follows—"I know from the *best* authority, your *own*, that your time has passed in a very different manner, nor do I object to it, amuse yourself, but leave me *quiet*, what would you have?—I go nowhere, I see no one, I mix with no society—I write when it is proper—these perpetual causeless caprices are equally selfish & absurd." &c. &c. & so on in answer to her description of her *lonely lovelorn condition*!!! much in the same sever*er* style.—And now this must end, if she persists I will leave the country, I shall enter into no explanations, write no epistles softening or reverse; nor will I meet her if it can be avoided, & certainly never but in society, the sooner she is apprized of this the better, but with one so totally devoid of all conduct it is difficult to decide.—I have no objection to her knowing what passed about A[nnabella]—if it would have any good effect, nor do I wish it to be concealed, even from others or the world in general, my vanity will not be piqued by it's development, & though It was not accepted I am not at all ashamed of my admiration of the amiable *Mathematician.*—I did not reproach C[aroline] for *"her behaviour"* but the *misrepresentation* of it, & her suspicions of mine; why tell me she was *dying* instead of *dancing* when I had much rather hear she was acting, as she in fact acted? viz—like any other person in good health, tolerable society & high spirits.— — In short I am not her lover, & would rather not be her friend, though I never can nor will be her enemy.—If it can be ended let it be without any interference, I will have nothing more to do with it, her letters (all but one about *Ld. Clare*[2] unanswered & the answer to *that* strictly confined to his concerns except a hint on vanity at the close) are filled with the most ridiculous egotism, *"how* the Duke's mob observed her, *how* the boys followed her, the women caressed & the men admired, & *how* many lovers were all sacrificed to this brilliant fit of constancy.["] —who wants it forsooth or expects it after sixteen?— —Can't she take example from me, do I embarrass myself about A[nnabella]?—or the fifty B. C. D. E. F. G. H's &c. &c. that have preceded her in cruelty or kindness (the *latter* always the greatest plague) not I, & really sans phrase I think *my loss* is the *most considerable.*— —I hear Ly. Holland is ill I hope *not seriously.*— Ld. O[xford] went today, & I am still here with some idea of proceeding either to Herefordshire or

[2] See Oct. 24, 1812, to Lady Melbourne. Lord Clare was in Ireland at the time. Caroline, knowing him to be a close friend of Byron, tried later to have him get a portrait of her former lover for her. See *Notes and Queries*, 1967, Vol. 14 (Vol. 212 of the continued series), pp. 297–99.

to Ld. Harrowby's, & one notion of being obliged to go to London to meet my Agent.—Pray let me hear from you; I am so provoked at the thought that our *acquaintance* may be interrupted by the old phantasy. —I had & have twenty thousand things to say & I trust as many to hear, but somehow our conversations never come to a clear conclusion. —I thank you again for your efforts with my Princess of Parallelograms, who has puzzled you more than the Hypothenuse; in her character she has not forgotten "*Mathematics*" wherein I used to praise her cunning.—Her proceedings are quite rectangular, or rather we are two parallel lines prolonged to infinity side by side but never to meet. —Say what you please for or of me, & I will mean it.—Good Even my dear Ly. M.—ever yrs most affectionately

[TO JOHN HANSON]   *Cheltenham Octr. 18th. 1812*

Dear Sir—With perfect confidence in you I sign the note, but is not Claughton's delay very strange? let us take care what we are about, I answered his letter which I enclose to you, very *cautiously*, the wines & China &c. I will not demur much upon but the *vase* & cup (not the *skull cup*) & some little coffee things brought from the East, or made for the purpose of containing relics brought from thence, I will not part with, & if he refuses to ratify, I will take such steps as the Law will allow on the [force?] of the contract for compelling him to ratify it.— Pray write, I am invited to Ld. O[xford] & Ld. H[arrowby]'s, but if you wish very much to meet me I can come to town.— —I suppose the tithe purchase will be made in my name.—what[1] is to be done with Deardon?[2] Mrs. M[assingberd] is dead, and I should wish something settled for the Daughter who is still responsible.[3] Will you give a glance into that business, and if possible first settle something about the Annuities.

I shall perhaps draw within a £100 next week, but I will delay for your answer on C[laughton]'s business.

Ever yours, sincerely and affectionately,
BYRON.

---

[1] From here to end of letter from *LJ*, II, 174–175. This part is missing from the MS.

[2] James Dearden held the lease of the coal mines at Rochdale.

[3] Mrs. Massingberd and her daughter had been co-signers of Byron's transactions with the usurers.

My love to all the family.

I wish to do something for young Rushton, if practicable at *Rochdale*; if not, think of some situation where he might occupy himself to avoid Idleness, in the mean time.

Robert,— I hope you continue as much as possible to apply yourself to *Accounts* and Land-Measurement, etc. Whatever change may take place about Newstead, there will be none as to you and Mr. Murray. It is intended to place you in a situation in Rochdale for which your pursuance of the Studies I recommend will best fit you. Let me hear from you; is your health improved since I was last at the Abbey? In the mean time, if any accident occur to me, you are provided for in my will, and if not, you will always find in your Master a sincere Friend.

B.

My dear Ly. M.—Tell A[nnabella] that I am more proud of her *rejection* than I can ever be of *another's acceptance*, this sounds rather *equivocal*, but if she takes it in the sense I mean it & *you* don't blunder it in the delivery with one of your *wicked laughs*, it will do for want of something better.—It merely means that the *hope* of obtaining *her* (or *any body else*—but skip this parenthesis) was more pleasing than the possession of St. Ursula & the 11000 virgins (being a greater number than have ever *since* existed at the *same time* in that capacity) could possibly have been to her "disconsolate & unmathematical admirer, X. Y. Z."— — —"Not a word to C[aroline]!" as you please.—*I* who do not write at all am in no danger of betraying our conspiracies.—I am not sorry to hear that she has written to a "Man" or "waltzed" because both *were in* the *articles*, of which I must take advantage at the proper time for the *infringement* & be angry enough to make a decent quarrel or rather defence when she falls upon me which she shall not if I can keep out of the way.—My terrific projects amount to this—to remain on good terms with Ly Cowper—[1] & Mrs. Lamb—[2] & on the

---

[1] Lady Melbourne's daughter, Emily Mary Lamb, married in 1805 Peter, fifth Earl of Cowper.

[2] George Lamb, fourth son of the first Lord Melbourne, married in 1809 Caroline Rosalie St. Jules.

best terms with *you*—being the three pleasantest persons in very different ways with whom I am acquainted, & to be as quiet or cool with C[aroline] as a mere *common acquaintance* as my wish to retain *your intimacy* will permit, if not & I must quarrel with one of the parties, it shall certainly be with *her*, & indeed I should prefer it at once on every account; I am sick & annoyed with the connection. I fear A[nnabella] is right that I cannot be indifferent—but change from love "to hate with the bitterest contempt."—Believe me I would not give up your friendship & that of three or four rational beings for five thousand Carolines were each five thousand times more *perfect* than she is the *reverse*.—What can I say or write to her? it will answer no end, I shall be bored with reproaches *exclamation declamation defamation* & perhaps she may set off to display a *vindication* in person. I mean (entre nous my dear Machiavel) to play off Ly. O[xford] against her, who would have no objection *perchance*. but she dreads her scenes & has asked me not to mention that we have met to C[aroline] or that I am going to E[ywood]—where by the bye I am not sure that I am going.— —In short if not by yourself—cannot any of your friends intimate or subordinate "varnish this tale of truth" for her, if it was a fiction there would be no difficulty, but certainly truth is an Artichoke particularly to *her*.—Not a word of Ly. O[xford] for the present to *C[aroline]* & *certainly* to *no one* else.—When C[aroline] returns she will commence some furious flirtation elsewhere which will give me the opportunity of breaking at once.—Perhaps Dublin has done it already.—Write to me & believe that whatever I am to A. B. C. &c. I am ever yours

most affectionately & sincerely

P.S.—My *Love* to *Ld. M.*

P.S.—Thanks for your "Examiner" Hunt[3] is a clever man & I should like to know his opinion—pray send it, it will be very acceptable.—I shall return it faithfully if required.—

[TO JOHN HANSON]   *Octr. 22d. 1812*

Dear Sir—I enclose you Mr. C[laughton]'s letter from which you yourself will judge of my own.—I insisted on the *contract* & said *if* I

---

[3] For Byron's relations with Hunt, see biographical sketch, Appendix.

gave up the wines &c. it would be as a *gift*.—He admits the validity as
you perceive.—I told him that *I* wished to avoid raising difficulties &
in all respects to fulfil ye. bargain.—I am going to Ld. Oxford's—
Eywood Presteigne—Hereford.—In my way back I will take Farleigh
if you are not returned to London before.—I wish to take a small
house for the winter anywhere not remote from St. James's.—Will you
arrange this for me?—& think of young Rushton, whom I promised to
provide for & must begin to think of it, he might be a *sub*-Tythe
collector, of a Bailiff to our agent at R[ochdale] or many other things,
he has had a fair education & was well disposed, at all events he must no
longer remain in idleness.—Let the Mule be sold & the dogs.—Pray
let me hear from you when convenient & believe me ever yrs. truly

                                                          BYRON

My best remembrances to all.—I shall draw for *fifty* this week.—
Is anything done about Miss M[assingberd]?—You have not mentioned her.—

[TO JOHN MURRAY]   *Octr. 23d. 1812*

   Dear Sir—Thanks as usual—you go on boldly but have a care of
glutting ye. public, who have by this time had enough of C[hilde]
H[arold].— —"Waltz" shall be prepared—it is rather above 200
lines with an introductory letter to the Publisher.— —I think of publishing with C[hilde] H[arold]—the opening lines of the C[urse] of
Minerva as far as the first speech of Pallas—because some of the
readers like that part better than any I have ever written, & as it contains nothing to affect the subject of the subsequent portion, it will find
a place as a *descriptive fragment*.[1]—The *plate* is *broken*—[2] between
ourselves it was unlike the picture, & besides upon the whole, the
frontispiece of an author's visage is but a paltry exhibition.—At all
events *this* would have been no recommendation for the Book.—I am
sure Sanders would not have survived the engraving, by the bye the
picture may remain with *you* or *him* (which you please) till my return.—
The *one* of two remaining copies is at your service till I can give you
a *better*; the other must be *burned peremptorily*.—Again—do not
forget that I have an account with you—& *that* this is *included*—I
give you too much *trouble* to allow you to incur *expence* also.—You

   [1] This description of a sunset seen from the Acropolis was finally put at the
opening of the third canto of *The Corsair.*
   [2] See Oct. 12, 1812, to Murray.

best know how far this "address Riot" will affect the future sale of C[hilde] H[arold].—I like the vol of "rejected A[ddresses]" better & better.[3]—The other parody which P[erry] has received is *mine* also (I believe), it is Dr. B[usby]'s speech versified.[4]—You are removing to A[lbemarle] Street[5] I find & I rejoice that we shall be nearer neighbors.—I am going to Ld. Oxford's but letters here will be forwarded. —When at leisure all communications from you will be willingly received by the humblest of your scribes.—Did Mr. Ward write the review of H. Tooke's life?[6]—it is excellent.— yrs.

[TO LADY MELBOURNE] *Octr. 24th. 1812*

My dear Ly. M.—I am just setting off through detestable roads for ——— [Eywood]. You can make such use of the incident of our acquaintance as you please with C[aroline] only do not say that I am *there* because she will probably write or do some absurd thing in that quarter which will spoil every thing, & I think there are enough of persons embroiled already without the addition of ———[Lady Oxford] who has besides enough to manage already without these additions.—This I know also to be *her* wish, & certainly it is mine.— You may say that we met at C[heltenham] or elsewhere anything but that we are *now* together.—By all means *confide* in Ly. "Blarney"[1] or —the Morning Post, seriously if anything requires a little *hyperbole*, let her have it—I have left off writing entirely & will have nothing more to do with it.— —"If you write anything to me" *she* is sure to have it!— How?— I have not written these two months—but *twice*— nor was your name mentioned in either.—The last was entirely about Ld. Clare between whom & me she has been intermeddling[2] & conveying notes from Ly. C[lar]e on the subject of a foolish difference between Clare & myself, in which I believe I am wrong as usual.— —

3 See Sept. 30, 1812, to Lord Holland (*b*), note 2.

4 See Oct. [17?], 1812, to Murray, note 1.

5 Murray, whose place of business was at 32 Fleet Street, opposite St. Dunstan's Church, moved in September, 1812, to 50, Albemarle Street, having bought the lease, the stock and copyrights of William Miller, bookseller. The firm of John Murray has remained there ever since.

6 J. W. Ward wrote the article alluded to. (See *Quarterly Review*, Vol. VII, p. 313.)

1 Lady Bessborough, Caroline's mother. See [Aug., 1812?], to Lady Melbourne, note 2.

2 See Oct. 18, 1812, to Lady Melbourne, note 2.

But that is over.—Her last letters to me are full of complaints against *you* for I know not what disrespectful expressions about the *"letter opened"* &c. &c.—I have not answered them nor shall.—They talk of going to Sicily, on that head I have nothing to say, you & Mr. Lamb are the best judges, to me it must be a matter of perfect indifference; & though I am written to professedly to be consulted on the subject what possible answer could I give that would not be impertinent?—It would be the *best* place for *her* & the worst for him (in all points of view) on earth, unless he was in some official capacity.—As I have said before do as you will—in my next I will answer your questions as to the 3 persons you speak of at present I have not time though I am *tempted* by the *theme*.—As to A[nnabella] that must take it's chance, I mean the *acquaintance*, for it never will be any thing more—depend upon it—even if she *revoked*—I have still the same opinion—but I never was *enamoured*—& as I very soon shall be in some other quarter—cosi finiva.—Do not fear about C[aroline] even if we meet —but allow me to keep out of the way if I can merely for the sake of peace & quietness.—You never were more *groundlessly* alarmed, for I am not what you imagine, in one respect; I have gone through the experiment before, more than once, & I never was separated three months without a perfect *cure*, even though ye. acquaintance was renewed.— —I have even stood as much *violence* as could be brought into the field on ye. present occasion.—In the first vol. of Marmontel's memoirs towards the end you will find my opinion on the subject of women in *general* in the mouth of Madame de *Tencin* [3]—should you deign to think it worth a moment's notice.—ever yrs most affectionately

B.

P.S.—If you write to Cheltenham my letters will be forwarded.— And *do* write—I have very few correspondents, & none but this which give me much pleasure—

[TO LADY MELBOURNE]   *Eywood. Presteign.—Octr. 30th. 1812*

My dear Ly. M.—Though you have not written to me lately I can account for the *prudential* silence & do not blame you although one of your epistles *anywhere* is a great comfort.—Every thing stands as you

---

[3] Mme Tencin's sage advice was, "gardez-vous bien d'être autre chose que l'amie" to a woman.

could wish, & as I wished & nothing more need be said on that subject. — — —I have had an epistle from Ireland, short & full of resignation, so that I trust your cares are nearly wound up in that quarter; at least I must appeal to you if I have not done everything in my power to bring them to a conclusion, & now I have more reasons than ever for wishing them never to be renewed.— — — — —The Country round this place is wild & beautiful, consequently very delightful; I think altogether preferable even to Middleton (where the *beauties* certainly did not belong to the *landscape*) although the recollection of my visit there will always retain its *"proper"* preeminence— —I am at present however a little laid up, for a short time ago I received a blow with a stone thrown by accident by one of the children as I was viewing the remains of a Roman encampment.—It struck me—providentially— though near the eye—yet far enough to prevent the slightest injury to that very material organ, & though I was a little stunned & the stone being very sharp the wound bled rather profusely, I have now recovered all but a slight scar, which will remain I rather think for a considerable time.—It just missed an Artery, which at first from the blood's flowing in a little spout, was supposed to be cut, but this was a false alarm, indeed I believe it has done me good, for my headachs have since entirely ceased.—This is my old luck, always *near* some- thing serious, & generally escaping as now with a *slight* accident.— An inch either way,—the temple—the eye—or eyelid—would have made this no jesting matter—as it is—I thank my good Genius that I have still two eyes left to admire you with, & a head (uncracked) which will derive great benefit from any thing which may spring from your own.— —I suppose you have left London, as I see by the papers Ld. & Ly. Cowper are returned to Herts.—If you hear anything that you think I ought to know, depend upon my seconding you to the ut- most, but I believe you will coincide with me in opinion that there is little apprehension *now* of any scene from C[aroline] & still less occasion even to have recourse to A[nnabella] as your "forlorn hope" on that account.— —I leave it to you to deal with *Ly. B[essborough]* *&c.*—say of *me* what you please but do not let any *other name* be taken in vain — particularly to one whom you so well know as that *ingenious hyperbolist* Ly. B[essborough]. I am sick of scenes & have imbibed a taste for something like *quiet.*—Do not quite forget me—for *every- where* I remember you.

ever dr. Ly. M. yr. most affectionate

P.S.—Why are you silent?—do you doubt me in the "bowers of Armida"? [1]—I certainly am very much enchanted, but *your spells* will always retain their full force—try them.—

[TO JOHN HANSON (*a*)] *Eywood. Presteign. Hereford. Octr. 31st. 1812*

Dear Sir—The inclosed bill will convince you how anxious I must be for the payment of Claughton's first instalment, though it has been sent in without due notice I cannot blame Mr. Davies who must feel very anxious to get rid of the business [1]—Press C[laughton] & let me have an answer whenever you can to this Place

yrs. ever
B.

P.S.—I am at *Ld. Oxford's* Eywood as above

[TO JOHN HANSON (*b*)]   *Eywood Presteign Octr. 31st. 1812*

Dear Sir—Do pray press Claughton as Mr. D[avies]'s business must be settled at all events—I send you his letter & I am more uncomfortable than I can possibly express myself upon the subject—pray [act?].

yrs ever
[BYRON]

[TO CHARLES HANSON]   *Novr. 2d. 1812*

My dear Charles—You see by the inclosed the additional expence your Clerks put me to & I *advised* your father before I left town—Pray pay it & the odd pounds—& tell the gentlemen in the office not to be quite so hasty because it is *insulting* to say no more.—I was sure *you* would not have done it

ever yrs. most truly
B.

P.S.—If Claughton pays *liquidate* Davies's demand.

1 Byron several times referred to his situation at Lady Oxford's as comparable to that of Rinaldo in the "bowers of Armida", the enchantress in Tasso's *Gerusalemme Liberata*, who kept Rinaldo from his duties as a Crusader.

1 On the expectation of Claughton's first payment, Byron had accepted Scrope Davies's bill for £1,500 (a partial payment of the loan of 1809). After Claughton paid £5,000 in November Byron was able to meet Davies's claim. See Nov. 8, 1812, to Hanson.

My dear Ly. M,—Thanks for the *notice* of which I shall duly avail myself.—I have throughout the whole of this you are convinced been perfectly sincere with *you* & surely not less so *now* than ever.—It must end & I see no purpose which any interview can possibly answer, & I wrote to say as much adding moreover another important *truth*— that I am *deeply* & *seriously* engaged elsewhere.— —All *our* wishes tend to quiet—& any scene of C[aroline]'s will merely involve others in very unpleasant circumstances without tending at all to reunion— which is now absolutely *impossible* even if I wished it.—Besides, as there will be more *breakings* off than one much precious mischief will ensue if her illustrious example (I mean C[aroline]'s) is to be imitated in all quarters.— — —In my last letter I stated that I was *attached*— but to whom even in allusion I did not think myself justified in mentioning.—As to Ly B[essborough]—what would she have?— have I not complied with her own professed wishes? did I not tell you that end how it would *she* would never forgive me for not being suf- ficiently *dramatic.*— —I am out of all patience with her & hers & come what may will have no explanations, no scenes, no *anything*, & if necessary I will quit London or the country altogether rather than subject myself to the renewal of the last years harass.—The sooner, the stronger—the fuller you state this the better—Good God—am I to be hunted from place to place like a Russian *bear* or *Emperor?*— — do pray—do what you can for me—I would not at this time have an eclât for the world.—This country is very much to my taste, & I have taken a seat of Ld. Oxford's (Kinsham Court about 5 miles off in a *delightful* situation) for next year, I believe some arrangements relative to it will call me here again at Christmas.—This is no secret, & need not be one if you think it worth mentioning.—I leave you full powers to say what you please to C[aroline]—she wont I trust be silly enough to torment any one but me [or] she will find it labour in vain.— You need not doubt me, by the bye, I am committing myself too much, but let that be a proof that I do not *doubt you.*—I am asked to Middle- ton after the 10th, shall you be there?—if so I will go.— —I do not know if my letter will reach Ireland in time—nor what further good it may do.—Ly. B[essborough] with her foolish prognostics—she does not wish them fulfilled half so much as I do.—She always said all *went* on as she wished—pray Heaven it may.— —I write in very bad humour—forgive it—only manage *her*—I am *sure* of *every one* else —even *myself*; the person least likely to be depended on.—My next shall be a pleasanter letter—pardon the peevishness of this.—

ever my *dearest friend yrs*

Eywood. Presteign. Novr. 6th. 1812

My dear Ly. M.—Not being aware of any amusement which can possibly last four & twenty hours by "Shrewsbury clock" sans intermission, I suppose one may look at a Roman encampment now & then & yet be exceedingly occupied nevertheless with more serious entertainments.—Your "Coach horse" is admirable but *not* apropos.—I am glad you recommend *"cupping"* I wanted to be so but Ly —— [Oxford] says I *shant* (God knows why) & you know I am too tractable to oppose a negative to anything.—I believe I mentioned in my last that I have taken Kinsham Court in this vicinity, with the description of which I shall not trouble you.—I shall be here at Christmas to look after my arrangements.—Seriously (and I am *very serious*) I have so completely rendered a renewal with C[aroline] next to impossible that you will at least give me credit for sincerity; & to mend the matter all this is infinitely more to my taste than the A[nnabella] Scheme, to which my principal inducement was the tie to yourself which I confess would have delighted me— —I have had a tremulous letter from Mrs. [George] L[amb] who is in a panic about C[aroline]—this I have answered & announced as a simple piece of information that I have taken a seat in Herefordshire; an intimation which with "Ly. *Blarney's"* marginal notes will have a miraculous effect on the arrival of Pandora (& her boxes of evil for all her acquaintance) at Tixal.—So—a new accusation of imposition! At M[iddleton]—& before—my memory really fails me—I never laughed at P—(by the bye this is an initial which might puzzle posterity when our correspondence bursts forth in the 20th century) nor can I possibly pronounce where all was *"proper"* who was the "properest" but I am sure no one can regret the general *propriety* half so much as I do.—Though *we* are very quiet & wish to remain so as much as *C[aroline]* & *others* may permit, yet *we* are also determined to abide by our articles & not to relinquish a single *right-* (read—*"wrong"*—instead if you like)—which devolves to the Conquerors on such occasions—As to the Ly. Blarney, though I expected some absurd dissatisfaction on her part, I own it provokes me.—"Unfair" *who* could act fairly with people who were sending couriers & threatening to follow them?— As to C[aroline] she will find her in *fits* for the Winter without me to help her, depend upon it—& unless Providence sends another illness & Journey it is all over with my sussessor—I guess at Webster[1] (who is now in Parliament & will be in town more) as the first essay, but I *doubt* the Bart. himself as somewhat of the coldest.—Besides he must sacrifice his senatorial duties, & do nothing else but attend to his perplexities, which will be manifold.— —I presume that I may now have access to the lower regions of Melbourne House from which my *ascent* had long excluded me.[2]—I doubt if C[aroline] & I will be on speaking terms, & it is on the whole much better we should not, but I trust the taciturnity is not to be general.—Your threatened visit of C[aroline] to this place would have no effect in this *quarter*, all being secure. I shall go to Middleton shortly after the twelfth Inst.—address your Answer *there* or to *Cheltenham*—I hope to find you at M[iddleton]—You see *nothing* makes me unmindful of *you*, & I feel but too much obliged by your reciprocal remembrance.—

ever my dear Ly. M. yrs most affectly.

[TO JOHN HANSON] *Novr. 8th. 1812*

Dear Sir—Not being able (& today being sunday also) to procure a stamp as the Post town is very remote, I must request this letter to be considered as an Order for paying fifteen hundred pds. to S. B. Davies Esqre.[1] & the same sum to your own account for the Tythe purchase— Mr. D's receipt can be indorsed on the bond.— — I shall be in London the latter end of the week, I set out from this place on the 12th.—As to Mr. C[laughton] the Law must decide between us; I shall abide by the Contract.—Your answer will not reach me in time, so do not write to me while here.—Pray let Mr. D[avies] be paid & you also— come what may.—I always foresaw that C[laughton] would *shirk*, but he did it with his eyes open, what question can arise as to the title? has it never been examined? I never heard of it before, & surely in all our law suits, that question must have come to issue.—I hope we shall meet in town, I will wait on you the moment I arrive. My best respects to your family believe me

ever yrs sincerely
BYRON

[1] Sir Godfrey Vassal Webster (1788–1836).
[2] Caroline and William Lamb lived on the second floor of Melbourne House.
[1] See Oct. 31, 1812, to Hanson, note 1.

I am no longer your lover; and since you oblige me to confess it, by this truly unfeminine persecution,—learn, that I am attached to another; whose name it would of course be dishonourable to mention. I shall ever remember with gratitude the many instances I have received of the predilection you have shewn in my favour. I shall ever continue your friend, if your ladyship will permit me so to style myself; and, as a first proof of my regard, I offer you this advice, correct your vanity, which is ridiculous; exert your absurd caprices upon others; and leave me in peace.

Your most obedient servant,

[TO LADY CAROLINE LAMB (*b*)] [*November 1812?*]

Lady Caroline—our affections are not in our own power—mine are engaged. I love another—were I inclined to reproach you I might for 20 thousand things, but I will not. They really are not cause of my present conduct—my opinion of you is entirely alter'd, & if I had wanted anything to confirm me, your Levities your caprices & the mean subterfuges you have lately made use of while madly gay—of writing to me as if otherwise, would entirely have open'd my eyes. I am no longer yr. lover—¹ I shall but never be less than your friend —it would be too dishonourable for me to name her to whom I am now entirely devoted & attached.

[TO LADY MELBOURNE] *Novr. 9th. 1812*

My dear Ly. M.—With yr. letter I have received an *Irish* epistle, foolish, headstrong, & vainly threatening *herself* &c. &c. To this I shall return no answer; & though it is of very great importance to me to be in London at this time, I shall if possible delay it till I hear from you that there is no chance of any scenes.—Mr. D. could hardly avoid guessing but too correctly, for not a servant in the house but was afraid to awaken me, & *he* was called home from a club for that purpose,

¹ The only copy of this letter is that published in Caroline Lamb's novel. It sounds Byronic, and Byron did not deny its authenticity when he read the book; he must have recognized it as in substance what he had written. It is ascribed to the hero, Glenarvon, who is obviously intended to represent Byron.

¹ This may be a portion of the letter which Caroline published in *Glenarvon*. See [Nov., 1812?], to Lady Caroline Lamb (*a*), note 1. In the novel, Caroline has dated the letter November 9, but in Byron's letter of Nov. 4, 1812, to Lady Melbourne, he said: "In my last letter I stated that I was *attached*—but to whom even in allusion I did not think myself justified in mentioning."

his first & natural question to the man was whence he came from whom & why, the answer to all which is obvious, but D. ought not to have mentioned it & so I shall tell him.— —Why he placed me in Notts. at this moment I cannot say, except that he knew no better.—Mr. C[laughton] may repent of his bargain for aught I know to the contrary, but he has paid part of the money.—If he fails—the Law will decide between us, & if he acts in an ungentlemanly manner, the remedy is still more simple.— —With regard to Ly. B[essborough] & Ly. C[aroline]—I have little more to say and I hope nothing to do.— —She has hurt & disgusted me by her latter conduct beyond expression; & even if I did not love another, I would never speak to her again while I existed, & this you have my full consent to state to those whom it may concern.—I have passed my time since her departure *always* quietly & partly delightfully, nor will I submit to caprice & injustice.—This *was* to be broken off, it is broken off; I had neither the hope nor the inclination to satisfy Ly. B[essborough] on all points; if it is unfair to comply with her own express wishes,—let her complain till she is tired, but I trust a little reflection will convince even her that she is wrong to be dissatisfied.— —C[aroline] threatens to revenge herself upon *herself*, by all kinds of perverseness.—this is her concern—all I desire is to have nothing more to do with them—no explanations—no interviews—in short I neither can nor will bear it any longer.—As long as there was a necessity for supporting her I did not *shrink* from any consequences, but when all was adjusted —& you agreed to overlook the past in the hope of the future; my resolution was taken & to that I have adhered & will adhere.—I cannot exist without some object of love—I have found one with whom I am perfectly satisfied, & who as far as I can judge is no less so with me; our mutual wish is *quiet*—& for this reason I find a double pleasure (after all the ridiculous display of last season) in repose; I have engaged myself too far to recede, nor do I regret it—are *you* at least satisfied with what I have done to comply with your wishes if Ly. B[essborough] is not? If Ly. C[aroline] wishes any interview pray explain for me that I WILL NOT meet her, if she has either pride or feeling this will be sufficient—all letters &c. &c. may be easily destroyed without it.—

[TO LADY MELBOURNE (*a*)]   *Novr. 10th. 1812*

My dear Ly. M.—Last night my hostess Ly. O[xford] received a long epistle from C[aroline] containing a number of *unanswerable* questions to all which I have persuaded her to give no reply whatever. —Is every one to be embroiled by C[aroline]?—Is she mad or mischievous only? I was in doubt whether Ld. O[xford] (who knew the writer by Ld. B[essborough]'s *frank*) would not take ye. alarm but we have foiled her there if that was her intention.—This morning *your* letter arrives—& really when I compare her *letter* to me, to Ly. O[xford]—& the contents of yours. I must pronounce C[aroline] to be the most contradictory, absurd, selfish, & contemptibly wicked of human productions.—What she may say of me, I can only surmise by what she has said of others, but she seems to outdo the usual outdoings of *gentlewomen* on such occasions.—Fortunately for me I have her own testimonies in my behalf; but if she will raise a storm, be it so, she will be the first to perish in it.—Her conduct as to Mr. L[amb] is of a piece with the rest; since my first acquaintance with her I have suffered nothing but discomfort of every description, nor can I at all foresee how it will end.—My own resolution is taken.—I do most sincerely wish that she would reflect for one moment, or that she was fully aware of my determination never to hold any kind of communication with her in future; I have written till I am tired. I can do no more—most assuredly come what may—she will never be received by me—*now* it is impossible—I could wish to feel towards her as a *friend*—but as she herself says she has resolved since she is "not loved to be *detested*".—Her letter to me expressed this agreeable sentiment—her letter to Ly. O[xford] was a long *German* tirade evidently to discover on what *terms* we were & the information contained in *yours* I need not comment upon.—The part about Mr. L[amb] is like Don Felix "she would engross all the Violantes in the Creation"[1]—if she loves *him*—why not permit me to be at rest, if *me*— why this affectation?—You may suppose Ly. O[xford] is not very much delighted with her new style of correspondence besides having a slight embarras of the same kind on her own hands on the same score.— In short we manage in our infinite love of quiet to disturb *Ireland* & *Scotland* besides some part of England & Wales.—In the mean time —the present is at our own disposal — & as no one can answer for the future—'tis a great consolation to lose as little of it as possible— How you will laugh at all this—so should I were I not one of the Dram. Pers.—Col. P's wound is slight—& Ly. B[essborough] must

[1] In Mrs. Susanna Centlivre's drama, *The Wonder: A Woman Keeps a Secret* (1714) Don Felix was a Portuguese nobleman in love with Violante. Byron may have seen the play, for it held the stage for a century and Don Felix was one of Garrick's best roles.

make the most of it with C[aroline].—It will answer like the illness if she does it as well.—

ever yrs my dr. Ly. M. most affectly

B.

[TO LADY MELBOURNE (*b*)]   *Novr. 10th.* [*11th*] *1812*

My dear Ly. M.—I trouble you again principally to restore through your hands to Ly. B[essborough] an Opera ticket with many thanks & proper speeches.—Yesterday I wrote you a longish dullish & testy letter, for a brilliant epistle from the other Isle had put me out of all patience, but I have already pronounced my *Amen* to that subject.—Amongst other excellent arguments you may make use of—I humbly take the following to be *decisive*—besides my other manifold imperfections—which I may say with Richard the 3d. incapacitate me "from skipping in a Lady's chamber" I am grown within these few months much *fatter*; & have a visible scar under my right eye—quite "balafre"; and I can't think of starving myself down to an amatory size.— —This with the A[nnabella] scheme—properly commented upon—& my *present abode* with all the concomitants might I think furnish out as pretty a maternal harangue as ever was pronounced in Cavendish Square— —I have written to you so much & so stupidly that I will now have mercy & stop where I never stopped before at the second page

ever yrs my dear friend

[TO LADY MELBOURNE]   *Novr. 14th. 1812*

My dear Ly. M.—This day a further dispatch from C[aroline] with letters to me & our hostess—the one to me rational enough but to *her* only calm at the commencement, the conclusion winding up in the old style & threatening if some unexpressed or unintelligible wish (about a picture I believe) is not complied with to visit Eywood in all her terrors.— —They leave Ireland on the 10th. so by this time are safe in England & for aught I know within a few miles of us for the roads are very near my present abode.—The floods have detained me beyond my time, indeed business requires me in town & I shall make an attempt for *Cheltenham* on the 16th.— — ——— [Lady Oxford] is very anxious that I should *not* be in town till C[aroline] has left it, so am I—& I think you will be of the same opinion—I have just this *moment* been called to the window of the room where I am writing, & it has been suggested that a longer stay would be better on *that account*—but I fear that I must go on Monday, if I remain much longer "il Sposo" may be seized with crotchets & as I return at Xmas —& I really have business, I determine on the journey.—My London letters all stop at Cheltenham so I know nothing but by cross posts.— If C[aroline] makes her debut here we shall have a pretty scene! She has received my letter avowing a penchant elsewhere, & though I did not specify the *idol*, her subsequent epistles shew that the *date* of my own letter had sufficiently expounded what was not stated & I do think has answered the purpose to a certain extent.—She requires FRIENDSHIP—but you know that with her disposition it is impossible; for some time at least we must come to a total separation. — —Besides ——— [Lady Oxford] is of that opinion—& whether right or wrong I have no choice, & I certainly shall not waver an instant between the two.—You will I hope prevent an interview— after all you have more weight with her than any one—Ly. Blarney always spoils every thing bad as well as good; never did anyone throw away such excellent experience—she does by accident all that Ly. Holland performs on purpose. If Ld. Jersey is not in town I shall stop at M[iddleton] in my way according to invitation but why are *you* absent? I expect to find letters from you at Cheltenham & upon your advice much will depend.— —I am perfectly satisfied with my *situation* & have no intention of *changing* it unless *others* set the ex- ample.—Everything goes on "sans peur & sans reproche" yet very unlike Bayard[1] for all that. I congratulate A[nnabella] & myself on our mutual escape.—That would have been but a *cold collation*, & I prefer hot suppers.—

dear Ly. M. ever yrs
B.

P.S.—I open my letter to say that I have just been conversing with ——— [Lady Oxford] on ye. subject of C[aroline] & her late strange letters to ——— & she wishes me to remain a few days longer—I shall therefore wait for your *answer* here; one *line* only to say where they are will reach me by Wednesday—pray write it & my move- ments will be accordingly.— —I thought & fully intended to have

---

[1] Bayard, le Chevalier "sans peur et sans reproche" was the embodiment of the chivalric virtues of his age (1473–1524), but in an addition to the Preface in the second edition of *Childe Harold* I–II, Byron suggested that in the age of chivalry the knights might have been "sans peur" but not "sans reproche".

finished the subject of C[aroline] forever but you perceive that it is impossible till she is more tractable. I am however thankful in one instance that she has hitherto made *no progress* in disturbing our arrangements— — —I shall wait for your answer here—as otherwise I may stumble on them on the road.—

My dear Ly. M.—A letter from Holyhead proves them in England —it is rational & calm though rather plaintive & still presses on the point of *seeing* for the purpose of vindication from I know not what which her friends & enemies have it seems been about during her absence.—To cut that short at once—a *promise* has been *requested* & *given* that I will not on any account consent to such an interview, & this if possible I must adhere to. *She* denies ever having abused me &c. &c.—now this you know & I know to be most contemptibly false; not only to her mother to Mrs. L[amb] & to you—but she even forgets a volume of reproaches to myself which I shall remember rather longer than I could wish.— —My hope now rests with you & your influence over her, which I know to be great over *all* who *know* you & more even *with her* than she is aware of.—Recollect whatever may be said that your name has not been mentioned in any letter to her for these last two months; that she at most can only *guess* at what has passed of our correspondence; you must use your own discretion with Ly. B[essborough] who is not the trustiest of her age & country—with her I have had no communication whatever since the letter which puzzled her in October.— ———— [Lady Oxford] received two letters from C[aroline]—the most imprudent of her imprudent proceedings —of course she has sense enough to take no notice by answer or otherwise—& if C[aroline] does not renew her epistles—I will take care that these do no mischief.—The roads are now impassable—but in a few days I shall attempt my voyage London-ward by Cheltenham. — — —You will now I trust my dear Ly. M. think that I have kept to the tenor of our *"bond"* that I have done all in my power to render a renewal impracticable—& I can assure you there are now obstacles in the way sufficient to satisfy Ly. B[essborough] if anything could satisfy a personage wavering between Nature & Art; her own fears for the consequences to C[aroline] & her anger that so interesting a heroine should not be adored in the oldest & most tedious fashion of feminine worship; she is doubtless very angry that *I* should change.—

I am sure I waited a decent time for ye. Lady to take the pas—& she may console herself with the reflection that it was nothing on *her part* from ye. beginning but—original sin—or *vanity, which* I cannot determine—but the next adventure with the newest Comer will probably shew to better advantage.— —You will tell me if Ly. B[essborough] & I are to be on terms & *how* & *why* & *wherefore* & *when* & *but* & *if* &c. &c. down to the very "pourquoi of the pourquoi". —In the interim I am ever my dear Ly. M.—yrs. most truly

[TO JOHN HANSON]   *Novr. 16th. 1812*

Dear Sir—The floods having rendered the road impassable I am detained here but trust by the latter end of the week to proceed to Cheltenham where I shall expect a letter from you to tell me if I am wanted in town. I shall not be in time for the Prince's address but I wish you to write down for my *Parliamentary robes* (Mrs. Chaworth had them at least Mrs. Clarke the mother) though I rather think those were the Coronation & not the House robes.—at least enquire.—I hope Mr. D[avies] is paid—& if Mr. C[laughton] demurs we must bring our action according to Contract.—I trust you are well & well doing in my behalf & your own.—

                                                    ever yrs. most sincerely
                                                                      B.

[TO LADY MELBOURNE]   *Novr. 18th. 1812*

My dear Ly. M.—I think it proper to apprize you that I have written by this day's post to Ly. B[essborough] in C[avendish] Square.— Conceiving that my *possible* arrival in town about the same time with *herself* & *hers* might awaken her alarms I thought it as well to explain that all was concluded between B[yron] & C[aroline]. Your name is not even *hinted at* in this epistle (which you will probably see) nor that of *any* other person save & except their *two Ladyships* B[essborough] & C[aroline] L[amb] & your humble servant.— —Since my last I have heard nothing of C[aroline]—I have only to request ye. continuance of your *good offices* to *cement* the *breach* or rather to *widen* ye. *separation.*—I have little doubt the task is over, nothing but the spirit of contradiction could render it difficult, for *love* is out of the

question.— —I am still here only sad in the prospect of going; reading, laughing, & playing at Blindman's buff with ye. *children*; a
month has slipped away in this & such like innocent recreations; my
eye is well, & my person *fatter*; but I shall soon return to my abstinent
system, & grow thin & austere as usual. I have *promised* not to see
C[aroline] (without *permission* which will not be granted for some
time) this you may be sure is not mentioned to *Ly. B[essborough]*—
& I think may as well be kept in petto unless it becomes *requisite* which
I trust will not be ye. case—Have not I done well for *you?*—all to
oblige your Ladyship & prove my devotion.— —
I set off on Saturday—

ever yrs. dear Ly. M.

[TO JOHN MURRAY]   *Cheltenham Novr. 22d. 1812*

Dear Sir—On my return here from Ld. Oxford's I found your
obliging note & will thank you to retain the letters & any other subsequent ones to the same address till I arrive in town to claim them
which will probably be in a few days.—I have in charge a curious &
very long MS. poem written by Lord Brooke (the *friend* of Sir *Philip
Sidney*) (which I wish to submit to the inspection of Mr. Gifford with
the following queries first—whether it has ever been published &
secondly (if not) whether it is worth publication?—It is from Ld.
O[xford]'s Library & must have escaped or been overlooked amongst
the M.SS. of the Harleian Miscellany.[1] The writing is Ld. Brooke's
except a different hand towards the close, it is very long & in the six
line stanza, it is not for me to hazard an opinion upon it's merits, but I
would take the Liberty if not too troublesome to submit it to Mr.
G[ifford]'s judgment which from his excellent edition of Massinger I
should conceive to be as decisive on the writings of that age as on those
of our own.—Now for a less agreeable & important topic—How
came Mr. Mac-somebody without consulting you or me, to prefix the
address to his volume of "*de*jected Addresses"[2] is not this somewhat
larcenous? I think the ceremony of leave might have been asked—
though I have no objection to the thing itself, & leave the "hundred &
eleven" to tire themselves with "base comparisons"—I should think

---

[1] In 1744 a collection of the manuscripts in Lord Oxford's Library was published
under that title.
[2] B. Macmillan published "Dejected Addresses" in 1812.

the ingenuous public tolerably sick of the subject, & except the parodies I have not interfered nor shall, indeed I did not know that the Dr. [Busby] had published his apologetical letter & postscript³ or I should have recalled them, but I confess I looked upon his conduct in a different light before its appearance.— —I see some mountebank has stolen Alderman Birch's name⁴ to vituperate the Doctor; he had much better have pilfered his pastry—which I should imagine the more valuable ingredient at least for a Puff.—Pray secure me a copy of Woodfall's new Junius⁵ & believe me Dr. Sir

yrs. very sincerely
Bn

[TO LADY MELBOURNE]   *Middleton Novr. 26th. 1812*

My dear Ly. Melbourne,—I perceive by ye. arrivals & departures in ye. papers that you will not object to my being in town (as I must be on Sunday) on business. I shall take my seat on tuesday, & not go to the romantic melodrama of monday notwithstanding the attraction of a royal Roscius.—¹ —I have been here these 2 days past in the palace of *propriety* with a picture of Lucretia in the act of—*suicide* over my chimney, & a tome of *Pamela* lying on ye. table, ye. first as a hint I presume not to covet ye. *mistress* of a house, & the last as a defensive treatise in behalf of the Maid.— —The decorations of my *last* apartment were certainly very different—for a print of Rinaldo & Armida² was one of the most prominent ornaments.— —On Saturday I left Herefordshire with more regret than need be inflicted in detail upon my correspondents—so no more upon that topic. I begin to think your rhetoric has had its proper effect on C[aroline]—I have written twice to the Lady B[essborough] to decline an interview.—I found at Cheltenham your letters, & C[aroline]'s & *spared* you on this eternal subject by a cessation of ink for three days, I trust this is nearly the last to be shed on the same theme.—She charges me with my *own* letters—I have heard that a man in *liquor* was sometimes

³ Dr. Busby wrote an apologetic letter published in the *Morning Chronicle* of October 23, 1812. See Oct. 17, 1812, to Murray, note 1, concerning Byron's parody of his Address.
⁴ A pastry-cook in Cornhill.
⁵ *Junius's Letters*, by Woodfall, 3 vols., was among Byron's books sold at auction April 5, 1816.
¹ Byron so designates the Prince Regent, whose Address to Parliament he was deliberately missing.
² See Oct. 30, 1812, to Lady Melbourne, note 1.

responsible for what he may have said & perhaps the same rule extends to *love*—if so pray make the amplest apology for me—The moment I came to myself I was sorry for it.—One thing the Lady forgets—For a very *long time* (in the Calendar of Asmodeus) my answers were the subject of endless reproach on account of *their coldness*—at last I did write to her without restraint but rarely without regret.—I do not mean to deny my attachment—it *was*—and is not.—It was no great compliment, for I could love anything on earth that appeared to wish it; at the same time I do sometimes like to chuse for myself.—I shall be in town (the post is waiting) at Batts' Hotel on Sunday—I wrote this to tell you as much as under the present circumstances we cannot meet (except perhaps at Ly. H[olland]'s) for some time, & I heartily acquiesce in your opinion upon the subject.—Believe me ever yrs dr. Ly. M.—

[TO JOHN CAM HOBHOUSE]   *Middleton Novr. 27th. 1812*

My dear Hobhouse—I have some hopes from what I hear that you are in parliament, if so—whatever part you take & of course it will be with your father I shall rejoice in the success of which I think you certain.—My time has been passed since I wrote to you last chiefly at Eywood, where you would have been a welcome guest & I think as pleased as pleasant.—In a few days I leave Ld. Jersey's for London where you will find me at Batts' Hotel, & at Xmas I return to Eywood, near which I have a taken seat of Ld. O[xford]'s called Kinsham Court. —From this you will probably infer that the connection with Ly. C[aroline] is completely broken off—it is—I have formed another which whatever it's advantages or disadvantages is at least less troublesome & more to my taste.—More it would not be fair to add even to *you* mon ami, but I leave you to your brilliant conjectures, & usual laugh at my egaremens.—Sure I am you will rejoice at my disentanglement from one who has plagued us both so frequently; & as my escape is not owing to my prudence, in future you will have some confidence in ye. Fates who have stood my friends, & will I trust not abandon one who leaves so much to their own good pleasure.— —I was once not very far from you, on your route from Wales you must have passed through Cheltenham.—I am still remote from *marriage*, & presume whenever that takes place, "even-handed Justice" will return me cuckoldom in abundance.—I only left E[ywood] on Saturday

& have since been chiefly here, where sundry of the nobility & gentry are assembled in one of the pleasantest of all possible houses.—Both Ld. J[ersey] & his Countess are delightful, & their hospitality is Oriental; & except the place which I lately left, I prefer that where I am to all *visiting* residences.—Your father it seems has accepted a baronetcy, but I hope he will not stop there; it would give me great pleasure to have you some day on our benches, to which I trust his dignity is but a preliminary step.—You will see me in town, but I shall not go to the opening, if I arrive in time even for the regency debut.— —Tuesday will be time enough to take my seat.—You must have been amused with all this *de*jected Address fracas; to me the joke is somewhat near but I can laugh at it though no Gainer.—I can tell you some odd things about it unknown to the Public.—It was quite unthought of & unsought by me.—How go on the Quartos?

ever yrs my dear H.

BYRON

[TO LADY MELBOURNE] *Batts' Hotel. Novr. 30th. 1812*

Dear Ly. M.—I am just arrived & have received exactly 36 letters notes &c. (as I write a 37th!) of all descriptions so that I have full employment for ye. present.—I find amongst them some from C[aroline] of yesterday's date (Welwyn)[1] I believe most incoherent &c. & to which in the name of all the Saints & martyrs what answer can I give but what has been given already?—Her *letters* I have already said of my own accord I will give up to *her* or destroy in *your* or *her* or any other's presence, so that the interference of any other person will only *mar* my good intention—I thank you for the *hint*—an answer to *Men* always depends upon the temperance & tenor of the question.—I am extremely glad that I did not receive yrs. of the 27th. till just now & that I had before from *Cheltenham* stated my intention already as to Letters "sans phrase" from any person—because I much doubt whether I could have given the like answer to a *peremptory* embassy.—As to Lady B[essborough] how many months did she spend in trying to make me believe the *whole* a *joke* &c. on C[aroline]'s part?—& now she is angry that I at last believed so.— —I have some trinkets which she wishes restored or rather *had* for God knows where they are by this time—I wish she would not think of returning *mine*

[1] Caroline was at Brocket Hall, the country house of the Melbournes near Welwyn, Hertfordshire.

as in that case I must search the Country for *hers* which will take some time & trouble.— —I shall endeavour to wait on you tomorrow—believe me

dr. Ly. M. ever yrs.

P.S.—The Letter of today is the most *wild* I ever read—I really have not PATIENCE for all this.—I cannot please every body—She & I must not meet—not that I dread a *past* weakness—but it must not be—as to *others*—I have really had so much plague on the subject—& been at so much pains to free you all from these inquietudes that I very much fear my *politeness* will not carry me much further. Ly. H[olland?] has been taunting her it seems—her answer to Ly. O[xford] is stuff—*we* nor *she* nor *I* sent any *whatever answer*—& I have implored Ly. O[xford] to be *silent*.—If you knew but *ten* of the *twenty* scrapes I am in at this moment you would (& will I hope) pardon my pettishness.—I do not [know] which are the worst Lawyers, friends, or the *fair sect*.—I know Ly. O[xford] has not answered her & will not I *trust*—but who can trust anything or anybody?—

[TO LADY MELBOURNE]   *Tuesday Even.—[December, 1812?]*

Dear Ly. M.—I have received a letter from Ly. C[aroline] which has been *opened*—the contents profess to have accompanied some money which (God knows why) she supposes herself to owe me but (I thank heaven) it has been pilfered by the way.— This is all her own imagination & my only motive in writing this is to vindicate myself from the meanness of being supposed to receive or accept that to which really I have no claim.—Will you use your interest to induce her not to torment me with such transactions; the person present when I received the letter saw that it had been opened & contained *nothing*— at which I rejoice—but do beg sincerely to have no more of this for I most certainly am not one of her Creditors & she talks of some further shillings & pence as due to me of which I *know nothing* & bequeath them to those who may have more right to her bounty.—Believe me dear Ly. M.

yrs. ever
B.

P.S.—As the best way to comply with your last request I have (or rather) *shall* send one of the pictures to Ly. B[essborough] the other the moment I can extract it from a trunk not at present in my rooms, & for the letters I wait the pleasure of any *female* relative or Ly. C[aroline] herself.—I think my own might as well be returned as is usual on such occasions, particularly as on the last similar one in July I destroyed a great number & on requesting my own *was refused*!—

[TO JAMES RIDGWAY[1]]   [*December, 1812?*]

Mr. Ridgeway—You will address my newspaper (the *Morning Post*) to Ld. Oxford's Eywood Presteign, I shall change for the present as the Morning Chronicle is there regularly delivered & we do not want a duplicate.— —Pray send to the same place addressed to me the Number of "Town Talk"[2] for *October* last; & observe my directions as to the Papers.—

yrs. &c.
B.

P.S.—Have the goodness to forward these as soon as possible.—

[TO LADY MELBOURNE]   *Decr. 9th. 1812*

Dear Ly. M.—You have long ago forgotten a certain ring which I am still in your debt, & I hope you will not reject the only thing I ever dared to present you, nor violate ye. conditions on which I accepted your own by refusing this.— — —I regret that I lost your party last night, but meeting with Hobhouse whom I had not seen for some time I was detained too long either to appear or apologize.— —As I shall not see you before I leave town, I most respectfully take my farewell, & assure you that as far as *I* am concerned the *amiable* & *sincere* Phryna[1] shall never be the cause of further uneasiness.—To yourself I ever am dr. Ly. M.

most truly yr. obliged & f[aithfu]l, St.
BYRON

---

[1] James Ridgway was a bookseller, with a shop on Piccadilly, who supplied Byron with books and periodicals.

[2] *Town Talk: or Living Manners*, a literary and theatrical paper, was published first as a weekly and later as a monthly, from 1811 to 1814.

[1] Perhaps one of the fanciful signatures of Caroline Lamb.

Dear Sir—I have to request that you will pay the bearer (my Groom) the wages due to him (12 pds. 10 S.) & dismiss him immediately as I have given up my horses, & place the sum to my account.

ever yrs.
BYRON

Dear Sir—I request your attention to the enclosed, which I believe is very true—see what can be done with Howard[1]—& urge Claughton—if this kind of thing continues I must quit a country which my debts render uninhabitable notwithstanding every sacrifice on my part.

yrs. ever
B.

My dear Ly. M.—The trinkets[1] are travelling (at least most of them) in all parts of England & Wales, they certainly are not in the possession of ———— [Lady Oxford]—indeed so anxious was I to get rid of them that most of them had disappeared before my acquaintance with *her*.—The truth is they were all *women's adornments* & looked so very out of place in my custody, that lest they should seem not *honestly* come by, I was too glad to find any one to take them off my hands.—This is all the answer I can give to a species of *bullying* which I presume the Lady has learned in Ireland.—She will not deliver up my letters—very well—I *will* deliver up hers nevertheless —& mine she may make the most of, they are very like the Duke of York's[2] & the Editor of any magazine will treat with her for them on moderate terms—Whatever my motive good or bad may be for resolving not to keep back her brilliant documents, I think it will not be imputed to fear, since by so doing without receiving my own, I leave

[1] Howard was Byron's principal creditor among the money-lenders. See Jan. 16, 1812, to Hanson.

[1] The trinkets were the gifts of Caroline Lamb to Byron.

[2] The Duke of York's letters to his mistress, Mary Ann Clarke, were sentimental and romantic. Some of them were made public at the time of the Parliamentary inquiry in 1809.

the story entirely to her own telling; & as she has just acknowledged that *her* letters would *"ruin her"* I leave my determination in this respect to her own construction which of course will be the worst possible.—*This* I will do on my return to town, to *you* & *you* only or Ly. B[essborough] save & except one *boxfull* which I must for certain reasons *burn* in *your* presence,[3] so pray, have a good fire & fireguard on my next visit, I repeat that I never will again request my own— let her keep them or what she pleases.— —I do not exactly understand who my "secret foes" & her ambushed "men in buckram" are;[4] all this we shall know in due time, I don't know whether I can fight but I presume like the redoubtable Nym "I can wink & hold out my cold iron"[5] as well as another.—This I know that if she does plunge me into a quarrel It will be a serious one, for I am tired of trifling, & if *any* noble blood is to be spilt in her behalf I had as lief the puddle was *Irish* as any other complexion.—She writes menacingly, & at the same time accuses me of *menaces*—what menaces have I used?—poor little weak thing!— —she says I "concealed" myself in town, that is —I took my seat in the house, & visited all my acquaintance every day.—The comparison of the Rattlesnake, or any other with which Polito can furnish her are very much at her service, I rejoice that she stopped at Exeter Change being rather apprehensive that she might have driven as far as Billingsgate for a metaphor. Dont interrupt her, & if she wishes you all to quarrel with me—pray indulge her.—If I *had* the trinkets I would *not* deliver them up to the threat of the "secret [bitter?] assistant knights" & I am rather glad that I have them not to deliver, her *letters* I give up because she has a *child*—the other things will be of no consequence, but will form pretty subject matter for dispute without hurting her; as I have some guess at her "daring champions" I shall not wait their good pleasure, but explain to them on the very first opportunity my sentiments of them & their conduct; in the mean time I shall not stir to right or left but pursue "the even tenor of my way."—This is my answer to *her* & *your* letter, tell Ly. B[essborough] whatever disturbance arises is not of my seeking, I have borne as much as man can bear, & even now *I* will put it out of my power to rely upon my own resolutions, lest fresh insults should get the better of my temper.—All I desire from you or Ly. B[essborough]

[3] Some of Caroline's letters which Byron thought should be burned were those referring to indelicate matters such as the one accompanying a gift of a lock of her pubic hair. See Elwin, p. 146.

[4] According to Medwin, Byron said Caroline "promised young Grattan her favours if he would call me out". (Medwin, Lovell ed., p. 218.)

[5] Shakespeare, *Henry V*, II, i, 8.

is to "nothing extenuate nor set down aught in *malice*"[6] the *last* part of the quotation is not addressed to *you*.—To *her* I have no reply, no observation of any kind "if she will perish let her perish."—If you hear anything further you will let me know—if not—at any rate write to me—& believe me

ever yrs. most truly

P.S.—I always thought that anything given to a person became their property & these things were *forced* upon me as she knows, but once *mine* I was at liberty to part with them which I did to different people almost immediately.—

P.S.—She says I abuse her everywhere, & yet *conceal* myself!! I do neither one nor the other.—If I mentioned her at all it would not be with praise—but it is a subject so utterly abhorrent to my feelings that I never do—& as to concealment *you* can answer that.—

[TO LADY MELBOURNE]   *Decr. 15th. 1812*

Dear Ly. M.—Contrary to my first intent I have answered her letter to me & enclose it to you for delivery.—If she writes to Ld. O[xford] I am almost sure that *he* will write to Mr. L[amb] if so— there will be a pretty scene—we had some difficulty to prevent this once before, & I suppose it would not be very desirable now.—He is tolerably obstinate, & it would be as well not to bring it to the proof— of course I should prevent it if possible—because eventually it would be unpleasant to all parties.—I should wish you to be present when she receives this letter & tell me the effect. ever yrs.

B.

Always take this with you—*you* are not mentioned in this letter nor is *any name* therein.

[TO HENRY FOX[1]]   *Decr. 15th. 1812*

My dear FOX—Your letter arrived just as I was setting out in the full hope of having "an agreeable companion in a Post Chaise" & I

[6] Shakespeare, *Othello*, V, ii, 344-45.
[1] Henry Fox, Lord Holland's son. Byron liked him, partly because, like himself, he was lame.

passed through Oxford at an hour when you were not likely to be found to hear my useless regrets.—After skaiting up a perpendicular road I arrived here & found every body well except ye. Lady Jane[2] who is laid up with the stiffest of all possible necks, but it is now just beginning to turn upon it's hinges though rather rustily.—I thank you for ye. inclosed letter & cannot sufficiently admire the device of *your* seal, which passed the inspection of all the family before it came into my hands.—We are all marvellously impatient for your coming & none more than yrs. ever sincerely

BYRON

P.S.—Will you write to me—Ly. Holland looked on me rather grimly in town, I do not very well know why, for I was in her good graces in the autumn.—She is rather better in health which *you* will rejoice to hear.—

[TO LADY MELBOURNE]   *Decr. 21st. 1812*

My dear Ly. Melbourne,—I have not written to you for some days which must be some wonder & great relief to yourself—I do not presume that my epistle to the most amiable of the Ponsonbys will have much effect & I fear Ly. B[essborough] will not deem it sufficiently "soothing."—As the Lady however seems to have imagined herself extremely terrific in my eyes I could not altogether humour the mistake, & leave it to the inhabitants of Chili (or where is it?) to worship the D——l —"Soothing!" quotha! I wonder who wants it most! I think at least some portion of that same soothing syrup ought to fall to my share.— — —We have some talk here of a voyage to Sicily &c. in the Spring—if so—I shall be of the party—but this is merely speculation for the present—Hobhouse & myself have serious thoughts of "Levanting" once more & I expect to hear from him soon on that & other subjects.—You will not be sorry to find me once more "on the wings of the wind" & I hope you will send me some English intelligence foreign & domestic.—I shall still retain Kinsham (the place I have taken) even if I go abroad;—if it will be any satisfaction to the

---

2 Lady Jane Harley, Lady Oxford's daughter. Lady Oxford had a number of beautiful children, whose paternity was uncertain; they were commonly referred to as the "Harleian Miscellany". Hobhouse was half in love with Lady Jane, but found her "*un peu libre*" in her conversation and conduct. (Broughton, I, 41.) Byron's favourite was Lady Charlotte Harley, then eleven years of age. He paid tribute to her in some stanzas "To Ianthe" prefixed to the seventh edition of Cantos I and II of *Childe Harold*.

respectable C[arolin]e to know that she has had some share in disgusting me with this country she may enjoy it to the full—if it were not
for *others* I would set sail tomorrow.—My resentment against her is
merely *passive*—I never will degrade myself into her enemy—notwithstanding *all* the provocatives so plentifully administered.—I
shall soon discover if she has been tampering with Clare, but shall not
interfere between them further than concerns *myself*—[1] she will make
nothing of him—he has too much sense & too little vanity to be
fooled like his friend.— —I wish much to see you on my return to
London which will not be before the 12th. of next month, if then—we
are all very happy & serene—no scenes—a great deal of music—
good cheer—spirits & temper—& every day convinces me of the
contrast—by the bye—this *travelling scheme* as far as regards *all*
except Hobhouse & myself must be a *secret*—being the *first* between
you & me & if you keep it well—I have *ten* more for your discreet ear
when we meet.—I have not received the letter you mention from Ly.
B[essborough] & have no great interest in it's safe arrival—I do not
want any recantations & the old or new excuses—whatever the impression may be on others on my mind it is indelible—but let that
pass—it is odd that her last letter to me (which came with yours)
contains nothing but more *general* menaces of vengeance & professions
of not unwelcome hatred—but no particular denunciations of a serious
description—the closing sentence is awfully amiable & I copy it—
"you have told me how foreign women revenge—I will show you
how an Englishwoman can"— —very like the style of Miss Matthews
in Amelia & Lucy in the Beggar's Opera—& by no means having
even the merit if Novelty in my ears.—A namesake of C[aroline]'s[2]
was much more polite in her expressions though equally angry—&
now—if I may trust the authority of several reputable gentlefolks—
Does me the honour after the interval of several years to speak of me
in very gentle terms—& perhaps in the year 1820 your little Medea
may relapse into a milder tone. Believe me dear Ly. M.

> ever yrs.
> *Bn.*

P.S.—I think your plan with her not so good as yr. general plans
are—as long as she is in ye. country & has nothing to do but gallop
on the turnpike & scribble absurdities she will be unmanageable—

---

[1] See Oct. 18, 1812, to Lady Melbourne, note 2.
[2] Mrs. George Lamb's name was Caroline. The two sisters-in-law were sometimes distinguished by the names "Caroline William" and "Caroline George".

but a fortnight in town—the *10th Uniform*, the first fool & the last comer will work wonders—commit her to C[avendish] Square & she will forget every thing if not herself into the bargain—but you know best after all.— — —

[TO LADY MELBOURNE]   *Decr. 23d. 1812*

My dear Lady M.—Your last anecdote seems to shew that our friend is actually possessed by "the foul fiend *Flibertigibbet* who presides over mopping & mowing" & if the provincial literati dont insert it in the St. Alban's Mercury, the collectors of extraordinaries ought to be dismissed for malversation & omission.—Seriously though all this forms *my* best justification—I very much fear it will not forward your interests at the next election except amongst ye. ballad-makers.— What will the Lady B[essborough] say? I fear it will go nigh to the recall of Sir W. Farquhar & the ancient disorder.—Was the "odious book" (which has just attained the *summit* of *fame* by giving a name to a *very slow race horse!*)[1] added to the conflagration? & what might be the pretty piece of eloquence delivered by her right trusty Henchman? My letter would have added very appropriately to ye. combustibles & I regret ye. omission of such exquisite ingredients.[2]— — —I wrote to you yesterday (franked & directed to B[rocket?] H[all?])[3] not having then received ye. mandate to ye. contrary) & do not know that I can add anything to my details in that sheet—we are completely out of the world in this place, & have not even a *difference* to diversify the scene or amuse our correspondents, & you know perhaps that the recapitulation or display of *all good* things is very insipid to auditors or beholders.—I wait the news of the reception of the same ineffable letter now in your hands though (as I tell her) I have no great hopes of it's doing the least good.—It is written a little gravely but very much nevertheless in the usual tone which Ly. B[essborough] is pleased to say is not "soothing."— —I am really become very indifferent as to her next proceedings, for what can she do worse than she has already done?—I am much amused with ye. tale of Ly.

---

[1] Such was the fame of *Childe Harold* that a racehorse was apparently named after Byron's hero.

[2] Caroline Lamb had sought a vicarious revenge on Byron by staging a dramatic scene at the country estate of the Melbournes, having some children dance around a bonfire in the park in which she burned "effigies" of Byron's picture and copies of his letters (she couldn't bear to part with the originals).

[3] The country house of the Melbournes in Hertfordshire.

Cowper's little girl—her Mamma has always had a great share of my *most respectful* admiration, but I dont desire to be remembered to any of you as I suppose the best wish you have is to forget me as soon as possible; besides which under ye. impression of C[aroline]'s correspondence Ly. C[owper] must conceive me to be a sucking Catiline only less respectable.—Bankes is going abroad, & as I said in my last it is not very unlikely that I may recommence voyaging amongst the Mussulmen.—If so I claim you as a correspondent; since you *wont* give me up to the reasonable request of the moderate C[aroline] & in truth I don't wish you should.—You know I have obeyed you in everything, in my suit to ye. *Princess* of *Parallelograms*,[4] my breach with little *Mania*,[5] & my subsequent acknowledgement of the *sovereignty* of *Armida*[6]—you have been my director & are still for I do not know anything you could not make me do or undo—& m'amie (but this you *wont believe*) has not yet learned the art of *managing* me nor superseded your authority.—You would have laughed a little time ago, when I inadvertantly said talking of you that there was nothing you could not make me do or give up (if you thought it worth while) a sentiment which did not meet with the entire approbation of my audience but which I maintained like a Muscovite enamoured of *Despotism*.—I hear little from London but the lies of the Gazette & will back Buonaparte against the field still.—Pray write—& tell me how your *taming* goes on—I am all acquiescence to you & as much yours as ever dr. Ly. M

B.

[TO WILLIAM BANKES]   *Decr. 26th. 1812*

My dear Bankes,—The multitude of your recommendations has already superseded my humble endeavours to be of use to you & indeed most of my principal friends are returned—Leake from Joannina[1]— Canning & Adair[2] from the City of the faithful & at Smyrna no letter is necessary as the Consuls are always willing to do every thing for personages of respectability.—I have sent you *three* one to Gibraltar which though of no great necessity—will perhaps put you on a more

4 Annabella Milbanke.
5 Caroline Lamb.
6 Lady Oxford.
1 William Martin Leake was British "Resident" or diplomatic representative in Janina when Byron was there.
2 Stratford Canning was First Secretary and Robert Adair was British Ambassador at the Sultan's court when Byron was in Constantinople in 1810.

intimate footing with a very pleasant family there.— —You will very soon find out that a man of any Consequence has very little occasion for any letters but to Ministers & Bankers & of these you have already plenty I will be sworn—it is by no means impossible that I shall go in the Spring & if you will fix any place of rendezvous about August I will *write* or *join* you.—When in Albania I wish you would enquire after Dervise Tahiri and Vascillie (or Basil) [3] & make my respects to the Viziers both there & in the Morea.—If you mention my name to Suleyman of Thebes I think it will not hurt you, if I had my dragoman or wrote Turkish I could have given you letters of *real service* but to the English they are hardly requisite, & the Greeks themselves can be of little advantage.— —Liston [4] you know already & I do not, as he was not then minister.—Mind you visit Ephesus & the Troad—& let me hear from you when you please—I believe G. Forresti [5] is now at Yanina, but if not—whoever is there will be too happy to assist you.—Be particular about *firmanns*—never allow yourself to be bullied—for you are better protected in Turkey than any where —trust not the *Greeks*—& take some *knicknackeries* for presents— *watches pistols* &c. &c. to the Beys & Pachas.—If you find one Demetrius [6] at Athens or elsewhere I can recommend him as a good Dragoman—I hope to join you however—but you will find swarms of English now in the Levant.—
Believe me dear B.

ever yrs.

B.

[TO GEORGE FORRESTI [1]]   *Decr. 26th. 1812*

Dear Sir—I recommend to your notice & kindness my friend Mr. W. Bankes a gentleman of the first distinction in character, family, &

[3] Byron's Albanian servants in Greece.

[4] Robert Liston succeeded Adair as British Ambassador in Constantinople in 1811, after an interim when Canning served as chief of mission.

[5] George Forresti, a Greek by birth, whom Byron had met at Malta, and who was in Tripolitza when Byron was visiting Veli Pasha (see letter of August 16, 1810, to Hobhouse), followed Leake as British Resident at Janina. It was he who encouraged Byron and Hobhouse to visit Ali Pasha. In his diary (September 5, 1809) Hobhouse gave the first name of the man they met at Malta as Spiridion. It is possible that George was his brother, but Hobhouse's description seems to point to the same man, and Byron appears to be writing to a man he has met.

[6] Demetrius Zographo, the Greek servant whom Byron brought with him to England, had returned to Athens.

[1] See Dec. 26, 1812, to Bankes, note 5.

fortune, in this country.—As he will be some time in Albania your acquaintance will be of great advantage to his pursuits, & if he finds it as agreeable as Mr. Hobhouse & myself did I trust he will remember it with the same pleasure.—I hope you & Ali Pacha go on well together—Leake is still in this country.—Believe me ever yrs.

BYRON

[TO LADY MELBOURNE]   *Decr. 27th. 1812*

My dear Ly. M.—I know very little of the P's[1] party & less of her publication (if it be hers) & am not at all in ye. secret, but I am aware that the advice given her by the most judicious of her "little Senate" has been to remain quiet & leave all to the P[rincess] C[harlott]e.—I have heard nothing of the thing you mention except in ye. papers & did not imagine it to be *hers*. I by no means consider myself as an attache to her or any party, though I certainly should support her interest in Parliament if brought forward in any shape—& I doubt the possibility of the divorce—firstly—because he would already if he could—2dly.—unless there is different law for Sovereign & subject she might recriminate (even were the charge proved) & by the law of the land as in Ld. Grosvenor & Duke C[umberland]'s case there could be no divorce[2]—3dly. it would hurt the daughter 4thly. if he married again & the Holy Ghost or any other begat him an heir— still there would be a party ready to bastardize the product of the 2d. marriage by maintaining the legality of the first & denying his divorce to be legal—& 5thly. the uproar would be prodigious & injure his nerves—for my part I care not & think this country wants a little "civil buffeting" to bring some of us to our senses. I shall not mention your name nor what you have said though I fully agree with you that it is much better for her to be quiet.—M'amie thinks I agree with her in *all* her politics, but she will discover that this is a mistake. She insists always upon the P[rincess]'s innocence; but then as she sometimes reads me somewhat a tedious homily upon her own, I look upon it in much the same point of view as I should on Mary Magdalen's vindication of Mrs. Joseph, or any other *immaculate riddle*.—I suspect from what you say & what I have heard that there will be a

1 The Princess Caroline had gathered a party about her in opposition to the Prince Regent. The liberals and radicals generally rallied around her, and her cause became a popular one. Lady Oxford was one of her friends and supporters.

2 Byron must have been thinking of the Duke of Cumberland (1721–1765) who wanted to divorce his wife for a mistress.

scene.—My proposed confidence to you will do for our meeting & consists merely of one or two slight domestic things on which I want to ask your advice, & you *know* I not only ask but *take* it when you please.— —I am glad C[aroline] is so quiet—her account of my letter is right—her inference from it wrong—if she knew anything of human nature she would feel that as long as men love they *forgive* every thing, but the moment it is over they discover fifty things on which to ground a plausible & perpetual implacability.—She could not renew it—& this she knows, but she is quite right to reserve a point for Vanity. In her last she says "she shall quit the room or the house the moment I enter it." I answered that she was to do as she pleased but that my carriage would be always respectful & as friendly as she thought proper to allow—an expression I now regret for she will interpret it into a wish to be again in her trammels which I neither would nor could.—Her letters were still more absurd than ever— telling me she had "perjured herself to Lady C[owpe]r & Mrs. L[amb]" &c. to whom it seems I betrayed her &c. (I can safely appeal to *both* as you will or may discover) & all this was my fault & so on.— Then comes a long account of the bonfire[3] still more ludicrous than *yours*, full of *Yeomanry*, *pages*, gold chains, *basket of flowers*—herself— & all other fooleries.— —Ld. O[xford] goes to town on Saturday next, & we shall follow him the week or fortnight after—in the mean time write to me—we are very quiet & happy—but I shall certainly attend to what you say on travelling "en famille."— Believe me dear Ly M

ever yrs
B.

P.S.—I just hear that *we* shall not be in town before the 20th.—

My dear Ly. M.—I have received several epistles from C[aroline] which I have answered as seemed best at ye. time—she has at last said that she heard of the proposal but is ignorant to whom[.] I have owned it but not added any names of any parties concerned though by this she probably knows, & it is quite as well she should.—Her letters are as usual full of contradictions & *less* truth (if possible) than ever, my last answer which was goodnatured enough but rather more

---

[3] See Dec. 23, 1812, to Lady Melbourne, note 2.

facetious than befits her taste has produced a pettish rejoinder, she has again written to Ly. O[xford] but *quietly* & *cunningly*. She has sent me a Banker's receipt for some money she swears she owes me, but which I will have nothing to do with, I have returned it, & if the money is not removed from Hoare's & my name withdrawn, I shall most assuredly dispatch it with *her* compliments one half to the *Magdalen asylum* & the other to *St. Luke's*[1] as a donation & return in kind for her *bonfire*—if she *will* play the fool I rather suspect that I shall be seized with a fit of repartee which will not be very "soothing" —this I beg you will hint as to the disposal of this money,—it is of no use to try "soothing" with so detestable a disposition, & my patience stands marvellously in need of repose.— —If Mr. N. is one of her confidants I regret it, against him I have no enmity, but through *her* means I was once before nearly involved in a dispute, & not improbably shall again—I do wish she would consider what the consequences may be of this perpetual system of irritation on my temper— I begin to look upon her as actually mad or it would be impossible for me to bear what I have from her already.— —We have no *scenes* here—& you do not know well if you suppose I covet them—I shall not entertain you with a long list of *attributes*, but merely state that I have not been guilty of once *yawning* in the eternity of two months under the same roof—a phenomenon in my history—we go on admirably in ye. *country*—but how Town may suit us I cannot foresee.—I hear Ly. H[ollan]d is *not* pleased with my present place of abode, no bad reason for liking it better myself.— —*We* shall have no quarrels about my visits to you, for you are a great favourite though suspected of *undue influence* (which you *deserve*) and were it otherwise, after your firm adherence to my cause, I neither would nor could desert your banners unless dismissed by your own express request.—I sent you so long a letter the other day on ye. subject of the P[rinces]s that I shall now no further trespass on your Xmas amusements than by wishing they may be pleasantly prolonged for the present, & often renewed hereafter.—This is the last day of the year —I shall hope to hear from you soon in the next—& like the Spaniards hope you "may live a thousand."—

ever yrs. dr. Ly. M.
B.

[1] The Magdalen asylum was a reformatory for prostitutes. St. Luke's was a hospital for lunatics instituted in 1751 on the north side of Old Street Road near the City Road.

LIST OF LETTERS AND SOURCES

Date	Recipient	Source of Text	Page

Date	Recipient	Source of Text	Page
		1811 (continued)	
July 23	John Cam Hobhouse	MS. Murray	61
July 24	John Hanson	MS. British Museum (Eg. 2611)	62
July 28	John Hanson	MS. British Museum (Eg. 2611)	62
July 29	J. Wedderburn Webster	MS. Murray	62
July 30	William Miller	MS. Murray	63
[July 30?]	[?]	MS. Murray	63
July 31	J. Wedderburn Webster	MS. Murray	63
July 31	John Cam Hobhouse	MS. Murray	64
July 31	John Hanson (*a*)	MS. British Museum (Eg. 2611)	66
July 31	John Hanson (*b*)	MS. British Museum (Eg. 2611)	66
Aug. 2	John Hanson	MS. British Museum (Eg. 2611)	67
Aug. 2	John Pigot	Text: Moore, I, 272–273	67
Aug. 4	John Hanson	MS. British Museum (Eg. 2611)	68
Aug. 7	Scrope Berdmore Davies	Text: Moore, I, 277	68
Aug. 10	John Cam Hobhouse	MS. Murray	69
Aug. 12	R. C. Dallas	MS. British Embassy, Athens	70
Aug. 12	Samuel Bolton	Text: Moore, I, 279–282	71
Aug. 16	Samuel Bolton	Text: Moore, I, 282	73
Aug. 20	Samuel Bolton	Text: Moore, I, 283	73
Aug. 20	James Cawthorn	MS. Robert H. Taylor Coll., Princeton University Library	73
Aug. 21	Augusta Leigh	MS. Murray	74
Aug. 21	R. C. Dallas	MS. Stark Library, University of Texas	75
Aug. 22	Francis Hodgson	Text: Moore, I, 284–285	77
Aug. 23	John Murray	MS. Murray	78
Aug. 24	J. Wedderburn Webster	MS. Murray	78

Date	Recipient	Source of Text	Page
		1811 (continued)	
Sept. 15	R. C. Dallas	MS. Stark Library, University of Texas	99
Sept. 15	John Hanson	MS. Stark Library, University of Texas	99
Sept. 16	John Murray	MS. Murray	100
Sept. 16	R. C. Dallas	Text: Dallas, *Correspondence*, II, 111–112	100
Sept. 17	R. C. Dallas (*a*)	Text: Dallas, *Correspondence*, II, 113–115	100
Sept. 17	R. C. Dallas (*b*)	Text: Dallas, *Correspondence*, II, 116	102
Sept. 20	John Cam Hobhouse	MS. Murray	102
Sept. 21	R. C. Dallas	MS. Mrs. C. Earle Miller	103
Sept. 23	R. C. Dallas	MS. Robert H. Taylor Coll., Princeton University Library	104
Sept. 25	Francis Hodgson	Text: *LJ*, II, 45–47	105
Sept. 26	R. C. Dallas	MS. Roe-Byron Coll., Newstead Abbey	106
Oct. 10	J. Wedderburn Webster	MS. Murray	107
[Oct. 10]	R. C. Dallas	MS. Beinecke Library, Yale University	109
Oct. 10	Francis Hodgson	MS. Meyer Davis Coll., University of Pennsylvania Library	109
Oct. 11	R. C. Dallas	Text: Dallas, *Correspondence*, II, 142–145; Fac. of last page Terry sale, Anderson Galleries, May 2, 1934, p. 43	110
Oct. 13	Francis Hodgson	Text: Moore, I, 303–305	111
Oct. 13	John Cam Hobhouse	MS. Murray	113
Oct. 14	John Cam Hobhouse	MS. Murray	114
Oct. 14	R. C. Dallas (*a*)	Text: Dallas, *Correspondence*, II, 146–147	115
Oct. 14	R. C. Dallas (*b*)	MS. Murray	116
Oct. 16	R. C. Dallas	MS. Bodleian Library	116
Oct. 22	John Cam Hobhouse	MS. Murray	117

Date	Recipient	Source of Text	Page
		1811 (continued)	
Oct. 25	R. C. Dallas	MS. Doris Rich Stuart	118
Oct. 27	Thomas Moore	Text: Moore, I, 309–310	118
Oct. 28	Mrs. Margaret Pigot	MS. Nottingham Public Libraries	119
Oct. 29	R. C. Dallas	Text: Dallas, *Correspondence*, II, 156	120
Oct. 29	Thomas Moore	Text: Moore, I, 311	120
Oct. 30	Thomas Moore	Text: Moore, I, 312	121
Oct. 31	R. C. Dallas	Text: Dallas, *Correspondence*, II, 159–160	121
[Nov. ? or 1812]	Miss Hodgson	MS. Carl H. Pforzheimer Library	122
Nov. 1	Thomas Moore	Text: Moore, I, 313	122
Nov. 1	John Hanson	MS. British Museum (Eg. 2611)	122
Nov. 2	John Cam Hobhouse	MS. Murray	123
Nov. 3	John Cam Hobhouse	MS. Murray	124
Nov. 4	Francis Hodgson	MS. Carl H. Pforzheimer Library	127
Nov. 7	Mr. Deighton	MS. Manuscript Division, N. Y. Public Library	127
Nov. 9	John Cam Hobhouse	MS. Murray	128
Nov. 15	Francis Hodgson	Text: Sotheby Catalogue, March 2, 1885	129
Nov. 16	John Cam Hobhouse	MS. Murray	129
Nov. 17	John Cam Hobhouse	MS. Murray	130
Nov. 17	Francis Hodgson	Text: *LJ*, II, 70–71	132
Nov. 18	John Hanson	MS. British Museum (Eg. 2611)	133
Nov. 19	Rev. Dr. Valpy	MS. Stark Library, University of Texas	133
Nov. 20	John Hanson	MS. British Museum (Eg. 2611)	134
Nov. 26	R. C. Dallas	MS. Haverford College Library	135
Dec. 3	John Cam Hobhouse	MS. Murray	135
Dec. 4	Francis Hodgson	Text: *LJ*, II, 72–73	136
Dec. 6	William Harness	MS. Stark Library, University of Texas	137

Date	Recipient	Source of Text	Page
		1811 (continued)	
Dec. 7	J. Wedderburn Webster	MS. Murray	138
Dec. 7	John Hanson	MS. British Museum (Eg. 2611)	139
Dec. 8	Francis Hodgson	Text: *LJ*, II, 82–87; Fac. of first page, Terry sale, Anderson Galleries, May 2, 1934, p. 40	139
Dec. 8	William Harness	MS. Stark Library, University of Texas	142
Dec. 9	John Cam Hobhouse	MS. Murray	143
Dec. 10	John Hanson	MS. British Museum (Eg. 2611)	144
Dec. 11	Thomas Moore	Text: Moore, I, 325	145
Dec. 12	Francis Hodgson	MS. Robert H. Taylor Coll., Princeton University Library	145
[Dec. 13?]	R. C. Dallas	MS. Morgan Library	146
Dec. 13	John Hanson	MS. British Museum (Eg. 2611)	146
Dec. 15	John Hanson	MS. British Museum (Eg. 2611)	147
Dec. 15	John Cam Hobhouse	MS. Murray	147
Dec. 15	William Harness	MS. Stark Library, University of Texas	148
Dec. 17	John Cam Hobhouse	MS. Murray	150
Dec. 17	R. C. Dallas	Text: Sotheby Catalogue, Feb. 10, 1948	151
[Dec. 25]	John Cam Hobhouse	MS. Murray	151
		1812	
——	Samuel Rogers (*a*)	MS. Stark Library, University of Texas	152
——	Samuel Rogers (*b*)	MS. Morgan Library	152
——	Samuel Rogers (*c*)	MS. Fac., Hofman & Freeman, Catalogue 33, Boston, April, 1971	152
——	John Hanson	MS. Murray	152
Jan. 4	G. Walleden[?]	MS. Morgan Library	153

273

Date	Recipient	Source of Text	Page
		1812 (continued)	
Jan. 4	John Hanson	MS. British Museum (Eg. 2611)	153
Jan. 14	John Hanson	MS. British Museum (Eg. 2611)	153
Jan. 16	John Hanson	MS. Murray	154
Jan. 16	John Cam Hobhouse	MS. Murray	155
Jan. 19	E. D. Clarke	MS. British Museum (Eg. 2869)	156
Jan. 21	Robert Rushton	MS. Murray	157
Jan. 25	Robert Rushton	Text: *LJ*, II, 94	158
Jan. 27	John Galt	MS. Murray	158
[Jan. 28]	Francis Hodgson	Text: Hodgson, *Memoir*, I, 221	159
Jan. 28	Susan Vaughan	MS. Lytton	159
Jan. 29	Thomas Moore	Text: Moore, I, 330	159
Feb. 1	Francis Hodgson	Text: *LJ*, II, 96; Sotheby Catalogue, March 2, 1885	160
Feb. 4	Samuel Rogers	MS. British Museum (Add. 51639)	160
Feb. 10	John Cam Hobhouse	MS. Murray	161
Feb. 12	John Cowell	Text: Moore, I, 334–335; Fac. last page, Maggs Catalogue 646, Summer, 1937	162
Feb. 16	Francis Hodgson	Text: *LJ*, II, 99–101	163
Feb. 21	Francis Hodgson	Text: Hodgson, *Memoir*, I, 223–224	164
Feb. 21	John Cowell	MS. Bergen University Library	164
Feb. 25	Lord Holland	MS. British Museum (Add. 51639)	165
Feb. 28	John Hanson	MS. British Museum (Eg. 2611)	166
March 1	James Perry	Text: *LJ*, II, 97n	166
March 2	John Hanson	MS. British Museum (Eg. 2611)	167
March 5	Francis Hodgson	MS. Huntington Library	167
March 5	Lord Holland	Text: Moore, I, 342	168
[March?]	Col. Greville	MS. Boston Public Library	168

Date	Recipient	Source of Text	Page
		1812 (continued)	
March 8	E. D. Clarke	Text: Walter H. Hill Catalogue 30, Chicago, April, 1910	169
[March 11]	R. C. Dallas	Text: Dallas, *Correspondence*, III, 23	169
March 25	Thomas Moore	Text: Moore, I, 356	169
[April 3?]	Thomas Moore	MS. National Library of Scotland	170
[April]	Lady Caroline Lamb	MS. Murray	170
[April–July?]	Lady Melbourne (*a*)	MS. Morgan Library	171
[April–July?]	Lady Melbourne (*b*)	MS. Murray	171
April 5	E. D. Clarke	MS. British Museum (Eg. 2869)	171
[April?]	William Bankes (*a*)	Text: Moore, I, 353	172
[April?]	William Bankes (*b*)	MS. British Museum (Loan MS. 60)	173
April 20	William Bankes	MS. Mrs. James Edward Fitzgerald	173
[April?]	Thomas Moore	Text: Moore, I, 356	173
[May?]	John Murray (*a*)	MS. Murray	174
[May?]	John Murray (*b*)	MS. Murray	174
[May?]	John Murray (*c*)	MS. Murray	175
May 1	Lady Caroline Lamb	MS. Lytton	175
May 8	Thomas Moore	Text: Moore, I, 356–357	176
May 10	T. J. Mathias	MS. Carolyn Manovill	176
[May 19?]	Lady Caroline Lamb	MS. Murray	176
May 20	Thomas Moore	Text: Moore I, 357	177
May 20	[?]	MS. Mayfield Coll., Syracuse University Library	178
May 27	E. D. Clarke	MS. British Museum (Eg. 2869)	178
June 1	Bernard Barton	MS. Roe-Byron Coll., Newstead Abbey	178
June 25	Lord Holland	MS. British Museum (Add. 51639)	180

Date	Recipient	Source of Text	Page
		1812 (continued)	
June 26	E. D. Clarke	MS. Robert H. Taylor Coll., Princeton University Library	180
June 30	Mr. Longman	Text: Maggs Catalogue 425, Summer, 1922	181
[July–Dec.?]	Lady Melbourne	MS. Murray	181
July 6	Walter Scott	MS. National Library of Scotland	182
July 29	Miss Mercer Elphinstone	MS. Marquess of Lansdowne	183
[Aug. ?]	Lady Melbourne (*a*)	MS. Murray	184
[Aug. ?]	Lady Melbourne (*b*)	MS. Murray	184
[Aug. ?]	Lady Caroline Lamb	MS. Murray (lithographed Fac.)	185
Aug. 3	Miss Mercer Elphinstone	MS. Marquess of Lansdowne	186
[Aug. 12?]	Lady Melbourne	MS. Murray	187
[Aug. 14?]	Lady Melbourne	MS. Murray	188
Aug. 17	John Hanson	MS. Murray	189
Aug. 23	John Hanson	MS. Murray	189
Aug. 31	John Hanson	MS. Mayfield Coll., Syracuse University Library	189
[Sept.]	Rev. Robert Walpole	MS. British Museum (last page only laid in *Childe Harold*—C.28.M.14)	190
Sept. 5	John Murray	MS. Murray	190
Sept. 10	Lord Holland	MS. British Museum (Add. 51639)	191
Sept. 10	Lady Melbourne	MS. Murray	192
Sept. 13	Lady Melbourne	MS. Murray	193
Sept. 14	John Murray	MS. Murray	196
Sept. 15	Lady Melbourne	MS. Murray	198
Sept. 18	Lady Melbourne	MS. Murray	199
[Sept. 19]	John Hanson	MS. Murray	201
Sept. 19	Lady Melbourne	Text: Airlie, *In Whig Society*, pp. 132–133	202
Sept. 21	Lady Melbourne	MS. Murray	202

Date	Recipient	Source of Text	Page
		1812 (continued)	
Sept. 22	Lord Holland	MS. British Museum (Add. 51639)	203
Sept. 22	Charles Hanson	MS. Murray	204
Sept. 23	Lord Holland	MS. British Museum (Add. 51639)	204
Sept. 24	Lord Holland (*a*)	MS. British Museum (Add. 51639)	205
[Sept. 24]	Lord Holland (*b*)	MS. British Museum (Add. 51639)	206
Sept. 24	Lord Holland (*c*)	MS. British Museum (Add. 51639)	206
Sept. 25	Lord Holland	MS. British Museum (Add. 51639)	207
Sept. 25	Lady Melbourne	MS. Murray	208
Sept. 26 [-27]	Lord Holland	MS. British Museum (Add. 51639)	209
Sept. 27	John Murray	MS. Royal Library, Windsor	211
Sept. 28	Lord Holland (*a*)	MS. British Museum (Add. 51639)	212
Sept. 28	Lord Holland (*b*)	MS. British Museum (Add. 51639)	213
Sept. 28	William Bankes	MS. Beinecke Library, Yale University	214
Sept. 28	Lady Melbourne	MS. Murray	216
Sept. 29	Lord Holland	MS. British Museum (Add. 51639)	219
Sept. 29	Charles Hanson	MS. Murray	219
Sept. 30	Lord Holland (*a*)	MS. British Museum (Add. 51639)	219
Sept. 30	Lord Holland (*b*)	MS. British Museum (Add. 51639)	220
Sept. 30	Lord Holland (*c*)	MS. British Museum (Add. 51639)	221
[Sept. 30?]	Lady Melbourne	MS. Murray (last two pages only)	222
[Oct. ?]	Lady Caroline Lamb	Text: Airlie, *In Whig Society*, p. 150	222
Oct. 2	Lord Holland (*a*)	MS. British Museum (Add. 51639)	223

Date	Recipient	Source of Text	Page
		1812 (continued)	
Nov. 16	John Hanson	MS. Murray	248
Nov. 18	Lady Melbourne	MS. Murray	248
Nov. 22	John Murray	MS. Murray	249
Nov. 26	Lady Melbourne	MS. Murray	250
Nov. 27	John Cam Hobhouse	MS. Murray	251
Nov. 30	Lady Melbourne	MS. Murray	252
[Dec. ?]	[Lady Melbourne]	MS. Murray	253
[Dec. ?]	James Ridgway	MS. Stark Library, University of Texas	254
Dec. 9	Lady Melbourne	MS. Murray	254
Dec. 10	John Hanson	MS. Murray	255
Dec. 14	John Hanson	MS. Murray	255
Dec. 14	Lady Melbourne	MS. Murray	255
Dec. 15	Lady Melbourne	MS. Murray	257
Dec. 15	Henry Fox	MS. Huntington Library	257
Dec. 21	Lady Melbourne	MS. Murray	258
Dec. 23	Lady Melbourne	MS. Murray	260
Dec. 26	William Bankes	MS. Colorado College Library	261
Dec. 26	George Forresti	MS. Stark Library, University of Texas	262
Dec. 27	Lady Melbourne	MS. Murray	263
Dec. 31	Lady Melbourne	MS. Murray	264

FORGERIES OF BYRON'S LETTERS

July 27, 1810: To His Mother. Schultess-Young, pp. 105–107; *LJ*, I, 292–293.

Aug. 29, 1811: To [Sir Godfrey] Webster. MS. Princeton University Library.

Sept. 1, 1811: To James Cawthorn. Sotheby Catalogue, Nov. 27, 1945.

Sept. 26, 1812: To Lady Davies [Davy?]. Schultess-Young, p. 156.

BIOGRAPHICAL SKETCHES

LORD HOLLAND

Henry Richard Vassall Fox, third Lord Holland (1773–1840) had married Elizabeth Vassall in 1797 two days after her first husband, Sir Godfrey Webster, had divorced her (naming Lord Holland as co-respondent). But they recovered from the scandal and reigned over the most recherché Whig society at Holland House, Kensington. Byron met Lord Holland, probably through Samuel Rogers, by early 1812. As a leader of the Moderate Whigs in the House of Lords, Holland welcomed a new Opposition member, and Byron sought his advice before making his maiden speech. If the radicalism of Byron's stand went beyond Holland's position, it made no difference in his friendly gestures. It was chiefly to please Lord Holland that Byron suppressed *English Bards and Scotch Reviewers*, which had some caustic comments on the Holland House circle. After Byron's fame with *Childe Harold* he was always a welcome guest at Holland House. Lady Holland, who had a sharp and gossipy tongue, was uniformly kind, and Byron paid both the Hollands the greatest deference. Lord Holland requested Byron to write the address for the opening of the new Drury Lane Theatre. He complied though it went against his grain to write a piece to order. Holland offered a kindly intercession in the separation of the Byrons but it was of no avail.

LEIGH HUNT

James Henry Leigh Hunt, born in 1784 and educated at Christ's Hospital, had started with his brother John in 1808 a weekly paper called *The Examiner* espousing liberal causes and expressing daring opinions, political and literary. For a "libel" on the Prince Regent in 1812 the brothers were convicted and sent to prison for two years. In May 1813 Moore took Byron to meet Hunt in the Cold Bath prison and thereafter Byron visited him frequently, bringing books useful to Hunt's writing of his poem *The Story of Rimini* (published in 1816 on Byron's recommendation by John Murray). After Hunt's release from prison in 1815 Byron paid him several visits. Hunt's sympathy and loyalty at the time of the separation Byron remembered with gratitude. When Shelley suggested that Hunt be invited to Italy to edit jointly with them a new periodical, Byron offered an apartment in his house and sent money for Hunt's passage. The drowning of Shelley shortly after his arrival left Byron with Hunt on his hands. Byron gave him all the help he could for the new periodical, *The Liberal*, including the free use of *The Vision of Judgment* and several other poems. But Hunt, though good-natured, was never able to strike the right note with Byron. He was either too deferential or too familiar and utterly feckless in money matters. Mrs. Hunt's superior moral attitude, and their numerous uninhibited children smearing Byron's walls, did not help matters. Though largely supported by Byron's contributions, *The Liberal* died after four numbers. Wholly dependent on Byron, Hunt's touchiness increased. And he was the cause of some unfortunate misunderstandings between Byron and Mary Shelley. Hunt took his revenge in *Lord Byron and Some of His Contemporaries* (1828). But he admitted his prejudice and made some kinder remarks in his *Autobiography* many years later.

THE HON. DOUGLAS KINNAIRD

An intimate friend of Hobhouse at Cambridge, Kinnaird met Byron there but they were not close friends until later. Born in 1788, the fifth son of the seventh Baron Kinnaird, he was educated at Eton, Göttingen, and Trinity College, Cambridge. He travelled with Hobhouse on the Continent in 1813–14. On his return Byron began to see more of him. It was at his request that Byron wrote the *Hebrew Melodies* to be set to music by Isaac Nathan, and the following year Kinnaird induced Byron to become a member with him of the subcommittee of management of Drury Lane Theatre. Byron enjoyed his bachelor dinners where the brandy and the talk flowed. He and Kinnaird frequently had to help Sheridan navigate homeward. As a partner in the bank of Ransom and Morland, Kinnaird became Byron's banker and business and literary agent after he went abroad in 1816. Kinnaird was in political sympathy with Hobhouse in the radical reform movement. He was elected to Parliament from Bishop's Castle in July 1819, but lost his seat the following year. Byron's letters to him are filled with much good humour and facetiousness as well as good sense.

LADY CAROLINE LAMB

Caroline was the daughter of Frederick Ponsonby, third Earl of Bessborough, and his wife Lady Henrietta Frances Spencer, sister of Georgiana, Duchess of Devonshire. Born in 1785, Caroline was three years older than Byron. She was lively, pretty, clever, and eccentric. She married in 1805 William Lamb, second son of Lord Melbourne (and later, as Lord Melbourne, Prime Minister under Queen Victoria). When Byron met Caroline in 1812 she retained the childlike freshness which in his eyes was part of her charm. She had, as Byron said, all the accomplishments of a lady, but "a total want of common conduct" and her heart was "a little volcano". It was her headlong indiscretion in the end which repelled him, and her persistence in making scenes. Her affair with Byron lasted only about three months, but she refused to leave him in quiet when he had turned to the more tranquil love of Lady Oxford. His image haunted her for the rest of her life. After he went abroad in 1816, she published her novel *Glenarvon* in which Byron was the thinly disguised hero-villain. She made a friend of John Murray and at one time forged a letter to get from him Byron's portrait, and Murray gave her advance copies of Byron's poems. She later had periods of mental derangement and died four years after Byron, in 1828.

LADY MELBOURNE

Elizabeth, only daughter of Sir Ralph Milbanke of Halnaby, Yorkshire, married in 1769 Sir Peniston Lamb, created an Irish baron as Lord Melbourne in 1770, an Irish viscount in 1780 and an English peer in 1815. She was past sixty when Byron met her in 1812 just after he had achieved fame with the publication of *Childe Harold*. Soon his liaison with Lady Caroline Lamb, wife of her son William, involved him deeply with her family. After the affair ended, Lady Melbourne became Byron's confidante. He was fascinated by her, respecting her wisdom and her tolerance. He spoke of her as "the best, the kindest, and ablest female I have ever known, old or young". He told Lady Blessington: "She was a charming person—a sort of modern Aspasia, uniting the energy of a man's mind with the delicacy and tenderness of a woman's. . . . I have often thought, that, with a little more youth, Lady M. might have turned my head. . . ." She relayed his proposal of marriage to her niece, Annabella Milbanke, gave him sage advice concerning the danger of his liaison with his half-sister, encouraged his flirtation with Lady Frances Webster as a distraction, and defended him during the separation. Byron was saddened by her death in 1818.

ANNABELLA MILBANKE (later LADY BYRON)

Anne Isabella, only daughter of Sir Ralph and Lady (Judith) Milbanke of Seaham, near Durham, was born in 1792. A spoiled child and a precocious one, she had read widely and had a penchant for mathematics. Her notebooks show her to have been rather smug in her moral judgments and confident of her ability to read character, though her social contacts had been few before she came to London in the spring of 1812. She first saw Byron at the home of her aunt, Lady Melbourne, just after the fame of *Childe Harold* had made him much sought after, when he was already coming under the spell of Lady Caroline Lamb. One or two conversations with him convinced her that it was her destiny to befriend and reform this fallen angel. Byron was strongly attracted by her innocence and intelligence. When he was seeking an escape through marriage from Caroline, he proposed to Annabella through Lady Melbourne. She gave him an involved negative but wanted to remain his friend. In the autumn of 1813 she began a correspondence which led in the following year to an engagement. Byron married her on January 2, 1815. On December 10 she gave birth to a daughter, Augusta Ada, and on January 15, 1816, she left for her parents' home and never returned. Two weeks later her father wrote to Byron asking him to accede to a quiet separation, which he resisted until he was convinced that it was Lady Byron's wish. She never revealed publicly her reasons for the separation, but did not counter or deny rumours detrimental to Byron and his sister. After he went abroad she systematically eroded Augusta's peace of mind, inducing her to show all her correspondence with her brother. Lady Byron's later years were devoted to "good works" and to self-justification. Despite her "policy of silence", she confided her story of the marriage to a great many people. She died in 1860.

THOMAS MOORE

Byron knew and admired Moore by reputation before they met in November 1811. The son of a Dublin grocer, he was born in 1779, was educated at Trinity College, Dublin, and early showed a facility for writing melodious verse. He had come to London in 1799 to study law at the Middle Temple, but his *Odes* translated from Anacreon

(1800), dedicated to the Prince of Wales, opened to him the houses of the Whig aristocracy and launched him on a very successful poetical and social career. His pseudonymous *Poems of the Late Thomas Little*, titillatingly amorous, was much admired by the youthful Byron, and it influenced his early poems. But Moore's reputation, when Byron met him, was based on his *Irish Melodies* and his ability to sing his own songs at social gatherings. Byron met him after they had avoided a duel that Moore threatened because of some lines in Byron's *English Bards and Scotch Reviewers*. The meeting took place at the home of Samuel Rogers, the banker poet, then one of Moore's closest friends. Byron took to Moore immediately and they became fast friends. When Moore was in town they were frequently together at parties and at the theatre. Moore had an agreeable appearance and personality but was something of a social climber. Byron said later, "Tommy loves a Lord". The friendship continued throughout Byron's life, and some of his most interesting letters were written to Moore. When Moore came to Venice in 1819 Byron gave him the Memoirs which he subsequently with Byron's approval sold to John Murray for posthumous publication. It was against Moore's protest that the Memoirs were burned after Byron's death. Moore used a few anecdotes he remembered from them in his "Life" of Byron which he published in 1830.

John Murray II

The first John Murray had established a bookselling and publishing business at 32 Fleet Street in 1768. His son (born in 1778) had become one of the most enterprising and successful of the London publishers when Byron submitted to him through Dallas the manuscript of the first two cantos of *Childe Harold* in 1811. He was one of the founders and the publisher of the powerful Tory *Quarterly Review*, edited by William Gifford, who was also his literary adviser. Murray had an impressive list of authors, and the publication of *Childe Harold*, and of Byron's subsequent works, added to his fame. And his prosperity over the next ten years was augmented by the immense popularity of Byron's poems. Ten thousand copies of *The Corsair* were sold the first day of publication. Murray was noted for his generosity to authors, and Byron profited also from the connection after he went abroad and had cast off his reluctance to accept money for his publications. Byron called him the "Anax of Publishers" and confided in him in both business and personal matters, so that his letters to Murray, especially those from Italy, are among his most entertaining and revealing.

In September 1812 Murray purchased from William Miller, the bookseller, the premises at 50 Albemarle Street which have been the seat of the publishing firm ever since. In Murray's parlour (now the Byron Room) gathered some of the most distinguished literary people of the day. There in 1815 Murray introduced Byron to Walter Scott. Byron quarrelled with Murray and left him for John Hunt as a publisher, but continued to value him as a friend.

LADY OXFORD

Jane Elizabeth Scott had married in 1794, when she was twenty-two, Edward Harley, fifth Earl of Oxford and Mortimer. She was a rector's daughter, brought up in the ardour of French Revolutionary thought. Lady Oxford's free views in politics and love permitted her to follow her penchant for handsome young men devoted to the reform movement. Her first lover was Sir Francis Burdett. As a by-product of her amours, she acquired a family of beautiful children of uncertain paternity, dubbed by wits the Harleian Miscellany. Her husband was too complacent and amiable to make it worth her while to leave him. When Byron met her in 1812, she was forty and he was twenty-four. She caught him on the rebound from his too tempestuous affair with Lady Caroline Lamb. Her "autumnal charms", as he told Lady Blessington, exactly suited him, and he spent blissful days in her company at Eywood, "in the bowers of Armida". In London she encouraged him in his "Senatorial duties" and drew him into the party of the Princess of Wales, who was her friend. The liaison died when she went abroad with her husband in 1813, expecting Byron to follow her. But he was drawn into other attachments and finally into his fatal marriage.

SAMUEL ROGERS

Rogers was 48 when Byron met him in 1811. The son of a London banker, he retired from active business on the death of his father in 1793 and devoted himself to poetry and social and artistic pleasures. His poetical reputation was established by *The Pleasures of Memory* (1792). Byron had admired his poetry as an embodiment of the Popean elegance carried into the Romantic nineteenth century. Rogers was one of the few poets to whom he gave unqualified praise in *English Bards and Scotch Reviewers*. Rogers cultivated the opulent life with good taste and he welcomed the young Byron with friendliness and exquisite tact. Byron saw him frequently during his years of fame, and Rogers treated him with uniform kindness. They published together two verse tales, Byron's *Lara* and Rogers' *Jacqueline* (1814). But after Byron went to Italy, he heard stories of the older poet's gossip about him and wrote a savage satire on Rogers ("Question and Answer", posthumously published). In his "Detached Thoughts" Byron gave Rogers credit for being a *"good* man; at least he does good now and then". But his muse was "all Sentiment and Sago and Sugar, while he himself is a venomous talker". But Rogers never said anything mean about Byron in print. He gave a fine tribute to him in his *Italy* (1822–1834). Rogers lived on into the Victorian period carrying his cadaverous figure and his memories of an elegant past into the salons of the new era.

JAMES WEDDERBURN WEBSTER

Where Byron first met Webster is not certain. Perhaps it was at Cambridge, since he was known to Hobhouse and other Cambridge friends of Byron. He was born in 1789. His grandfather was Sir A. Wedderburn. His father took the additional name of Webster. Webster was at the famous party at Newstead before Byron went abroad in 1809, and was already something of a butt and buffoon. Byron apparently liked him but viewed him as somewhat absurd. Webster married, in 1810, Lady Frances Annesley, daughter of Arthur, first Earl of Mountnorris and eighth Viscount Valentia. Some of Byron's most amusing letters to Lady Melbourne recount the progress of his flirtation with Lady Frances when he visited the Websters at Aston Hall in 1813. She passed love notes to him under the nose of her conceited, philandering, and jealous husband. In the same year Byron gave Webster £1,000 as a loan, which was not repaid. In later years Webster was separated from his wife, and, while pursuing other women, solicited Byron's intervention to effect a reconciliation. Byron made an honest effort but was not successful.

INDEX OF PROPER NAMES

Page numbers in italics indicate main references and Biographical Sketches in the Appendix. Such main biographical references in Volume 1 are included in this index and are in square brackets.

Burney, Fanny (Mme D'Arblay), 143;
Cecelia, 143; *The Wanderer, or
Female Difficulties*, 143n, 146
Busby, Dr. Thomas, 227; *Rejected
Address*, 228n, 235, 250 and n
Butler, Dr., translates *Charlemagne*,
136n, 141n, 197n
Butler, Samuel, *Hudibras*, 126
Byron, Augusta Ada (later Lady Love-
lace), B.'s daughter by Annabella,
284
Byron, Mrs. Catherine Gordon, [*Vol. I,
273–4*]; at Newstead, 4, 9, 51–2,
61; values B.'s property, 46;
attacked by Hewson Clarke, 65
and n, 67; death, 65n, 67–9;
deposition of her Scotch property,
72 and n, 133 and n
Byron, George Anson (later seventh
Baron), [*Vol. I, 41 and n*]; heir to
peerage, 71, 81–2
Byron, George Anson, f. of above, 82n
Byron, George Gordon, sixth baron;
Works:
Address Spoken at the Opening of
Drury Lane Theatre, 204–14
passim, 219–27 *passim*
Anacharsis; proposed translation into
Romaic, 32n, 40n
'Away, Away, ye notes of woe',
139–40
'The Barmaid' (unpublished), 91n
Beppo, 128n
Childe Harold, on Fauvel, 11n; submitted to Miller, 63 and n;
Elgin, 65–6, 156, 172n; title page,
75–6, 83; to be shown to Gifford,
78, 98–9, 101; commemorative
stanzas, 84; disquisition on literature of modern Greeks, 91; defended by B. against Dallas, 92;
changes in proof, 96 and n, 103
and n, 104, 106, 115–17; Notes,
99, 100, 102 and n, 103, 104
and n, 115 and n, 130, 172n;
Edleston, 116n, 121 and n; Wingfield, 118n; identification of
Harold, 122 and n; nears publication, 130, 151; Dodona, 134n;
Earl of Aberdeen, 156 and n;
publication (Cantos I and II), 167
and n, 168, 283, 284; measure,
210; parodied in 'Cui Bono', 221n;
Preface to 2nd edition, 246n; race
horse nominee, 260n; reviewed

by: *Anti-Jacobin Review*, 197 and
n, *British Critic*, 174n, *British
Review*, 181 and n, *Edinburgh
Review*, 174n, *The Satirist*, 225 and
n, 228–9
The Corsair, 228n, 234n, 285
The Curse of Minerva, 131, 136, 228
and n, 234
'Detached Thoughts' (Journal),
125n, 215n; Sotheby, 128n;
Rogers, 287
Don Juan, 13n, 128n, 141n; ridicules
British Review, 181n
English Bards and Scotch Reviewers,
43, 45n, 281; subsequent editions,
44, 53, 127, 131; Hewson Clarke's
lowly birth, 65n; Kirke White and
Bloomfield, 76n; makes Augusta
laugh, 88; gives offence to Moore,
118n; praises Campbell and
Rogers, 128n, 286; Sotheby, 128n;
Edinburgh reviewers, 168n; Col.
Greville, 168n; Scott, 182 and n
'Farewell to Malta', 126 and n
Fugitive Pieces, 'The Cornelian',
119n
Hebrew Melodies, 282
Hints from Horace, 42 and n, 43, 53–
54, 75, 127, 131; addressed to
Hobhouse, 45–6, 49; 'Ad Pisones',
49; with Cawthorn, 59, 74, 80, 81,
83n, 90, 104, 109; Townsend, 82n;
ridicules Southey, 101n; Method-
ism, 112 and n; Annual Register,
112 and n; difficulty of proof-
reading, 112
Lara (with Rogers), 287
'An Ode to the Framers of the Frame
Bill', 166 and n
'Parenthetical Address, by Dr.
Plagiary', 228 and n
Poems on his Domestic Circumstances,
126 and n
Pope on Buckingham (parody), 15
'Question and Answer', 287
'Sons of the Greeks, arise!', 135n
'Sympathetic Address to a Young
Lady', 183n
'To Ianthe', 258n
The Vision of Judgment, 282
The Waltz, 228 and n, 229, 234
Byron, Julia, 82n

Cameron, Miss, B.'s mistress in
Brompton, 8 and n

Campbell, Thomas, 127, 128 and n; to read *Childe Harold* MS, 130; attacked by Coleridge, 140, 141, 142, 147; at Sydenham, 147 and n, 149; *Pleasures of Hope*, 140 and n, 147

Canning, George, 23n

Canning, Stratford (later first Viscount Stratford de Redcliffe), [*Vol. I, 242n*], 23n, 40, 261 and n, 262n

Carapanos, Constantin, and Dodona, 134n

Carlisle, Frederick Howard, fifth Earl of, [*Vol. I, 76n*], 85 and n

Caroline, Princess, 263 and n

Cawthorn, James, *English Bards*, 44, 57–8; *Hints from Horace*, 58, 59, 74, 81, 83 and n, 90; Hobhouse, 61 and n, 65 and n; Miss Burney, 143, 146, 147

Cazenove, James, 41 and n

Centlivre, Mrs. Susanna, 244n

Cervantes, *Don Quixote*, 194

Charlotte Augusta, Princess, 183n, 263

Chatterton, Thomas, 82

Chaworth, Mrs., 248

Choiseul-Gouffier, Count, 11n

Churchill, Charles, 206, 207 and n

Cibber, Theophilus, *Lives of the Poets*, 197n

Cicero, *De Oratore*, 138n

Clare, John Fitzgibbon, second Earl of, 230 and n, 235, 259

Claridge, (Sir) John Thomas, [*Vol. I, 176n*], 102–3, 113n, 115, 126 and n, 127

Clarke, Edward Daniel, 103, 117 and n, 157; *Childe Harold*, 169 and n, 171 and n; B. quotes his letter, 172 and n, 178; *Travels* (6 vols.), 61 and n, 66 and n, 117n, 125, 180 and n, 181 and n

Clark, Hewson, [*Vol. I, 167n*]; personal attack on B. in *The Scourge*, 65 and n, 67 and n, 68

Clarke, Mary Ann, mistress of Duke of York, 194 and n, 255n

Claughton, Thomas, 231, 233–4; purchase of Newstead, 28n, 188n, 190n, 238 and n, 241, 255

Clonmell, Lady, 183

Coates, Robert, 143 and n, 144

Cockerell, Charles Robert, 24n, 29n, 30 and n, 37 and n

Coke, Rev. Richard, 95n

Coleridge, Samuel Taylor, lectures on Shakespeare, 138 and n, 140 and n, 141, 142, 147 and n, 149

Collet of Staines, 95

Colman, George, 178; *Bluebeard, or Female Curiosity*, 20n; *The Review, or Wags of Windsor*, 138 and n

Colman, George, the Elder, 210 and n

Congreve, William, 206

Coray, M., translator of Strabo, 102n

Coul Pasha, 114, 125

Courtney, Lord, 124 and n

Cowell, John, 162 and n, 164

Cowper, Peter, fifth Earl of, 215n, 232n, 260–1

Cumberland, Richard, 82 and n

Cumberland, William Augustus, Duke of, 263 and n

Dallas (later Byron), Henrietta Charlotte, 82n

Dallas, Robert Charles, [*Vol. I, 274–5*], 53n, 84, 175n; performance of his farce, 20 and n, 132; in B.'s will, 72 and n; *Childe Harold*, 92, 100, 101, 104; recommended to Southwell, 110–11

Dalrymple, Capt. John Henry William, 108 and n

D'Arblay, Mme *see* Burney, Fanny

Darwin, Charles Robert, *Origin of Species*, 7n

Darwin, Erasmus, *The Botanic Garden*, 7n

Darwin, Dr. Francis, 7 and n

Davies, Edward, on *Church Union* (*British Critic*), 174 and n

Davies, Scrope Berdmore, [*Vol. I, 184n*], 60, 77, 83, 93; B.'s indebtedness, 28 and n, 45 and n, 123 and n, 162, 238 and n, 241; character, 102–3; in B.'s will, 71, 72–3; in Cambridge, 95, 117, 118

De Bathe, Sir James Wynne, Bt., 126 and n

D'Egville, possible identification, 8

Deighton, Mr., 127

Demetrius Poliorcetes, 113 and n

Demosthenes, 'Lantern', 12 and n

Dermody, Thomas, 175 and n

Devonshire, William George Spencer Cavendish, sixth Duke of, 96 and n, 160

Djezzar Pasha, at Acre, 181 and n

Downshire, Marquis of, 160

Greville, Col., and Argyle Institution, 168 and n, 169
Grey, Charles, second Earl, 167n, 171n, 211n
Grey, Lady, w. of above, 171 and n
Griffiths, George Edward, publisher of *Monthly Review*, 164 and n, 167
Grossius, agent of Lord Aberdeen, 156
Gruter, Jan, *Corpus Inscriptionum*, 145 and n

Haller von Hallerstein, Karl Freiherr, 27n, *30 and n*, 33 and n, 37 and n
Hamilton, William Richard, 12n
Hannibal, on Phormio, 138 and n
Hanson, Charles, 25
Hanson, Hargreaves, 25, 120n
Hanson, Harriet, 25
Hanson, John, [*Vol. I, 275*]; fails to write to B. in Greece, 4, 8, 16–17, 18; suggests he should sell Newstead, 25, 26, 28, 32, 41, 45; Wymondham purchase money, 39; Rochdale property, 39, 40, 41, 45, 57, 94, 201 and n; account of B.'s affairs, 42–3; in B.'s will, 71; Newstead rents etc., 153 and n; Newstead's sale, 188n, 189
Hare, Naylor, 87 and n
Harley, Lady Charlotte (later Lady Bacon), 258n
Harley, Lady Jane, d. of Lady Oxford, 258 and n
Harness, William, [*Vol. I, 154 and n*], 136, 140; at Newstead, 142, 145, 148, 155
Harrowby, Dudley Ryder, first Earl, 167 and n, 227 and n
Haygarth, William, 33 and n, 37
Heath, Rev. Robert, 82n
Hobhouse, Benjamin, first Bt., 252
Hobhouse, John Cam (later first Baron Broughton de Gyfford), [*Vol. I, 275–6*], 282; to return to England, 4, 8–9, 26; in *Pylades*, 7n; encounter with Lady Hester Stanhope, 21; specimens of Greek sculpture, 45 and n, 47 and n, 48, 56, 60; projected society, 46; quarrels with his father, 46–7, 47n; indebtedness to B., 47n, 161 and n; uncertain future, 54–5, 56; in Ireland with his regiment, 64 and n, 76, 96, 155; Elgin, 66 and n; Matthews' death, 70, 74, 77, 93;

in B.'s will, 72; *Arnauts*, 113; Lady Jane Harley, 258n; *Imitations and Translations*, 11; B. on its price, 16, 19, 22, 55; poems by B., 26n, 75; stationary sales, 45, 49, 53, 55, 59; *A Journey through Albania and Other Provinces of Turkey*, 26, 61n, 66n, 81, 103, 104 and n, 109, 113n, 131, 135, 155 and n; notes by B., 125 and n, 135 'Weeks at Bath', 65 and n, 81
Hodgson, Rev. Francis, [*Vol. I, 276–7*], 83, 86, 87n, 95n, 130, 143; his father's death, 27 and n; 'loans' from B., 27n; to be ordained, 113; retains Moore's letter to B., 118n, 120–1, 129 and n; at Newstead, 148, 149, 155; asked to review Galt's *Voyages*, 164 and n; tale from Boccace, 127; *Lady Jane Grey*, 87 and n; *Sir Edgar*, 20 and n, 55, 145 and n; songs, 97, 113; *Translations of Juvenal*, 45, 95 and n, 101n
Hodgson, Miss (unidentified), 122 and n
Holland, Dr. Henry, 124n
Holland, Lady (née Elizabeth Vassall) (divorced w. of Sir Godfrey Webster), 180, 253, 265, 281; in Ireland, 189n, 192 and n
Holland, Henry Fox, third Lord, [*Vol. I, 281*]; overture to B., 128, 281; B. seeks his advice, 160–1, 281; and Nottingham weavers, 161n, 165–6; and B.'s maiden speech, 167 and n; presented with *Childe Harold*, 168; attacked in *English Bards*, 168n; asks B. for a Drury Lane Address, 191 and n, 193, 197, 204n, 281; at Bowood, 223 and n; leader of Whig Society, 281; and B.'s separation from his wife, 281
Hookham, Thomas, jr., 16 and n, 45
Horace, 11, 13 and n; imitation of 'De Arte Poetica', 42 and n, 43 and n; *Carmina*, 96 and n; *Odes* ('To Venus'), 14 and n, 47 and n
Hornby, Capt. of *Volage* frigate, 50, 53
Howard, Hon. Frederick, 75 and n
Howard, money-lender, 60, 154, 255 and n
Hume, David, 97
Hunt, James Henry Leigh, 233, *281–2*

293

Murray, John, II.,—*Contd.*
228, 285; asks B. to moderate some expressions, 91n, 92, 99; submits MS. to Gifford, 98–9, 101, 109, 130; arouses B.'s anger, 105, 107; Scott, 182 and n, 286; publisher of Lucien Bonaparte, 197; moves to Albemarle St., 235 and n, 286; publishes Leigh Hunt, 281; Caroline Lamb, 283; founder of *Quarterly Review*, 285

Napoleon, 41n, 197 and n
Nathan, Isaac, music to *Hebrew Melodies*, 282
Neale, Mr., 153 and n
North, Lord (later fifth Earl of Guilford), 5 *and n*, 10, 170n
North, Catherine, d. of above, 170

Oakes, General Sir Hildebrand, [*Vol. I, 239 and n*]; Commander in Malta, 50, 55, 126 and n, 198 and n
Ossulston, Lord (Charles Augustus Bennet, Earl of Tankerville), 185n
Ossulston, Lady (née Corisande Armandine, d. of Duc de Gramont), w. of above, 185 and n
Otway, Thomas, 77 and n, 197 and n, 206
Oxford, Edward Harley, fifth Earl of, 257; Harleian Miscellany, 249 and n
Oxford, Countess of (née Jane Elizabeth Scott), 215, 227, 233, 286; likened to 'Armida', 108n, 238 and n, 250, 261, 286; B.'s attachment to, 235, 283, 286; Eywood estate, 237; children of uncertain paternity, 258n, 286; supporter of Princess Caroline, 263 and n

Paul, Mr., Imperial Consul, 7 and n
Payne and Mackinlay, 101 and n, 113
Peel, Sir Robert, Bt., 128 and n, 131
Penn, Granville, *The Bioscope*, 196 and n; 'Christian Knowledge', 196 and n
Perceval, Spencer, shot by Bellingham, 177n, 192
Perry, James, 166 and n, 225n, 226, 228, 235
Peterborough, Charles Mordaunt, third Earl of, 114
Petrarch, 172
Petronius, *Satyricon*, 14 and n

Philips, Ambrose, and Racine's *The Distrest Mother*, 210 and n
Pigot, Elizabeth Bridget, [*Vol. I, 93n*], 119–20
Pigot, John, practices in Chester, 67 and n
Pope, Alexander, 114, 187; lines on Buckingham, 15 and n; *Arbuthnot*, 43n; 'Elegy to the Death of an Unfortunate Lady', 211; *Essay on Criticism*, 69 and n; 'Prologue' to Addison's *Cato*, 210n; *Rape of the Lock*, 21 and n
Pope, Alexander, actor, 204 and n
Porson, Richard, ed. of Euripides, 124 and n; 'The Lexicon of Photius', 124 and n
Portland, William Henry Cavendish, third Duke of, 196n
Portman, Edward Berkeley, 216 and n
Pratt, Samuel Jackson, and Blackett, 53 and n, 76, 80, 132
Prior, Matthew, 179 and n
Pye, Henry James, 180 and n

Queensbury, Catherine Douglas, Duchess of, 114

Racine, Jean, *The Distrest Mother*, 210 and n
Rawdon, Francis, Baron Rawdon (later Earl of Moira), 215 and n, 216
Rawdon, Miss, admired by B., 216
Raymond, stage-manager, 205 and n
Raynal, *History of the Indies*, 211n
Reeve, John, 82n
Rich, John, pantomimist, 212 and n, 214
Richardson, Samuel, pirating of his works, 144 and n; *Pamela*, 250
Ridgway, James, 16 and n, 30 and n, 254 and n
Roberts, William, ed. *British Review*, and *Childe Harold*, 181n
Robinson, Henry Crabb, 147n
Rogers, Samuel, 119 and n, 122, 127, 286–7; friendship with B., 128, 129, 131, 285; attacked by Coleridge, 140 and n, 142; to see B.—Moore correspondence, 152 and n; position in society, 179; on tour in the north, 192 and n; friendship with Moore, 285; and destruction of B.'s Memoirs, 285; *Italy*, 287; *Jacqueline, Lara* (with B.), 287; 'Pleasures of Memory', 123, 286

Rolle, John, nominee of the *Rolliad*, 221 and n
Romanelli, Dr., 14–15, 19
Roque, Dudu and Phokion, 13 and n
Rose, George, 196 and n
Rose, William Stewart, s. of above, 196n
Rowe, Nicholas, *Fair Penitent*, 143 and n, 144, 149
Rushton, Robert, 232; in B.'s will, 71, 232; rudeness to Susan, 157, 158; to be found a place at Rochdale, 232, 234

St. John, Henry, Viscount Bolingbroke, 114
St. Ursula, 232
Sanders, George, 4, 18, 224 and n, 234
Sandwich, John Montagu, fourth Earl of, 32n
Saraci, Spiro (Andreas), 48 and n, 153n, 157 and n, 167
Scott, Sir Walter, 59n, 132 and n; admired by Prince Regent, 180n, 182 and n, 183; and *Childe Harold*, 182 and n; meeting with B., 286; 'Gilpin Horner', 113 and n; *Helvellyn*, 192 and n; 'Lady of the Lake', 20, 182; *Lay of the Last Minstrel*, 182; *Marmion*, 46, 182n; *Rokeby*, 191 and n, 197
Scudéry, Madeleine de, *Artamène*, 194 and n
Seneca, *Troades*, 89 and n
Seward, Anna, *132 and n*
Shakespeare, William, 219, 221; *As You Like It*, 201; *Henry V*, 44, 46, 256 and n; *Macbeth*, 76, 110, 160, 214 and n; *Merchant of Venice*, 210n; *Much Ado About Nothing*, 141 and n; *Othello*, 257 and n; *Richard III*, 245; *Twelfth Night*, 207 and n
Shelley, Mary, 282
Shelley, Percy Bysshe, 16n, 282
Sheridan, Richard Brinsley, 20, 210, 225n, 282; *The Critic*, 195, 207 and n; *Monody on Garrick*, 219–20; *The Rivals*, 14, 201, 219 and n; *The Trip to Scarborough*, 227 and n
Sheridan, Thomas, s. of above, 20 and n
Siddons, Mrs. Sarah, 147 and n, 225n
Skinner, John, *Theological Works*, 174n
Sligo, second Marquis of (formerly Lord Altamont), 3n, 49, 160; with B. in Greece, 3–4, 7–8, 16; his brig and entourage, 5–6, 11, 13–14; alleged abduction of a seaman, 117 and n, 118; in Ireland, 132
Smith, Mr., B.'s indebtedness, 99
Smith, Mrs. Constance Spencer, [*Vol. I, 224 and n*]; love affair with B., 198 and n, 199
Smith, James and Horace, *Rejected Addresses*, 221n, 228 and n, 235
Smith, Sir Sidney, defence of Acre, 181 and n
Smollett, Tobias, 'The Tears of Scotland', 211 and n
Smyth, William, Ode to Duke of Gloucester, 92 and n
Socrates, 29
Sotheby, William, 128 and n, 129, 131; *Oberon, Georgics*, 128n
Southey, Robert, 101n; and Kirke White, 76n; 'Curse of Kehama', 137; 'Queen Orraca and the Five Martyrs of Morocco', 138 and n
Spencer, Lady Henrietta Frances (later Lady Bessborough—*see under*)
Spencer, John, first Earl of, 174n
Spencer, Lady, w. of above, 174 and n
Spencer, W. R., B. reviews his poems in *The Monthly Review*, 156n
Spenser, Edmund, 210
Spinoza, Baruch, 136
Stanhope, Lady Hester Lucy, *21n*, 49–50
Stewart, Princess Annabella, 68 and n
Strabo, Geography, 102n, 134
Strané, English Consul at Patras, 6, 7, 8 and n, 10
Suleyman of Thebes, 262
Swedenborg, Emanuel, 98
Swift, Jonathan, 45n, 114
Swinburne, Henry, *Travels in the Two Sicilies*, 155 and n

Tahiri, Dervise, 262 and n
Tasso, Torquato, *Gerusalemme Liberata*, 108 and n, 238n
Thomson, James, *Alfred*, 180n
Thornton, Thomas, 106, 115
Tonson, Jacob, 30
Tooke, Horne, life of, 235
Townsend, Rev. George, *82 and n*; *Armageddon*, 82 and n; *Poems*, 82n
Tucker, Surgeon, 54 and n, 58
Twiss, Horace, 191 and n, 193

Valentia, George Annesley, Lord (later Earl of Mountnorris), 50, 124 and n, 125, 128, 131, 148; to stand for Wexford, 108 and n; marriage of his daughter, 126 and n, 287

Valpy, Rev. Dr., probable identity, *133 and n*

Vanburgh, Sir John, *The Relapse*, 227 and n

Vassall, Elizabeth (later Lady Webster and Lady Holland), 281

Vaughan, Susan, 131 and n, 151 and n, 155, 157; B. bids her farewell, 159 and n, 160

Velly Pasha, [*Vol. I, 226 and n*], 21; receives B., 9–10, 11, 16, 19, 22, 262n

Vergil, *Aeneid*, 90–1, 137 and n; *Eclogue*, 33 and n

Viscille (Vescille), 10 and n, 13, 262 and n

Voltaire, François Marie Arouet de, 89n, 98 and n

Vondel, Joost Van, *Gysbrecht van Amstel, 112 and n*

Von Stackelberg, Otto Magnus Freiherr, 27n

Wallace, Capt., 8 and n, 28 and n

Walleden, G. (?), 153 and n

Walpole, Rev. Robert, 190 and n, 197

Ward, John William (later Lord Dudley), 125 and n, 128, 129, 131, 140

Ward, J. W., review of life of Horne Tooke, 235 and n

Wardle, Col. Gwyllym, [*Vol. I, 197 and n*], 194n

Warton, Thomas, 54; Ode in honour of George III's birthday, 221n

Watson, George, 13 and n

Watson, Richard, 136, 140; *An Apology for Christianity*, 136n

Webster, Sir Godfrey Vassal, 241 and n; divorces his wife, 281

Webster Wedderburn, Lady Francis, 126; and B., 131, 287; poems addressed to, 200 and n

Webster Wedderburn, (Sir) James, [*Vol. I, 171 and n*], 62, 131, 287; marriage, 50, 126n, 148, 287; carriage deal with B., 62, 64 and n, 78–9; absurd conversation, 124, 287; in trouble with the press, 125, 128

Wedderburn, Sir A., f. of James, 287

Wellesley, Sir Arthur (Duke of Wellington), 91n, 216n

Wellesley, William Pole, marriage, 142 and n

Westmorland, John, tenth Earl of, 173n

Whitbread, Samuel, *211n*, 212 and n, 213–14

White, Henry Kirke, *76 and n*, 82

Whittington (unidentified), 157

Wingfield, John, [*Vol. I, 101 and n*]; death, 69 and n, 70, 77, 81, 92–3, 118n, 119n

Wolcot, John (Peter Pindar), 49

Woodfall, Henry Sampson, *Junius's Letters*, 250 and n

Wordsworth, William, 215n

Wright, Walter Rodwell, 20n; Consul-General in Ionian Islands, 111 and n; *Horae Ionicae*, 92; Ode to the Duke of Gloucester, 92n

York, Frederick Augustus, Duke of, 194 and n, 255 and n

Zantachi, Andreas, 10 and n, 13 and n, 16, 29, 32n

Zograffo, Demetrius, 48 and n, 60, 102, 124, 130; in B.'s will, 71; Arnaut dialect, 84, 102, 103, 113 and n; Hobhouse's travel book, 113 and n, 129 and n, 150, 155 and n, 162; to return to Greece, 153n, 167, 262 and n